A Cultural Poetics of Bhasha Literatures

A Cultural Poetics of Bhasha Literatures

In Theory and Practice

Edited by

E. V. Ramakrishnan

Orient BlackSwan

A CULTURAL POETICS OF BHASHA LITERATURES:
IN THEORY AND PRACTICE

ORIENT BLACKSWAN PRIVATE LIMITED

Registered Office
3-6-752 Himayatnagar, Hyderabad 500 029, Telangana, India
Email: centraloffice@orientblackswan.com

Other Offices
Bengaluru, Chennai, Guwahati, Hyderabad,
Kolkata, Mumbai, New Delhi, Noida, Patna

First published by Orient Blackswan Private Limited 2024

ISBN 978-93-5442-987-3

041711

Typeset in Minion Pro 11/13 *by*
Shine Graphics, Delhi 110 094

Printed at
Avantika Printers Private Limited, New Delhi 110 020

Published by
Orient Blackswan Private Limited
3-6-752, Himayatnagar, Hyderabad 500 029, Telangana, India
Email: info@orientblackswan.com

Contents

Acknowledgements

This volume has been long in the making. The delay was mainly due to the disruption caused by the Covid epidemic and its aftermath. Most of the papers included in the volume were presented in a National Seminar organised by the Forum for Contemporary Theory (FCT), Baroda, on the subject, "The Literary across Cultures: Cultural Poetics of Bhasha Literature" held on FCT campus, Baroda during 25–27 February 2019. But for the whole-hearted support of Professor Prafulla Chandra Kar, the Director of the FCT, and his team, the national seminar could not have been held in such a grand manner. I thank Professor Kar and his staff for all the assistance they extended to the scholars who attended the seminar.

Professor Gulammohammed Sheikh had delivered the key-note address to the Seminar. As a painter-poet and translator, he had many insights to offer on the cultural poetics of bhasha literature.

Dr Tonisha Guin, who was an Academic Associate at the FCT at that time, supervised all the communications related to the Seminar, and later assisted me in editing the revised papers to prepare the first draft for submission to the publisher's scrutiny and peer-review. But for her initial help, I could not have gone ahead with this volume.

I am extremely grateful to the eminent scholars from various parts of the country who participated in the seminar and actively contributed to the discussions on the subject. Among those present were Dr Mrinal Kaul, Professor Dipti R. Pattanaik, Professor Nirmal Selvamony, Professor Sachin Ketkar, Professor P. P. Raveendran, Professor Rajendra Chenni, Dr Vipin K. Kadavath, Dr Sukanya Sarbadhikary, Dr B. S. Bini, Dr Zarana Maheshwari, Dr Tonisha Guin and Dr Hiren Patel. They represented some of the major literary traditions of India.

It was felt that efforts should be made to get scholarly papers by eminent Indian authors belonging to the significant literary traditions which were not represented in the volume. All the senior scholars we contacted agreed to write for us: Professor Anisur Rahman, Professor Subha Dasgupta, Professor C. Rajendran and Dr Dhurjjati Sarma have contributed valuable papers to the volume. But for their kind support, the volume would have been much impoverished in content. We put on record our gratitude for their learned contributions.

The essay "A Local Habitation and a Name for Knowledge: the Case of Odiya Bhasha Literature" was jointly written by Dipti R. Pattanaik and Debendra K. Dash (1954–2022). In the untimely death of Professor Dash we lost a remarkable bilingual scholar of Odia literature. We are extremely grateful to Geetanjali Dash, for granting us permission to use the article co-authored by her husband, in this volume.

We had invited Dr Shamsur Rahman Faruqi (1935–2020), the doyen of Urdu literature to deliver the key-note address. However, ill-health prevented him from travelling to Baroda. His demise in 2020 was a great loss to Urdu language and literature as well as Comparative Indian Literature. Before his passing, he had given consent to us to use one of his uncollected essays, "Toward an Indian Poetics" published in an issue of *Bahuvachan*, an occasional publication edited by Krishna Baldev Vaid, J. Swaminathan and Ashok Vajpeyi from Bharat Bhavan, Bhopal. Subsequently Professor Baran Farooqi, his daughter, granted us written permission to use her father's essay in the present volume. We greatly appreciate her help.

A different version of P. P. Raveendran's essay, "The Social Imaginary and the Evolution of Modern Indian Literature" appeared in his volume, *Under the Bhasha Gaze: Modernity and the Indian Literature* (OUP, UK, 2023). We would like to thank the Oxford University Press for granting us permission to use the present essay.

I have incurred debts of various kinds to my friends in editing this volume and preparing its introduction. In this regard,

I would like to specially mention P. C. Kar, Anisur Rahman, K. Satchidanandan, P. P. Raveendran, Gulammohammed Sheikh, Ganesh Devy, Subha Chakraborty Dasgupta, T. S. Satyanath and Udayakumar, for their suggestions and inputs.

I am deeply indebted to S. Sreenath of Orient Blackswan for taking up our proposal and seeing through its publication. Aditi Jha has done a meticulous job as a copy-editor, doing full justice to the volume's multi-lingual/literary content. Her interventions have enriched this volume.

I would like to mention the support of my wife, Gowri, my son, Dhiraj and daughter, Ramya in all my intellectual pursuits, though it keeps me away from them for considerable time. What gives me strength even in these days of failing health, is my strong faith in the relevance of disciplines like comparative literature, culture studies and translation studies to comprehend the complexity of the composite and syncretic cultural traditions of India.

E. V. Ramakrishnan

Introduction

A Transregional, Transcultural and Translational Poetics for Bhasha Literatures

E. V. Ramakrishnan

(1)

The present volume of essays resulted from a national seminar which addressed the topic, "The literary across cultures: Cultural poetics of *Bhasha* literatures in theory and practice". The idea was to explore the interrelations between languages, literatures and cultures in the context of South Asia in general and India in particular. Despite belonging to four different language families, the literatures of India have evolved in dialogue with each other. There are shared metaphors, symbols, tropes and forms of expression among them, which have roots in the collective lived experiences of the peoples belonging to different social strata, religions, regions, geographical locations, climate and cultural practices. However, "Indian Literature" in the singular should not be taken to mean that homogeneity exists in matters of literary practices, templates of culture or social environments. "Indian literature" as a possibility can be realised only "in a cultural environment where *bhasha*s interact with a spirit of mutual filiation and inter-animation" (Raveendran 2023, 98). The ideas of circulation, negotiation, translation and exchange constitute the contours of the literary field in South Asia. But these values hardly find any mention in the literary histories or critical discussion of literary texts, nor are they reflected in the theoretical debates on aesthetics that have shaped critical evaluation of poetry and prose in the major languages of India.

Traditionally, the word *bhasha* denotes Indian languages other than Sanskrit. *Bhasha*s have had an ambivalent relationship with Sanskrit, as its hegemonic status in the subcontinent created a hierarchy among languages. *Bhasha*s used translation and appropriation as modes of negotiating the rich legacy of Sanskrit language and literature over the centuries. While *bhasha* literatures were rooted in the everyday world of the subaltern and marginalised sections of people, Sanskrit maintained an elitist aloofness, becoming the language of philosophical debates and aesthetic enquiries. As Sanskrit poetics evolved over centuries, its focus was on art as a subjective experience, and the representation of human emotion in the literary text. The debates within this rich argumentative tradition were exclusively focussed on the world of the text in its manifold forms. In his introduction to *A Rasa Reader*, Sheldon Pollock says: "Furthermore, almost everything outside the literary realm, let alone, the cultural realm, remained outside classical Indian aesthetic analysis" (2017, 2). As aesthetics emerged as a discipline in the West in the eighteenth century, as seen in the writings of Alexander Baumgarten (1714–1762), Immanuel Kant (1724–1804) and Georg W. F. Hegel (1770–1831), it gave rise to a secular domain of knowledge devoted to the study of art in terms of questions such as what constitutes taste, beauty and emotion as manifested in the literary text. However, in India, it was in the pre-modern era that the dominant schools of aesthetics emerged as well-defined systems of thought. Pollock argues that to understand *rasa* as a historical form of thought, one has to recognise that it is "a theory clearly contingent on a nonmodern worldview and understanding of literary art" (ibid., 44). He sees several pre-modern systems of thought being instrumental in shaping the *rasa* theory: "Its full conceptualization is intimately tied to a number of primary, uncontested, and largely, non-transferable Indian presuppositions—about the threefold psychophysiology of Samkhya, for example, or the storage of memories of past lives, or even transmigration" (ibid.).

Pollock's readings in *rasa* theory convey the impression that "Indian aesthetics" is confined to the Sanskrit theory of *rasa-dhvani* and the long lineage of debates it entailed over the centuries. Even a cursory look at Pollock's *A Rasa Reader* reveals that the Sanskrit aesthetics attained its dominant position across India during the first seven centuries of the second millennium. The second chapter of the book is titled "The Great Synthesis of Bhoja, 1025–1055" and the sixth chapter that ends the book is titled "Rasa in the Early Modern World, 1200–1650". This is an exclusivist, essentialist view of Indian aesthetics which lacks a conception of India and South Asia as a pluralist multilingual society.

That a separate aesthetic had taken roots in the classical Tamil with an emphasis on the underlying relation between the emotional states and the patterns of landscape, widens the discussion of cultural poetics in the Indian context. *Tholkappiyam,* a treatise on the Tamil aesthetics that dates back to the second century BC, posits a unique semiotic system where each emotion corresponds to a landscape, further each shade of emotion to specific flora and fauna, seasons of the year and even times of day. A mere mention of a flower can ignite a chain of associations across several symbolic systems, with remarkable economy of words, as the text is transformed into an intertext. A. K. Ramanujan, in the elaborate "Afterword" to his translations of Sangam poetry, comments:

> The poet's language is not only Tamil: landscapes, the personae, the appropriate moods, all become a language within language. Like a native speaker he makes "infinite use of finite means," to say with familiar words what has never been said before; he can say exactly what he wants to, without even being aware of the ground rules of his grammar. If the world is the vocabulary of the poet, the conventions are his syntax—at least one of the many kinds of poetic syntax. (1985, 251)

Cultural poetics of the kind we see in classical Tamil demonstrates how its mode of signification varies from the *rasa* theory of Sanskrit. Beyond these two traditions there exist diverse systems of oral poetics rooted in the folk-cultures across the various regions of India. Folk tales and songs, *kirtan* and other forms of worship involving music and dance and the popular visual representations of the epics and mythological narratives—all of these point to the need for abundant descriptions of cultural practices. Some of the essays in the volume attempt informed documentation of such oral practices.

(2)

Richard Eaton's book, *India in the Persianate Age 1000–1765*, covers the same period of Indian history which Sheldon Pollock examines from the perspective of Sanskrit aesthetics. One of the stereotypes of India that Eaton challenges in his book is that of India "as an essentially self-generated Hindu and Sanskrit civilization that evolved on its own, rather than a hybridized composite produced from protracted interaction with other peoples and cultures" (Eaton 2020, 3–4). It was in the nineteenth century that two competing narratives of India based on religious beliefs emerged in the Indian historiography. The British historians replicated the tripartite model based on the ancient, medieval and modern periods used in the writing of European history to represent the past of India. In the process, they equated the period between 1000 CE to 1800 CE to the decadent period of Islamic rule mired in obscurantism and religious bigotry. The ancient period was equated with the classical Hindu age of great achievements. This enabled the British to justify the colonial conquest of India, as harbingers of modernity. Eaton rightly comments that "the reading of history in terms of mutually exclusive religions has, however, come at enormous cost" (ibid., 9). It has completely erased from our view a large number of cultural practices and expressions that were rooted in the vision of a cross-cultural, syncretic view of society and culture that transcended narrow sectarian boundaries. These practices did not have any religious affiliations and could not be termed Hindu, Muslim or Sikh, and were rooted in the experience of everyday collective living.

In the second millennium, between 1000 and 1600, *bhasha*s underwent radical transformations. From being merely "spoken" languages, they came of age as "literary" languages with their own written traditions. It was through their dialogic interactions with Persian and Sanskrit that *bhashas* found their moorings.

The larger cultural space occupied by the classical languages came to be occupied by *bhashas* through adaptations, translations and accommodations that entailed reception, interpretation and assimilation. As Eaton suggests, "much of India's history between 1000 and 1800 can be understood in terms of the prolonged multi-faceted interaction between the Sanskrit and Persianate worlds" (ibid., 13). The process of "vernacularisation" was not a process of imitation and influence as Pollock would like us to believe (2011, 330–338). It was made possible by the creative confidence of thinkers, poets and performers who had emerged from the margins to the mainstream, as part of a larger political assertion of the regions which they represented. The enabling role played by Persian/Arabic poetics in the transformation of *bhasha*s into full-fledged literary languages needs to be underlined. Sufi poetry and the Islamic cosmology were crucial factors in shaping the poetic discourse of Bhakti. The emergence of *bhasha*s into modern *literary* languages happened in the context of a resonant multilingualism that rendered borders between linguistic and cultural domains porous and fluid.

The emergence of *bhasha*s as independent literary languages has the makings of an Indian Renaissance as argued by M. Govindan in his introduction to the volume, *Poetry and Renaissance* (1973, 5–18). In European Renaissance we witness the shifting of power from sacred languages to the local languages, large-scale translations of classics for those unfamiliar with the classical languages, and an accompanying assertion of the salience of local cultures against the hegemonic power structures of religion and imperial powers. Modern Indian languages looked within, towards the margins of society as well as to the pan-Indian cosmopolitan world for sustenance. The cultural poetics of *bhasha*s was defined by a willingness to engage in dialogue, and a strong sense of resistance to dogmas in matters of faith and belief. Its oppositional discourses permeate the literary world in the form of interactive and relational discourses that emphasise openness and mobility.

Aesthetics as we understand it today, is a codification of rhetorical and imaginative features of literary texts as revealed in their interpretation. They attain canonical status over a period of time as they come to regulate the protocols of reading and interpretation in a society. *Bhasha*s as they developed in the second millennium, did not feel the need to codify their aesthetics as they distrusted "theoreticism" (the compulsion to codify experiences into theories) which could result in domination and colonisation. Their irreducible multilingualism and insistence on accommodating contradictions without cancelling them out and homogenising them has to be seen as the hallmarks of an alternative aesthetics in the making.

Multilingualism is a feature that goes beyond mere competence in many languages. It is a dialogic mode of understanding that enables one to be in relation with the other. A poet like Amir Khusru (d.1325) wrote in Persian, Hindwai and Brajbhasha, and was fluent in Turkish and Arabic. Christian Lee Novetzke shows how Namdeo's performance of *kirtan* impacted languages across India: "Namdeo is a key figure in Maharashtra as well as central, western, and northern India, and virtually ubiquitous in the Hindu and Sikh religious-literary traditions of these regions from the fifteenth century to the present, a period spanning Sultanate, Mughal, Maratha, and British rule as well as post-Independence India" (2008, 1).

The "vernacular" world was deeply grounded in the cultural practices of communities which were multilingual and their migrations and mobility created shared metaphoric worlds that continue to animate the literary creations in Indian languages. The origin and development of a language like Dakhini was made possible in the fourteenth century through dialogues between the Sufis and the *sant*s. Eknath's poem, *Hindu-Turk Samvad*, which has an undercurrent of satire directed against the priestly class in both Islam and Hinduism, speaks of new forms of belonging that looked beyond fixed and fossilised religious identities. Its spirit of defiance against dogmas answers to a deep urge within the *zeitgeist* (the general set of ideas, beliefs and feelings that is common to a particular period) to open up the frontiers of experience and expression beyond the normative. The term "early modernity" has gained currency in recent times in the context of the creative surge that revamped the apparatus of language and expression across the subcontinent. That will require a separate chapter for detailed exposition.

The question of "aesthetics" or "poetics" in the Indian context is complicated by the penetration of distinctively polyglot, hybridised discourses which could accommodate contradictions and ambivalence. Words such as "local" or "cosmopolitan" cannot be used with any degree of certainty in the context of the intercultural exchanges between communities of people who followed different faiths, spoke different languages and lived simultaneously in multiple worlds, without succumbing to the compulsion of surrendering to the simplistic notions of homogeneity. Their sense of complex living and difficult dialogues in conjunction with a searchingly reflective and nonconformist attitude to authoritarian ideology are at variance with what stands for "official and canonised" aesthetics. It manifests itself in the transregional, translational, travelling poetics of the subcontinent which is interactive, intertextual and intercultural. The volume of essays collected here addresses these issues from multiple perspectives rooted in separate linguistic and literary traditions. They elaborate the nature of dialogues that have shaped the poetics of living cultures in the context of modern Indian languages, moving from the general to the particular, from the theoretical to the practical, and identifying the multivalent elements that constitute a text, a cultural practice or a literary trend.

(3)

When Stephen Greenblatt used the term "cultural poetics" in the context of Shakespeare studies, he meant "the study of the collective making of distinct cultural practices and enquiry into the relations among these practices" (1988, 5). The idea of "collective making of distinct cultural practices" and their interrelations finds resonance in the discussions presented here. However, the scale and scope of complexity that informs the cultural practices of the oral, written, visual and performance texts in Indian languages and their mutual interactions have no parallels with the monolingual textual traditions of the West.

One of the ways in which this can be done is by looking at translation as a form native to modern Indian languages. Here translation must be taken as a form, as suggested by Walter Benjamin (1996, 254). The rise of *manipravalam* in Malayalam literature as the standard of poetic discourse will help us illustrate this point further. Wherever Sanskrit went, it blended with the local language to create a hybridised literary language. Sanskrit and Prakrit were fused in some of the early literary texts in some parts of India. As a literary style in South Indian languages, *manipravalam* comes into being from the beginning of the second millennium. The term literally means "ruby and coral"—the local language, Malayalam standing for ruby and Sanskrit standing for coral. While the vernacular tradition of *pattu* (songs) existed as an oral tradition for centuries, the fusion of this tradition with Sanskrit dates to the time Malayalam emerges as a literary language. While *pattu* was constituted by Dravidian words exclusively, the harmonious blending of Malayalam and Sanskrit gave rise to the new discourse of *manipravalam*. As Malayalam had to define itself against the hegemonic traditions of Tamil and Sanskrit, the invention of this new discourse was a mode of negotiating power relations. In interpreting the grand style of Sanskrit to suit the local conditions of a newly assertive speech community, the poets who used *manipravalam* cleared a cultural space which was not available earlier (Ramakrishnan 2011, 150–52). The defining feature of this new cultural poetics is its ability to address the high and the low, the Sanskrit-knowing elites and the Malayalam-speaking common people. The making of a translational poetics was clearly laid out in its emergence as the standard poetic idiom of Malayalam for the next five centuries. In an insightful study of the politics of *Leelathilakam*, the treatise in Sanskrit that outlined the rules of *manipravalam* in the fifteenth century, M. R. Raghava Varrier argues that it marks a moment of affirmation of the self-identity and cultural autonomy by Malayalam, distancing itself from the hegemonic domination of Sanskrit and Tamil. This suggests a proto-nationalistic narrative taking shape in the social imaginaries of the fifteenth century (Varrier 2016, 24, 64–66). Translation of the kind implicit in *manipravalam* is implicated in the politics of imagining new social identities.

The same "translational", dialogic sensibility is at work in the nature of interaction and influence between Sufism and Bhakti. Many great Sufi seers and poets visited India and settled down in India during the thirteenth and fourteenth centuries. While India had its own tradition of divine worship through song and dance, the kind of frenzy that accompanied them in the medieval times had the stamp of Sufism. Suniti Kumar Chatterji, after mentioning this point, adds: "Yet it appears quite reasonable to assume that a form of Sufi worship through a sort of frenzied singing or repetition of divine name … which raised religious emotion to the highest pitch, acted as a stimulus upon a similar path or line of Vaishnava religious *sadhan* in Medieval India" (Chatterji 1946, 29). Sufi saints, much like the Bhakti poets, came from the artisan class of lower castes and were opposed to priestly authority. In his essay, "The Mad Lover", Sisir Kumar Das has argued how "a state of madness (became) an integral part of the lives of many saints in medieval India and what striking resemblance it had with the general behaviour of the Sufi mystics" (Das 2003, 161). As these poets composed for the common people, much of their folklore and common beliefs found their way into their articulations. While discussing a poem by Guru Nanak which describes devotion in terms of frenzy and madness, Das points out that he uses "common words such as 'betala', 'diwana' and 'baurana', all ordinary words used to designate madness" (ibid., 215). Such use of everyday idiom points to a new aesthetics of communication. Unlike the distilled wisdom and ascetic detachment of the Upanishads and the Vedas, we find here open display of emotion, sensuous engagement with lived reality and immersion in interpersonal relations. Theories of *rasa* or *dhvani* may not be particularly illuminating in interpreting the expressive mode of this poetic discourse; we need an alternative vocabulary of cultural poetics rooted in the social imagination of the people to explicate the wider intertextual and intercultural dimensions of this affective articulations. The essays on Chaitanya and Sankardeva included here grapple with the need for an alternative cultural poetics that puts the performing body at the centre.

During the medieval period the Sufi romance or *premakhyana* became a favourite form in north and east India. Muhammad Jayasi (d. 1542) composed *Padmavat* (1540) in this tradition not to celebrate the triumphal march of brave armies but to enact the search for the divine self as revealed by love. His narrative is deeply rooted in the local and the regional. Eaton comments: "For him (Jayasi), the Indian's annihilation at Chittoor becomes a metaphor for the Sufi's ultimate mystical quest, namely annihilation of the self (*fana*) by way of achieving an abiding presence of God" (2020, 135). In an interview with me, Gulammohammaed Sheikh, the well-known painter and poet, pointed out that the Persian translations of the Ramayana were painted by Hindu and Muslim artists at the Mughal court (Sheikh 2021, 112). One of the finest Ramayana versions with over 400 folios was painted at the court of Maharana Jagat Singh of Mewar in the seventeenth century by Sahibdin along with Manohar. The popular culture of the times also exemplifies a similar hybridised mix of diverse traditions and cultural practices. In rural and tribal heartlands, their "heterogenous forms remained alive on their own mettle, often fighting the forces of the dominant urban styles" (ibid.). The amazing plurality and polyphony of Indian artistic and literary traditions and practices are, however, conspicuously absent from the kind of aesthetics taught in the literary and educational systems. As Sheikh puts it, "we need to construct an alternative aesthetic of ideational and practiced multiplicity, diversity and heterogeneity instead of being stuck to an aesthetics of finality based on shastras, a desi-margi divide, or the contested syndrome of unity in diversity" (ibid.).

On closer examination, the cultural contexts outlined above can be seen to be "contact zones" where different cultural trajectories meet, mingle and reinvent themselves in response to the changing contexts of the speech communities (Greenblatt 2010, 251). The Parsi theatre in the nineteenth century may be briefly mentioned here as a further example of a contact zone, where an alien tradition (Shakesperean theatre) gave rise to an indigenous form of theatre that moved between Hindustani, Marathi and Gujarati and went even beyond the boundaries of these languages. Inspired by the spectacular staging of the plays of Shakespeare, these plays soon borrowed stories and themes from Persian, Hindu, Islamic and folk mythologies to widen their appeal to the domestic audience. That Parsi theatre shaped the indigenous tradition of *sangeeth-natak*, and even impacted the visual dynamics of the Indian cinema at its inception, testifies to the robust intercultural networks that animate our cultural production. Parsi theatre thus becomes a meeting point of multiple traditions of music, performance, visual presentation and narrative modes. In his essay, "A Historiography of Modern Indian Theatre", Ananda Lal remarks that popular Indian theatre scaled the high-water mark of popularity between 1870 and 1930: "Moreover, for the first time a pan-Indian populist theatre emerged in the nationwide reach and influence of heterogenous, fairly cosmopolitan Parsi companies that toured productions in a lingua franca of Hindustani, even travelling abroad to southeast Asia and east Africa" (quoted in Bhatia 2009, 34).

It was to the folk and the marginal performance traditions that modern Indian theatre turned when it had to reinvent its basics in response to a new set of sociopolitical transformations.

(4)

Against this outline of the need for an alternative aesthetic, the essays in the volume examine the cultural practices of authors, critics, commentators and translators from multiple local traditions with their separate histories. Various facets related to the cultural poetics of Indian literatures as they have evolved over the centuries are taken up for treatment, with no attempt to integrate them into larger wholes. They open the possibilities of approaches to texts and ideas that have their genesis in the meeting points between the sociopolitical and artistic–cultural contexts, each with their own dynamics. They remind us of the truth of Bakhtin's observations in a letter to the editorial staff of *Novy Mir*:

> In our enthusiasm for specification we have ignored questions of the interconnection and interdependence of various areas of culture; we have frequently forgotten that the boundaries of these areas are not absolute, that in various epochs they have been drawn in various ways; and we have not taken into account that the most intense and productive life of culture takes place on the boundaries of its individual areas and not in places where these areas have become enclosed in their own specificity. (1986, 3)

It is to peripheries and margins that we turn to discover how centres and canons come into being and how they shape our practices and theoretical dispositions. In doing so, we have to see how literary works break through the boundaries of their own time and belong as much to the past as to the present.

The opening essay by Mrinal Kaul sets the tone for the essays that follow by suggesting that the potentiality of the idea of creativity in the South Asian context lies in its open-endedness. While applying the modern concepts to the pre-modern thought patterns, we are bound to face contradictions and paradoxes. If we can isolate some concepts and pursue them in their development and map their transformations through history, we may be nearer to a method of dealing with the complexity of the enormous corpus of aesthetic thought generated over centuries. A single text such as Kalidas' *Abhijnanashakuntalam* is part of a network of texts, creating a history of intertextuality that will go back to the Mahabharata and return us to Tagore. The only way of answering the question, "Is there a South-Asian Poetics?" is to see the very question as part of an ongoing debate on the need for an open-ended approach to the cultural poetics of South Asia.

Mrinal Kaul quotes Shamsur Rahman Faruqi as suggesting that for South Asian poetics a metaphor is as real as anything, unlike for the Western thought which questions its reality. In his essay, "Toward an Indian Poetics", originally published in *Bahuvachan* (1988), Faruqi argues that the poetics of a language or culture is bound by its concerns and contexts, and may not have much relevance for readers elsewhere. "Indianness" is an attribute which would be understood better by a non-Indian. The Victorian–Western ethos that still controls our imagination limits our capacity to appreciate heterogeneity in the arts as a value. The Indian view of fine arts as interlinked and mutually interlocking is an idea that has its relevance still. The formulation that all fine arts are so interlinked as to be in symbiosis with each other, is central to the enquiry into a cultural poetics of the literatures of *bhashas*.

Anisur Rahman raises the question whether *razmia* or epic is conspicuous by its absence in Urdu. In the West, the epic was considered a pure genre and had its subject matter, structure and style strictly defined. In Eastern tradition, this genre exhibits much variety and diversity in style, mode and substance. Through a nuanced analysis of the rich tradition of narrative poetry in Urdu, in all its plurality, he documents the features of the epic tradition in Urdu which may not conform to all the defining features in other cultures. Obviously, its incarnation in Urdu embodies the literary culture and ethos of the language. The earth-bound nature of the cultural poetics of Indian languages needs to be emphasised here. The concerns and contexts of the speech community determine the choice of genres and their defining features.

C. Rajendran's essay, "Scripture or Poetry? Anandvardhana on How to Read an Epic" begins by making a distinction between the Western epics which are read primarily as literary works and Indian epics like the Ramayana and Mahabharata which have acquired a religious aura. The question of interpretation of the epics, thus, is complicated in the Indian context. A poet–critic of the ninth century, Anandvardhana, takes the epic as a unified whole. Through a close analysis of the Ramayana as a *kavya* in the light of *rasa* theory, Anandvardhana highlights its enactment of *karuna* (compassion) *rasa*. While he is able to retrieve the Ramayana as a literary epic, he encounters problems in the status of the Mahabharata. Reading it as *kavya* to the exclusion of its multiple facets would pose problems. The text's ability for plurisignification renders it *kavya* and *shastra* at the same time. Anandvardhana invokes the concept of *shanta* (tranquillity) *rasa* to characterise its emotional appeal. His reading marks an important moment of reception for the Mahabharata, as his arguments find echoes in subsequent interpretations of the text. In invoking a *rasa* which is not part of the canonical *rasa* theory, Anandvardhana breaches the canon, while remaining within its larger tenets. The concept of plurisignification is thus an enabling concept that may be invoked in the context of other complex texts belonging to different genres.

In his essay, "Reinventing the Literary: Two Moments in the History of the Kannada Tradition", Rajendra Chenni discusses two significant points of departure in the literary history of Kannada literature, both of which contributed toward reformulating the idea of the literary. Between the ninth and eleventh century CE, Kannada became the medium of public proclamations as well as poetic expression. *Kavirajamargam* (875 CE), a major poetic treatise that examines the emergent cultural poetics of literary compositions, has much to say on the relations between *marga* and *desi*, framing the relations between Sanskrit and Kannada. The bilingual elite of the times negotiated the regional *desi* as a medium of literary expression on the terms set by Sanskrit poetics. In the actual poetic practice of Pampa, considered the *adikavi* (the first major poet) one can see how he departs from the tenets of Sanskrit poetics by speaking in a hybridised poetic discourse that leans towards the local. However, it was in the twelfth century, with the appearance of the *vachana* movement—with poets such as Allama, Basava, Mahadeviyakka breaking away from the Sanskrit conventions—that a new *desi* literary culture came to the fore in Kannada. As these poets spoke in their own voice, emphasising the here-and-now of the everyday world, resisting all conventions of Sanskrit poetics, a new poetic took shape in Kananda, its ethical vision creating a new bond between the popular and the poetic. Chenni illustrates his essay with several examples from the literary history of Kannada. While the two moments outlined in this essay have parallels in languages like Marathi, they appear to be fused into a single moment in languages like Gujarati and Malayalam. The moment of Narasinh Mehta in Gujarati or that of Ezhuthachan in Malayalam marks the emergence of a poetic unique to the bhasha tradition that resists and redefines the conventions of Sanskrit poetic.

Dipti R. Pattanaik and Debendra K. Dash examine the case of Odia in the context of the creation of a vernacular poetic rooted in the local and the regional. It was through translations of the canonical texts in Sanskrit, Prakrit and Pali that a vibrant Odia literary culture came into being. During the fifteenth century, with the decline of Sanskrit, advancement of Muslim rule in central parts of India, and the rising pre-eminence of Kannada and Telugu, Odia was required to negotiate a new poetic rooted in the popular and the local. The authors discuss in detail the works of Sarala Das from *Bichitra Ramayana* onwards, to demonstrate how his works exemplify the linguistic and cultural negotiations of the period. Once Odia attains a stable state, the radical poetic of Sarala Das is altered from within. Writers like Balaram Das appropriate the cosmopolitan knowledge systems to create a poetic which, as in the translation of *Bhagavata,* shows the influence of a pan-Indian culture. The authors conclude that the story of Odia literary culture is one of continuous negotiation between "local aspirations for knowledge and cosmopolitan hegemonic structures of power/culture".

Nirmal Selvamony examines two major pre-modern traditions of love poetry where the relations between lovers form the substance of the poems. His accent is on the nature of conventions that control the expression of the various shades of love relationships. Erotic passion dominates the articulation of love in Gahas whereas spousal harmony characterises the emotional tenor of *akam* poems. Even before *Tholkappiyam* came to be written, the poetic conventions regarding love were codified in Tamil. But there was no such codification of conventions in the tradition of Prakrit love poetry. Selvamony feels that Prakrit Gahas must have followed the conventions codified and embodied in Tamil texts; this confirms the larger outline proposed in the earlier part of this introduction regarding a travelling and translational poetic for Indian literatures.

Sachin Ketkar in his essay, "World Literature and Literary Historiography of Pre-colonial South Asian Vernaculars" shows how the notion of world literature is underpinned by the world-capitalist system, exemplifying neo-liberal attitudes towards culture. Disregarding these limitations of the concept, he follows a more productive model of "world literature" proposed in the writings of Dionyz Durisin using the concept of "inter-literariness". He examines the literary culture of Marathi during the medieval period spanning from the twelfth to the fifteenth centuries, when multiple literary worlds interacted in close proximity. He shows how conventional histories of Marathi literature, following the British model of historiography, have viewed the Islamic period as one of decadence and decline. This is disproved by the innovative literary productions of the period. Namdev's pilgrimages brought him into contact with the multiple worlds of Persian-Arabic as well as Sanskrit poetics, shaping a new intercultural consciousness. Further, the bardic *shahiri kavya* in the popular culture and the precolonial historic *bakhar* literature in the bureaucratic circles resulted from the dynamic interactions between Marathi and Dakhani literatures, in a context where the Sanskrit cosmopolis and Persian cosmopolis were in dialogue with each other. All the major Marathi Bhakti poets such as Namdev, Eknath, Tukaram and Ramdas wrote in Hindustani as well. Ketkar rightly concludes that all literary communities across the South Asia and beyond share interliterary processes with "world literary" traits.

Sukanya Sarbadhikary demonstrates how the biography of the saint Chaitanya (1486–1533) becomes the locus of discourses on the significance of *uddanda nritya* as an example of a living experience of ecstatic devotional dance. *Chaitanya Charitamrita* articulates the theology of *achintya-bhed-abhed*, giving rise to a tradition of participatory performances. The essay opens up several possibilities of relating performance traditions to literary texts, to bring out the dialogical process that is at work in the pre-modern culture as a whole.

Dhurjjati Sarma's essay examines the subliminal layers of the visual poetics that informs the multilingual and multimedial aethetics of Vaishnavism in Assam during the fifteenth and sixteenth centuries. The visionary–saint Sankardeva (1449–1508), who founded and nurtured the faith into a popular movement, had visited the major centres of Vaishnavism in India, and stayed at Puri for long to interact with scholars and deliver discourses. His translation of the tenth book of *Bhagavata Purana* into Assamese led to the production of its illustrated version, *Chitra Bhagavata.* Subsequently, he translated more books of *Bhagavata Purana* and refashioned them into musical, visual and performative versions, creating a set of multimedial productions which captured the imagination of the masses. This integration of Bhakti into diverse forms and meanings was made possible by Sankardeva's familiarity with the pan-Indian traditions of art and literature and their expressive potential from his familiarity with several languages. The cult of Chaitanya was particularly influential in shaping Sankardeva's multimedial poetics. Sarma examines at length the illustrated manuscripts of the *Chitra Bhagavata* and *Gita Govinda* to highlight the interface between the oral, the written and the visual in the Vaishnava literary culture.

P. P. Raveendran critically examines the literary histories of Malayalam in "The Social Imaginary and the Evolution of Modern Indian Literature" to problematise their evolutionary teleology borrowed from the Western models. He shows how they fail to grasp the social dynamic at work behind the literary practice as well as the role of creative imagination in the construction of literary sensibilities and social identities. The practice of literary historiography reveals conflicts and contradictions that inform their basic assumption. He shows how several of the eminent Malayalam poets may not answer to the categories such as "the romantic" or "the modernist" without misrepresenting the nature of their poetry. He rightly comments that the social imaginary that informs these works need to be studied further, as it shapes the social identities of a people. This approach has significance beyond

Malayalam when it comes to questions of literary historiography in our times.

It is the Indian novel which has documented our confrontations with modernity and its ideological baggage. Subha Chakraborty Dasgupta in her essay, "The Search for Form and Authenticity in Bangla Novels: A Reading of Debes Ray's *Tistaparer Brittanta*" argues that the Indian novel had to struggle against its form as derived from the West to represent the nuances of the Indian social reality. It is reflected in its anxiety of authenticity. She examines the use of the indigenous narrative resources in Bibhutibhusan Bandopadhyay's *Pather Panchali,* Tarashankar Bandopadhyay's *Hansuli Banker Upkatha* and Satinath Bhaduri's *Dhorai Charit Manas.* The voices of the marginalised and the displaced come alive in these novels through the digressive, non-linear forms of *upkatha, charit* and *panchali,* each of which has its own geneology that goes back to the medieval times. Her detailed exposition of Ray's *Tistaparer Brittanta* shows how, in his search for an authentic representation of "the story of the poorest 6.7 crore", the author has to deploy a wide range of narrative devices such as shifting perspectives, non-mimetic narratives, double-voiced story-telling and epic references. Ray's rural characters are down-to-earth and their bleak lives are trapped in endless cycles of betrayal and oppression by the power structures which are not accountable to any authority. The surplus of events and details in the novel do not tell the story, but enact it, with its unspeakable sorrow at the gradual breakdown of a community, and the mindless destruction of the forest, the river, the mountains and trees. The Indian novel can realise its ethical vision only by decentering the European form of the novel, and in the process embodying the perspective of the underprivileged in its very structure.

Vipin K. Kadavath's explication of Kumaran Asan's narrative poem, *Chintavishtayaya Sita* (Sita Lost in Thought, 2019) raises complex questions of ethics and aesthetics that inform this rewriting of the Ramayana. He characterises it as an "*im*-possible ethics that spills over into modes of political action reducible neither to a self-assuring individualism nor the colonial technologies of community". The idea of "thought" as something enacted through language as performance endows the narrative with the power to critique the prevailing morality of the hegemonic power structures. Kadavath finds that in Asan's prose writings the burden of ethical experience of responsibility transmutes into a form of political action.

Tonisha Guin discusses the popular representation of the Mahabharata in the Amar Chitra Katha series in relation to the narrative traditions in modern Indian literatures. Do they signify Hindi nationalistic themes through their visual narration? She goes back to the tradition of calendar art and chromolithographs to document their different textual traditions and their manner of significations; identifying the unresolvable aporias that mark their visual and verbal articulations.

B. S. Bini's essay on *Aithihyamala* deals with a moment in the life of modern Kerala when orality meets print, creating a disjunction in the very nature of textuality. This volume of loosely narrated folklore about local heroes, places, elephants, black magic, ayurvedic practitioners with miraculous powers, etc., served a certain purpose at the turn of the twentieth century when the novelistic genre had not acquired a hegemonic form. Reading the stories between the lines, Bini shows how they reveal intersections between multiple social worlds which included animals as well.

Colonial modernity forced native intellectuals to reorder the relations between the domestic and the public spheres. Zarana Maheshwari in her essay, "Domestication of English, Education and Perpetuation of Sexual Difference: A Reading of Govardhanram Tripathi's *Leelavati Jeevankala*" reads Govardhanram Tripathi's iconic text in relation to the emerging social conflicts in the wake of English education and the assertion of women's rights. The biography legitimates Leelavati's virtuous Hindu way of life as an exemplary model of woman's conduct. In the process it reinforces a hierarchical social structure, centred on the male's dominant role in the social sphere. The biography contrasts the merits of English and Sanskrit educations, and establishes the classical Indian language as a repository of wisdom and knowledge.

The essay raises larger issues regarding the relation between tradition and modernity which are often seen as mutually exclusive binaries. They often function as versions of a deeper schism which cannot be resolved within the available moral economy.

The prose-centred literary genres altered the literary landscape of Gujarati in the nineteenth century, as part of Gujarati language's attempt to negotiate the ideology of colonial modernity. It is through translations that these negotiations took place. Hiren Patel's essay, "Quest for a New Discourse in Literary Criticism in the Nineteenth Century: Interface between Gujarati and English, 1850–1890" discusses at length how a new critical consciousness arose in the literary sphere as a response to a felt need to evaluate the new prose genres. He discusses the essays that were published in some of the prominent literary periodicals like *Buddhiprakash* in the late nineteenth century. The new critical discourse shows the impact of the critical concepts of the alien literary tradition Gujarati is forced to contend with, along with traces of lingering effect of native critical thought.

E. V. Ramakrishnan in his paper, "From the Poetics of Self-knowledge to the Politics of Social Change" discusses the life and works of Sree Narayana Guru as a philosopher–poet and social reformer against the background of social reforms and colonial modernity. Guru reconstitutes the social discourse of reforms in the light of his deep engagement with poetic and philosophical traditions of Tamil Shaivism and Advaita, his poetic compositions enabling him to formulate an intercultural space of thick pluralism. In this sense, Guru may be considered a contemporary of poets like Kabir, Jnandev and Tukaram who reimagined the social through their philosophical poetry.

The essays included in the volume contribute to a better understanding of the intercultural and intertextual processes that have shaped the cultural poetics of modern Indian languages over the centuries. The social dynamics that inform these processes point to the subliminal pulls and pressures that have shaped the political formations in the country. Though we are not suggesting any one-to-one correspondence between the larger sociopolitical formations and the cultural poetics of Indian literatures, each has a stake in the other, and their mutual awareness is suggested by shared epistemes in critical moments of sociopolitical transitions. The larger objective of a volume like this is not to resolve issues of poetics and politics one way or the other, but to open up new modes of critical thinking and alternative models of evaluation in the interest of a genuine search for interactive spaces of dialogism in Indian critical thought.

Works Cited

Bakhtin, Mikhail. 1986. *Speech Genres and Other Late Essays.* Translated by Vern W. McGee. Edited by Caryl Emerson and Michael Holquist. Austin: University of Texas Press.

Benjamin, Walter. (1996) 2004. "The Task of the Translator." In *Selected Writings Vol. 1, 1913–1926,* edited by Marcus Bullock and M. W. Jennings, 253–63. Cambridge: Harvard University Press.

Bhatia, Nandi. 2009. *Modern Indian Theatre: A Reader.* New Delhi: Oxford University Press.

Chatterji, Suniti Kumar. 1946. "Islamic Mysticism, Iran and India." *Indo-Iranica*: 29.

Das, Sisir Kumar. 2003. "The Mad Lover." *Indian Literature* 47, no. (3), 215 (May-June,): 149–78.

Eaton, Richard M. 2020. *India in the Persianate Age 1000–1765.* Penguin Books.

Greenblatt, Stephen. 1988. *Shakespearean Negotiations.* Berkeley: University of California Press.

———. 1990. *Learning to Curse: Essays in Early Modern Culture.* New York: Routledge.

———, ed. 2010. *Cultural Mobility: A Manifesto.* U.K.: Cambridge University Press.

Novetzke, Christian Lee. 2008. *Religion and Public Memory: A Cultural History of Saint Namdev in India.* Columbia: Columbia University Press.

Pillai, Ilamkulam Kunjan, ed. With commentary. 1995. *Leelathilakam* (in Malayalam). Kottayam: Sahitya Pravarthaka Sahakarana Samgham.

Pollock, Sheldon. 2006. *The Language of Gods in the World of Men: Sanskrit, Culture and Power in Premodern India.* Ranikhet: Permanent Black.

———, ed. and trans. 2017. *A Rasa Reader: Classical Indian Aesthetics.* Delhi: Permanent Black.

Ramanujan, A. K., trans. 1985. *Poems of Love and War: From the Eight Anthologies and the Ten Long Poems of Classical Tamil.* Delhi: Oxford University Press.

Ramakrishnan, E. V. (2011) 2017. *Locating Indian Literature: Texts, Traditions, Translations.* Hyderabad: Orient BlackSwan.

Raveendran, P. P. 2023. *Under the Bhasha Gaze: Modernity and Indian Literature.* Oxford: Oxford University Press.

Sheikh, Gulammohammed. 2021. "Towards an Alternative Visual Language: An Interview with Gulammohammed Sheikh by E. V. Ramakrishnan". *Frontline,* June 19–July 02, 101–14.

Varrier, M. R. Raghava, and Kesavan Veluthatt. 2016. *Manipravala Charcha* (Debates on Manipravalam). Kottayam: Sahitya Pravarthaka Sahakarana Samgham.

ONE

Is There a "South Asian Poetics"?

Mrinal Kaul

kartarah sulabha loke vijnataras tu durlabhah

(Bhasa, *Svapnavasavadattam*, act IV, verse 9)

Let me begin by posing a question that I have chosen to be the title of this paper—"Is there a 'South Asian poetics'?" Before I discuss why exhorting such a question is important, let me briefly say what I mean by asking this. In other words, the answer to this question lies, I believe, in profound understanding of the question itself. To examine my title—I purposely use the present subjunctive verb "is" and not past "was" for if I use the past verb, it would mean that I am focusing on "poetics" as a historical category *alone*, while my intention in raising this question is to situate it in *our* understanding (whatever it may be) of poetics or the discourse about it in the *present*. In other words, how do we address and answer this question at present if we have to locate such an answer in its historicity as well. Furthermore, I think it would be wrong to use a definite article "the" and hence I use the indefinite article "a" in the title bearing in mind there can never be a definite category like "the poetics", particularly in case of South Asia. A partial answer to this is also embedded in accosting a very complex question that I will not attempt to answer here—what is South Asia? Or if approached from a pre-modern point of view, then to use Sheldon Pollock's expression—where *was* this "South Asia"? [emphasis in italics mine]. To use the past tense in the latter question also means to problematise the idea of pre-modernity itself. Without defining South Asia and its pre-modernity as categories of our concern, it remains futile to approach the question of "poetics". Scholars like Sheldon Pollock have already dealt with the complexity of such categories and I am indeed taking a cue from his critical engagement. However, I will only focus on a part of the complexity of "poetics" in its history and how we understand it today, particularly focusing on Sanskrit literary culture. For doing this, I will build on my argument using materials from the pre-modern South Asian poeticians themselves. What I will argue is that the potentiality of the idea of creativity in the South Asian context lies in its open-endedness, that is, its flexibility and catholicity. In other words, it lies in the complete autonomous agency of how a certain experiencing subject wants to think about his/her own experience. To understand this, I use a constructed category that I name "South Asian poetics" that eventually will need to be deconstructed/dissolved and is only being used here to problematise the idea at hand. We never really imagine or explore the linguistic or cultural maps of South Asia and if we misinterpret the political as cultural, the territory of our concern becomes even more evasive.

But what does this constructed category of "South Asian poetics" mean and what would it be? Where does its ontology lie—in the past itself or in the present? Or in both or in neither? I do agree with Pollock (2006, 2) when he says that the term literature "needs to be understood pragmatically rather than ontologically, as pointing to ways certain texts are used rather than defining what those texts inherently and essentially are" or when he mentions "literary is a functional rather than an ontological category, comprising something people do with a text rather than something a text truly and everlastingly is, but the fact that people are constantly induced to do whatever that something is, and to do it variously because 'every specific situation is historical'" (2003, 9).[1] While I agree with Pollock, my interest lies in exploring the ontology of the aesthetic phenomenon itself and to do this by exploring the pre-modern literary traditions in South Asia, one has to be able to perceive this aesthetic phenomenon in its historical context as well. This indeed raises a further set of fundamental

[1] Also see Pollock (2003, 18–19).

questions in the context of "poetics": what did creativity mean for literary practitioners in pre-modern South Asia and where did this literariness lie? Rather, where was this literary newness and what was it? These questions have to be asked in their history and to pose and answer these questions, the category of "literary history" itself has to be complicated (Pollock 2003, 2–22). To be able to do this one needs to reconsider and re-look at the literary categories themselves and further inquire into them in the South Asian context. But the engagement with these questions will be incomplete if we do not consider a further question—what is the locus of creativity and literariness *now*?

For me, a partial answer to this question lies in our approaches to answer such problems. In other words, how are we meaningfully making sense of such categories, problematising them systematically while subjecting them to ruthless but meaningful criticism, understanding their critical development in their history, and how then we present a narrative that may be called meaning-making. In this way what I am also suggesting is that we need to explore the continuities from the pre-modern to the modern, where we are located at present. These questions have already been addressed by scholars like Sheldon Pollock, Shamsur Rahman Faruqi, Velcheru Narayan Rao and David Shulman using different methods and I am not suggesting anything new.

To summarise the problem, if one wants to have a fresh look at the pre-modern structures themselves one has to be able to displace or de-institutionalise the already prevalent approaches and has to go back to where pre-modernity began. This is quite fundamental. In other words, one has to be able to do justice to pre-modern authors themselves and understand their structures in their own terms before we bring them to the comparative platforms for ruthless analysis (Pollock 2003, 14–15). Might I add that an important tool to achieve this aim is philology about which I will not talk much here. But a note of warning should be issued to those who think philology is a colonial device and has no serious or meaningful role to play in our postcolonial understanding of South Asian texts. Philological pursuit is, as

Pollock puts it, *making sense of texts* (Pollock et al. 2015) and it is something perilous and difficult to accomplish; otherwise, our misunderstanding, misinterpreting or misleading the context of a text, even if minimal, might prove to be precarious and we may be inadvertently discharging injustice to the concerned author or the tradition they belong to. We should also be careful while employing the modern structures in the context of pre-modern literary traditions of South Asia. We are aware that the Orientalist comparative models should not be used, like many early researchers did in colonial times, and many others still afford to do it under the veil of colonial hangover (in both East for different reasons and in West for yet other reasons), for the sake of fitting the Eastern models into the Western. That is not to say that we cannot use non-Orientalist comparisons as Pollock would plead or as Daya Krishna (1989, 59–60) would strongly emphasise in the context of Indian philosophy, that one may follow "comparative 'comparative studies'" instead of doing comparative studies with a Eurocentric bias. This can be done without getting entangled in the dichotomies of the East and the West; we should learn how to generate a narrative that is beyond these dichotomies. A large picture of South Asian intellectual cultures on a very wide canvas should be brought in where we can portray its universal picture in comparison to various other grand intellectual cultures of the world. In this case, I think, one should keep in mind the work of Velcheru Narayan Rao and David Shulman. The exercise they have been engaged with is long overdue in the case of South Asian literary cultures. But our problem does not end here. One does not only need to re-evaluate the history of ideas, but also needs to dislocate and challenge the earlier flawed interpretations and understanding/evaluations, and I do believe that one of the most constructive ways of doing this is the way both Narayan Rao and Shulman have done it over the past few decades.

To illustrate my point further, I will take a few examples in case of the pre-modern Sanskrit literary culture. One problem we often face is how Sanskrit literary trends have been evaluated by early writers, both colonial Indologists and South Asian scholars often trained under colonial Indologists, writing in or translating into (in many cases for the first time) English. Such interpretations have become canonical trends. Two examples could be that of *dhvani* (suggestion/resonance) and *slesha* (pun/simultaneous narration).[2] Taking a cue from Pollock, two excellent studies in recent years have dealt with such issues presenting their studies on *dhvani* and *slesha* in the new light. I am referring to Lawrence McCrea's *The Teleology of Poetics in Medieval Kashmir* and Yigil Bronner's *Extreme Poetry, The South Asian Movement of Simultaneous Narration*. McCrea's argument is that Anandavardhana's poetics of *rasa-dhvani* brought about an analogous paradigm shift in normative expectations of how a Sanskrit poem was read. Anandavardhana's fame obscured almost all other innovative theories of poetics. On the other hand, modern researchers rebuked him for being over-critical and not really focusing on what he should have focused on—what makes good poetry? This is what, for instance, K. Krishnamoorthy (1968, 214 quoted in McCrea 2008, 6) had to say:

> We, who study the Dhvanyāloka at this distant date, separated by more than a thousand years from its author, are apt to take objection to one feature in which the work abounds, viz., the preponderance of minute classification, subtle hair-splitting and at times even logic-chopping; It may rightly appear to us so much waste of energy on matters insignificant in respect of literary criticism. But while making such an estimate we should not blind ourselves to the fact that Anandavardhana is an ancient writer living in an age when the whole atmosphere was permeated with a love for philosophical argument and logical subtlety; and if Anandavardhana errs, sometimes on the side of too much brevity and at other times on the side of over-subtlety, it is because he was a typical product of that age and he was merely following the *zeitgeist*.

As far as the second example is concerned, Bronner highlights the bias that modern scholars had generated towards what almost appeared to be like an anti-*slesha* movement. He says,

---

[2] One more example could be seen in Lawrence McCrea (2015).

"The prevalent disregard for this literary movement has partly been the result of a strong distaste for *sleṣa* among modern scholars, both Western and South Asian. The vast amounts of energy Indologists have invested in writing against *śleṣa* is quite remarkable, particularly when it is compared with the relatively small amount of scholarly work that has been produced about it". The implicitly crucial remark that Bronner is making here is that much of our understanding about pre-modern literary texts is based on the interpretations of early researchers and there is a need to have a totally fresh look at much of this literature that also involves re-translating and re-interpreting many of them critically; he also points out how the biases of early scholars have percolated down to us smoothly and how comfortably we have accepted much of it at its face value. For instance, we need to relook at the following interpretation of *slesha* (Balasubramaniyam quoted in Bronner 2010, 9):

> The author is always very verbose and never cares for the plot. He is fond of using all kinds of similes—unnatural and disgusting through some of them are—for the purpose of giving free scope to his extreme partiality to *slesha* [*śleṣa*] or pun upon words. The introduction traces the origin of this deceased imagination which appears to have exercised so much influence on Subandhu as to make him not to care for anything else except the use of a string of words and phrases full of *slesha*. From this it will be clear how the process of deterioration has proceeded and how the story, the necessities of the circumstances, the dictates of reason, of nature and even of decency, were all set aside for the author's inordinate love of profuse verbosity and dry pun.[3]

In the above lines we also have to think why "verbosity" is essentially considered to be deterioration by Balasubramaniyam. Was being verbose understood as an essential characteristic of creativity by the pre-modern Sanskrit craftsmen themselves?

---

[3] J. K. Balasubramaniyam, in his preface to *Vāsavadattā* of Subhandu, with commentary by R. V. Krishnamachariar; the introduction he refers to is by R. V. Krishnamachariar, the editor.

Is pun a dry trope or does it generate more nuanced relish for connoisseurs—obviously provided the connoisseurs are sensitive to the idea of punning, provided they understand both the literal word and the layers of meanings it conveys. But Sanskrit literature was not unique in receiving such treatment. There were no exceptions as is clear from what Faruqi Sahab (2001, 15), for instance, says about Urdu literature:

> When Urdu literary histories or historical-literary-theoretical accounts of Urdu literature came to be written, the first one as early as 1880, their authors took pains to blame Urdu literature for lacking in 'originality'. That the Urdu poets 'chewed morsels that had already been chewed over and over again' became a favourite among the charges most commonly framed against them. Literature was seen as a social-functional, and not an aesthetic-artistic, object, Urdu literature seemed to fail on this count too. Literary history was seen as a history of individual departures and initiatives, leading to 'change'. Continuity was seen as 'no-progress'.

One can possibly list a number of such methodological problems and also contemplate how to address them. But let me not digress from our main question—Is there South Asian Poetics? If yes, what is it? Let me clarify what I mean by "poetics" here. By poetics I do not mean the manuals of literary injunctions *alone* (obviously them as well), I do not *only* mean how literariness was practised either, I do not *only* mean who talked about what constitutes literary newness or what comprises what one may call cultural poetics *alone*, yet I do mean all of these together simultaneously. But why should I sound paradoxical? I think the need to be paradoxical emerges out of the complexity of the situation—both in space and time. The enormously vast literary landscape that we have in front of us in its history is not easy to deal with. It is even more complicated to make repeated attempts to deal with it meaningfully. Even if one focuses on the cosmopolitan literary culture alone, that is, Sanskrit, we find ourselves dealing with Bharata sometime in between second BCE to second CE all the way up to Panditaraja Jaganatha in seventeenth CE (Pollock 2003, 42–43). This cosmopolitan literary culture was by no means a homogenous category in itself. How could it be? After all, even if at one point of time there was active presence of Sanskrit from Afghanistan to Java, as Pollock would say, yet it was always able to survive in all these different practices along with the local or indigenous traditions both synchronically and diachronically (Faruqi 2001, 13). If that was not the case, we would not have had Abhinavagupta (*fl.c.* 975–1025 CE) arguing for the ontological status of the ninth rasa (*shanta*) or Rupa Gosvami (1489–1564 CE) pleading for a tenth rasa (*bhakti*) or we would not have had a Mullah Sa'dullah "Masih" Panipati (seventeenth CE) translating Rama of Valamiki's Ramayana as a proto-Muhammadan prophet in his *Masnavi-i Ram va Sita* (Keshavmurthy 2018). We should neither have expected Amir Khusrau (1253–1325 CE) to be writing in the unique style of language that he did, nor should we have expected early Telugu poets like Nannaya (eleventh CE), Tikkana (thirteenth CE) and Errana (fourteenth CE) to be writing the renderings of the Mahabharata in highly Sanskritised Telugu and yet creating in them "an atmosphere closer to Telugu domestic life" (Rao 2016, 43). And this was not only ensuing at the level of language, retellings, translations, new presentations of literary critical ideas or the attempts at defining "literary newness" or "creativity" but also deeply somewhere at the level of engaging with the idea of developing a rich profusion of heterogeneously variegated methods. One dynamic principle that was inherent to this literary newness was "change" (Faruqi 2001, 13).[4] By "change" I do not mean here what Faruqi Sahab is mentioning in the context of "social-functional" above.[5] What I mean by "change"

---

[4] Pollock (2003, 9) also quotes M. M. Bakhtin referring to the idea of change in literature. I think it is worthwhile to mention the quote here (I am quoting directly from Pollock and have not referred to Bakhtin in the original): "After all, the boundaries between fiction and nonfiction, between literature and nonliterature and so forth are not laid up in heaven. Every specific situation is historical. And the growth of literature is not merely development and change within the fixed boundaries of any given definition; the boundaries themselves are constantly changing."

[5] See also Pollock (2003, 102).

is that every changing literary dynamic was seen as bringing in a newness. If looked from the diachronic point of view, certainly the idea of “change” was inevitable, but it is not at all absent in the synchronic approach either. What I mean to say is that the strength of this literary newness lay in how many different ways could one approach the same reality while we are situated in the present contemporary world. To explain, if, for instance, we take an example of an object of art—an apple or an image of an apple—we need to focus on how creatively and differently this object of art has been defined in the past and in how many different ways this piece of art can be defined in the present by many of us. In any case an apple will always remain what it is, but what will change is the various ways of describing it. Those creative approaches lie within our minds albeit without allowing any change in the apple itself. Also, in the present, that is, while you are reading this paper, twenty different creative craftsmen can project the same object of beauty—the same apple—in completely multifarious ways. The object of art will always remain what it is, but the locus of creative newness lies in the subject of the appreciation of art, that is, the connoisseur. The real existence of an object of art thus lies in the mind of an aesthete.

But this does not answer our question about what possibly South Asian poetics is? Does it? I don’t know, but surely it raises another question—is it that what people do is always more important than what they think, as Pollock (2006, 7–8) would ask, or vice versa. This “doing” which is a form of literary practice is what one needs to look at closely. As I would conclude towards the end of this paper, what we can do in the present is what David Shulman is doing—not comparing and contrasting methods and applying them to the South Asian literary cultures (understand I am not against it at all), but focusing on a few important literary concepts like “imagination” in the literary history of South Asia and mapping its territory. By mapping this territory all the way from the cosmopolitan age to the vernacular age, like for instance, in Shulman’s *More Than Real* (2012), he establishes an unsaid method. I say “unsaid method” because he is following a very tight structured method allowing a vast amount of literature spread over eons covering an enormous landscape to speak for itself through the literary and non-literary works, characters therein, the literary trends they follow, conceits they choose and so on. This is done without invoking any preset structures and academically popular methodological tools and without attempting to appropriate any South Asian ideas using such tools. This allows a probing deep into the pre-modern South Asian minds to get a glimpse of how they perceived what "imagination" is. Shulman attempts to let the un-presented and under-represented South Asian mind speak for itself perspicuously. This is a daunting task, but certainly more significant than naively eulogising about its richness and historicity. This can also be achieved by unostentatiously providing the standard and careful translations of literary works like how Shulman and Narayan Rao have done in case of Telugu literature, and alternately this can be accomplished by studying the medieval translation factories like in the Mughal court as is presented by Audrey Truschke (2016).

I must mention that the inspiration of the present title of the paper comes from a lecture of Jenab Shamsur Rahman Faruqi that he delivered in CSDS, Delhi[6] asking what do we really mean and what are we referring to when we use the expression "Indian Poetics" or "South Asian Poetics" and where does it lie. Can we posit there *is* a category called Indian/South Asian poetics? Is this poetics hybrid and plural as opposed to being pure and homogenous? Can any poetics function in cultural isolation, no matter how rigid it has been over the course of its development in history? Will it not influence the literary or linguistic practices outside its own domain one way or the other, or will it not itself become influenced by literary practices other than its own irrespective of whether it does or does not ever come into close

---

[6] Pratiman Release: Lecture by Shamsur Rahman Faruqi on Urdu Adabi Riwayat Ki Sachi Triveni organised by Centre for the Study of Developing Societies, Delhi. Accessible on https://www.youtube.com/watch?v=XTC769HYy2Y (Accessed on 11 June 2024).

proximity with parallel literary practices elsewhere in the world owing to various historical trajectories? Who can prevent this? Or why should one prevent this at all? Should this change be considered a creative literary development in that literary tradition or should it be considered interfering with the pure nature of it? Who has the agency to decide it? And the most compelling question—is a connoisseur not a part of this project, that is, is the assimilation of reader/listener/receiver of such traditions also not a part of this poetics? How sagacious is it on part of the meaning-maker, for instance, as Faruqi Sahab would ask, to read Ghalib in isolation from *rasa* theory or Kuntaka's theory of oblique speech (*vakrokti*) even if Ghalib would have never known or read about what *rasa* theory or *vakrokti* was? Of course, I do not mean to say that Ghalib cannot be read or interpreted bereft of the *rasa* theory, but being constantly involved in the phenomenon that this cultural poetics has evolved into, we should be compelled to explore the contrary trajectories that transpires into this process of novel meaning-making. We must discuss this. This influence may not be phonetic (*shabda*), literal, may not even be very evident or may not be verbatim influence, but it might be present subtly or semantically (*artha*) or in generating the receptive meaning as Anandavardhana of the ninth century CE or his commentator Abhinavagupta would have posited. In fact, Faruqi Sahab (2003, 856 quoted in Pollock 2003) seems to argue that the notion of *kaifiyat* is similar to Abhinavagupta's notion of *dhvani* that is defined as "a state of subtle and delicious enjoyment such as one derived from tragedy or a sad piece of music". Perhaps a comparison with *rasa* or *rasa-dhvani* in particular might have been better, if I may suggest. Faruqi Sahab further compares the literary tropes in the two literary cultures like *ma'ni* and *vyanjana* (2003, 852 quoted in Pollock 2003) or *iham* with *slesha*[7] or *tab'-i-vaqqad* and *sahrdaya* (2003, 827 quoted in Pollock 2003). It should be recognised that these theories did not emerge only

[7] Faruqi (2003, 856) in Pollock (2003).

on the basis of Sanskrit literary theory; rather, they emerged by way of assimilation with it (Faruqi 2003, 835 quoted in Pollock 2003). But what does Faruqi Sahab mean by this "assimilation"? Like he would say (ibid.):

> While his general debt to Arabic and Sanskrit poetics is obvious, it is hard to pinpoint exactly where their influence lies. Rather, there is an air of assimilation, an indirect intimation of connections and continuities. Like Khusrau in his Persian, Shaikh Ahmad is constructing not so much from the past as for the benefit of the present and the future. Anticipations of what will come to be called the "Indian style" of Persian poetry can be seen. They are not dominant yet, but they are clearly the most prominent element in the Shaikh's poetics. The emphasis on abstract, subtle thought; the centrality of metaphor; the global reach of the imagination; and the value placed on figures of speech—all these are characteristics of the "Indian style."

The point I want to make is that there is no scope for a solitary interpretation of this poetics or the "Indian style" of it and it can only be engaged with in its myriad phenomenon since the intrinsic development of this poetics is syncretic by nature. This tradition skeptically practiced this syncretism in the heterogenous hermeneutics of its history that was gradually assimilated by what we are hypothetically calling "Indian style" or "South Asian poetics". As an illustration, one may only think of the answer that many Sanskrit literary theorists have attempted to the question—what is the essence or soul of the literature (*kavya*) or literariness? They all had different answers to this problem. For both Bhamaha (c. 650 CE) and Dandin (c. 700 CE) the question remained confined to the problem of word (*shabda*) and its meaning (*artha*). However, both Bhamaha and Dandin did not have the same kind of challenges in front of them as did Anandavardhana. Later, neither Anandavardhana nor Abhinavagupta had in mind what perhaps Mahimabhatta (c. 1025 CE) and Jagannatha (c. 1650 CE) were planning to 'do' with this question. Yet all of them had similar concerns based on a certain skepticism that continued to question literariness. The poetic style was changing, so were poetic idioms, tropes, diction, conceits, concerns, etc., and yet a unique question connecting all these concerns was—what is literariness? Is the literary newness hidden in the word or in the meaning, is it concealed in the literal expression or metaphorical tropology? Or is it a category completely distinct—a suggested meaning that is context-dependent and the agent enjoying the absolute agency of appreciation to generate a new meaning each time depending on how it is received or interpreted? Or is this literary newness completely dependent on emotions (*bhava*) or to be precise, a response to emotions (*rasa*)? Who can answer such questions—poets themselves who are the practitioners of this trade or poet–philosophers who wonder what creativity ought to be?

This also reminds us of the two major intellectual and creative practices in pre-modern South Asia, *kavya* and *shastra* (Pollock 2003, 49–52). *Kavya* was creative and descriptive and *shastra* was scientific and prescriptive. Thus, the *kavya-shastric* manuals were philosophising the notion of literary newness or literary creativity—what it is and what it ought to be, or as they would say, what is the best form of poetic creativity. However, the poets themselves, and not poeticians or poet–philosophers, were never really troubled by this. They seamlessly continued to compose *kavya*. For most of them, to avoid all sorts of complexities, they were generally engaged in what one may call creative re-use of language, both at the level of word and meaning, and using twists in presenting their narratives, most of which were already present in grand epics like the Ramayana and the Mahabharata. But these interventions, even if tiny, were crucial. If one were only to take examples of Bhasa or Kalidasa, it evidently becomes clear how they practised literary newness in their works by developing shorter scenes or episodes from these grand epics, sometimes not even adhering to the principles of Sanskrit dramaturgy too strictly. To use illustrations in different contexts, the same strategy was used in the legend of the literary character of Sakuntala right from its inception in the Mahabharata or the Padmapurana: the twists fitting the plot in the play called *Abhijnanashakuntalam* by

Kalidasa, further depictions, adaptations, etc. in popular culture, along with depictions by the Orientalists like William Jones and Monier-Williams, Tagore's exploration of "Its Inner Meaning" (Thapar 2011) and so on and so forth. One could even take the example of "many Ramayanas"—as many Ramayanas, so many Ramas (Ramanujan 1999)—as well as Bhavabhuti's Rama who is nothing but compassion (*karuna*) (Shulman 2001). All the above examples illustrate to us the heterogenous functionality of the phenomenon that is the cultural poetics.

We must also revisit the crucial question about taxonomies viz., discussions and clarifications about classifications, or should I say modern classifications. Where was the demarcation between what in modern terms we call literature and philosophy? This is probably true about every pre-modern intellectual culture. J. L. Masson (1971) and Phyllis Granoff (2001) have already problematised this issue. The broader taxonomies in practice, as just mentioned above, seemed *kavya* and *shastra*, and yet texts like the Mahabharata that were strictly understood as *itihasa* were proclaimed by Anandavardhana along with Valamiki's Ramayana and Kalidasa's *Abhijnanashakuntalam* as the only great works of poetry (*kavya*) ever composed. In fact, exaggeration itself seems to be a sort of a taxonomic category for these pre-moderns who also put important texts like the Mahabharata, Natyashastra and later Ramacharitamanasa written in Avadhi in the category of the fifth Veda. To this one should add if the following literary craftsmen were "doing" literature or practicing philosophy—the *vachanakaras* in old Kannada, the hymns of the *alvars* and *nayanmars* in old Tamil or Sufis writing *vaks* and *shruks* in old Kashmiri. I am purposely posing this question since the above mentioned "poets" do not find a place in the canonical space that is dominated by the doctrinal philosophical teachings taught in the Sanskrit language preaching Shaiva or Vaishnava faiths or philosophies. Can these questions be answered? Why have we generously contributed to the widening of the gulf between literature and philosophy that can otherwise be interpreted as a homogenous category? In the South Asian context, the pursuit of philosophising did not only mean rationalising. The relationship—if at all we understand philosophy and literature as two distinct categories—between the two was complicated, as mentioned by J. L. Masson (1971, 168):

> What can we say about ancient India? When we speak of a philosophy of aesthetics, of underlying philosophical notions in literary criticism, what precisely do we mean? What did it mean to be a philosopher in ancient India? Is it merely a question of training in philosophical doctrines? This all literary critics shared. The very nature of education in ancient India was such that we cannot imagine a literary critic who was not well-versed in *nyāya*, *mīmāṃsā*, *vedānta* and grammar. Poetics uses all of these disciplines. But does this mean that it is founded on any particular philosophy? Is there, in fact, any system in Sanskrit poetics that could be described as philosophical that is more than just the use made of other systems?

Are the famous allegorical plays like the *Prabodhachandrodaya* of Krishna Mishra (c. 1000 CE) that teaches the non-dual Vedanta philosophy, a good example of addressing this problem? Is this a book of philosophy or literature? Do such texts present the "newness" through their distinct genre or through the "newness" of the doctrinal and philosophical teaching? What is "new" about Krishna Mishra's Vedanta? Another such example could be the *nyaya* logician Jayanta Bhatta (c. 820 CE–c. 900 CE) and his play titled "Much Ado About Religion" (*Agamadambara*) (Dezsö 2005). I consider *Agamadambara* a wonderful textbook of Indian philosophy that portrays in front of us invigorating scenes of a graduate school where students and teachers engage in lively discussions about the rivalry philosophical schools like *nyaya*, Buddhist and *mimamsa*. It is hard to appreciate these literary pieces of art if one is not trained in the philosophical tenets they are presenting. Mark the following words of J. N. Mohanty in his foreword to the play titled "The Rise of Wisdom Moon" (*Prabodhachandrodaya*) translated into English by Matthew Kapstein (2009, xv):

> "The Rise of Wisdom Moon" belongs to a literary genre that requires from readers both philosophical knowledge and literary sensibility

> in order to be able to appreciate it. The work cannot be reduced to a merely philosophical treatise, so compelling is its literary and dramatic effect. The cast of characters, each representing a power of sensible, erotic, intellectual and spiritual life, is at first confounding, but soon, as one identifies each power's characteristic, familiar role, the entire story of conflict, struggle, and eventual resolution coheres in its depiction of man's inner life, and is comparable in this respect to Hegel's "Phenomenology of Spirit." For while Hegel's is a philosophical treatise cast, rather severely, as a dramatization, Krishna·mishra's is ostensibly a drama meant to be staged, but is also explicitly philosophical.

To come back to our question of where this literary newness really lay or lies, and taking an example of the Ramayana once again, one can cite an example from what Ajay Rao has shown us about the commentarial tradition of Shrivaishnavas on the Ramayana from 1250–1600 CE in the south India. Over the course of time, Rao has illustrated, how the history of reception of Ramayana transformed gradually as the hermeneutic project reconceptualising Rama's story by applying "innovative interpretive techniques to the *Rāmāyaṇa* as a text. Specific interpretative techniques included allegorical reading, *śleṣa* reading (reading a verse as a double entendre), and the application of vernacular performance techniques such as word play, improvisation, repetition and novel forms of citation" (Rao 2015, 9–10). This indeed was nothing unique. It was the functionality of what we called literary newness that was percolating into the vernacular age even if the hermeneutic project was still very much being practised in Sanskrit. Another example is what Deven Patel has illustrated to us about the history of the reception of the immortal poetic work of Shriharsha named the *Naishadhiyacharitam*. Taking as an example the commentarial literature on the *Naishadhiya*, Patel notes that what is missing is "serious discussions about an individual Sanskrit poem's reading communities and their reading *practices*, a sense of what tied a particular work's readership together over centuries, and what the dynamics of difference between these audiences, separated by time and space, were" (Patel 2014, 2). Patel's work manages to fulfil this gap while attempting to answer the following crucial questions: "What are the different types of readerships a Sanskrit poem attracted across centuries? What were some of the diverse explanatory or interpretative practices readers brought to the text? What tied all of them together?" (ibid.). Was it some kind of homogeneity of the heterogeneous tradition? This homogenous category, as Patel puts it, was or is exemplified by "reading practices of empirical readers and reading communities in specific historical situations in order to reconstruct the contributions of human agents in forming the *Naiṣadhīya* tradition as it exists for us today" (Patel 2014, 5).

Thinking about such possibilities does make us run into other problematic realms—how do we define a text and how do we define a tradition, and yet another more important question—how do we read the relationship between the two? Remember I quoted Pollock in the beginning in this context, where he argues for defining literary as a functional rather than a fossilised category, that is, something we *do* with a text rather than defining a text merely as a relic. When Paul Ricoeur (1984) asked the question "What is a text?" one possible answer, we can think of, comes from Philip Lutgendorf's *The Life of a Text: Performing the Rāmcaritmānas of Tulsidas* (1991). Does a text reside in the physical book, in the tradition, in the narrative or in the oral or performative narrative? Is it out there or is it in how we imagine it to be? Does the reality of a certain literary text lie, in the words of Pollock, in what "something people do with a text"? In other words, how do *we* respond to this literariness? How does the life of an otherwise dead text on a piece of paper or its narrative or the characters therein become conscious entities in our imagination? Is it something like what you experience as a part of the audience of a certain powerful *dastan* performance where everything is being imagined on the spot and thrown unto you for imagining and you suddenly infuse life into Amir Hamza or Hoshruba? *Dastan* narratives are a part of such unruly and autonomous imaginative practices that they cannot be chained in any rules of poetics, yet Musharraf Ali Farooqui (2000; 2009) had to create its poetics. If you are sensitive enough to experience through imagination a certain aestheticised emotion, this is what Abhinavagupta calls the phenomenon of *rasa* and this is what David Shulman means by saying—to use the title of his fundamental work—imagination for South Asian poetics is "More Than Real". The "more" aspect here is to introduce or emphasise the ontology of the phenomenon that I referred to in the very beginning. Like Faruqi Sahab would say, that for "South Asian Poetics", a metaphor is as real as anything unlike the Western obsession with whether a metaphor is true or not. Here a certain metaphor is not only real, but it is more than real because it is a part of the subjective imagination of the connoisseur. One possible answer to Ricoeur's question would be that this real imagination itself transforms into a text.

Here another set of crucial questions should be invoked. In the literary history of South Asia, what was global about "Sanskrit-ness"? Was it the language itself or the literariness of the narratives that pushed it to become global? And why and how did it influence the making of vernacular or bhasha literary traditions? What changed when global was slowly transforming into local? Or was there any global at all at the first place? And what qualified for "creativity" when we were already in the age that was vernacularised? This has been discussed by Pollock in detail and I am not attempting to engage with these questions in this short paper, but I can only present a brief point of view. As argued by Rao and Shulman (2012, 25), in some cases the situation was contrary to what Pollock suggests. For someone like the coastal Andhra poet Shrinatha of fourteenth CE, to take an example, who wrote in highly ornate Sanskritised Telugu style, and was effectively re-Sanskritising Sanskrit (to use Rao and Shulman's idiom), this is what good poetry meant:

> A little crooked
> like the crescent moon on Śiva's head,
> sharp as the contours
> of the firm, quickened breasts of the goddess
> roused to fury at the end of time,
> yet soft and delicious:

> good poetry is all of this together,
> wherever poets live. (Rao and Shulman 2012, 4)

In the above definition of poetry, the concern had gradually moved away from *shabda* and *artha*, or the dialectics of subject of aesthetic emotion and object of it. Now we are dealing with Shiva's head and the goddess' breasts and our concern is "where poets live", rather than the locus of the aestheticised emotion and its ontology. Unlike Shrinatha, there are cases of the *mangalakavya*s in Bangla or the *vachana*s in Kannada which seem straightforwardly wanting to move away from Sanskrit literary forms and yet there are cases like that of Narmad (1833–1886 CE) in Gujarati literary culture who is wanting to bring back Sanskritic forms and is writing the *Pingal Pravesh*, the *Alamkara Pravesh* and the *Rasa Pravesh* in Gujarati. Works like the *Kavirajamargam* in Kannada, the *Lilatilakam* in Malayalam and the *Chaitanya Charitramrita* in Bangla are the manifest examples of "cosmopolitan vernacular" that eventually, as Pollock argues, are also being replaced by "regional vernacular". There is a big shift taking place and yet it is not completely bereft of Sanskrit and its literary culture. In fact, one can argue, as A. K. Ramanujan does, as opposed to "structure", gradually it is "anti-structure" in play and this is not only transpiring at the level of the choice of language, form or genre that literati are choosing to write in, but also society that is playing an important role. In fact, one may even make an assertion that functionality of literary-newness was no more the practice of literati alone, but now also in the agency of practice of commoners.

An important point to bear in mind is that in the early phase of the development of literary theory, I do not think that literary was meant to have any social concerns as Pollock (2001) would think, but the social and the political at the epistemic level was the domain of the practitioners of the legal and moral philosophy represented in the texts of the *dharmashastra*. This is not to suggest that no poet was thinking about social or moral or ethical issues. If we quickly jump back in time—in the tenth-eleventh CE Kashmir where the master aesthetician Abhinavagupta was writing his most celebrated commentary on the Natyashastra and not too far away from his spatio-temporal world was Kshemendra, a master satirist, who has been completely neglected by the modern Sanskritits or Indologists for even though he was writing in Sanskrit, he was prejudiced against for using uncultured/rustic/vulgar (*ashlila*) vocabulary and expressions that was unacceptable to the "civilised" Sanskrit literati and thus objectionable. In his writings, he invoked prostitutes, pimps and mother-prostitutes, ostentatious priests and pontiffs, corrupt officials, young women being married to old men, students visiting brothels instead of attending universities, etc. Are we not reminded of Manto and Chughtai in the twentieth century? Kshemendra himself was a poetician who finds a lauded place amongst Sanskrit poeticians for his theory of propriety (*auchitya*), but his satires that are a sturdy manifestation of his social consciousness in his *kavya* depicting the unique scenes of social realism of his own time are yet to be addressed thoughtfully. Social critique emerges as a dominant literary theme in Kshemendra's writings. Kashi Gomez has proposed in her thesis that "the application of the author's unique take on the concept of propriety is not only evident in his satires, but that his satires and his literary theory actually utilize the same function of negation and incongruity to engender social critique" (2012, 2). We do also have examples like that of Chakradhar (c. 1194 CE) and Jnandev (c. 1271 CE) in the early Marathi literature whose voice and concerns involved the issues of language, caste and gender (Novetzke 2016) and these are not obviously the only examples. In such cases, as proposed by Christian Novetzke, the process of vernacularisation itself needs to be contemplated upon. In the Marathi literary tradition, the texts like the *Lilacharitra* and the *Jnaneshvari* "self-consciously represented the 'vernacular turn' and did so, in part, through a social critique" (Novetzke 2016, 3). In case of Urdu literature when Faruqi Sahab said "Literature was seen as a social-functional, and not an aesthetic-artistic, object,…", did he mean to say that the idea of literariness had traversed from *akam* to *puram*, to use the literary categories of Tamil Cankam poetry? In other words what was the poetry of the "inner world" which had now become the "public poetry" (Ramanujan 1999, 198ff) or was it that both the concepts viz., "social" and "aesthetic" were undergoing a substantial change over a longer period of time? In fact, as argued by Nirmal Selvamony, a fourth century CE text like the *Tholkappiyam*, even though a text of grammar, logic, ethics, prosody and rhetoric, also had an active social function (Selvamony 2023). The prescription of the structure of poetry had a functionality in the socio-political milieu. On the other hand, another striking example of this "change" from the inner world to the outer world is clearly reflected between the deep concerns Lal Ded or Sheikh Noor-ud-din-Noorani had in fourteenth CE and Ghulam Ahmad Mahjoor (1887–1952) and Dinanath Nadim (1916–1988) had in twentieth CE Kashmir. The poetic philosophy of the prior two was completely laden with deep Shaiva-Sufi concerns and the interest of the latter two was evoked by the socioeconomic and political renaissance (Kachru 1981). Both Lal Ded and Sheikh Noor-ud-din's concerns were deeply soteriological and yet altruistic. In their Kashmiri literary forms called *vak* and *shruk*, they often draw teachings based on what one may call yogic phenomenology that paved a path for every mortal being to achieve the highest good. Of course, the definition of this highest good can be attempted in many ways. For Nadim, phenomenology was not yogic. The Kashmiri voice of Nadim was on the one hand struggling with his poverty and on the other hand fighting the oppression of the poor. His poetics was obviously Marxist. In other words, the question to ask is what had changed from Bharata to Marx in the poetics of South Asia? An exploration into the history of this voyage is a prerequisite.

Let me come back once again, this is the last time I promise, asking the same question with which I began—is there a South Asian poetics? I am aware that I have not been able to answer this question, at least not fully. Yet I have attempted to contextualise it. There are a lot of categories left undiscussed, those of religion, language, the social, culture-power, historical reconstruction, and more importantly if the social is aesthetic or vice-versa or what does that even mean. However, when in the beginning of this paper I argued that the potentiality of the idea of creativity in the South Asian context lies in its open-endedness, I did not only mean that such has been the case with South Asian poetics in its history alone. What I also meant was that the most important level of creativity that is exercised through our approach and methodology fundamentally lies in this open-endedness. If there *is* a definition of creativity, as Anandavardhana might posit, then how can it be called creativity at all? Defining means creating limitations while creativity should have none. To take a cue from Anandavardhana himself, and radically so, the definition of creativity is that there is no definition of creativity. It can only be defined in as many ways as one can and there is where the potentiality of creativeness lays. An illustration of such a creativity in the contemporary literary world is the David Shulman's *More Than Real* that has significantly helped us understand how the idea of imagination was understood in the literary history of South Asia and how he is also establishing the ontological status of imagination with respect to it.

Works Cited

Bronner, Yigal. 2010. *Extreme Poetry, The South Asian Movement of Simultaneous Narration.* New York: Columbia University Press.

Dezsö, Csaba, ed. & tr. 2005. *Much Ado About Religion* by Bhaṭṭa Jayanta. Clay Sanskrit Library. New York: New York University Press/JJC Foundation.

Farooqui, Musharraf Ali. 2000. "Simurgh Feather Guide to the Poetics of Dastan-e Amir Hamza." *Annual of Urdu Studies* 15: 119–67.

Farooqui, Musharraf Ali. 2009. "The Poetics of Amir Hamza's World: Notes on the Ghalib Lakhnavi/Abdullah Bilgrami Version." *Annual of Urdu Studies* 24: 89–97.

Faruqi, Shamsur Rahman. 2001. *Early Urdu Literary Culture and History.* New Delhi: Oxford University Press.

Gomez, Kashi. 2012. *Where Upside Down is Right Side Up: A Study of Ksemendra's Narmamala and His Theory of Aucitya.* UC Berkeley: Library. Retrieved from https://escholarship.org/uc/item/0xf7t1qv.

Granoff, Phyllis. 2001. "Portraits, Likenesses and Looking Glasses: Some Literary and Philosophical Reflections on Representation and Art in

Medieval India." In *Representation in Religion: Studies in Honor of Moshe Barasch*, edited by Jan Assmann and Albert L. Baumgarten. Leiden: Brill.

Kachru, B. B. 1981. *Kashmiri Literature: A History of Indian Literature.* Wiesbaden: Otto Harrassowitz.

Kapstein, Matthew, tr. 2009. *The Rise of Wisdom Moon.* Clay Sanskrit Library. New York: New York University Press.

Keshavmurthy, Prashant. 2018. "Translating Rāma as a Proto-Muḥammadan Prophet: Masīḥ's Masṇavī-i Rām va Sītā." *Numen* 65: 1–27.

Krishna, Daya. 1989. "Comparative Philosophy: What It Is and What it Ought to Be." In *Interpreting Across Boundaries: New Essays in Comparative Philosophy*, edited by Gerald James Larson and Eliot Deutsch. Delhi: Motilal Banarsidass.

Krishnamoorthy, K. 1968. *The Dhvanyāloka and its Critics.* Mysore: Kavyalaya.

Lawrence, McCrea. J. 2008. *The Teleology of Poetics in Medieval Kashmir*, Harvard Oriental Series 71. Cambridge: Harvard University Press.

———. 2015. "The Conquest of Cool—Theology and Aesthetics in Māgha's *Śiśupālavadha*." In *Innovations and Turning Points: Towards a History of Kāvya Literature*, edited by Yigal Bronner, David Shulman and Gary Tubb, 123–41. New Delhi: Oxford University Press.

Lutgendorf, Philip. 1991. *The Life of a Text: Performing the Rāmcaritmānas of Tulsidas.* Berkeley: University of California Press.

Masson, J. L. 1971. "Philosophy and Literary Criticism in Ancient India." *Journal of Indian Philosophy* 1: 167–80.

Novetzke, Christian Lee. 2016. *The Quotidian Revolution: Vernacularization, Religion, and the Premodern Public Sphere in India.* New York: Columbia University Press.

Patel, Deven. M. 2014. *Text to Tradition: The Naiṣadhīyacarita and Literary Community in South Asia.* New York: Columbia University Press.

Pollock, Sheldon. 2001. "The Social Aesthetic and Sanskrit Literary Theory." *Journal of Indian Philosophy* 29: 197–229.

———, ed. 2003. *Literary Cultures in History—Reconstructions from South Asia*, Berkeley: University of California Press.

———. 2006. *The Language of the Gods in the World of Men: Sanskrit, Culture, and Power in Premodern India.* Berkeley: University of California Press.

Pollock, Sheldon, Benjamin A. Elman, and Ku-ming Kevin Chang, eds. 2015. *World Philology.* Cambridge: Harvard University Press.

Ramanujan, A. K. 1999. *The Collected Essays of A.K. Ramanujan.* Edited by Vinay Dharwadker. New Delhi: Oxford University Press.

Rao, Ajay. 2015. *Re-figuring the Ramayana as Theology: A History of Reception in Premodern India*. London and New York: Routledge Hindu Studies Series.

Rao, Velcheru Narayana, and David Shulman. 2012. *Srinatha, The Poet who Made Gods and Kings*. New York: Oxford University Press.

Rao, Velcheru Narayana. 2016. *Text and Tradition in South India*. Albany: SUNY Series in Hindu Studies.

Ricoeur, Paul. 1984. *Time and Narrative*, vol. 1–3. Translated by K. McLaughlin and D. Pellauer. Chicago: Chicago University Press.

Selvamony, Nirmal. 2022. "Logic in tolkāppiyam". In *Handbook of Logical Thought in India*, edited by S. Sarukkai and M. Chakraborty. New Delhi: Springer.

Shulman, David. 2001. *The Wisdom of Poets: Studies in Tamil, Telugu, and Sanskrit*. New Delhi; New York: Oxford University Press.

———. 2012. *More Than Real, A History of the Imagination in South India*. Cambridge: Harvard University Press.

Thapar, Romila. 2011. *Sakuntala: Texts, Readings, Histories*. New York: Columbia University Press.

Truschke, Audrey. 2016. *Culture of Encounters: Sanskrit at the Mughal Court*. New York: Columbia University Press.

TWO

Toward an Indian Poetics

Shamsur Rahman Faruqi

Suppose our world has a visitor from outer space. Suppose he can read all our languages and is interested in poetry. Suppose he reads all, or much of the poetry there is. Will he then conclude that this little, insignificant dot in the immensity of the universe has one poetry, or many poetries? Will he find traces of Sophocles in Wang Wei, echoes of Bhavabhuti in Shakespeare, pointers to Rumi in Virgil? Can there be an all-comprehensive, all-comprehending view of the world's poetry? The answer, I fear, should be in the negative. I have always held that there must be some general rules of poetic excellence, rules which are somehow programmed into our brains, and which make us recognise excellence in poets far removed from us in culture, space, or time. But recognising excellence is not the same as knowing a kindred spirit, unless the act of recognition is itself triggered by a perception of similarity, real or imagined. But if the similarity is more imagined than real, or if the similarity is perceived falsely, due to circumstantial irrelevances, then the whole edifice collapses, and we are back at the root question. Do we recognise excellences in different kinds of poetry through a visceral, gut level reaction, or do we have only delusions? Going back to the visitor from outer space, one wonders if he could understand our human poetry at all, unless he shared our biological, anthropological and cultural characteristics to some extent.

So, the parable of the extra-terrestrial visitor reading our poetry poses the following questions:

1. Does poetry have intransitiveness? That is, can it be enjoyed per se? If so, what is the source of that enjoyment?

2. How different are the poetries of different peoples and cultures? Are there any common marks of excellence in all poetries, marks which can be perceived across the differences?
3. Is our poetry specific to our kind of biology?
4. How do theories of poetry originate? To what extent are those theories relevant to our enjoyment of poetry?

If poetry is intransitive, then our visitor from outer space will have no difficulty in enjoying it, and the source of that enjoyment could be the feeling of play that poetry generates in us. But some people might deny that poetry generates a feeling of play. They might hold that poetry is serious and sacrosanct. But seriousness and sacrosanct-ness do not give enjoyment, at least, not always so. Some people must then believe that poetry is not intransitive. You can enjoy it only when the ideas it conveys to you are welcome in the chamber of your psyche. The visitor from outer space may have ideas very repugnant to those conveyed by our human poetry. So, he won't enjoy our poetry. But if that is so, what right do we poets have to exist? If poetry is idea-bound, then the poet's word has no universality.

There is, no doubt, the phenomenon of poets coming alive for us across time and space. This is an argument in favour of universal, intuitively observed standards of excellence in poetry. But the theories of poetry, constructed often to explain or justify poetry, teach us otherwise. The theory of poetry which explains or justifies, say, Chinese poetry, does not say much to me. But I enjoy Chinese poetry all the same. Is it because Arthur Waley or Edward Fenollosa have conditioned me? Or is it because the theories themselves are irrelevant? But theories of poetry originate in poetry itself or follow poetry closely. So, they can't be entirely irrelevant. Theories are made with the view of describing and explaining a phenomenon and predicting the occurrence of similar or even identical phenomena if the conditions set or described by the theory are met. There would be no theories of poetry if there were no poetry. But the theories' power to predict is sadly limited where poetry is concerned. In fact, one and the same body of poetry often gives rise to several mutually contradictory theories. But we have lived with theories of poetry for so long that it is impossible to claim that enjoyment of poetry is fully possible without any knowledge of the theory or theories built around the poetry.

So, there is a massive confusion of poetries and theories of poetry. Perhaps we can hope for all poetries themselves to have some meeting point, enabling us to enjoy poetry. Such a meeting point, one might almost say, is in our biology rather than in the poetry.

It is we who, in some sense, embody poetry within us. As T. S. Eliot said of music in the section "Dry Salvages" of his *Four Quartets*:

> ...music heard so deeply
> That it is not heard at all, but you are the music
> While the music lasts. (http://www.davidgorman.com, Accessed on 4 June 2024)

Or am I giving to poetry too exalted a position by claiming that it resides in our biology? I hope not. For I do not want to reinforce the platonic delusion that some poets and most politicians have about poetry, to the effect that poetry can change the world, or the society, or that poetry is a power for good, or evil. I claim no such power for poetry. The greatest danger to poetry in India today is from politicians and poets who believe, or fear, that poetry is a powerful force in social and political affairs, or that the poet has an extra poetic obligation toward society. Let me digress here a bit and quote from Joseph Brodsky (quoted in Wiseman 2018): "If a poet has any obligation toward society it is to write well...society on the other hand, has no obligation toward the poet. A majority by definition, society thinks of itself as having other options than reading verses, however well written".

There cannot be a world poetics, but there can perhaps be a poetics distilled from the poetries of the world, a sort of immanent poetics, not always evident. Similarly, there can be, and in fact is, an

Indian poetics, distilled from all the poetries written by our poets in their different languages. This poetics would be characterised by Indianness, just as the total poetry of the world would seem, for the visitor from outer space, to be characterised by Humanness. And just as the Humanness would be more readily obvious to a non-human observer, so the Indianness would be more readily observable by a non-Indian. But this should not close the door for us Indians to try and define Indianness.

Learned and stimulating papers written about Indianness or Indian poetics seem often to assume that Indian and Hindu are synonymous. One need not appeal to the well-worn notion of unity in diversity to support or refute the contention that Indianism means Hinduism. The truth is far more complex. There must, surely, be a way of thinking and feeling which can be described as Indian without needing recourse to a religion or philosophy to ratify that way of thinking and feeling. When F. Schlegel (1968, 101) described Romanticism as a "way of feeling", he did not limit that "way" to Christians, or Protestants, or Pagans. If there is an Indian poetics, it should be common to all languages, one way or another. That such a poetics exists, cannot be disputed. When Indian poets began writing in Persian, they created, quite unconsciously, an Indian style of Persian poetry; it was a style quite distinct from, and disclaimed by the Iranian Persian poets. The English poetry of Michael Madhusudan Dutt and Toru Dutt remains Indian in spite of its conscious effort to sound English; the so-called Indian poem of Thomas Moore, "Lalla Rokh", remains an English poem in spite of its effort to sound Indian. And the reason is not linguistic. True, there are words and phrases in Indian Persian and Indian English which are specific to India. Some of them are not standard Persian or English. But this is a surface phenomenon. Chinua Achebe and Wole Soyinka are not English writers, even if they, deliberately and often to ironic purpose, imitate the various idioms and sub-languages used by different classes of people in Britain today. Their sensibility is African even if their language is standard English.

Indian poetics no doubt originates in Sanskrit poetics. But it goes beyond that. Sanskrit poetics informs all Indian poetry in some way or the other. But it is not a stultifying force. It is a vitalising force. Some years ago, some Urdu critics expressed the view that no poem can be considered modern if it cannot be successfully translated into a Western language. The underlying assumption was that modernist sensibility was predominantly, if not solely, Western. I do not want to open here the can of worms called the theory of translation. But I should think that translatability is no criterion of excellence, or even of modernity. And I should say that just as there are local sensibilities, so there are sensibilities common to a whole age, everywhere in the world. Indian poetry today is no exception to this. But there is an Indian way of looking at things; there is an Indian ethos, and it should be reflected in our poetry.

What is that Indian ethos? To my mind, the greatest inhibition against the Indian ethos surfacing unmistakably in our poetry is the intellectual and emotional dominance over us of a Victorian-Western ethos, not about life and universe, but about literature. It seems to me that we still reject, at least unconsciously, the classic Indian view of poetry as a play of words, and of words as a way to refashion the world in our imagination. We have forgotten what the Sanskrit theoreticians termed "Kavi Vyapara". We are still not out of the emotional strangle-hold of Plato, mediated to us through Victorian-Protestant moralists. The Protestant ethic taught that no work is valuable unless it is useful. More than 150 years ago, the West began to reject this view of the world and began its long, though not quite finished, effort to come to terms with reality as seen by the perceiving mind. Gautier declared in 1835 that all useful things are ugly. One need not go that far to reassert the position of poetry in society. But one must indeed defend poetry's position against those who would, like Plato, have poetry exist only to serve their ulterior ends.

One way, and perhaps the best way, of combating the tendency to use poetry as a pawn in the game of power is to reaffirm the ancient Indian formulation that all fine arts are so intimately interlinked as to be in symbiosis with each other. The kind of architecture that a people develop is determined by the kind of poetry or painting that it develops. The arts are therefore mutually interlocking. You cannot have music go one way and architecture another way.

Indianness does not deny the West. It welcomes it, but on its own terms. Is it not, though, somewhat ironical that the insights about literature and literariness, developed by the Russian formalists in the early nineteen-twenties, and now being used in most modern Western criticism, have an unconscious parallel in the poetic theory that developed long ago in India? Victor Shklovsky said that everything in a work of art exists in order to make the work of art meaningful. This insight would have found a happy echo in medieval Iran and ancient India. Let a restatement of Indian poetics take on from here.

Works Cited

Schlegel, Frederich. 1968. *Dialogue on Poetry and Literary Aphorisms.* Translated by Ernst Behler and Roman Struc. University Park: Pennsylvania State University Press.

Wiseman, Rachel. "Switching Off: Joseph Brodsky and the moral responsibility to be useless." *The Point* (April 23, 2018). https://thepointmag.com/examined-life/switching-off/. Accessed on 12 June 2024.

THREE

Revisiting Urdu Literary Culture

The Curious Case of Razmia

ANISUR RAHMAN

An Excuse for a Parameter

Acomparative reading of Urdu literary history seems to create a general impression that *razmia*, or epic, in its supposedly pure and proper form, as defined universally with reference to its grandeur of experience and expression, has been conspicuous by its absence in the Urdu language. Although I do not wish to engage here with the definition of epic coming to us either from the East or the West, or even to contemplate over the question whether epic could be defined in a holistic manner, I do wish to engage with what constitutes an epic in Urdu and whether it is present, or absent, in its literary tradition spread over more than six centuries.[1] It should be pertinent to state here that this impression about the ostensible absence of *razmia* in Urdu has arisen from the misplaced notion of comparison between two, or more than two literary traditions. While in the larger Western traditions epic is a pure genre with a given subject matter, structure and style, there are remarkable variations in the Eastern traditions with reference to its immense thematic variety and wide-ranging historical and sociocultural representations. In the case of the former, it held a high position

---

[1] I refer to this span of time with reference to Fakhr-e-Din Nizami's *Kadam Rao Padam Rao*, which is supposed to be the first *mathnawi* (long narrative poem) in Urdu written during 1421–34. Although it is not easily comprehensible because it used Urdu along with Sanskrit and south Indian languages, its value lies in the way it laid the foundation of a genre that was developed prominently in the succeeding ages.

in the literary hierarchy of genres but in the case of the latter it emerged as a genre of poetry that grew alongside the indigenous traditions of narration and developed simultaneously alongside various interrelated literary forms.[2] With my understanding about the way the map of reading or misreading is created, most often inadvertently, I intend here to help lay at rest the doubt about the very existence of *razmia* in Urdu. I have two arguments in hand to do so. First, I should like to propose that the presence of epic in major Western or Eastern languages and cultures does not make it necessary for all other languages either of the West or the East to imbibe it in a similar fashion. This implies that the case of *razmia* in Urdu need not be examined necessarily with reference to other traditions, howsoever potent they might be, but in its own historical and literary context. Second, I must also posit that as every literature produces its own version of a literary genre, so did Urdu but surely with a difference which ultimately helped distinguish its literary culture.

I have to make yet another point here. This relates with the response of Urdu critics and literary historians who have dealt with the so-called absence of *razmia* in two ways. Most of them have either remained silent or indifferent to this issue, but one of them has tried to find reasons for its hypothetical absence.[3] He has offered five reasons to explain why *razmia* as a separate genre of poetry could not grow in Urdu. First, he posits that *razmia* called for a kind of language that was rich in creative expression and Urdu could not meet this requirement. Second, he says that Urdu spread out at different cultural locations in different ways that resulted in the loss of a uniform literary culture; this implies,

---

[2] Major epics from the European tradition that define this genre include *Aenid, Beowulf, Iliad, Le Morte d'Arthur* and *Odyssey*. Remarkable among those that represent the important Asian traditions are *The Epic of Gilgamesh, Bahman Namah, Mahabharata, Ramayan, The Book of One Thousand and One Nights, Shahnamah* and *Silappatikaram.*

[3] This refers to Qasim Yaqoob's *Urdu Shaa'iri per Jangon ke Asaraat* (2010).

according to him, that cultural uniformity was imperative for the writing of *razmia*. Third, he suggests that Urdu was unable to reflect the cumulative intellectual identity of the subcontinent as it was was too large and too diverse to be contained in one language. Fourth, he submits that Urdu poets remained confined to courts and wrote only a certain kind of poetry that was much easier than writing a *razmia*; and fifth, he points out that political chaos within the land sealed the possibility of developing broader ideological representations in Urdu poetry which resulted in the absence of *razmia*.

To counter these, I would extend certain arguments in a sequence rather briefly which, in turn, would also define Urdu's literary culture with all its essential markers. I would question, first, that if the paucity of creative expression was a reason for the absence of *razmia*, then how did ghazal acquire its root and flourish as one of the finest expressions of poetry in the Urdu language? By this, I clearly mean that Urdu which had its roots in Arabic and Persian first and then in several avatars of Hindavi, was enriched from age to age and gathered enough strength as a literary language to represent all shades of human experience. Second, I would argue that the spreading of Urdu at various locations in the southern and northern parts of India contributed, in fact, to its enrichment and comprehensive growth rather than causing its impoverishment. This would be borne out well by the brief exposition that I bring later in this chapter regarding the development of poetical genres in Urdu both in the north and the southern parts of India especially since the sixteenth century. Third, I would suggest that instead of remaining aloof, Urdu absorbed the multiple intellectual traditions of the land which empowered it to develop its own literary discourse. By this, I underline the hybridity and openness of Urdu as a language and the catholicity of its practitioners who have not stayed in segregation from the larger sociocultural matrix of the land and have liberally drawn upon the mixed cultural resources to enrich its literary capital. Fourth, I would contend that only some of the Urdu poets received royal patronage and even they did not necessarily remain helplessly subservient to their patrons. The stories of poets and their patrons from Khusro to Ghalib only negate this much-too-general observation regarding their role in the court and their own growth as poets. Fifth, I must propose that social and political forces do not always work negatively; instead they are known to create space for diverse ideological representations in literature and develop liberal discourses of belonging. This holds well in the case of Urdu as it strengthened its literary tradition from one generation to another at both the locations—Deccan and Delhi—ever since the thirteenth century. I should like to finally assert that the reasons extended to explain the absence of *razmia* in Urdu are more in the nature of unqualified apologies which do not stand ground. The fact of the matter is that Urdu's evolving map of literary representation from Deccan to Delhi and other habitats ever since the very beginnings of this language and its literature have a different story to tell.

The Veiled Presence of *Razmia*

With reference to what has been argued above, it would be pertinent to posit that the history of Urdu poetry is in a major way a history of the birth and growth of the long poem. This long poem, classified as *mathnawi* (long narrative poem), *marsiya* (elegy) and *qasida* (panegyric), originated in Arab, developed in Iran, and found a suitable clime in India, especially the Deccan, to begin with. While *mathnawi* developed as a genre of narrative poetry, or romance, *marsiya* matured as a genre of elegy, and *qasida* flourished as one of panegyric. However, in the entire trajectory of the long poem, as presented in Urdu literary histories, *razmia* finds no mention as a distinct category of poetry even though it has had an unmistakable, albeit subdued, presence in all other genres of *mathnawi*, *marsiya* and *qasida* from the very beginning. Before substantiating this argument, it would be proper for us to keep in mind that *razm*, which in Persian means war, is also the root of *razmia* which emerged in the Persian language as a long narrative poem that principally represented the history of the land,

and delineated the experience of battles in the grandest possible terms. As Urdu literary historiographers and critics did not engage with Persian models in strict terms, they did not consider how, for example, Firdausi had represented his land and all its glory in his *Shahnama*.

It would be pertinent to argue here that the language which came to be known as Urdu only in the late eighteenth century, was developing differently at least since the thirteenth century,[4] and also configuring itself as a literary language with an intermixing of Persian, Hindavi, Hindi, Dehlavi, Gujari, Deccani and Rekhta in different parts of the land. As it passed through various stages of growth and development, it also kept evolving its own models of the long poem rather than following the Persian models in strict terms. As such, the long poem in Urdu written as *mathnawi*, *marsiya* or *qasida* had to be different from the Persian models insofar as it incorporated the elements of one into the other. So, the Urdu long poems also drew upon the elements of *razmia* that represented the history and politics of society and community as regulated and defined by imperial, economic, mercantile, religious, cultural and ideological considerations.

This brings us to trace the emergence of the long poem in Deccan since the early fifteenth century. Even before the breaking up of the Bahmani Sultanate in 1527, the Deccan had started experiencing internal skirmishes, upheavals and external threats from the Mughals with Aurangzeb finally expanding the Mughal

---

[4] One may substantiate this point by referring to the role of spiritual masters like Fariduddin Ganj-i-Shakar (1173–1265), Sheikh Sharfuddin Bu Ali Qalandar (1209–1324), Khwaja Nizamuddin Auliya (1238–1325), Amir Khusro (1253–1325) and Sheikh Sarfuddin Ahmed Yahya Maneri (1263–1381) who played significant roles in the development of what came to be later known as Urdu. It must also be noted that this was a time of great linguistic experimentation and growth of dialects resulting into the growth of Urdu as a language. A couplet from Sheikh Bu Ali Qalandar may be quoted to show how the language used by him comes close to modern-day Urdu: *Sajan sakaarey jayengey aur nain marengey roye/Bidhna aisi rayn kar bhor kadhi na hoye.*

Empire in this region in 1680. These provided material for the poets to write about their times especially in their *mathnawis*, *marsiyas* and *qasidas*. With the fall of the Bahmani Sultanate in 1527, however, and its division into five states—Ahmad Nagar, Bidar, Berar, Bijapur and Golconda—it was only in Bijapur Sultanate (1490–1686) under the Adil Shahi rulers and Golconda Sultanate (1512–1687) under the Qutubshahi rulers that Urdu literature found the most fertile ground for its growth. The long poem emerging as *mathnawi*, *marsiya* and *qasida* found its practitioners in a number of poets in Bijapur. As *razmia* was supposed to highlight bravery in the battlefield, it also found its kindred spirit in these three genres which were written as gripping poetical narratives of emotional surfeit representing the intriguing paradigms of human behaviour. A brief account of the development of these genres would help me make my point but it is important before that to say that there are two forms of *mathnawis* that are identifiable as *razmia mathnawis* and *bazmia mathnawis*. As their names suggest, *razmia mathnawis* describe battle and bravery in grandiloquent terms, while the *bazmia mathnawis* narrate stories of love and romance in fanciful terms. I would like to consider the case of *razmia mathnawis* here to show that *razmia* is not really absent from Urdu poetry; it rather exists as an important but largely unacknowledged constituent of the genre of *mathnawi* in Urdu.

The historical account of the *mathnawi* must begin with Fakhr-i-Din Nizami's *Kadam Rao Padam Rao* (1421–34). Even though it does not strictly exemplify this genre but it surely paved the way for the writing of the long poem which came to be identified as *mathnawi*, or a fanciful romance, in subsequent stages. Supposed to have been written during the second and third decades of the fifteenth century, this text has not been available in full but is reported to be spread over 2000 lines by one account even though it was left unfinished by the poet.[5] It has been established

[5] "It is a poem of great length; the manuscript comprises 1032 verses (2034 lines)—and is incomplete" (Faruqi 2003, 824).

to be an Urdu poem with a liberal sprinkling of Sanskrit and south Indian languages. With all the features of the classical stories of the olden times, this poem makes use of supernatural machinery to tell the story of king Kadam Rao's incarnation into a bird, the goodness of Padam Rao, his vizier, and the misdemeanour of Jogi Akkhar Nath who used his magic to dislodge the king and usurp the throne. I do not wish to suggest that this poem has the typical elements of *razmia* but I would like to say that it seems to create a condition for the writing of the long poem which could afford space for developing the narratives of battles and bravery.

Apart from Nizami's incredibly long poetical narrative *Kadam Rao Padam Rao*, another important mention in the account of the long poem must be that of Ashraf Bayabani (1459–1528) who developed an extended narrative in the genre of *marsiya* in 1503 and spread it over nine sections to appropriately call it *Nausirhar*. Coming closer to *razmia*, this poem described the events of Karbala and the martyrdom of Imam Hussain, which happens to be the stock theme of *marsiya*s in general. It was designed as an oral narrative which *marsiya*s also aspired to become and it, therefore, suitably drew upon conversational idiom meant to appeal to larger sections of audiences and readers. We have had since then a series of long poems written in the genres of *mathnawi* and *marsiya* that introduce the elements of *razmia* in terms that can hardly be neglected. In the series of the long poems detailing the victories and defeats in war, a mention should be made of a less celebrated poet called Mirza Muqeem who wrote *Fatehnama Bakheri* in 1637 and recorded a history of war in verse and made a contribution to the genre in general. He glorified the conquest of Bakheri following a fight between Raja Apabhadra and Mohammad Adil Shah who ruled for 30 years from 1627 to 1657. This tradition was followed by Rustami who wrote *Khawarnama* in 1649 and glorified the military expeditions of Ali, the son-in-law of Prophet Mohammad. Yet another mention should be made of a *razmia mathnawi* entitled *Fateh Nama-i-Nizam Shah* written in 1565 by Hasan Shauqi (1540–1632). He presented an account of the battle of Talikota, fought in 1565, where Hussain Nizam Shah is shown to have won over Raja Ram Raj of Vijaya Nagar. In the annals of Urdu poetry of the Deccan we have yet another poet of considerable merit called Nusrati (1600–1674) who wrote *Alinama* in 1670. This *mathnawi* described the situation during the first ten years of the reign of Ali Adil Shah II (who reigned from 1657–72) and went on to develop a dramatic narrative focussing on the fight between the forces of Ali Adil Shah against the forces of Shivaji (1627/30–80). This poem is generally compared with Firdausi's *Shahnama* for its grandeur and for the way it described battle and bravery to draw the attention of readers while recording the history of his times. Two years later, he wrote *Fatah Nama Bahlol Khan* in 1672 which is also known as *Tareekh-e-Askandaria.* Falling in the same genre of poems about battles, this poem also described the battle between Askandar and Shivaji. We have some other examples in this genre of poetry which celebrate valour and victory. These include Syed Azam Bijapur's *Dastan-e-Fath-e-Jung* written in 1666, Lateef's *Zafar Nama* written in 1684, Sevak's *Jungnama-i-Mohammad Haneef*, written in 1691 and Ghazanfar Hussain's *Jung Nama Alam Ali Khan* written in 1720. The first and probably the only *razmia mathnawi* with battle as its theme entitled *Waqaa-i-Sana*, was written in the north by Syed Zahid Sana. This poem described the third battle of Panipat fought in 1761. Even this broad survey of early Urdu poetry in the Deccan brings home the idea that the long poem which found its most fertile ground there, also defined the genres of *mathnawi*, *marsiya* and *qasida* as well as *razmia*, although literary historians have not put the long poems celebrating valour and victory in the battlefield in the category of *razmia* even though they clearly demonstrate the elements of this genre. This must have led towards the marginalisation of the genre in the subsequent ages and helped reiterate the opinion that *razmia* is almost non-existent in Urdu.

It would be interesting to note here, however, that this tradition of writing long poems in the genre of *razmia mathnawi* did not last long. With the passing of time and changing of political conditions, battles were no longer the only way to establish authority and governance. This must have led, one may surmise, towards the decline of *razmia* as a genre and the emergence of other genres instead. This could be marked rather prominently in the case of the Deccan. Although the writing of long and short poetical narratives in the form of *mathnawi*, *marsiya* and *qasida* continued even in the following ages in the north, they developed along different lines with respect to language and treatment.

Having said this, I must reiterate that the above account relates only to the *razmia mathnawi*s that made battle and bravery their main subject. There is another rich tradition of *mathnawi*s that grew both in the Deccan and the north and narrated stories of romantic love and passion, creating fascinating worlds of romance. *Bazmia mathnawi*s, written in Bijapur, prominently include Mirza Mohammad Muqeemi's (d. 1665) *Chandra Badan-o-Mahyar*, a tragic tale of unrequited love, suffering and death. In a study of classical Urdu literature, this poem has not been considered "an outstanding work of art but it deserves mention for philosophical reasons" (Schimmel 1975, 138). Among others, we have Ameen's (d. 1675) *Bahram-o-Husn Bano* and Malik Khushnood's *Hashst Bahisht*. Those written in Golconda in a similar strain comprise Mulla Wajhi's (d. 1555) *Qutub Mushtari* (1609), Ibne Nishati's (d. 1645) *Phool Bun* (1655–66), as well as Tabaee's *Behram-o-Gul Andaam*. A special mention may be made here of Ghawwasi's *Saif-ul-Muluk-o-Badiul Jamal* (1625) which narrates the love story of an Egyptian prince for a Chinese princess. Spread over 14000 lines, it is considered to be a "Deccani version of a story in the Persian *Arabian Nights*" (Bailey 1932, 24). This tradition of *bazmia mathnawi* continued in Gujarat and the north also. The more prominent works of this kind are Ameen Gujarati's *Yusuf Zuleikha* (1697), Mohammad Afzal's (d. 1625) *Bikat Kahani*, Mirza Shauq Lucknowi's (1773–1871) *Bahar-e Ishq, Zahr-e Ishq* (1861) and *Fareb-e Ishq*, Meer Hasan's (1736/7–86) *Sehr-ul-Bayan* (1770), and Dayashankar Naseem's (1811–1845) *Gulzar-e Naseem* (1838). These are the prominent texts that literary history has recorded and critics have paid attention to as major contributions of the genre. To substantiate this case, it may be said that at least three *mathnawis—Sehr-ul-Bayan* (1770), *Gulzar-e-Naseem* (1838) and

Zahr-e-Ishq (1861)—canonised the genre and drew it closer to the epic.

Considering these works which have been traditionally categorised as *mathnawi*, it would be eminently possible to argue that the long poem in Urdu quite often blended the two forms of *mathnawi* and *razmia*, whereas in the Western traditions it remained classified in grand, sacrosanct and non-negotiable categories like epic, ballad, elegy and romance. I may submit, therefore, that *mathnawi* in Urdu is a liberated kind of poetry which corresponds closely with *razmia*, and approximates the stylistic flourish of a genre like *qasida* which is written to eulogise the heroes of Islam as well as kings and nobles. Similarly, another significant genre which comes much closer to *razmia* is *marsiya* which draws upon the tragedy of Karbala and makes dramatic representations of the battle fought by Imam Hussain and his supporters against Yazid and his army.

To elaborate the genre of *marsiya* further in order to establish its stature as a grand poem approximating the standard of *razmia*, it may be added that a proper *marsiya* is written in seven sections called *chehra*, or exposition; *saraapa*, or appearance; *rukhsat*, or departure; *aamad*, or arrival; *rajz*, or exhortation; *shahadat*, or martyrdom, and *bain*, or lamentation. In two of its parts—*rajz* and *shahadat*—it acquires the stature of epic with respect to subject matter and treatment. With the use of elevated language and rhetorical devices, the poet creates an environment within the poem that keeps the reader emotionally charged. It may thus be argued that in spite of their characteristic features, the *mathnawi*, *marsiya* and *razmia* draw commonly upon philosophical and ethical themes that emanate from the larger hinterlands of love and war and reflect upon the turns of history, politics and human destiny.

A Paradigm for Urdu *Razmia*

Before I try and develop a possible paradigm to examine the absence or presence of *razmia* in Urdu, let me put forward some contextual and generic questions that might help develop a proper context. These questions include: (a) What are the broader constituents of *razmia* as a form of poetry in Urdu? (b) Is war an essential and the only subject to serve as the primary material for the writing of a *razmia*? (c) Under what conditions could *razmia*, or poems approximating *razmia* be written in Urdu? (d) Can *razmia* be only a poetical composition, or can it also be written in prose? and finally (e) Is the time for the writing of *razmia*, or even the long poem in Urdu over now?

In attempting broader answers to these questions, I would like to posit the following:

(a) It may be justifiably argued that extended length and lofty treatment of material are the two major constituents of a *razmia*. A *razmia* may further draw upon a historical period, develop a philosophical foundation, create a variety of situations, introduce a set of congruent and incongruent characters, use a certain kind of diction, and exercise control over form to create a sense of unity through the entire narrative. This is well exemplified by the epics written in any of the Western or Eastern traditions.

(b) Although the word *razmia* is indicative of war and epics have generally executed the experience of war but this is not a regulative principle as all epics, in direct and indirect manners, draw upon the vast expanse of history and culture, as can be seen in the case of Firdausi's *Shahnama* in Persian. This implies that *razmia* casts a wider net and encompasses a whole set of references that characterise a people and their culture. It implies, therefore, that wars alone could not be the only subject of a literary composition approximating *razmia* in Urdu; it could also be written appropriating other subjects drawn from the domains of history, culture, romance and larger philosophical discourses.

(c) It is true that historical conditions and literary trends determine circumstances under which certain genres receive greater attention and acceptance than others. This also indicates that some genres have remained more popular than others in a certain age—like long poems of any genre have been more acceptable in the classical age and shorter compositions in the modern age. However, this is not a dictum which constricts writing preferences as there have been variations in all ages—shorter poems have also been written in the classical past as well as longer poems in the modern age.

(d) There has been a general understanding through all ages that *razmia* by its innate nature chooses poetry rather than prose for itself. The segregation of genres into prose and poetry, being a purely classical construct, has been constrictive. In modern age, the text is liberated and literary writing has moved beyond essentialist frameworks of genres to become essentially intertextual, making way for inter-relatedness of genres. It could be mentioned here that *razmia* also extends its frontiers to incorporate prose works. Examples of James Joyce's (1882–1941) *Ulysses* (1922) and Qurratuain Hyder's (1927–2007) *Kaar-e-Jahan Daraaz Hai* (2003) that reach the standards of epic may be quoted in this context. The way the idea of literature and literary writing has undergone changes in our times; it appears that the writing of epic in poetry or prose form can no longer follow the traditional poetics and it can only be revisited to evolve into a new form and a new identity both in poetry as well as prose.

(e) If one believes that war alone is the only subject fit for *razmia,* then it would mean that the time for the writing of *razmia* is indeed over. Today, as a literary text is a complex web of the word and the world in conversation with each other, it could be argued that all genres exist simultaneously, that is, no genre is indeed extinct. It is extinct, if at all, only to the extent that since the long poem is less and less practised now, *razmia* in its traditional sense too would no longer be written although it might have its presence in other textual configurations irrespective of the length of text and scope of experience to be represented. A modern

> work of art may thus be of especial nature even without being too long in a formal sense.

In view of the above, it would be justifiable to suggest that *razmia* in Urdu is not non-existent as it is generally supposed to be; it has existed in different forms in the genres of *mathnawi*, *qasida* and *marsiya*. Ever since their beginnings, all these genres have both mourned the loss and celebrated the gains that life and history bring to people just as epics do in other cultures and languages. In its veiled presence through *mathnawi* and *marsiya*, the Urdu *razmia* has also originated in history and culture, as well as in faith and philosophy, as epics generally did in the classical past. What distinguishes the long Urdu poem with predominant elements of *razmia*, however, is that it has obliterated the boundaries of literary forms and appropriated a language that was typically suitable for the subject. The long Urdu poems of this nature, like epics in other cultures and languages, were written as literary representations of history and culture but with the elements of *razmia* introduced into them; these poems in Urdu acquired a mixed tone and tenor. With reference to length and treatment of material, it has had a covert presence in *marsiya* in particular and *mathnawi* in general. This may be exemplified by referring to the poems mentioned above.

In this context, I should posit further that *marsiya* stands out quite prominently as the most appropriate example of *razmia* poetry in Urdu. In fact, *marsiya* re-defines the genre of *razmia* in its own way. The essential features of this genre have been succinctly summed as follows: "The *marsiya*s have redeemed the credit of Urdu poetry. Moral in their tone, a pleasing contrast to the sensual poetry of the school of Nasikh, freed from turgid bombast and extravagant hyperbole, vivid in their description of scenes and realistic in their portrayal of human emotions, the marsiyas have rendered a great service to Urdu literature and language " (Saksena 1990, 18). The most valued of the *marsiya* poets in Urdu, Meer Babar Ali Anis (1802–1874), immortalised the tragic events of Karbala and the martyrdom of Hussain and his companions in his *marsiya*s. As he re-created a chapter of Islamic history and represented a religio-cultural legacy of the Sh'ite sect in his highly charged poetical narratives, he demonstrated his mastery over dramaturgy and rhetoric. Anis is remarkable for his inimitable skills of plot construction and characterisation, as well as his imaginative vitality and psychological studies of characters and events associated with them. His *marsiya*s exemplify a poet's unique command over language to tell a tale of suffering as well as courage and valour. They also demonstrate his keen perception of his subject, art of dramatisation and narration with the use of lofty literary devices.

Anis' narration, marked by tonal variation, is remarkable for the choice of diction that he made to construct his grandiloquent narrative. He created drama, evoked sentiments, and imparted a moral understanding of suffering and sublimation. His *marsiya*s can be justifiably considered as epics for two reasons: he helped them grow into a strong genre of poetry, as also a robust genre of drama. The most remarkable aspect of his *marsiya*, in the ultimate analysis, is the quality of its orality, which has kept it alive ever since he wrote them. Its recitation in the month of Muharram has become a highly respectable tradition which also underlines, by proxy, the socio-religious function of poetry.

It would be meaningful to add here that the long poem which owes its origin in the oral tradition both in the East and the West, found its manifestations in multiple forms in Urdu. In its earliest phase in all its locations, the long poem remained synonymous with the telling of heroic tales, celebration of communal history and valorisation of culture. These were marked for being the mirrors of races and cultures in both the oral and written forms. The *marsiya*s of Mir Anis also represent these aspects of religious, cultural and communal history of a people both in the oral and written forms. Even though his *marsiya*s have been stereotyped as a medium of mourning the tragedy of Karbala, it goes far beyond and defines the larger issues of living a life, appropriating a language and evolving the art of poetry.

It would be pertinent to posit further that *marsiya* as a genre represents a fine case for the study of intertextuality in relation to other narrative forms of Urdu/Persian poetry and their inter-literary relationship. It also presents a case for the study of the genre itself with reference to its specific linguistic nature, as well as its relationship with oral tradition within an Islamic sect, and interestingly enough, for its survival through a tradition that approximates *shruti* and *smriti* traditions. In describing a war of good against evil, the *marsiya* also opens up horizons of expectations for the reader and projects, in turn, issues in philosophy and sociocultural epistemology that also characterise a faith in turn.

Urdu literary culture evolved in different schools before it grew out of geographical and cultural confines to become a part of larger literary habitats in the Indian subcontinent. It is marked for reaching its various genres to their height. There are religious representations in *hamd*, *munajat*, *naat*, *manqabat*, *marsiya*, *nauha*, *soze* and *salam*; secular narratives in *mathnawi*, *qasida* and *shahr ashob*; and cultural configurations in *geet*, *qawwali*, *sehra*, *hajw*, *wasokht* and *rekhti*. Even in this long list of genres, we have no mention of *razmia*. Yet one may not justifiably assert that *razmia* in Urdu is non-existent. I would rather posit that *razmia* exists in Urdu poetry but not in the way it does in other languages and cultures under the separate nomenclature of epic. In Urdu, it has had only an implied existence; it is unnamed, indirect and muted. It appears in different styles of written and verbal expression—now religious, now secular, now cultural—and authenticates the genre in each of these expressions.

Works Cited

Bailey, T. Grahame. 1932. *History of Urdu Literature*. London: Association Press (Y.M.C.A.).

Faruqi, Shamsur Rahman. 2003. "A long History of Urdu Literary Culture Part I: Naming and Placing a Literary Culture." In *Literary Cultures in History: Reconstructions from South Asia*, edited by Sheldon Pollock. Berkley: University of California Press.

Saksena, Ram Babu. 1990. *A History of Urdu Literature*. New Delhi/Madras: Educational Services.

Schimmel, Annemarie. 1975. "Classical Urdu Literature from Beginning to Iqbal." In *A History of Indian Literature* 8, fasc. 3, edited by Jane Gonda. Wiesbaden: Otto Harrassowitz.

Yaqoob, Qasim. 2010. *Urdu Shairi Per Jungon Ke Asaraat*. Faisalabad: Misal Publications.

FOUR

Scripture or Poetry?

Anandavardhana on How to Read an Epic

C. Rajendran

When we use the term epic in the Indian context, as in the present title, to denote works like the Ramayana and the Mahabharata, it is not altogether devoid of some methodological problems. "Epic" is a loaded literary term that has been historically used in the very special sense of a type of poetry comprising works like the *Iliad* and *Odyssey*. In Western tradition, epic stands for "a long narrative poem on a great and serious subject, related to an elevated style, and centered a heroic or quasi-divine figure on whose actions depends the fate of a tribe, a nation, or a human race" (Abrams 1988, 49). Homer's *Iliad* and *Odyssey* are the archetypal epics of ancient Greece and works like *Beowulf*, Virgil's *Aeneid* and Milton's *Paradise Lost* are some of the celebrated specimens of the genre. However, the term has been used in the extended sense of *itihasa* in the Indian context, ever since Western thinkers started exploring ancient Indian literature. It is used to denote mega-narratives in other cultures too. The term *itihasa*, which etymologically would mean "thus it happened" (*iti ha asa*) has been used in the sense of semi-scriptural narratives in India. However, its grand narrative framework, universal interest in the hero and his companions' dealings with the vicissitudes of life and literary qualities would suggest that such identification of it with the epic genre is not altogether inappropriate. Nevertheless, many comparatists and literary critics of the past have been enthused at the prospect of epics of all cultures gaining a universal stature. In one remarkable passage, Saint Beuve speaks about the universality of the very notion of epic poetry as capable of being applied to works belonging to other cultures (quoted in Mohan 1989, 6–7):

> Homer, as always and everywhere, should be first, like a god, but behind him, like a procession of the three wise kings of the east, would be seen three great poets, the three Homers, so long ignored by us, who wrote epics for the use of old people of Asia, the poets Vālmīki, Vyāsa of the Hindus, and *Firdausi* of the Persians, in the domain of taste; it is well to know that such men exist and not to divide the human race.

The problems of the universality and didactic nature of comparative literature implicit in the passage apart, it throws much light to the critical assumptions of nineteenth-century Europe which was trying to comprehend other cultures in terms of its own literary tradition. Of course, such interlinking is not bereft of its own share of problems arising from the fusion of two different literary traditions. It has been noted that Indian epics are not "mere narratives of heroic deeds" and that they are not concerned with a tension between man and his gods, but are "finished products of a bardic tradition aimed at recalling the path of human destiny as has been" (*Encyclopedia* 1996, 1191–92). Further, it is maintained that compared to the Greco-Roman epics, Indian epics might "appear to be more consciously philosophical" in the sense that the focus is on the dominant ethos, as against mere sense of destiny.

The reception accorded to Indian and Western epics in their respective cultures also varies. In Western tradition, epics like *Iliad* and *Odyssey* have always been looked upon as literary works; their structure and content as well as poetic style and characterisation are all matters of literary discussion at least from the time of Aristotle. Had they been treated as philosophical discourses, Aristotle would not have any problems in including them in the curriculum of the young Alexander, which he did after some deliberations. On the other hand, in India, epics have never been treated singularly as literary works. Of course, Valmiki, as the author of Ramayana has been regarded as *adikavi*, the first poet. Similarly, in a magnificent tribute on the first page of *Harshacharita*, Banabhatta describes Vyasa, the author of Mahabharata as the *kavivedhas* ("creator among poets"). The Ramayana and the Mahabharata have been inexhaustible sourcebooks for hundreds of plays, poems and other artistic representations for ages (a tradition which continues till date). But, over the ages, they have also acquired a religious aura. Their authors have been venerated as sages and their recitation, even in their avatar as translations has acquired a ritualistic nature as an act of piety.[1] There were even institutional arrangements for the regular recitation of the epics in temples. The heroes of the epics have been regarded as real divinities, with even temples built for them; folkloristics is galore all over India and sometimes even outside in far-off countries about the locations of the depicted events of the epics. It is probably because of this that *itihasa* as a class is often segregated from secular poetry in works on poetics; as a literary genre it is not available to poets to experiment with. Understandably, works on poetics which give precise structural rules for types of plays and poetry are silent about this.

The ambivalence about the status of epics as a class of literature vis-à-vis religious scripture is present in literary works also. Thus, Rajashekhara, in his *Kavyamimamsa* is circumspect in locating the place of the epics among various literary genres. On one hand, he accords a sacred stature to them, making the *itihasa* a "subordinate scripture" (*upaveda*). On the other, he also groups *itihasa* with *purana*, and further divides them into epics of single hero and many heroes, illustrating these divisions with the Ramayana and Mahabharata respectively. In any case they are not regarded as creative literature, which goes by the name of *kavya*. Bhattanayaka differentiates between three types of linguistic expressions, viz., *shastra*, *akhyana* and *kavya* (Sastri 1940, 87). Among these, *shastra* stands for the revealed scriptures encompassing the Vedas and *kavya* is a comprehensive term used to denote all creative literature, including those composed in prose and verse, and all types of plays. The term *akhayana* or

[1] For example, in Kerala, Thunchathu Ezhuthachan's *Adhyatma Ramayanam* was supposed to be recited with a lighted lamp in the month of Karkitaka every year.

the more prevalent term *itihasa* denotes a class of writing which stands somewhat in between these two and is understood in the sense of "tradition" or "history" (Warder 1989, 1). Poeticians like Mammaṭa argue that the *shastras* command, *itihasas* speak like friends and *kavya* advises like a spouse (Dwivedi 1986, 4).

All this shows that in Indian tradition, the literary aspects of epics are sidelined even though poeticians accept the authors of epics as poets. This ambivalence can create problems about the way epics have been read. The ritualistic aura surrounding such reading can be comprehended if we go through the elaborate tips given to start the recitation of Ramayana in each of its separate cantos. The Gita Press edition of the Ramayana has in fact an introductory section called "The Method of Recitation of Srimadvālmīkirāmāyaṇa" (*Srimad Valmiki Ramayanasya Pathavidhih*) and it is further stated that there are different methods of recitation according to different schools of thought (*sampradaya*) (*Srimadvalmikiramayana* 1993, 29). In the case of the Mahabharata (called *Jaya* at the beginning of its varied history), the very first verse enjoins one to recite the text after saluting Narayana, Nara, Goddess Sarasvati and Vyasa: *narayanam namaskrtya naram chaiva narottamam devim sarasvatim chaiva tato jayam udirayet/*

From Banabhatta's *Kadambari*, we can understand that there were regular practices in temples for the recitation of the Mahabharata.[2] Needless to say, such ritualistic instructions are conspicuous by their absence in secular *kavya* literature, which is indicative of the special stature enjoyed by epics in Indian tradition.

It is against this backdrop that we have to analyse the perceptions of Anandavardhana, the celebrated poet critic of ninth century AD, on epics. Anandavardhana is one of the few critics in Sanskrit who always turn to epics to illustrate his poetic theory and never loses sight of the fact that both the Ramayana and Mahabharata are primarily creative literature (*kavya*).This is very significant

---

[2] Banabhatta, *Kadambari*, p. 104.

since Bhattanayaka, who comes slightly later makes a structural difference between *kavya* and *akhyana*, arguing that in *akhyana* (comprising *itihasa* and *purana*), what is said is important while in *kavya*, it is the processes unleashed by poetic language which is the most important element. According to him, "(They say) *śāstra* is to be distinguished on the basis of the prominence of the word. Narrative (*ākhyāna*) is that where meaning it the prominent element. When both word and meaning are subordinated to the *process*, it is poetry" (Sastri 1940, 87).

Dhananjaya, the author of *Dasharupaka*—arguing that the sole aim of drama is pleasure—makes a passing reference to *itihasa*, which, in contradistinction to it has only instruction as its aim: "As for any simple man of little intelligence who says that from dramas, which distil joy, the gain is knowledge only, as in the case of history (*itihasa*) and the like-homage to him, for he has averted his face from what is delightful" (Haas 1962, 3). However, Anandavardhana does not entertain any such difference between the epics and creative literature and takes it for granted that *itihasa* is first and foremost poetry.

This perspective is evident in Anandavardhana's evocation of Ramayana and Mahabharata in connection with his assertion that the concept of suggestion, although unknown to poeticians, is present in all great poetry. Here, it is significant that he refers to the Ramayana and the Mahabharata as *lakshya* (target), making clear that he is very clear about them being poetry (Sastri 1940, 38). He profusely quotes from both these epics to illustrate the principle of suggestive art.

With reference to the Ramayana, we find in Anandavardhana an approach different from traditional scriptural hermeneutics and modern historical/philological method relying on textual criticism and textual history. He takes the text of Ramayana as a unified whole. This can be contrasted with the fragmented picture of the text as having a "kernel" portion to which some portions like the Balakanda and the Uttarakanda (the first and the last books respectively) were added, a view which has gained currency in modern Indological studies. Anandavardhana always regards the epic as the handiwork of a gifted poet with a unified vision. The view that the Ramayana is a collection of songs of wandering bards, *kushilavas* as they are called (from which modern scholars derive the names of Kusha and Lava) also does not find any possibility in Anandavardhana's understanding.[3] As such, in the Ramayana, he expects an organic structure in the work, triggered off by an intense and genuine emotional experience in the poet and not as an assortment of fragments written anonymously at different points of time. According to him, "In the *Rāmāyaṇa*, the *karunarasa* (the flavor of compassion or tragic mood) is prepared by the first of the poets himself, where he says that his 'grief became verse'. He carries out the same *rasa* throughout his compositionup to Rāma's final, irreversible separation from Sītā" (Ingalls et al. 1990, 690).

This emotive element permeates and pervades the entire work, as a "compositional suggestion" (*prabandhadhvani*) (Sastri 1940, 329–44). In this perspective, the well-known story of the genesis of the Ramayana assumes significance. According to this story, the very first verse of the epic was a spontaneous outpouring of the poet, overwhelmed by the grief of the *krauncha* bird. Anandavardhana takes this as the starting point of the epic, the logical culmination of which is the eternal separation between Rama and Sita. Thus, according to him, the epic, an epitome of pathos, begins with a tale of grief and ends in the denouement wherein grief is the dominant emotion.

There is no doubt that there is a symbolic relation between the *krauncha* episode and the Rama story in Anandavardhana's perspective. It has far-reaching implications, not always spelt out by the critic. There are some puzzles unsolved in the citation of the *krauncha* episode in the *Dhvanyaloka*. According to the original Ramayana story, it is the male bird which is being killed and

[3] Recently, Sheldon Pollock has pointed out that the account of oral transmission of the epic contained in it is a "fiction of written culture", cognising orality from outside orality impossible in a world ignorant of writing. See Pollock (2006, 78).

Valmiki's grief is aroused at the sight of the wailing female bird: *tasmat tu mithunadekam pumamsam papanishchayaḥ/ Jaghana vairanilayo nishadastasya pashyatah//* (*Srimadvalmikiramayana* 1993). But in Anandavardhana's account, it is the female bird which is killed and the male bird who wails. Many commentators like Kuppusvami Sastri and Pt. Badari Nath Sarma have tried to tide over this discrepancy by interpreting Anandavardhana's passage in a farfetched manner into which we need not enter. But as Ingalls, following Masson, points out, Anandavardhana seems to have altered the text of Ramayana to suit his purpose (Ingalls et al. 1990, 114).

What could be Anandavardhana's purpose then? His interpretation is clear: just as the *krauncha* episode brings to the fore the tragic predicament of the male bird, the Ramayana story culminates in the tragedy of Rama who stands helplessly as his wronged wife descends to Mother Earth, never to return. Such a tragic end is significant in the case of the Ramayana where Indian tradition sometimes stops with the coronation of Rama and ignores what happened thereafter. Most of the Sanskrit poets and playwrights who have borrowed from the theme of Ramayana either focus on the earlier part of the epic or, as in the case of Bhavabhuti, attempt drastic changes to it to have a happy ending. Kalidasa, in his *Raghuvamsha* fearlessly treads the path of Valmiki and portrays the tragic plight of Sita without any inhibition. However, in the grand narrative of the poem, the Rama story is only an episode to be subordinated and subsumed by the history of a whole race. Thus, Anandavardhana's vision of Ramayana stands in bold relief against the conventional reception accorded to the epic. It unravels a tragic vision permeating the epic, raising several ethical questions about the story, especially as related to the unwarranted repudiation of a chaste woman, which becomes the seed of the tragedy. A tragic end always signifies unresolved moral issues and puts a question mark on our conventional wisdom based on societal norms.

The vision also goes against the grain of a teleological perspective which is usually adopted in the reading of religious scriptures.

Such texts usually do not end in tragedies with unresolved moral issues; rather, they are designed to dispel moral dilemmas and to give proper instruction. No doubt, the moralist in a literary critic also may insist on moral instruction in creative literature, but it is doubtful if this goes hand in hand with a tragic vision. It may be noted here that within traditional poetics, when it is claimed that literature gives moral instructions like "one should act like Rāma and not like Rāvaṇa (*rāmādivadvartitavyam, narāvaṇādivat*)" (Dwivedi 1986, 4), a tragic world view is not intended at all.

Thus, it is clear that Anandavardhana approaches the Ramayana primarily as a literary text and focuses on the human predicament as revealed in a literary work.[4] This is actually a sort of retrieval of a literary text from the labyrinth of scriptural and didactic interpretations which are caused by its religious dimensions accrued over a period of time. But it should be remembered that as a pluralist, Anandavardhana does not deny the possibility of liturgical or philosophical interpretation of a text of the stature of the Ramayana and Mahabharata, as we are going to see presently.

Anandavardhana's unstinted admiration of the vision of the poet makes him very circumspect against the tampering with classics like the epics. This may be the reason why he is wary of poets who are fond of modifying the plot to their whims and fancy, a practice rampant among Sanskrit playwrights. According to him, "There are sources of stories like the *Rāmāyaṇa* which are famous for perfected *rasa*. One must not join matter of one's choice with them if it contradicts this *rasa*" (Ingalls et al. 1990, 434).

In short, Anandavardhana proposes a reading of the Ramayana taking the entire narration into consideration, marking the

[4] Even in literary works, pathos is never accepted as a dominant emotion, and tragic ending is scrupulously eschewed in Indian tradition. Abhinavagupta asserts that pathos, unlike love or enthusiasm or anger, can never be a dominant emotion in plays as it is not directly related to the four ends of life. But to Anandavardhana, who believes in an autonomous life of a literary text, no such consideration seems to be relevant.

beginning and the end, and exploring the aesthetic emotion embedded in it. He allows the text to speak by itself and the design of the poet to gradually unfold on its own. He does not want it to be overburdened by predetermined agenda and seldom mentions the instructive aspect of it. In short, he is not unduly concerned with non-literary cultural baggage in his critical engagement.

In the case of the Mahabharata, however, things are far more complicated, for the consensus seems to be that it is more of a moral scripture than poetry. There is a famous saying that the [Maha]Bharata is "veritably the fifth Veda". The epic itself claims that:

> *dharmecharthe cha kame cha mokshe cha bhartarshabha*
> *yadihasti tad anyatra yan nehasti na tat kvachit*
>
> "In *dharma*, *artha*, *kama* and *moksha* whatever is found elsewhere is here and whatever is not here cannot be found elsewhere" (*Mahabharata*, I.56.33)

Against such a formidable tradition, it is not easy to assert that the work is an imaginative artifice, a *kavya*. Anandavardhana wants to categorise it as a *kavya* and calls the author "poet creator Krishnadvaipayana" (*kavivedhasa krishnadvaipayanena*). But reading the epic as a *kavya* to the exclusion of its other facets is nearly impossible. In retrieving the *kavya* stature of Mahabharata, Anandavardhana relies on its plurasignification, claiming that it is both a poem (*kavya*) and an instructive treatise (*shastra*), which are not mutually exclusive. According to him, it is a *shastra* partaking the nature of a *kavya*. This is very interesting since in the Indian tradition, there has always been a dichotomy between *kavya* and *shastra*. According to Bhamaha, poetry is spontaneous, and the unpredictable outcome of creative intuition called *pratibha*. On the other hand, *shastra* is something which can be mastered "even by dull witted people" (Sarma and Upadhyaya 1981, 3). What Bhamaha means is that creative intuition is not a prerequisite for mastery over *shastra*. In a similar vein, Bhatta Tauta states: "Goddess of speech has two ways, one *śāstra* and the other poetry. The former is born of intellect, the latter from imagination" (Sreekantaiya quoted in Raghavan and Narendra 1970, 61). Anandavardhana does not see any contradiction between these two roles of the epic. The epic culminates in the tragic end of the Vrishnis and the Pandavas. The final import of it as a *shastra* is to produce disenchantment with this world, thereby paving the way for the final release (*moksha*) and along with it, in its capacity as a poem, the development of the aesthetic emotion of serenity (*shanta*).

The reference to the serene mood (*shanta rasa*) is very significant because Anandavardhana is one of the pioneers to have argued for its recognition as a *rasa*. Though commentators like Abhinavagupta evoke the authority of Bharata for its acceptance, we do not find it mentioned in the original Natyashastra. The first author to have mentioned it seems to be Udbhata, who, in his *Kavyalankarasarasangraha* (IV. 4) enumerates nine *rasa*s (Masson and Patwardhan 1969, 35). Anandavardhana maintains that such a *rasa* exists and that happiness arising from the destruction of desires (*trishnakshayasukha*) is the permanent mental state appropriate to it. He maintains that this *rasa* exists in *Nagananda*, a play of King Harsha with a Buddhist theme, dealing with the self-sacrifice of Jimutavahana. Such a *rasa* became prominent in medieval times due to the growth of ascetic ideals and the recognition of emancipation (*moksha*) as an ideal to be achieved in this life itself. By interlinking this *rasa* with the epic text, Anandavardhana was trying to supersede the assertion of this-worldliness in the epic through the celebration of final release.

This unified vision of the Mahabharata throws light to the methodology with which one can make sense of mega texts which are staggering due to their sheer size and the labyrinth of tales and sub-tales they unfold to the bewilderment of a reader. A single emotive tone for a macro text is a novel contribution introduced by Anandavardhana in literary criticism for the first time and he demonstrates that it is a valid method of making sense of a text. But there are many hurdles in proposing and maintaining such a perspective for a work like the Mahabharata. The problem of the multi-layered nature of the text, which is formidable for a modern reader, may not have been an issue in ancient times when it was assumed to have been composed by a single author at one stretch. Anandavardhana bases his interpretation on the hints contained in the text: that the Mahabharata culminates in the tragic end of the Vrishnis and the Pandavas. He quotes a verse from the text (*Mahabharata* 12.168.4) to reinforce the argument, without specifying the person who utters it:

> The more the world's affairs
> go wrong for us and lose their substance
> the more will disenchantment with them
> grow, there is no doubt. (Ingalls et al. 1990, 691)

This verse has been uttered by Bhishma, who is talking with the grieving Yudhishthira, but it seems that it can be taken as the authorial voice also, given Bhishma's moral stature in the epic. The verse has a superseding effect on the entire story of the Mahabharata. If we take this verse as the key statement of the epic, it would mean that, contrary to the generally accepted view, the ideal propagated by the epic would be the final emancipation resulting from the disenchantment with the ways of the world, rather than worldliness founded on dharma. However, Anandavardhana also maintains that one can ignore this final import and focus on parts of the text which give us other emotive experiences and prompt other aims of life. There can indeed be beauty in a subordinate rasa or human aim, just as there can be beauty in the body, though it is subordinated to the soul (Ingalls et al. 1990, 691).

Do we require authorial statements to determine the import of a literary work? Anandavardhana anticipates this problem while referring to the objection that the introductory summary (*anukramani*) contained in the epic is silent about either *moksha* or *shanta* and it merely states that the epic contains all human aims and all *rasas*. In reply to this valid objection, Anandavardhana relies on his own pet theme: the most significant things a poet wants to convey are never expressly stated; they are always suggested, lying beneath the expressed meaning to be imaginatively explored by a discerning reader.

There are two clues identified by Anandavardhana which reveal to us the final import of the Mahabharata. One is the following statement found in the introductory summary referring to the topics contained in the epic, specifically verse [1.1.193ab]: "And the blessed Vasudeva, the everlasting is here glorified" (Ingalls et al. 1990, 691).

According to Anandavardhana, this statement means:

> The adventures of the Pāṇḍavas and others which are here recounted, since they come to a miserable conclusion, represent the elaboration of worldly illusion, whereas it is the blessed Vāsudeva, representing ultimate truth, who is here glorified. Purify your minds, therefore, in blessed God, the all highest. Form no passion for insubstantial glories, nor let your minds dwell whole heartedly on virtues such as statesmanship, modesty, courage, or the like, so as to regard, them as sufficient in themselves. The word "and", graced with the full powers of a suggestor, appears clearly to be hinting that one should farther [in the book] and see the worthlessness of all worldly life. The verses which immediately follow, "for He is the truth" etc. [Mbh.1.1.193c] are seen to reveal within themselves the same sense. (Ingalls et al. 1990, 691–92)

The second hint mentioned by Anadavardhana is the composition of *Harivamsha* as a conclusion of the Mahabharata. This is very interesting, since most of the modern critics take this to be an apocryphal portion interpolated later. The appending of *Harivamsha* to the text results in the generation of total devotion to the truth lying beyond worldly life. As a result, all worldly activity now becomes a premise being rejected by it. He further argues that all the other descriptions like the power of gods, places of pilgrimage and asceticism assume a new significance once we accept the attainment of the final emancipation resulting from the disenchantment with the ways of the world as the import of the epic. They all become ancillaries to this purpose.

It may be argued, not without reason, that when Anandavardhana goes deeper into the text of the Mahabharata, it is the devotee in him who gains the upper hand, rather than the critic. Though he concedes that the Mahabharata has a dimension of a literary composition, in addition to its stature as a scientific treatise, it is its accent on the Vaishnavite version of absolutism that becomes projected in his analysis. The aesthetic dimension gets only a cursory glance. However, the stray observations he makes about the import of the text do shed some light on the perspective which emerges when one reads the text as a literary composition. Anandavardhana demonstrates that the text teaches us not to be carried away by "insubstantial glories" and not to be obsessed with virtues like statesmanship, modesty, courage, and the like, which are not sufficient by themselves. This is a new way of looking at the text which may baffle us with its infinite nature if a focal point is missing in our perspective. We get glimpses of Anandavardhana's perspective in his analysis of the famous dialogue between the vulture and jackal (*grdhragomayusamvada*) also (*Mahabharata* 12.149), where the hypocrisy of the vulture and the jackal who speak high philosophy just to serve their ends finally resolves in *shanta rasa.*

What makes the analysis of the epics by Anandavardhana remarkable is the fact that it is a novel attempt to retrieve their stature as creative literature on one hand and on the other it makes use of a methodology for reading a macro text to find out what it is all about. Anandavardhana focuses on the genesis story, the structural design, the recurring motifs, and many other aspects of the literary text to explore its hidden meaning. Of particular importance is the way in which the text begins and ends. Sometimes a stray passage may throw much light to the text's inner meaning. However, Anandavardhana's literary analysis does not touch upon vital aspects of the epics like characterisation and aspects of the narrative thread.

We now live in an intellectual climate which persuades us to believe that there is no final import in any text and once we enter it, what waits for us is a labyrinth of signs and significations from which there is no escape. In such a situation, Anandavardhana's attempt to retrieve the authorial vision may appear to be a far cry. However, the fact remains that literature, among other things, is also a creative work through which the author strives to approximate his vision through his medium, however unsuccessful he is bound to be in this attempt. In the Indian context especially, Anandavardhana wants to remind us that epics are primarily literary works composed by poets, to be read and actualised through imaginative identification and to be experienced in their full emotive significance.

Works Cited

Abrams, M. H. 1988. *A Glossary of Literary Terms.* Madras: Macmillan India Ltd.

Dwivedi, R. C., ed. 1986. *The Poetic Light: Kāvyaprakāśa of Mammata,*Vol. I. Text with translation and *Sampradāyaprakāśinī* commentary of Śrīvidyācakavartin. Delhi: Motilal Banarsidass.

Encyclopedia of India Literature, Vol. II. 1996. New Delhi: Sahitya Akademi.

Haas, George C. O., tr. 1962. *The Daśarūpa by Dhanamjaya.* Delhi: Motilal Banarsidass, Delhi.

Ingalls, Daniel H. H., J. Moussaieff Masson, and M. V. Patwardhan. 1990. *The Dhvanyāloka of Ānandavardhana with the Locana of Abhinavagupta.* Harvard: Harvard University Press.

Kale, M. R., ed. (1928) 1968. *Bāṇa's Kādambarī.* (Fourth Revised edition) Delhi: Motilal Banarsidass.

Kane, P. V., ed. 1997. *The Harshacarita of Bāṇabhaṭṭa.* Delhi Motilal Banarsidass.

Krishnamoorthy, K. 1982. *Dhvanyāloka of Ānandavardhana.* Delhi Motilal Banarsidass..

Mahabharata—The Critical Edition. 1933–1966. Bhandarkar Oriental Research Institute.

Masson, J. Moussaieff, and M. V. Patwardhan. 1969. *Śāntarasa and Abhinavagupta's Philosophy of Aesthetics.* Pune: Bhandarkar Oriental Research Institute.

Mohan, Chandra, ed. 1989. *Aspects of Comparative Literature.* New Delhi: India Publishers and Distributors.

Pollock, Sheldon. 2003. *Literary Cultures in History: Reconstructions from South Asia.* New Delhi: Oxford University Press.

———. 2006. *The Language of the Gods in the World of Men: Sanskrit, Culture, and Power in Premodern India.* California: University of California Press.

Raghavan, V., and Nagendra. 1970. *An Introduction to Indian Poetics.* Bombay: Macmillan.

Sarma, Batuka Nath, and Baldev Upadhyaya. 1981. *Kāvyālaṅkāra of Bhāmaha.* Varanasi: Chowkhamba Sanskrit Sansthan.

Sastri, P. N. Pattabhirama, ed. 1940. *The Dhvanyāloka with Locana and Bālapriyā Commentaries.* Varanasi: Chowkhamba Sanskrit Series Office.

Srimadvalmikiramayana. 1993. Gorakhpur: Gita Press.

Warder, A. K. 1989. *Indian Kāvya Literature,* Vol. I. Delhi: Motilal Banarsidass.

FIVE

Spouses in *thiNai* Songs and *Gaha Sattasai*

A puththiNai *Reading*

Nirmal Selvamony

This essay views spousal relation in Tamil *thiNai* songs and *Gaha Sattasai*[1] through the lens of the critical theory, *puththiNai*. The application of this theory to the songs of both traditions shows how the songs belong to two different types of communitarian order, namely, *thiNai* and state, and manifest the characteristic traits of each communitarian order.

Before turning to spousal relation in the songs in Tamil and Prakrit, a brief outline of the basic framework of *puththiNai* will be in order. According to the ancient Tamil sages, the basic constituents of *thiNai* are

1. *muthal poruL*, the three ultimate ends, *aRam* (ethicalness), *poruL* (substantialness), and *inpam* (happiness) based on *anpu* (love) (Tholkappiyam III. 3. 1)
2. *muthal* (place-time);
3. *karu* (naturo-cultural generative elements), and
4. *uripporuL* of *akam thiNai* aspects and *uripporuL* of *puRam thiNai* aspects.

These four constituents, which constitute the *thiNai* community called *vizhuththiNai* (*Purananuru* 27: 1–3; literally, excellent *thiNai*; Selvamony 2024), find, in *puththiNai*, their equivalents, *tanmai* (hereafter, T) *munnilai* (hereafter, M) and *padarkkai*

[1] *Gaha Sattasai*, an anthology of seven hundred songs in Prakrit, is dated to second century ACE.

(hereafter, P) (Selvamony 2001; 2002; 2003–2004; 2009; 2012; 2014; 2018; 2020), which form a primordial triadic praxic community. If the ultimate ends of *muthal poruL*, place-time of *muthal*, and the naturo-cultural features of *karu* could be subsumed under P, the actions of *uripporuL* could be under T and M. The triadic personaic community constituted by T, M and P is primordial because all actions presuppose such a communitarian framework. These three personae are members because each is organically related to the other just like the organs of an organism.

Of the three members of this framework, T (*tan* – self + *m* intensive consonant + *ai* – stem suffix = *tanmai* self; Gnana Prakasar 2000) is an intentional instrument-using agent or agentive persona, the source of not only linguistic acts such as making utterances but also various non-linguistic physical and mental acts. T intends to perform an act using some instrument or the other. If the intention is a part of T's action, the latter's instrument may be purely physical as an implement or physical and metaphysical as spoken or written language or wholly metaphysical as an idea.

Everything that is not T in the praxic community falls under two categories: M and P. M (*mun*, front + *nilai*, standing = *munnilai*, standing before or that which stands before) is the patient or patient-persona which stands before T, whereas P is that on which T and M stand. M makes itself vulnerable and available to T, especially through relational action. As part of P, M shares everything that is part of the place-time it occupies, both physical and metaphysical. But T does not act upon the elements of P shared by M because those elements are part of P.

P (*padar* to extend + *k*, intensive consonant + *ai*, stem suffix = *padarkai*, extending > *padarkkai* (noun), that which extends, (that which extends beyond *tanmai*) is that which extends beyond T and M; it is the naturo-cultural and axiological contextual member or context-persona, which cannot be acted upon by T because it extends beyond the reach of T. Whatever cannot be acted upon by T will be part of P: place-time (rather than place and time) and the end or purpose of action. T cannot act upon place and time because they are not objects. Like objects they are immanent but unlike objects they are transcendental too. When place-time refers to the location where *tanmai* acts, it is *kaLam* (stage/arena); when it denotes the territory of T, it is *kaTchi* (*Purananuru* 157: 10); whereas, the regional space-time that extends beyond *kaLam* and *kaTchi* and surrounds them is *tuRai* (a meeting place; Selvamony 2021).

Place and time are not empty categories; they are already filled with natural phenomena, living things including people and also the latter's tradition (*marapu*) and metaphysical systems, which are part of *vazhakku*, the good conventions and values approved by the ancestors and the noble people of the community (*Tholkappiyam* III. 9. 94). A vital part of the metaphysical system is the end of the action which lies beyond the grasp of T making it also transcendental like place-time.

Effectively, there are three types of P: the locational (place-time; known as *muthal* in *thiNai*), the generative (physical and metaphysical entities of *kaLam*, which include all naturo-cultural entities, other people and the worldview T shares with the people who are a part of its *kaLam*, all of which are collectively called *karu* in *tiNai* theory because all of these generate T's action), and, the teleological. The last is called *mutal poruL* or the three ultimate ends, which are part of *uyarntha paal* (literally, transcendental division) because they are transcendental and the highest ends of life. *uyarntha paal* is also the abode of godhood (*kadavuL*), and spirit beings (*teyvam*). Though the sacred resides in the world itself in the form of *aNangku* and *chuur*, and worshippable as *teyvam*, *uyarntha paal* of P is transcendental and not manipulable by humans. Similarly, the locational P is also available to humans and beings other than humans, but it is not manipulable by them.

Though humans cannot manipulate P, they can ennoble their actions and make the latter reflect the nature of *uyarntha paal* through the praxis of love. From *Tholkappiyam* one learns that love characterises an action as an ethical one (*aRam*), enables the action to prioritise (*poruL*) the ultimate end, and brings happiness (*inpam*) to the parties involved in the action. Therefore, love, which connects *uyarntha paal* and T is the basis of the three ultimate values.

It is *uyarntha paal* which enables T to perform positively teleological actions, and validates T's relation to M as a familial one blending spousal or *iNai*, kin or *kiLai*, friendly or *naTpu*, positively tensive or *naRpakai* relational modes (*Cilappatikaram* 8: 33). This relation is governed by conventions of haptic contact, which determine the degree of intimacy of physical contact between two persons. If spousal relation allows sexual intimacy, kin relation does non-sexual haptic contact, friendly relation does not depend on haptic contact and tensive relation is marked by the absence of such contact. The familial interrelationship based on all the four modes of haptic contact among T, M and P is the normative one.

To reiterate briefly, if T acts, M is that which is acted upon, and P is that which cannot be acted upon by T. Neither M nor P can occupy the role of T. When M does, it is no more M but T. In the case of P, it is neither agent (T) nor the patient of T. Only T can act; neither M nor P can. Further, to act is to relate. As the agent, T initiates a relation with M. The initiated relation could also be regarded as T's response to M's call. As M cannot act in the praxic community, its call can only be presupposed. However, being the agent, T is the central persona in the community of action.

Though T, M, and P are the three fundamental correlates of any praxic community, the mode of relation of the correlates (which expresses itself in the actions of T) in one type of community is not the same as it is in another. For example, in the primal community, the mode of relation among the correlates is familial whereas in the state society, it is characteristically, organisational. Being egalitarian and non-egalitarian at once, familial relation of primal community circulates power in a heterarchic (Crumley 1995) manner, whereas the state society is non-egalitarian and its organisational relation among its correlates negotiates power hierarchically (Bondarenko 2006).

The mode of relation also tells us about the nature of the community and its worldview represented in an event or text.

If an event or text represents more than one mode of relation (as many do), the type of community corresponding to the mode of relation may also be inferred. The different relational modes may be profitably compared to understand any action or relationship. This essay attempts to understand spousal relationship in *thiNai* songs and the Prakrit *gaha*s by examining the relational modes that obtain in these songs.

In *thiNai* community, the most fundamental communitarian institution is the family (which also goes by the name, *thiNai*) and its central personae, *kizhatti* (chief female persona) and *kizhavan* (chief male persona), are spouses or an *iNai* (couple) whose relationship is also called *iNai*. The noun *iNai* derives from the verbal base *iN* "to join" (Selvamony 1990). Significantly, it is also the nominal base, which yields the word, *thiNai* (*th* + *iNai*, to join = *thiNai*), which, in turn, is a community that results from the union of humans and beings other than humans specific to a particular land area. It is *thiNai* because its members (humans and non-humans) stand in an *iNai* relation to each other. Similarly, *iNai* denotes spousal relationship as it is the most harmonious one possible between any agent and patient.

Besides denoting spouses, and spousal relationship, *iNai* also means one of the four types of tonal relationship. The other three are *kiLai*, *naTpu* and *pakai*. While *iNai* means the fifth relation, *kiLai* or kin-like does the fourth, *naTpu* or friend-like does the third, and *pakai* or foe-like does the second, sixth and seventh. Unlike the other three, *iNai* (*Cilappatikaram* 8: 33–34; Selvamony 2008; 2016; 2017; 2018) is the tonal relation between the tonic and the dominant (say, for example, C and G). In a well-tuned stringed musical instrument, when the tonic and the dominant notes are produced simultaneously, they are almost indistinguishable. If they sound like two different pitches, better tuning is required. The pitches are different, yet they sound identical. This is the highest level of achievable harmony between two notes in an octave. A Prakrit song from *Vajjalaggam* calls attention to the blissful experience of listening to this harmony:

> Even other melodies
> Give a lot of pleasure
> If they are sung properly.
> But, the bliss that the *Panchama* note brings
> Is totally different. (Sharma 2014, 759)

Such "harmony" is called *iNai* because the pitches enjoy maximal identity and minimum difference and necessary tension due to instability. Among living beings, such harmony is found only among spouses and not in any other praxic relationship. This is the reason why the spouses are also referred to as "*iNai*". From early Tamil songs we learn that non-human beings like birds and animals were the ideal examples of spousal harmony.[2]

At first, the spouses appear to be only two personae and the fifth relation only two correlates. But at closer look, there are three: two relata and the common ground on which the relation obtains.

---

[2] The spousal pair of the bird known as *makanRil* (*KuRuntokai* 57; *AingkuRunuuRu* 381) is the archetypal example (rather than metaphor) of spousal harmony. The two individuals pair for life and if one were to die the other would perish soon. When they pair, they are said to achieve a kind of union in which they appear to have a single head despite their two distinct bodies. Scholars seem to attribute such ideal union to another bird known as *anRil* also (*NaRRiNai* 124: 1–2). The former is a water bird of *marutham thiNai*, monogamous like its European counterpart, Bewick's swan, whereas *anRil* is an arboreal one that prefers the palmyrah palm of *neythal thiNai*. Etymologically, *makanRil* means, excellent *anRil* (*maku*, excellent + *anRu*, without + *il*, not being = excellent *anRil*, [which does] not [exist] without [its spouse]; probably because *makanRil* is considered a superior type of *anRil*. M. Krishnan (son of A. Madhaviah), a renowned Tamil naturalist, is the one who had identified *anRil* as Indian black ibis (also known as The Red-naped ibis (*Pseudibis papillosa*). Interestingly, the clinching evidence for the identification was the prevalence of the name *anRil* (for Black ibis) among Tamil villagers in 1986. But Krishnan was not too sure that this bird mated for life (Guha 2001, 93–95). But this was averred by A. O. Hume, a British ornithologist of colonial India, who endorses the characteristic trait of this bird: "They certainly pair for life and palpably exhibit grief for the loss of their mate…on two occasions, I have actually known the widowed bird to pine away and die." (Viveksundar 2021; Ganesan 2016)

In the case of music, this applies to the two pitches that stand in fifth relation, and the octave that gives identity to the pitches and also differentiates them. The three tonal relata are comparable to the three correlates in action, T, M and P. Evidently, P which manifests as *vazhakku*, is the equivalent of the octave in music. When the three correlates unite maximally, the result is the type of harmony called *iNai*.

From the above discussion, it is evident that the chief characteristics of *iNai* harmony are: identity, difference and instability. Identity is a state of oneness that results when two or more entities unite. In *thiNai*, *kizhatti* (wife) and *kizhavan* (husband) exemplify paradigmatic identity. Difference is a state of separation in which the agent could either affirm autonomy or assert herself or himself or dominate the other or be indifferent to the other or attempt all of these. The greater the difference the lesser the identity. Instability is a kind of difference that anticipates resolution to identity (Randel 1986, 197).

INai is neither a state of oneness in which difference is non-existent, nor is it one of twoness that privileges individual autonomy. It distributes power bimodally in the form of equality as well as authority. Identity (in *iNai*) privileges an egalitarian relation, whereas difference (in *iNai*) does authority-oriented one. The seemingly contradictory nature of the spouses is evident in their being egalitarian and authoritative at once. Such a contradictory nature is unstable and renders the relation heterarchical. Does such a relationship exist between the spouses in *tinai* songs and in the Prakrit *gahas*?

Spousal relationship manifests itself through the actions of the spouses. In their praxic contexts, often each occupies either the role of T or M, and rarely, of P. At this point, it might be appropriate to consider a *thiNai* song which deals with spousal relationship. The ninety-fifth song in the early Tamil poetic anthology called *Ainkurunuru* depicts a typical spousal praxic context of a *thiNai* aspect called *marutham*, in which a husband returns home at dawn and attempts to cajole his sulking wife. In such a context, his wife who occupies the role of T, addresses a buffalo that has broken its tether to graze in the adjacent ripe paddy field. Here is the song:

karungkooT Terumai kayiRu parinthasaii
nedungkathir nellin naaNmeeya laarum
punalmuR Ruuran pakalum
padarmali yarunooy cheythana nemakee

The black-horned buffalo
breaks loose from its tether
and grazes at dawn
the ripe fresh paddy on long stalks,
and the man of the village
surrounded by water,
has caused great grief
that grows on me even at day
(*Ainkurunuru* 95; translated by Nirmal Selvamony)

When her husband (M) is standing right before her, the wife, the T in this context, points to the buffalo and speaks about it, which is a non-participatory M here, while she actually intends to address her husband directly.[3] The buffalo is a sort of proxy M when she speaks to it and yet does not speak to it, but speaks about it to vent her anger at her husband by identifying him with their buffalo. The buffalo causes her intense grief even during day time because it does not stay tethered; it breaks loose and grazes where it is not supposed to. This she can say about the buffalo. But if her husband were the direct M in this praxic context, then, she could *not* have told him (according to the praxic conventions

[3] According to the commentator, the addressee in this song is not the husband but a messenger. The message that the wife wants to convey to her husband is most dramatically conveyed to him only if she looks at the buffalo and says what she says when he is within hearing distance. Were the husband absent in the scene of action, the song would only be a desperate complaint without the dramatic verve it is meant to have. If her addressee is a messenger, as the commentator says, the effectiveness of the message will depend on the rhetorical skills of the messenger rather than the wife. Therefore, this situation does not call for the presence or mediation of a messenger.

in *thiNai* community) that he caused her intense grief because he left home to spend the night to indulge in forbidden pleasures.

If the metaphor of the buffalo is applicable to her husband, there must be an equivalent of the forbidden paddy. The equivalent can only be that which has the potential to be the cause of the wife's sulking. Such an equivalent can only be spending the night in the company of some other woman/women. By suggesting that her husband has done what was forbidden, when in fact, he has not, she strengthens the cause of her sulking. It is true that he spent the night outside home, and it is probably true that the night was spent in the company of another woman or other women. But even if he had, what he had done would not be forbidden or immoral in his community. However, the hypothetical charge levelled against her husband is good enough to cause the necessary instability, a sort of discord (*pakai* or tensive relation) in spousal relationship in order to test its potential for resolution to harmony (*iNai* relation).

Spousal harmony is not possible between unfaithful spouses who would stand in negative tensive relationship to each other. If the *kizhavan* of *marutham* were guilty of infidelity as several scholars aver (Vellaivaranan 1983, 126–37; Srinivasa Iyengar 1989, 81; Varadarajanar 1957, 353; Thani Nayagam 1966, 112; V. S. P. Manickam 1962, 165–75; V.T. Manickam 1982, 151; Tamizhannal 2012, 119; Sivathamby 1998, 19; Balasubramanian 1976, 44; Ramanujan 1970, 110; Kuppusamy 1984, 135)[4], neither will *marutham* qualify as a *thiNai* aspect nor will its chief male persona as a *kizhavan*. As the very term *thiNai* means (harmonious) conduct (Selvamony, "*thiNai* Studies"), especially that of the spouses, which is nothing other than *iNai* or spousal harmony, it is incompatible with infidelity and prostitution. Scholars represent

---

4 Discussing the question of prostitution, V. S. P. Manickam is of the view that prostitution is part of *thiNai* society, but not of *ainthiNai* or the five *thiNaikaL* based on love, and that it should be relegated to *perunthiNai* or the theme of excessive passion, which is not based on any ecoregion as the five *thiNaikaL* are (1962, 165–175).

paraththai, one of the female partners of *kizhavan*, as a prostitute. But this representation is not supported by evidences in early Tamil *thiNai* songs.

The central male persona's relationship with *paraththai* has deluded the Tamil scholars for a long time. Many of them have mistaken *paraththai* for a prostitute and based on such a misconception they have averred that *kizhavan's* illicit relationship with such a woman is the major cause of sulking, the appropriate action (*uripporuL*) of *marutham*. Such a reading of *marutham thiNai* vilifies not only *paraththai* but also *marutham thiNai* itself and posits prostitution and infidelity as essential features of this *thiNai*. Dating back to the days of the earliest commentators of *Tholkappiyam*, denigratory representations of *paraththai* and *marutham thiNai* can be traced to a hermeneutic fallacy, I may call, "mishistoricization," which consists in assigning an entity to a wrong historical period. Scholars had assigned the phenomenon, namely, prostitution, a feature of state society, to *thiNai* community, which has resulted in imagining *thiNai* as a state rather than as a primal community. It must be added that prostitution found among some indigenous communities all over the world is attributable to one external pressure or the other which denatures the community and the new practice probably becomes acceptable to the community due to the loss of the earlier axiological basis of the community.

One of the reasons for mishistoricization of *thiNai* was the idea the scholars have had about the central male persona (*kizhavan*) of *marutham*. One of his names is *makizhnan*, an aptronym which literally means "he who is merry, given to fun and frolic" (Selvamony 1998, 108–09) and derives from *makizh*, meaning, "toddy". A typical *thiNai* dweller, *makizhnan* enjoys his drink, song, dance and swim especially in mixed company often until dawn leaving behind his wife who is all by herself the whole night. Such adventurous merriment is often the cause of the wife's sulking, and the wife does not fail to blame it on *paraththai* and her husband's other female acquaintances. If *makizhnan* were a debauch, he would undermine the characterological definition advanced by *Tholkappiyam* according to which the central male persona is expected to be noble and resolute (III.3.7).

Though *thiNai paraththai* has been stigmatised as prostitute by several scholars for a long time, recent studies have tried to redress the wrong (Selvamony, 1998, 22, 37–38; Selvaraj 2012, 84–85; Theynmozhi 2014, 68–69). It must be remembered that *makizhnan*'s partners, *kizhaththi*, *kaamakkizhaththi*, and *paraththai* with whom he has sexual contact are taken in marriage of one kind or the other. If *kizhaththi* is central female persona the man falls in love and marries, *kaamakkizhaththi* is the latter wife taken in marriage if the man could afford a second household, and *paraththai* is another woman the man marries but does not establish a separate household with. While *kizhaththi* and *kaamakkizhaththi* are mostly homebodies, *paraththai* is often an outdoor companion of *kizhavan* (Ramakrishnan 1982, 102).

Kizhaththi, *kaamakkizhaththi*, and *paraththai* attain the status of wife through public or non-public marriage, an important *vazhakku* of *thiNai* (*Tholkappiyam* III. 3. 50; Singaravelu 2001, 191–201). *Tholkappiyam* avers that there has been a long-standing tradition that had upheld the following eight types of love-based marriage as licit ones (III. 3. 1):

1. *iyaRkaip puNarchchi*: literally, natural union; the marriage vow taken by *kizhavan* and *kizhaththi* when no one except them was present (*Kuruntokai* 25)
2. *udanpookku/pookku*: elopement of *kizhavan* and *kizhaththi* (*Tholkappiyam* III. 3. 25: 8; III. 4. 2: 2; *Akananuru* 221); *udan*, together + *pookku*, going = going together, the couple fleeing from home to get married
3. *koNDukaivaliththal*: carrying away the spouse; *kizhavan* carrying away *kizhaththi* as in *Narrinai* (4: 5–7) or *paraththai* whisking away *kizhavan* as in *Akananuru* (76: 13)
4. *koduppak koLvathu*: receiving when given (*Tholkappiyam* III. 4. 1: 3; also known as *tamarin peRuthal* or "receiving from relatives," (*Tholkappiyam* III. 8. 184: 1; *Akananuru* 86: 1–20; 136)

5. *perumporuL vathuvai: kizhavan* marrying *kaamakkizhaththi*; *perum*, large + *poruL*, wealth + *vathuvai*, marriage = large wealth marriage; a man marries because he has lot of wealth (*Tholkappiyam* III. 4. 31: 1)
6. *paraththaik kaLavu maNam*: marrying the female companion secretly (*Akananuru* 36)
7. *kizhavan illaththil paraththaik kaRpu maNam: kizhavan* marrying *paraththai* in his own house (*Akananuru* 46; 336), and
8. *paraththai illaththil kaRpu maNam*: marrying *paraththai* in her house (*Akananuru* 56: 8–14).

The first three types of marriage occurred without the knowledge of the society. Of these, *iyaRkaip puNarchchi* was a type in which the marriage vow, probably invoking the sacred, joined the couple in marriage without any witness. Apparently, there were instances of failure of this marriage due to lack of any public witness. *Tholkappiyam* observes that the elders devised rituals (*karaNam*) in order to strengthen the marital bond weakening due to moral lapses (*Tholkappiyam* III. 4. 4). When the parents did not permit the couple to get married, the latter eloped and subsequently, the marriage was arranged by the parents of *kizhavan*. This type of marriage was called *udanpookku*. The third type was taking away from the family a consenting partner, which was called *koNDukaivaliththal*.

The fourth was the predominant form of marriage of *kizhavan* and *kizhaththi* in the presence of family and other kin, and the fifth of *kizhavan* and *kaamakkizhaththi*. When *kizhavan* had enough wealth, he married *kaamakkizhaththi* and this marriage was called *perumporuL vathuvai* or marriage made possible by adequate wealth.

The sixth, seventh and eighth were three different types of marriage of *kizhavan* with *paraththai*—marrying her without anyone's knowledge except that of *paaNan* (musician), marrying her publicly in her own house and marrying her in his house. These show that marriage with *paraththai* is counted as a licit one.

In *thiNai* community only sexual relationship between spouses of licit marriage was acceptable. However, *thiNai vazhakku* did not consider casual heterosexual bodily contact taboo when persons of both sexes bathed, danced and participated in such social events as festivals. These casual female acquaintances were known by several names: *uuran peNDir* (women of *uuran*, *Ainkurunuru* 13:3; his women; 40: 2–3; your women, 70:4), *puthuvor* (the new persons, *Ainkurunuru* 17:3), *nallor* (literally, the good persons, particularly, women, *Ainkurunuru* 61:4), *palar* (many persons, *Ainkurunuru* 67:4), *ivvuur mangkaiyar* (girls of this village, *Ainkurunuru* 62:3), *punalaadu makaLir* (women who play in the water, *Ainkurunuru* 15:2), *udan aadu aayam* (a bevy that plays with a woman, *Ainkurunuru* 31:4), and so on. The relation between *kizhavan* and casual female acquaintances is described by the bards metaphorically. Even as children who play with the play-cart do not enjoy a ride in it but can only amuse themselves by drawing it with their hands (*Kuruntokai* 61), the raft a swimmer uses does not reciprocate the embrace of the swimmer (*Akananuru* 186: 7–9), and such is the relationship not only among those who play in the water but also *kizhavan* and his casual female acquaintances. The analogies make it clear that the relationship between the casual female acquaintance and *kizhavan* is physical but not sexual. In short, *kizhavan*'s relationship with women other than the ones he had married conforms to the norms (or *vazhakku*) of haptic contact in *thiNai*.

The *vazhakku* of the indigenous Tamil people governed the morality or *aRam* of *thiNai* society. As morality or ethicalness is an ultimate end which is inseparable from the supernatural, which is also a part of the *uyarntha paal* of P, reverence for the supernatural helped sustain morality. For example, the vow the spouses took in marriage in the name of the spirit being called *chuur* validated their marriage (*Kuruntokai* 53; Bowra 1962, 186–87). This was most probably the ancestral spirit being known as *kula teyvam* revered by the boy or the girl or both.[5] Even today Tamil people travel

[5] Even as the masculine suffix was added to *muruku* (a form of sacred) to derive the name, Murukan, the masculine name of the spirit being, *chuuran*

great distances (from whichever part of the world they live in) to take their marriage vow before their *kula teyvam* located in the original homestead of the family. Moreover, the belief that the spirit being guarded the morality of the society was also a part of *vazhakku*, which distinguishes the licit from the illicit.

Vazhakku is not breached but put to severe test in *marutham*. In other *thiNaikaL* the temporary separation of the couple challenges spousal relationship to some extent. But only *marutham*, especially its appropriate action, sulking, stresses spousal relationship maximally in order to demonstrate the strength of love and harmony (*iNai*), characteristics attributable to *thiNai* itself. Further, as spousal identity is expressed through spousal difference, the difference between fidelity and infidelity, as well as socially acceptable heterosexual contact and sexual deviance are probed in-depth in *marutham* songs. However, what counts as infidelity or deviance in *thiNai* is a matter settled by the authority of noble conventions (*vazhakku*) rather than by the authority of law or scripture or codified absolute ethical principles.

In fact, in *thiNai* conformity to *vazhakku* (which is a part of P) is rated higher than adherence to personal ethics. In other words, to T, P is of higher value than oneself. As T shares *vazhakku* with the public, public chatter called *alar* (literally, that which blossoms) matters a lot in situations of spousal relationship (*Kuruntokai* 393). Like sulking, it too plays a significant role in spousal relationship by bringing about a creative instability in the relationship. Both sulking and public chatter eventually prove to be catalytic praxes. But the radar that steers the course of the turbulent spousal relationship is love.

It is *anpu* or love which expresses the true nature of spousal relationship or *iNai*. The latter is heterarchical because it is marked

---

was derived later from the neuter form, *chuur* (a form of sacred). Though *chuuran* originally meant a warrior, later on he was represented as an evil power as in the case of Chuurapanmaa, an *achuuran* slain by Murukan. Degradation of meaning appears to be the fate met with by other names of *kula teyvangkaL* (or clan deities) too such as *muni* and *chudalai*.

by the biaxiality of love, horizontal egalitarianism and vertical authority. The partners are both equal and unequal. In some contexts, the husband exercises authority whereas in others, the wife does as in the *Ainkurunuru* song discussed earlier. The locus of both equality and authority shifts in love according to the need of the context. For example, when the husband returns home and seeks admission, the wife is in charge of the situation but only until he embraces her or their child. In one of the songs the wife admits that the moment her husband embraces her she loosens up like soil tilled by the plough (*Akananuru* 26).

The assumption of authority and equality as well as the relinquishing of them requires T to seek identity with M and diminish the difference that exists between them. In order to seek identity, T ought to lose itself by surrendering its power to manipulate M. Such losing of oneself is the crux of love. Love, in which identity is maximised and difference minimised, is harmony whose value can be understood only in terms of the common ground or *vazhakku* of P that brings the spouses together.

Without love tiff could only be a disastrous blame game ending in separation (which is a state of excessive difference). On his part, the loveless male partner would be a self-centred libertine unworthy of the character expected of him, and on her part, the loveless female partner would be someone waiting to settle her scores with her man. On the contrary, in *marutham thiNai*, the spouses embody the virtues pertinent to each and love each other selflessly.

Love is an aspect of ethicalness, which is an ultimate end that cannot be manipulated by a T because it is both immanent and transcendent. What T can do is speak about it, describe and define it, and choose to do something which is likely to result in love. When we describe an action as an act of love, it is not what T does which is love but the consequence of T's action. Put differently, T can lay its hands on the idea of love, and choose to do something that will result in love, and yet cannot apprehend love itself.

In order to describe or define love and describe someone's action as ethical or unethical, T may use bivalent logic. But this type of logic cannot vindicate a situation where what does not seem to be love is in fact love, or the ethical is representable as the unethical, whereas, *nayam*, the fuzzy logic of *thiNai*, is at once bivalent when it allows the definition of love and the ethical enabling the choice of an action that embodies love or a position that is ethical, and multivalent when it allows the representation of love as not love or the ethical as the unethical. As an action is performed in a definite place and time, the choice of one action and not another is a bivalent one, whereas the consequence of that action is a multivalent one as it is an ultimate end that can neither be chosen nor manipulated by T. For example, in the *Ainkurunuru* song discussed earlier, the husband's action of spending the night in mixed company can be represented either as an act of love or not as an act of love or as an ethical one or an unethical one, and the wife chooses to represent it neither as an act of love nor as an ethical one and sulks. The wife's representation is based on the bivalence accommodated by *nayam*. But the reader who is familiar with *thiNai vazhakku* knows that the personae of *thiNai* can only perform ethical actions and that *kizhavan*'s overnight enjoyment in mixed company was, in reality, not unethical at all and that it is only represented thus (as unethical) by the wife in order to make sulking effective. The reader's representation of the husband's action invokes *vazhakku*, a part of P, which lies outside the song as a part of the *thiNai* master narrative, in order to show how the wife represents love as not love and the ethical as the unethical. It is the positively teleological orientation of the action which resolves its ambivalence.

In fine, what is determinate about a particular praxiological situation (like the one described in the *Ainkurunuru* song) in *thiNai* is T's choice of a particular action that conforms to *vazhakku*, namely, the husband enjoying mixed company ethically, and what is indeterminate about the same situation is the ethical ambivalence associated with it, which can be resolved only by *vazhakku* of P. The bimodality of action (in *thiNai*), determinateness and indeterminateness, neither allows the bivalent categorisation of the agent (T) as good or bad nor the non-bivalent typology, which includes the middling persona who is neither wholly good nor wholly bad (as the Aristotelian hero with a flaw or the *madhyama nayaka* in Sanskrit drama). The middling type is also not part of the *thiNai* world if the action of such a type of persona is not positively teleological (*vazhakku* of P).

From what is said about the persona shows that love is not an ontological category that can be located in a persona, but a praxiological one that points to the ultimate end (*payan*) of action rather than to the action itself. So, one can only speak about the actions of a persona, not about her or his nature, and this renders the critical category "characterology" inapplicable to *thiNai* personae. The ethicalness of a persona can be spoken of only in relation to what the persona does rather than what the persona is.

Now it may be appropriate to see how the relationship between the spouses is represented in the *gahas*. This relationship is one of the major subjects of the Prakrit songs as exemplified by the following song:

> The husband laughed at his wife's face
> Which, smudged with soot
> That stuck to her hand from kitchen work,
> Looked more than ever like the moon.
> (Khoroche and Tieken 2014, 63; cf. Basak 2010, 4)

The spouses are part of a family, which is understood as a type of organisation in which they stand in a hierarchic relation to each other. This relation distributes power among the personae, T, M and P in a unimodal manner; only in the form of authority. Therefore, the female partner of the putative spouses in the *gahas* figures as a subordinate of a dominant husband. Consider the following songs:

> Instead of criticism, smiles,
> Instead of grievances extreme, politeness,
> Instead of quarrels, tears,
> Such is the way of good wives.
> (Khoroche and Tieken 2014, 83)

> Laughing without showing her teeth,
> Moving around without crossing the threshold,
> Looking without raising her face:
> Such is the way of a virtuous wife.
> (ibid., 83–84)

When a *thiNai* wife is free to criticise her husband, the wife spoken of in the song, "Instead of criticism" can only smile. Even if she has a grievance against her husband, all she can do is to be polite with him. When her husband provokes her, she can cry as much as she wants but not quarrel with him. The wife in the song, "Laughing" is also a perfect image of submissiveness. Unlike the ideal wife in *thiNai* who is both humble and authoritative, her counterpart in the Prakrit songs is expected to be only submissive. This means that the relationship between the spouses in the Prakrit songs is hierarchic[6] and not heterarchic. Evidently, hierarchic relation cannot be normative *iNai*.

Hierarchic relation between spouses may be founded on the hierarchic social order such as the caste system or a philosophical anthropology that imagines the human as *homo hierarchicus* (Dumont 1981; Appadurai 1986). But both the caste system and the hierarchical philosophical anthropology undermine harmony of spouses and their relationship with the members of the community (especially, with the non-human ones; Leiss 1972; Bookchin 2005). The interrelationship among T, M and P is no more familial and heterarchic as in *thiNai* but organisational and hierarchic as in a state society. The spouses of the *gaha*s form a dyadic group of two individuals brought together by certain social conventions which undergird the organisation of the hierarchic society. Potentially such individual spouses are monads who are not bound by love. Consider the following song: Let faithful wives/ Say what they like,/ I don't sleep with my husband/ Even when I do. (Mehrotra 1991, 66)

---

[6] The normative spousal relationship in the *Kama Sutra* is also hierarchical (Part IV, chapter 1, Upadhyaya 1978).

The speaker in this song ("Let faithful wives") is a wife who frankly admits that she fakes sexual relationship in her husband's presence and that she is not faithful to him. Khoroche and Tieken have grouped (in their translation of *Gaha Sattasai*) two dozen songs under the head, "Faithless Wife." The adultery on the part of the wife is matched by the waywardness of the husband (Kuppusamy 1984, 136):

How much happiness
Can my errant husband get
From the sidelong glances
Cast by women starved of love?
(Khoroche and Tieken 2014, 97)

In fact, if we trust the speaker of the following song, the wife herself seems to encourage her husband's multiple sexual contacts:

O god, please
Let my husband form other attachments,
For men who have experience of one person only
No longer appreciate what's good and what's bad.
(Khoroche and Tieken 2014, 95)

In the context of the Prakrit songs, the phrase, "other attachments" may not be taken to mean "polygamy" as there are quite a few songs that deal with adulterous wives and husbands. Therefore, the spousal relationship implicit in the song quoted above can neither be counted as love nor as identity.

When identification with the partner is made impossible by the force of subordinating difference, true love is substituted by its fake counterparts. One such is love as irrational passion. Consider the following song: Love's like stretching out:/ The bedstead shaky, one leg/ Falling off. (Mehrotra 1991, 67)

If lying down means taking the least active position, the agent cannot avert an impending disaster unlike someone who could run away from it had he/she been standing instead of lying down. In the Prakrit poet's opinion, love is at best an inactive condition in which one courts disaster. It is such because while in the grip of erotic passion, one's rationality loses its original controlling power. In other words, the song speaks of love as a kind of (irrational) passion.

Love is also imagined as a kind of *rasa* or flavour. Even as boiled water loses its original fresh *rasa*, love is not the same after an experience of unpleasantness caused by one's partner. The following song conveys this idea:

> Love
> Estranged and patched up again,
> Once its dissolution is plain to see,
> Will never taste right again
> Like water that has boiled then cooled.
> (Khoroche and Tieken 2014, 123)

Significantly, scholars aver that the major theme of the *gahas* and their later imitations is a *rasa* known as *shringara*, and that all these compositions belong to a genre called *shringara muktaka*[7] (Kuppuswamy 1984). Evidently, *shringara* and love are not the same thing. While the former is a *rasa* (sentiment or passion), the latter is an ethical state of being marked by selflessness. *Rasa* is subjective experience even when it denotes aesthetic emotion. It is valorised by the experience of the present moment. Though love

---

[7] *muktaka* derives from Ta. *muththakam* from Ta. *muthu*, ripe > *muththu*, pearl as that which ripens within the shell of an oyster > Skt. *mukta*, pearl; *mukti*, liberation as the fully ripe stage; *muthu* > *muRRu* to ripen, to end + *akam* inside = *muRRakam* ripening/ending within; *muRRakam* > *muththakam* that which ripens/ends within the stanza; *muththakam* > Skt. *muktaka*. However, "*muththakam*" is not understood in *thiNai* and the Prakrit song the same way. It must be pointed out that subsuming the Prakrit compositions under the genre called *shringara muktaka* is an attempt to Sanskritise the Prakrit tradition. Ethnocentric Sanskritists attempt to erase the differences between the two traditions in more than one way. One such attempt is the Sanskritization of the Prakrit name of the anthology. Translators call *Gaha Sattasai* (the original Prakrit name) by its equivalent Sanskrit name, *Gatha Saptasati*. Determined to fight Sanskritisation, the Prakrit composers candidly express their hostility to Sanskrit verse, which is in evidence in some Prakrit songs in the anthology, *Vajjalagga* (Sharma 2014, 754–55).

includes subjective experience, it is valorised not by experience but by the end (that is beyond experience) it envisages, namely, selflessness, which facilitates accommodation of the other. If the Prakrit songs and their imitations in different languages are all *shringara*-based, the Tamil *thiNai* songs are love-based ones.

In the Prakrit songs, love is reduced to *shringara*, a *rasa*, which is a T-centric concept. T-centricity, which is characteristic of hierarchic spousal relationship (as in the *gaha*s), diminishes the importance of P, especially the positively teleological P. Superior to both M and P, T is invested with power or authority to deny equality and power to M, and bracket off the positively teleological P, if any. Such bracketing off is compensated by privileging of T. Though T does not necessarily have to abuse power by virtue of its superiority, it is an irresistible temptation. The female spouse attests to the possibility of abuse of power in the following song: "We have nothing to do with bad and good persons. Therefore, a mediocre man is rather better (for us). For, just as a bad man, when unseen, causes affliction, so also a good man, when unseen, does the same" (Basak 2010, 51).

In the song quoted above, the three categories of the chief male persona, namely, good, bad and middling (Pkt. *majjimo*; Skt. *madhyama*) are mentioned (plausibly) by the chief female persona probably under the influence of the *Natyasastra*. As the dramaturgy in the latter text is shaped by the hierarchic nature of the state society in which it originated, the three categories of the chief male persona mentioned by the chief female persona also stand in a hierarchic relation to each other. She would rather have a man who is neither entirely good nor entirely bad, a type she calls, "*majjimo*," which literally means "middling" (rather than "mediocre" as in Basak's translation as the latter has negative connotation and often implies less skilled) because the good man is likely to abuse his moral supremacy.

Goodness, like love, is not an ontological category that can be located in a persona, but a praxiological one that points to the ultimate end of action rather than to the action itself. But in the song under discussion, the goodness the female persona refers to is not an aspect of the ultimate end, ethicalness, but a mere description of a T that projects itself as a good person before the others, and misbehaves at the slightest opportunity. Such projection is considered an organisational necessity in a hierarchic society. Therefore, the "goodness" the female persona speaks of is not an aspect of P, but a mere characterological descriptor of T.

The T of the *gaha*s can project itself appropriately as it occupies a dominant position in the family and society. This is possible because T has freed itself from the control of P, especially *vazhakku*. The source of *vazhakku* in a hierarchic universe is T which depends on power rather than on P. The dismissal of *vazhakku* and the privileging of T undermines spousal harmony, and these have to be understood in light of the dismissal of locational P, the basic characteristic of *thiNai*.

The following song shows how *vazhakku* is regarded in the universe portrayed by the Prakrit songs: Because the jealous world must drive/ A pestle through a pinhole,/ My eyes can never dwell/ On him, though he lives in my village. (Mehrotra 1991, 40)

The world out there is the social P and this part of P is characterised by the speaker as "jealous world." While "the world" is "*ulakam*" (world), which, as a part of *vazhakku*, helps maintain social decorum in *thiNai*, it is something to be avoided in the state society. In fact, we have songs that disrespect decorum, and (consequently) encourage explicitness in matters of sex (not unlike the erotic sculptures in the temples of Khajuraho). This is borne out by the manner in which the human body and sex are treated in the songs ("He finds", Mehrotra 1991, 39; "Always wanting me" Mehrotra 1991, 50). Such explicitness seems to contradict the scholarly view that suggestiveness is an important aesthetic device in the *gaha*s (Selby 1991, 76–77). In Tamil *thiNai* songs the literary device, namely, suggestiveness is not a mere literary device; it derives from the good conventions (*vazhakku*) in real life. But in Prakrit songs, the fantasies of T supersede the primacy of *vazhakku*.

There is evidence of gross abuse of *vazhakku* or what has been referred to earlier as the positively teleological P. Incest is a case in point. This song is about an incestuous relationship a mother has with her son: Why *mahua* flowers, son?/ Even if you grabbed my skirt,/ Who'd hear me in the forest?/ The village's far, and I'm alone (Mehrotra 1991, 65).

What is more, the social P in these songs could also collude with a deviant wife. The following song makes this point clear:

> Though distressed by the death of her relatives
> The hostage made eyes at her kidnapper
> Who was a handsome youth.
> For who begrudges anyone
> His good points?
> (Khoroche and Tieken 2014, 132)

The wife in the song is someone who arranges her own abduction and enjoys it. This is evidence of the failure of *vazhakku*. When *vazhakku* fails, the vacuum is filled by the indulgent T, which expresses itself promiscuously. If promiscuity is doing what one pleases, it shows total disregard for *vazhakku* as in the case of the following song: Her father-in-law said no,/ Her languish yes/ To the traveller asleep/ In the terrace (Mehrotra 1991, 22).

Having discussed the various aspects of spousal relationship in both the *thiNai* songs and Prakrit songs, some general observations could summarize the discussion. While *puththiNai* interprets *thiNai* as the triadic personaic community, it does not abandon the ancient Tamil *thiNai* theory but embraces it. Put differently, *puththiNai* is a happy blend of both the ancient *thiNai* theory and a neo-*tinai* theory. Therefore, a *puththiNai* reading of the *thiNai* songs and the *gaha*s provides insights into various aspects of spousal relationship from a *thiNai* perspective, shows how a communitarian order other than *thiNai* is represented in the songs, and helps to historicise the content of the songs.

When the *thiNai* songs and the *gaha*s are seen from the perspective of *thiNai*, the following points are noteworthy. The foundational principle of the *thiNai* song is *thiNai* itself, the primal community, which is much larger than the family and its basic spousal relationship. Neither any tradition of love poetry nor *Gaha Sattasai* seems to be based on *thiNai*. Therefore, *thiNai* songs cannot be treated as another kind of love poetry as some Tamil scholars do.[8]

Each *thiNai* song, which depicts one aspect or the other of *thiNai*, is only an episodic strand of the master narrative. Such a technique may be called synecdochic composition, which is possible only when the listeners and viewers know the whole story or at least several parts of the master narrative.[9] They need to know enough about the dramatis personae, their interrelationships, their roles in the plot and their praxic conventions.

But a non-Tamil imitation of *thiNai* presupposes a commonsensical understanding of the family and community, not prior knowledge of *thiNai* tradition. For example, the *Ainkurunuru* song discussed earlier cannot be read properly without invoking the *vazhakku* regarding the central personae's true nature that forms a part of the *thiNai* foundation of the song but not mentioned in the song itself. But to read the Prakrit song, "Her father-in-law said no," a reader needs no prior knowledge of what *thiNai* tradition calls *kuuRRu* or speech situation except common sense.

An unbroken tradition of *thiNai* exists only in Tamil Nadu. Therefore, the notion that there was a common source in the Deccan from which *thiNai* songs and the Prakrit songs derived

---

[8] The *thiNai* songs are not mere love songs as Vaiyapurip Pillai represented them (1956, 45; Mathivanan 1978). The label "love poetry" is ambiguous as it takes different meanings in different cultures. To subsume *thiNai* songs under the generic rubric of love poetry is quite unhelpful as there is no corpus of love poetry in the world that is based on the *thiNai* system as the Tamil Cankam songs are. It must also be added that not all Cankam songs represent the *thiNai* or primal society. However, in all the *thiNai* songs, the central *vazhakku* is *thiNai* though love is indeed the ultimate end of *thiNai*. As *thiNai* songs are about *thiNai*, they are best identified as "*thiNai* songs" rather than "love poetry."

[9] It may be profitable to compare what I have called "synecdochic composition" with a feature of oral poetry Ramanujan calls, "a language within language" (1996, 250–51) and "second language of poetry and narrative" (1996, 269–70).

is baseless. Refuting this non-Tamil source notion, Kuppusamy says, "there was neither a manual nor tradition (either in Prakrit or Sanskrit) which preserved and propagated the poetic conventions on which the Prakrit songs were based" (Kupppusamy 1984, 143–44; Hart 1975).[10]

From the indigenous Tamil *thiNai*-based performative tradition sustained by the Tamil musicians called *paaNar* and *pulavar*, Prakrit (and later Sanskrit) poets borrowed such conventions as synecdochic composition, dramatic monologue, the employment of typological personae, dyadic central personae and their interactions and so on. However, the Prakrit songs did not scruple to flout a Tamil convention or two and a striking example, besides precedence to ultimate values (*muthal poruL*), is the convention of anonymity. According to *thiNai* theory, the spouses cannot be named in *akam* songs that deal with the relationship between *kizhavan* and *kizhaththi*, and the Tamil *thiNai* songs faithfully follow this rule. But in some Prakrit songs the spouses are named Krishna-Radhika, and Parvati-Pasupati (Basak 2010, 21; 26; 16). In fact, the Prakrit song is neither governed by conventions pertaining to *muthal poruL* nor *uripporuL* (appropriate action of *thiNai*) nor *muthal* (place-time) nor *karu* (generative elements of place-time). If so, it has borrowed only some features of a *thiNai* song, not *thiNai* itself.

---

[10] As the Prakrit *gaha*s are not based on a *thiNai* framework, attribution of *tinai* to them is irrelevant. It is unfortunate that scholars like George L. Hart (1975) and Mathivanan (1978) have made such attempts. The *nayaka-nayika bheda* in the *Natyasastra* may bear partial comparison to *akapporuL* (heterosexual love) in Tamil. But the relationship between the central heterosexual personae is only one aspect of *uripporuL* of *thiNai*, and evidence for this aspect in the Prakrit songs is not adequate to argue that the latter are based on *thiNai*. Kuppusamy states that the Tamil *akapporuL* tradition "inspired many Sanskrit poets, including the great Kalidasa, and later blossomed into a long Sanskrit *Sringara Muktaka* [tradition] that ran continuously for several hundred years producing in its course many anthologies like *Amara Sataka*, *Catur Pancasika*, *Arya Saptasati* etc. before it fructified into Hindi *Rīti* poetry (1700–1800 AD)." (1984, 149).

The concepts of *puththiNai* provide significant insights into both traditions. With the help of the concept of *iNai* as a mode of interrelationship that distributes power in a complex manner blending equality and authority, *puththiNai* could describe the relationship between the spouses in the *thiNai* song as a heterarchic one and its counterpart in the Prakrit songs as a hierarchic one. The concept of heterarchy of *puththiNai* shows how *thiNai* is a familial type of community, and how the state and the triadic personaic community in the Prakrit songs are organizational and hierarchic rather than familial and heterarchic.

If the familial, heterarchically constituted *thiNai* is the normative *thiNai* or *vizhuththiNai*, the organisationally and hierarchically (often, homoarchically) constituted community (as in the Prakrit songs) may be called *viizhthiNai* or fallen *thiNai* as the latter is a denatured form of the original *vizhuththiNai*. In the contemporary industrialist age, there is a growing trend of rejection of heterosexuality and embracing of asexuality which renders spousal relationship impossible.[11] In other words, anarchisation of sexual relationship results in *althiNai* or "no *thiNai*" because *thiNai* itself is destroyed when *inai* or spouse-like relationship is annihilated.

INai connotes a familial relation, and also the very nature of *thiNai* itself. As it is a kind of harmony that expresses itself as love between the spouses, and not mere erotic passion or *shringara*, it also shows how the generic name, "*shringara muktaka*" is an inappropriate descriptor of a *thiNai* song. Imitations of *thiNai* songs were named so probably because the imitators did not realise that the originals were songs about *akaththiNai* and the central concern of these songs was *thiNai* rather than erotic relationship. This could be the reason why the imitators did not prioritise *thiNai* principles over erotic relationship.

---

[11] The following verse titled "Asexuality" expresses the ideology of *althiNai*:

> They tell me I'm missing out / That I should find a person to be my home / But I am not lacking/ I am whole / All on my own (Willow 2022)

Though the Prakrit songs borrowed the theme of spousal relationship, they could not depict a heterarchic spousal relationship because they reflected the philosophical anthropology of the state society in which they were composed. Accordingly, they prioritised T instead of the positively teleological P. By postulating *thiNai* as a triadic personaic community, *puththiNai* establishes the P-orientation of the *thiNai* songs, and the T-orientation of the Prakrit imitations. As the hierarchic relation is a corollary of T-centricity, the spousal relationship in the Prakrit songs represents the negatively teleological values of T. T-oriented goal like pleasure with no commitment to morality and ultimate values could be pursued only in a hierarchic relationship, where T occupies positions of power and gives free reign to its desires and base instincts. This is the reason why instances of promiscuity, adultery, and incest are in evidence in the Prakrit songs. As the latter did not borrow the principle of P-centricity, they could not privilege the key element of the *thiNai* songs, namely, *iNai* or spousal harmony because it is an impossibility in the hierarchic state society which produced the Prakrit songs. This study shows that, despite imitation, there is unbridgeable distance between the *thiNai* songs and the *gaha*s, and that distance is not just time, but the kind of harmony the Tamil sages identified as *iNai*.

WORKS CITED

Ainkurunuru
https://sangamtranslationsbyvaidehi.com/ettuthokai-ainkurunuru/ Accessed on 16 August 2024.

Akananuru
https://sangamtranslationsbyvaidehi.com/ettuthokai-akananuru-1-120/
https://sangamtranslationsbyvaidehi.com/ettuthokai-akananuru-121-300/
https://sangamtranslationsbyvaidehi.com/ettuthokai-akananuru-301-400/ Accessed on 16 August 2024.

Appadurai, Arjun. “Is Homo Hierarchicus?” *American Ethnologist.* 13.4 (Nov. 1986): 745–761. <http://www.arjunappadurai.org/articles/

Appadurai_Is_Homo_Hierarchicus_A_Review_Essay.pdf> Accessed on 16 August 2024.

Balasubramanian, C. 1976. *The Status of Women in Tamilnadu During the Sangam Age*. University of Madras.

Basak, Radhagovinda, trans. 2010. *The Prakrit Gatha Saptasati*. Kolkata: The Asiatic Society.

Bondarenko, D. M. 2006. *Homoarchy: A Principle of Culture's Organization: The 13th–19th Centuries Benin Kingdom as a Non-state Supercomplex Society*. Moscow: KomKniga.

Bookchin, Murray. 2005. *The Ecology of Freedom: The Emergence and Dissolution of Hierarchy*. Oakland, CA: AK Press.

Bowra, C. M. 1962. *Primitive Song*. London: Wiedenfeld and Nicolson.

Cilappatikaram. 1985. Ed. U. V. Saminatha Iyer. Thanjavur: Tamil University.

Crumley, Carole, L. "Heterarchy and the Analysis of Complex Societies." *AnthroSource* (Jan. 1995): 1–5. https://doi.org/10.1525/ap3a.1995.6.1.1

Dumont, Louis. 1981. *Homo Hierarchicus: The Caste System and Its Implications*. Chicago: University of Chicago Press.

Ganesan, N. 2016. "*Kampanil oru keeLvi: kiravuncham*" (A question with regard to the poet, Kampan). https://groups.google.com/g/vallamai/c/TMDvEonVomU/m/wDkDmL1bAgAJ. Accessed on 16 August 2024.

Guha, Ramachandra, ed. 2001. *Nature's Spokesman: M. Krishnan and Indian Wildlife*. OUP.

Hart III, George L. 1975. *The Poems of Ancient Tamil*. California: University of California Press.

Khoroche, Peter and Herman Tieken, trans. 2014. *Hala's Sattasai (Gatha Saptasati in Prakrit): Poems of Life and Love in Ancient India*. Delhi: Motilal Banarsidass Publishers Private Limited.

Kuppusamy, T. S. 1984. "Tamil *akam* Poetry: Forerunner of Indian *Srngara Muktaka* Tradition." *Journal of Asian Studies* 1.2 (March 1984): 127–151.

Kuruntokai
https://sangamtranslationsbyvaidehi.com/ettuthokai-kurunthokai-1-200/
https://sangamtranslationsbyvaidehi.com/ettuthokai-kurunthokai-201-400/ Accessed on 16 August 2024.

Leiss, William. 1972. *The Domination of Nature*. New York: George Braziller.

Manickam, V. S. P. 1962. *The Tamil Concept of Love*. Tirunelveli & Madras: The South India Saiva Siddhanta Works Publishing Society Tinnevelly Ltd.

Manickam, V. T. 1982. *Marutam: An Aspect of Love in Tamil Literature*. Karaikudi: Tema Publishers.

Mathivanan, R. 1978. *aanthira naaTTu Akananuru* (*Akananuru* of the Andhra country). Chennai: Thaay Nadu Pathippakam.

Mehrotra, Arvind Krishna, trans. 1991. *The Absent Traveller: Prakrit Love Poetry from the Gathasaptasati of Satavahana Hala*. Delhi: Ravi Dayal Publisher.

Narrinai. https://sangamtranslationsbyvaidehi.com/ettuthokai-natrinai-1-200/ https://sangamtranslationsbyvaidehi.com/natrinai-2-2/ Accessed on 16 August 2024.

Purananuru. https://sangamtranslationsbyvaidehi.com/ettuthokai-purananuru-201-400/ https://sangamtranslationsbyvaidehi.com/ettuthokai-purananuru-1-200/ Accessed on 16 August 2024.

Prakasar, Gnana. Rev. 2000. *An Etymological and Comparative Lexicon of the Tamil Language*. Chennai: International Institute of Tamil Studies.

Ramakrishnan. 1982. *akaththiNai maanthar: oor aayvu* (Personae of *akaththiNai*: A Study). Madurai: Sarvodaya Ilakkiya Pannai.

Ramanujan, A. K., trans. 1970. *Interior Landscape: Love Poems from a Classical Tamil Anthology*. London: Peter Owen.

———. 1996. *Poems of Love and War From the Eight Anthologies and the Ten Long Poems of Classical Tamil*. OUP.

Randel, Don., ed. 1986. *The Harvard Dictionary of Music*. Cambridge, MA, London: The Belknap Press of Harvard University Press.

Selby, Martha. 1991. "Afterword." In *The Absent Traveller: Prakrit Love Poetry from the Gathasaptasati of Satavahana Hala*. Selected & Translated by Arvind Krishna Mehrotra. Delhi: Ravi Dayal Publisher, 71–82.

Selvamony, Nirmal. 1990. "An Alternative Social Order." *Value Education Today: Explorations in Social Ethics*. Eds. J.T.K. Daniel, Nirmal Selvamony. Tambaram: Madras Christian College and New Delhi: AIACHE, 215–236.

———. 1998. *Persona in Tholkappiyam*. Chennai: International Institute of Tamil Studies.

———. 2001. "*mozhi*: The Personaic Nature of Language." *thiNai 1*. Chennai: Persons For Alternative Social Order, 27–36.

———. 2002. "From Sign to Persona." *thiNai 2*. Chennai: Persons For Alternative Social Order, 15–20.

———. 2003–04. "Oikopoetic Method." *thiNai 3*. Chennai: Persons For Alternative Social Order, 44–56.

———. 2008. "Water in Contemporary Tamil Literature." *Words on Water: Literary and Cultural Representations*. Ed. Maureen Devine and Christa Grewe-Volpp. Trier: Wissenschaftlicher Verlag Trier, 89–101.

———. 2009. "Home: The Tryst of the Ecocritical and the Postcolonial." IV International Conference of OSLE-India. National College, Tiruchi. Unpublished Paper.

———. 2012. "*thiNai* and Language Theory." *Contemporary Contemplations on Ecoliterature*. Ed. Suresh Frederick. Delhi: Authors Press, 15–31.

———. 2014. "Authorship in the Light of *thiNai*." *Culture and Media: Ecocritical Explorations*. Cambridge Scholars Publishing, 170–188.

———. 2016. "What is A fig?" *Ecodocumentaries: Critical Essays*. Ed. Rayson K. Alex. Palgrave Macmillan, 135–154.

———. 2017. "Development Poetics." *Aesthetics of Development: Art, Culture and Social Transformation*. Ed. John Clammer and Ananta Kumar Giri. Palgrave Macmillan, 231–252.

———. 2018. "*Communitas Harmonia* in Wordsworth: A Musicosociological Glance." *Transformative Harmony*. Ed. Ananta Kumar Giri. New Delhi: Studera Press, 741–762.

———. 2020. "Neo-*thiNai* Poiesis." Discussion on Neo-*tinai* Poiesis in the online workshop titled "Soundarya and the Sahridaya: Aesthetic Discourses in India & the West," organised by Padasala in association with Sree Sankaracharya University of Sanskrit-Kalady and Sahapedia, 26 November 2020. https://www.youtube.com/watch?v=aq3iFiEaARo. Accessed on 16 August 2024.

———. 2021. "Justice and *thiNai*: The Strange Meeting of *thiNai* and Industrial Societies." *Contemporary Contemplations on Green Literatures*. Ed. Suresh Frederick, Samuel Rufus. New Delhi: Authorspress, 11–35.

———. 2024. "*kaLam* in *thiNai* and post-*thiNai* societies: An introduction to *puththiNai*." "Folk and India" (Special Section), *Folk, Knowledge, Place* (online journal) (invited paper to be published).

Selvaraj, Silambu, N. 2010. *tolkappiyattil maNa muRaikaL* (Types of marriage in *Tholkappiyam*). Chennai: Kavya.

Sharma, T. R. S. 2014. *Ancient Indian Literature: Tamil and Kannada*. Delhi: Sahitya Akademi.

Singaravelu, S. 2001. *Social Life of the Tamils: The Classical Period*. Chennai: International Institute of Tamil Studies.

Sivathamby, Karthigesu. 1998. *Studies in Ancient Tamil Society*. Chennai: New Century Book House Private Ltd.

Srinivasa Iyengar. 1989. *History of the Tamils: From the Earliest Times to 600 A.D.* Asian Educational Services.

Subramanian, S. V. 2013. *cangka ilakkiyattil maruthap paadalkaL* (*muulamum teLivuraiyum*) (*marutham*... songs in Sangam literature [original text and explanatory commentary]). Chidambaram: Meyyappan Pathippagam.

Tamizhannal. 2012. *cangka marapu* (Sangam Tradition). Madurai: Meenakshi Puthaka Nilayam.

Thani Nayagam, Xavier S. 1966. *Landscape and Poetry: A Study of Nature in Classical Tamil Poetry*. Asia Publishing House, 2nd ed.

Theynmozhi, M. 2014. *cangka kaalat tirumaNa muRaikaL* (Types of Marriages during Cankam age). Chennai: Kavya.

Tholkappiyam muulam: paada veeRupaadukaL: aazh nookku aayvu. (*Tholkappiyam* original with textual variations from a research perspective). 1996. Ed. K. M. Venkataramaiya, S. V. Subramaniam, and P. V. Nagajan. Thiruvananthapuram: The International School of Dravidian Linguistics.

Upadhyaya, S. C., trans. 1978. *Kama Sutra of Vatsyayana*. Bombay: Taraporevala.

Vaiyapurip Pillai.. 1956. *History of Tamil Language and Literature*. Chennai: New Century Book House.

Varadarajan, M. 1957. *The Treatment of Nature in Sangam Literature*. Tirunelveli & Madras: The South India Saiva Siddhanta Works Publishing Society Tinnevelly Ltd.

Vellaivaranan, K. 1983. *Tholkappiyam poruLathikaaram: kaRpiyal*. Compendium of commentaries. Madurai: Madurai-Kamaraj University.

Viveksundar. 2021. Instagram message about *anRil*. https://www.instagram.com/p/CMa8SZvM0gC/. Accessed on 16 August 2024.

Willow, S. R. 2022. "Asexuality." https://hellopoetry.com/tag/asexual/ Accessed on 16 August 2024.

SIX

Re-inventing the Literary

Two Moments in the History of the Kannada Tradition

Rajendra Chenni

I intend to discuss two moments in the history of Kannada tradition when the notion of the literary was reinvented under the pressure of the historical and cultural forces. These were moments which Stuart Hall would have described as conjunctures (Hall and Massey 2010). I also believe that there is sufficient evidence to treat the two moments as instantiations of a continuous process in the Kannada tradition—the process of reformulating the notion of the literary for enabling it to express a changing Yugadharma.[1] The process takes place within a recognisable space and with the help of familiar tools, but what gets shaped is something radically new.

The first moment is the period from the ninth century CE to the eleventh century CE, the period described by Sheldon Pollock as marking the beginning of the vernacular cosmopolis or the cosmopolitan vernacular. Decades before Pollock's work, M. M. Kalaburgi in his PhD dissertation (1973) had analysed the sudden shift in the linguistic medium of the inscriptions during this period and discovered that instead of Sanskrit or Prakrit as in the past, Kannada had become the preferred language of the inscriptions. Pollock sees this as indicating a shift in the political will of the emerging vernacular polity. It now asserts its confidence in Kannada by making it the language of public, political acts

[1] Yugadharma zeitgeist, spirit of the age

(Pollock 2006, 331–36). Similarly, D. R. Nagaraj (2012, 31–33) describes the inscriptions as "public narratives" and agrees with Pollock that the shift in language of political communication was emblematic of a shift in the political will. In the political arena, vernacular polity was on the rise. Kannada was also rapidly becoming the vehicle of serious literary expression (Pollock 2006, 331). Though the earliest inscriptions in Kannada are estimated to belong to the fifth century CE, it is now that it becomes a pliant and mature medium of literary art.

Kavirajamargam (875 CE) is a manual for the poets, a full-fledged theoretical work of Kannada poetics. Though it borrows from the works of Bhamaha and Dandin so heavily that some scholars had treated it as a work of translation, three leading Kannada scholars—K. R. Nagaraj, D. R. Nagaraj and K. V. Subbanna—have treated it as a major statement of the cultural politics of the time. Subbanna (2000) compares it to the Spanish Grammar composed by Nebrija with the political motive of supporting Spanish nationalism/colonialism. D. R. Nagaraj (2012) sees it as a statement of politics in the guise of poetics. K. R. Nagaraj (2012) offers a distinctive analysis by arguing that the author of the work was articulating the need to fashion a standard Kannada dialect out of the many dialects in the Kannada *nadu* so that a Kannada polity would be supported by it. Alternatively, the work whose authorship is attributed jointly to Srivijaya and Nrupatunga, proposes that the Rashtrakuta Kannada empire could become the imagined Kannada *nadu*, both a geo-political entity and a polity itself. What is significant is that in *Kavirajamargam* the literary in Kannada is invented as a constituent element in the making of the Kannada vernacular polity. This convergence of the literary and the political is supported by the fact that every significant formulation in the text is described as the approved opinion of the king emperor. Unfortunately, historical studies of the early medieval period in Karnataka are very few and one has to surmise the factors which led to the hegemonising of the literary. From the text itself and the poetical works which followed soon it is evident that there was a bilingual literary cultural elite (with mastery over

Kannada and Sanskrit) centred around the court which functioned as the reading public and connoisseur. This also set the standards and taste of/for the literary. From the example of Pampa, it is also clear that the literary flourished under royal patronage and that political power itself considered the recognition and fame through literary works as very important.[2] Within less than a century, Pampa gave a powerful expression to this collaboration by allegorising his patron Arikesari as Vikramarjuna, the brave hero Arjuna in his Kannada retelling of the Mahabharata. While some traditional critics considered the allegory as awkward, others saw it as Pampa's tribute to his patron. However, Pampa's great epic is more than an elaborate poetic tribute. Its major preoccupations are far more serious. It is probably the first major literary effort to use pan-Indian Sanskrit model and material to express a regional sensibility, a regional politics and a way of life specific to a time and a place. Sheldon Pollock (2006)[3] who has written perceptively on both *Kavirajamargam* and *Vikramarjuna Vijayam*, uses all his arguments to construct the idea of a trans-regional Kannada vernacular which like the Sanskrit cosmopolis he constructs is at once of the region and supra-regional. One may or may not agree with Pollock's notion of a Sanskrit cosmopolis which somehow enjoyed an abstracted existence, with very little to do with temporal power or cultural hegemony. But the relationships between the Kannada vernacular polity and the vernacular cosmopolis were clearly political and part of the cultural politics of the time.

The court(ly) poetry of the Champu poets was not only patronised by the royal court but was a major constituent of

---

[2] Pampa is known as *adikavi*, the first or archetypal poet who wrote two great epics in Kannada namely *Vikramarjuna Vijayam* (950 CE) and *Adipurana* (939 CE). His patron was Arikesari, a feudatory lord who is allegorised as Arjuna in *Vikramarjuna Vijayam.*

[3] He discusses this in the chapter "Vernacular Poetries and Politics in Southern Asia" and in fact throughout the book.

the court itself.[4] However, this statement should not be wrongly construed to suggest that Pampa wrote a merely eulogistic poem. The epic poem is fraught with serious contradictions mirroring the conflicts of the age. Pampa, born in a Shaivite Brahmin family records that his father though born in a "high caste/religion" (a brahmin by birth), converted to Jainism which he describes as "the greater faith". This does not prevent him from writing a *loukika* (this-worldly) epic celebrating the martial values of war and heroism. While paying tribute to warrior kings, he also lashes out at the foolish "lords of the land" (kings) who do not understand the consequences of their actions. He allegorises his patron as Arjuna but in the end describes Mahabharata as "Karna Rasayana" and advises readers/listeners to "remember Karna for his truth (*nanni*)". He is sarcastic about the great sages unable to control their lust. It would be difficult to decide whether the mood of nihilistic war weariness in the epic owes itself to the original Mahabharata or is a comment on the violence of the age. The latter interpretation finds powerful support in Pampa's *Adipurana* which he claims is a celebration of the *agama* (religion, the spiritual or Jain religion itself). Its sources are the *Mahapurana* in Sanskrit by Jinasena and other religious sources.[5] Though it is structured as a hagiography of the first Tirthankara, the second half of the work is a powerful attack on the violence and greed on which temporal power and empire building depend. Bahubali, the brother of the all-conquering Bharata and a mightier warrior renounces all power realising its absurdity. Even though he was reconstructing a narrative based on the sources of his religion (Jainism), Pampa must have been aware of the powerful critique

---

[4] Champu is a poetic style used by Pampa and many poets after him. It is, among other things, a mix of poetry and prose, though poetry dominates. The term also refers to an open-ended style employing several different prosodic forms.

[5] Pampa acknowledges the *Mahapurana* (ninth century CE) profusely, attributed to Jinasena and Gunabhadra, two Jain ascetics. Professor Settar argues that this text was widely known in India.

his epic was offering of the endless strife, war and violence which characterised the feudal world of his times and of which his patron was also a celebrated hero. Thus, the martial values celebrated in *Vikramarjuna Vijaya* are powerfully deconstructed in *Adipurana*. In this epic, Pampa says that the epic based on Jain *agama* would itself bring eternal fame to him. He asks what greater things could others give, thus looking askance at the system of patronage too. *Adipurana*, which deals with the immersion in the pleasures of the world and the sudden turning away from it in every life of the protagonist in the cycle of lives, is also replete with eroticism and the male gaze at the woman's body. But then Pampa's readers perhaps saw in the work the integration of the two human impulses which we latecomers cannot.

Just as *Kavirajamargam* is accommodative of all approaches/ modes such as those of the North and South, Pampa's poetry also does not subscribe to the binaries of *marga* and *desi*.[6] In the oft quoted passage which describes Pampa's own poetics, he does not employ the terms as perhaps they later came to be used. For him, (good) poetry is that which enters the *desi* and pushes through the *marga* and acquires its aesthetic appeal. He seems to treat the two "ways" as equally useful and necessary. The following is Pollock's translation of the stanza in which Pampa comments on *marga* and *desi*:

> In its imagination (a poem) must be new, and the texture of the composition must be supple. Thus constituted, the composition must partake of the idiom of place (desiyol puguvuda) and at the same time must penetrate into the idiom of the way (margadol talvudu). In this way it becomes truly beautiful—as beautiful as a tender mango

[6] North and South are descriptive of styles and their relation to geo-cultural regions is tenuous. *Marga* and *desi* are two terms endlessly debated in Kannada poetics. There is no consensus on their etymology; the general perception that *marga* refers to the classical, Sanskrit-oriented, very sophisticated and stylised and that *desi* refers to the indigenous, non-formal is certainly a latter-day construction more like a cultural "backformation". Pampa uses the terms as descriptive of two styles which he claims to blend in his own poetic style.

> tree in springtime, drooping under the heavy weight of flowers and new shoots, and crowded with bees, and with the cuckoo singing, and only the cuckoo. (Pollock 2006, 357)

I would like to emphasise that not much can be gained by reading Pampa in the light of the binary terms, simply because like most of the Kannada poets Pampa uses popular terms prevalent in Sanskrit poetics but has little theoretical or practical interest in them. Like most Kannada poets of the pre-modern period, he has his own poetics which cannot be fitted into the framework of Sanskrit poetics. Pampa is a very learned poet, deeply immersed in the poetic and philosophical traditions of his times. There is such tremendous intertextuality of every kind in the texture of his poetry, that one has to reformulate the very co-ordinates of a text. With all this, he seems to be unaffected by the major theoretical formulations of Sanskrit aesthetics in the best parts of his poetry. Nor is he participating in the project of making Kannada translocal. A close analysis of the verbal texture of his poetry demonstrates the hybridity of the registers and lexis employed by him; it is a truly motley verbal world like Shakespeare's. The distinctions of *sama-sanskrit*, *gramya*, *deshya* do not help us in either analysing or responding to this complex texture. His immense creative energies are invested in embodying the highly conflictual, ambivalent sociopolitical world of his times. The ideal world he wants to bring into existence through poetry, a world in which "all mankind is one" is in contrast to the actual world torn apart by *varna*, caste and power. I would argue that Pampa constructed his own poetics to deal with this world and that this poetics had a tenuous relationship with the Sanskrit poetics of the age.

In his highly original examination of the Tamil Kannada relationships in the ancient times, S. Settar (2007), erudite historian, has many interesting things to say about the poetics and practice of Sangam Tamil poetry. He underlines the essential cultural differences between Sanskrit poetics and Sangam poetics. While Sanskrit poetics valorises the trans-regional and the universal, Sangam poetics systematises the specificities of time, season and space/place. It is bound inalienably with a regional way of life.

Comparing *Kavirajamargam* with *Tholkappiyam* he finds the Kannada author accommodative and integrationist in approach. He has no new conceptual terms to offer other than *rasa*, *dhvani* and *auchitya* (even these are not elaborately theorised by him). The *Tholkappiyam*, on the other hand, reformulates poetics as a discourse on the actual world of living. Some of the contemporary literary theoreticians in Kannada such as Nataraj Budal (2016) and Laxmipathi Kolar strongly assert that Tamil poetics is Dravidian poetics and is a counter paradigm. I should immediately add that these two are serious scholars trying to reconstruct Kannada *Meemamse* (poetics) as a very different cognitive order altogether, though it is forced into the grids of Sanskrit poetics.

Years ago, Kuvempu (2003, 737) had said that Kannada poetics had remained a shadow of the Sanskrit poetics. He had also warned that it would be probably worse if it were to become a shadow of Western poetics. The recent efforts in Kannada have been towards retrieving Kannada poetics which has had a suppressed existence. It is sought in the practices of the oral and subaltern traditions of the folklore and the *tatwapadakara*s.[7] It is an attempt to reconstruct a poetics from a set of practices. The philosophical roots of this "poetics in practice" are sought in the Buddhist Madhyamika tradition and the *vachanakara*s. Support is also sought in a somewhat vague historiography of the cultural domination of the North (Aryan) over the South. The archive of the massive compositions of the *tatwapadakara*s is now being researched. It is clear that outside the elite literary culture, vibrant oral and folk traditions have co-existed and also that a distinctive poetics seems to be at work behind them.

---

7 *Tatwapadakara*s are poets/composers of philosophical, spiritual lyrics and songs in colloquial, dialectal variations of Kannada. They are spiritual practitioners and mostly artisans from villages in many parts of Karnataka. They belong to the oral tradition and their compositions have been recently collected in nearly thirty volumes—an extraordinary tradition of many centuries and still continuing. I have not been able to locate any translations into English.

Let us take a look again at the complex picture emerging from the preceding sections of the essay.

(a) There was a hegemonic and powerful literary culture based on the Sanskrit traditions which had consolidated itself between the fourth and ninth centuries CE.
(b) All vernacular traditions including that of Kannada had to reinvent their literary identities and construct the notion of the literary by negotiating with this Sanskrit cosmopolis.
(c) However, this negotiation led to selective adaptation, resistance, accommodation and also imitation. Both *Kavirajamargam* and the great works of the period from the tenth century CE demonstrate the sustained effort in the Kannada tradition to reconstruct its literary culture showing both dependence and independence.
(d) According to Pollock the effort led to the formation of a cosmopolitan vernacular which was translocal. I have suggested that the "vernacular" was not something which could be abstracted from the actual history of the age.
(e) D. R. Nagaraj and others point out that the *desi* for which space was created in the poetics of the time was a *desi* constructed by the cosmopolitan vernacular and did not include the powerful oral/folk traditions.
(f) The present critical project in Kannada is towards examining the marginalised but vibrant subaltern traditions to reconstruct a poetics out of the practices in these traditions.

From this perspective the "real" Kannada poetics is distinctive and even adversarial to the dominant Sanskrit poetics which has been wrongly perceived as Kannada poetics.

The debates summarised in the preceding paragraphs gain a sharper edge as we turn towards the second moment of the reinvention of the literary—that of the *virasaiva vachanakaras* of the twelfth century. We could follow D. R. Nagaraj's—who follows Pollock closely in the use of these terms—argument that until the *vachanakara* movement, the *desi* was nothing but a construction of the cosmopolitan vernacular itself (2012, 89–93); it was something that could be accommodated easily into the elite literary culture patronised by the royal court and addressed to a small group of the literary cognoscenti. Most of the time, *desi* was a matter of lexical choice, expressions and gestures which would add variety to a literary style which generally followed the fixed conventions. An example of this is Pampa's description of the *soolegeri*, a colony of the *veshya*s. The description of the *soolegeri* is one of the obligatory conventional eighteen descriptions but Pampa uses it to give us extraordinary glimpses of the erotic practices of the time with graphic details of a lifestyle which is alien to the courtly tradition. It is a tour de force bringing in *desi* elements but the epic narrative quickly returns to the world of the palace.

The *vachanakara*s began a radically egalitarian movement under the leadership of Basava and others challenging at the same time the *varna* and caste systems, gender inequality, hollow Vedic rituals and sacrifice, superstitious populist practices and above all temple culture. It was a collective rebellion by the *sharana*s (devotees and followers of the new religion). The extraordinary feature was the induction of ordinary men and women from all professions including the untouchables. They followed an ethical religion of body labour, reverence towards all professions, worship of the *istalinga* (the personal god in the form of a *linga*) and a rational critical enquiry into all forms of authority. The *vachana*, the form of expression they invented was a short lyrical/philosophical statement mixing prose and poetry. *Vachana* is the spoken word believed to have been composed and articulated extempore. This perception has much to do with the format used by the editors of the latter-day narrative anthologies compiled by various individuals from the fifteenth century onwards known as *Shunya Sampadane*.[8] In these compilations a continuous narrative

---

[8] *Shunya Sampadane* is a unique genre, a mix of narrative, anthology and exegesis. Essentially, they are attempts to narrativise incidents involving the twelfth century *vachanakaras* (*virasaiva* saint poets) placing the *vachana*s in the narratives. There are several *Shunya Sampadane* works composed between the sixteenth and seventeenth centuries.

with some dramatic situations is created and the *vachanas* are introduced as spoken at the particular moment by a *vachanakara*. It is also generally argued that the *vachanas* were a byproduct of a revolutionary movement and in that sense were not meant to be literary expressions. This is only partially true. On the one hand most of the *vachanas* are addressed to the personal deity and record with startling honesty and intensity, the most private spiritual struggles of the *vachanakaras*. On the other hand, behind the spontaneity and simplicity of expression there is a profound sense of form, a feel for the texture of the words and enormous verbal dexterity in the use of all modes—ironic, satirical, lyrical, argumentative, rhetorical, etc. It would be more appropriate to see in the *vachanakara* movement the birth of a new literary culture which grew out of its total rejection of the literary as it existed in the tradition. It is a reinvention of the literal thought as the expression of the great movement which is always considered more important than the aesthetic-literary domain.

It is even possible to see the Anubhava Mantapa—where the *sharanas* gathered to discuss and debate—as a public sphere or a reading public because many *vachanas* directly address the issue of language, communication and authenticity of expression. The fundamentals of the traditional poetics are consciously deconstructed and rejected. Allama (Basvaraju 2001, 138)[9] dismisses past poets as "a flock of parrots" and even abuses them as the sons of his slaves. A large number of *vachanas* by those who come from the marginalised section express suspicion about the rhetoric of poetry itself. What is valorised is authentic expression supported by one's actions. Scathing attacks are made on the artificiality of the literary conventions. In a famous poem, Basava claims that he knows little of the art of music and singing, but he wants his body itself to be transformed into a musical instrument to help him to "sing as he pleases". Akka Mahadevi, a very accomplished poet herself, also constructs a poetics of the transparent self, emphasising spontaneity. Clearly, this is a rejection of the set

[9] See Basavaraju (2001)

protocols, conventions and formal practices of the Sanskrit literary culture. For the first and the only time before the twentieth century, a poetics which did not address the court or the literati was created.

While much attention has been paid to the social and ideological content of the *vachana*s, their poetics was brought into literary critical discussions very late. As literary historians have noted very surprisingly, *vachana*s were rediscovered only in the twentieth century and it was S. S. Basavanal and F. G. Halakatti who (re)discovered that the *vachana*s had to be typographically arranged as poetic expressions and not as prose renderings as the earlier scribes had done. It took some more decades for critics to notice the stylistic aspects of the *vachana*s such as parallelism, internal rhyme, use of metaphors symbols and polysemy. The major features of their poetics are as follows:

(a) It is a poetics which is grounded on the principle of the expression of the self in the making. The poetic utterance has to be an authentic record of the complex process of the making of the self. The central experience of the *sharana* is this process through which she/he "becomes" a *sharana*. The *virasaiva* philosophy is founded on the notion of "becoming" and not "being".

(b) The expression is dialogic. The *sharana* is either addressing his personal deity, the other *sharana*s or the people of the world. The *vachana*s carry a strong communicative force. To use a distinction made by Kannada critics, *vachana*s are closer to the "poetry of the ear" (to be heard, listened to) than the "poetry of the eye" (to be read). The rhetoric therefore has to adjust itself to the form of address, using a number of persuasive tones. In tune with this feature the register has to be conversational or colloquial.

(c) The *vachanakara*s rejected poetic conventions including the clichéd images and metaphors as well as the notorious *kavisamaya*s (improbable and fantastic elements used in rhetorical devices). Instead, they drew from the living world especially the world of labour. Since labour (*kayaka*) is considered sacrosanct and all skilled professions respectable, the *vachanakaras* choose their images from the world of quotidian work. For the first time, everyday words associated with labour enter the realm of Kannada poetry. In one stroke the *vachana* poetics resolves the issue of "poetic diction" by opening up poetry to aspects of the material world.

(d) *Vachanas* have a clearly stated ethical purpose. At the individual level the *sharana* has to pass through the various stages of spiritual evolution to be able to experience the divine. At the social level he has to admonish, cajole and sometimes force the men of the world to keep away from sin and superstition and follow their conscience. The poetics has therefore to blend the individual and the social. It has to provide space for the complexities of the mystical experience by creating the *bedagu* mode (like *sandhya bhash* of Bhakti poetry).[10] The binaries of body and mind, this-wordly and the spiritual are rejected by the *vachanakaras*. Therefore, the classical poetics which partitioned experience into the ordinary and the spiritual has to be replaced by a poetics reflecting a radically different world-view asserting the sanctity of everything.

D. R. Nagaraj builds up a very novel and interesting argument in his work *Allama mattu Shaiva Pratibhe*, an extraordinary work by all accounts (1999). His argument is that Allama's poetry and poetics are consciously and wholly opposed to the dominant poetics of *rasa*. Originally popularised by Bharata, the *rasa* theory allied itself to the mystical notion of merging oneself with the divine. It also meant that the signifier and the signified merge into

---

[10] In most Bhakti poetic traditions, deep metaphysical thoughts are expressed in a highly symbolic language which on the surface appear like a verbal puzzle. *Sandhya bhash* is one of the names given to this mode of writing. *Vachanakaras* use *bedagu* to describe the same.

oneness. As a result, Bhakti poetry compares religious experience to the *shringara bhava* and the pleasure of union with the divine pleasure of coitus. This is certainly true of Akka Mahadevi and many others who write in the "*Sharana sati, linga pathi bhava*" mode.[11] Allama, the metaphysical rebel, comes down heavily on this aspect of Bhakti. He is against the unitary state of the ultimate bliss, the coitus-like oneness with God.

Allama derides a poetics which supports this. He is all for a dynamic poetics which avoids the dangers of imitating the Indian schools of *rasa*. His poetics thus is a poetics of a total metaphysical rebellion against the *rasa* theory and those parts of Kashmir Shaiva which speak of the unity of the self and the divine. Without entering this debate one can say that *vachana* poetics offered an altogether different epistemology and understanding of the cosmos.

Settar's recent work on *Prakrit Jagadvalaya* (the Prakrit Cosmopolis) challenges many of the accepted notions of Kannada poetics. He emphasises the fact that the Prakrit cosmopolis existed and co-existed with Sanskrit for nearly a millennium. Though derided by some scholars as merely a corrupt form of Sanskrit and as the "language of snakes", Prakrit was not merely a language but a world-view. It would be erroneous to believe that Prakrit and Sanskrit co-existed without exchange and mutual influence. Didn't there exist a Prakrit poetics? Weren't many of the major aspects of Sanskrit poetics derived from Prakrit? With two major religions not opting for Sanskrit as their language and going on to shape the Kannada ethos for so long, can we accept the view that it was Sanskrit poetics which dominated over Kannada poetics? These questions should further complicate the discussion of Kannada poetics. With the study of Prakrit texts now restricted only to a small group of Jain scholars, we may not be in a position to answer these questions with any certainty. In many cases Kannada poets make direct references to well-known Sanskrit works of poetics

---

[11] In this mode, the *sharana* imagines himself as wife and the personal deity (here described as *linga*) as husband.

and aesthetics. However, though there is evidence that most of the major poets knew Prakrit well, such direct references to Prakrit works of poetics are very few.

Works Cited

Basavaraju, L., ed. 2001. *Allamana Vachana Chandrike*. Bellary: Lohiya Prakashana.

Budal, Nataraj. 2016. *Kannada Kavya Meemamse*. Hampi: Prasaranga Kannada Vishwavidyalaya.

Hall, Stuart, and Doreen Massey. "Interpreting the crisis: Doreen Massey and Stuart Hall discuss ways of understanding the current crisis." *Soundings*, no. 44 (2010): 57+. *Gale Academic OneFile*. https://link.gale.com/apps/doc/A237137517/AONE?u=anon~bf817a49&sid=googleScholar&xid=a8471b77. Accessed on 25 June 2024.

Kalaburgi, M. M. 1973. *Kavirajamarga Parisarada Kannada Sahitya*. Dharwad: Prasaranga, Karnataka University.

Kuvempu. 2003. "Introduction." *Bharatiya Kavya Meemamse* collected in *Samagra Gadya*, edited by Shivareddy. Hampi: Prasaranga Kannada Vishwvidyalaya.

Nagaraj, K. R. *Tereda Patya*. Edited by Nataraj Huliyar. Bengaluru: Kannada Pustaka Pradhikara.

Nagaraj, D. R. 1999. *Allama Prabhu Mattu Shaiva Pratibhe*. Heggodu: Akshara Prakashana.

———. 2012. *Listening to the Loom*, edited with an introduction by Prithvidatta Chandra Shobhi. Permanent Black.

Pollock, Sheldon. 2006. *The Language of the Gods in the World of Men*. Berkeley and Los Angeles: University of California Press.

Settar, S. 2007. *Sanga Tamilagam Mattu Kannada Nadu Nudi*. Bengaluru: Abhinava.

———. 2018. *Prakruta Jagadvalaya*. Bengaluru: Abhinava.

Subbanna, K. V. 2000. *Kavirajamarga Mattu Kannada Jagattu*. Heggodu: Akshara Prakashana.

SEVEN

A Local Habitation and a Name for Knowledge

The Case of Odia Bhasha Literature

Debendra K. Dash and Dipti R. Pattanaik

For long, may be due to orientalist historiography, the Indian knowledge system created by the priestly class in Sanskrit has been given a superior epistemic status in comparison to the bhasha écriture which has been perceived as inferior and derivative. According to this line of thinking the Indian bhasha literatures have been derived from the dominant écriture written in Sanskrit. This paper is a preliminary attempt to interrogate this simplistic discourse and present an alternative and complex narrative, taking Odia literary culture as a case study, which may provide a better explanation for the emergence of Indian bhasha literatures.

It is common knowledge that most of the great literary traditions of the world, in their formative stages at least, are appropriation of texts in other traditions and/or development of oral forms of communication and aesthetic artefacts. These appropriations/adaptations take place through a complex process of cultural–linguistic negotiations. A study of that complex process can be fruitful in several ways. First, it can shed light not only on the status of various languages and literatures in a given society where such a negotiation takes place but also on the relative strengths of the languages involved in terms of their knowledge-content, expressive sophistication and extent of dispersal. Second, since languages encode structures of culture and different forms of state apparatuses, an examination of the asymmetric relationship existing between them could help us in decoding the governing ideology and power-relations at the site of such negotiations. The case of the emergence of Odia bhasha literature and its subsequent consolidation presents us an example of a series of such negotiations. In our earlier essays (Dash and Pattanaik 2006; 2007) which historicise translational praxis in Odia we had demonstrated how the iconic texts of early Odia literature are creative transformations of earlier Sanskrit, different forms of Prakrit, Pali and other texts of already developed bhasha languages and how translational practice in Odia has been implicated in an ideological struggle to assert a caste-based regional identity.

The contours of that discourse, like all other identity discourses, have been unstable and have undergone redefinition from time to time with change in the context. The works of the individual translators belonging to different eras though united by the common thread of aspiration for asserting linguistic nationalism, show a remarkable diversity in their approach in terms of the choice of texts, methods of transformation and uses of language. Though not explicitly stated anywhere, their subtle strategies of transformation have had an impact much wider than the immediate task of carrying forth a text from one language into another. Because of their enormous influence in the Odia literary "polysystem" to borrow a term from Even-Zohar (2012), these texts have legislated an aesthetic paradigm that has shaped the entire Odia bhasha literature. The present paper will examine the strategies of aesthetic transformation of a few such texts and map out their overall impact in the shaping of the Odia bhasha literature. We argue that the negotiating strategies and the aesthetic principles they spawned resonate in the history of genesis and canon-formation of all bhasha literatures in India. There may be a few differences between one bhasha literature and another in terms of the time of their efflorescence and the precipitating sociopolitical context, but the key impulse that governed their proliferation is their relationship with the *deba bhasha* of Sanskrit and the master texts in that language (Pollock 2007). In the absence of a self-conscious theory of aesthetics to study bhasha literatures—before the bhasha languages could consolidate to an extent when activities like creative enterprise and professional abstract critical theorisation could be pursued as distinct intellectual activities, they were overtaken by Western critical/aesthetic theories imbibed through colonial contact—this kind of meditation will help us frame an indigenous aesthetic theory to study Indian bhasha literatures. This could perhaps be the most important outcome of the study of early translational negotiations which were not merely a process of rewriting but what can be termed as implicit literary criticism.

Indian society has always been multicultural and multilingual. Various mother tongues have, over the years, served the function of natural expression of folk life. Those languages were the carriers of primitive knowledge systems and literary expressions such as folksongs, proverbs, riddles, folktales and religious rituals. As the societies moved on from primitive knowledge systems to more sophisticated ones, Sanskrit gradually assumed a predominant position (Dash and Pattanaik 2005; Pollock 2007). As a language Sanskrit had acquired such sophistication that even the heterodox religions which had used the earlier forms of languages like Pali and Prakrit for their wider reach, ultimately adopted Sanskrit towards first century CE. Sanskrit became the medium of elite cultural expression, a language of power, knowledge, religion and literature while mother tongues got marginalised, remaining confined to their role as a medium of natural expression. Even literary expressions in the mother tongue had to be retold in Sanskrit in order to give them some kind of permanence and intellectual legitimacy. The case of Gunadhya's *Badat Katha* in Paishachi language getting wider dissemination through Somadeva's Sanskrit rendering *Katha Sarita Sagar* could be one such example. Such phenomena was so common that it was instrumental in creating the illusion that Sanskrit was the "original" language and the others in circulation were derived from it. Even when some languages like Tamil resisted Sanskrit's widespread hegemony, pockets of Tamil-speaking community belonging to priestly castes got identified with Sanskrit.

The widespread dominance of Sanskrit, however, did not remain unchallenged. Although the cognate Aryan languages were more or less overwhelmed by the dominance of Sanskrit after the first century CE, there were challenges from Dravidian languages of the South against this hegemony. In an earlier essay (Dash and Pattanaik 2007) we have elaborately discussed the nature of relationship between Sanskrit and the cognate Indo-Aryan languages and between Sanskrit and the Dravidian languages. One can sum up these relationships into four major categories. Tamil, for example, had an undiluted resistance to Sanskrit's influence, since it had an existing tradition of written literature beginning from the third century BCE prompting such resistance. The other Dravidian languages like Kannada and Telugu had a semi-independent status vis-à-vis Sanskrit eschewing the extreme form of resistance by Tamil. A third kind of development can be discerned in the emergence of various forms of Prakrit literary culture in Maharashtri, Sauraseni and Magadhi Prakrit. These written literatures were both competing and colluding with Sanskrit literary culture. The growth of Odia bhasha literary culture may represent a fourth category which had elements of all three above processes at various points of its evolution.

Before the third century BCE, Aryan languages like Pali and Prakrit co-existed peacefully with primitive language groups of Odisha like Austric and Dravidian. With the entry of Sanskrit after the first century CE—especially during the Gupta period—there was a decline in the usage of Pali and Prakrit. Most of the royal charters and epigraphs were written in Sanskrit. Unlike the other parts of northern and western India we do not come across adequate evidence of a parallel development of Prakrit literary culture. Even though most of the kings of the Bhaumakara dynasty which ruled over Odisha were Buddhists by faith, the copper plates written during their reign were in Sanskrit rather than in Pali or Prakrit. This does not mean Odisha witnessed a continuous vibrant literary culture in Sanskrit. The establishment of a vibrant literary culture had to wait till the eleventh century CE although there was the manifestation of a rich cultural life in the interregnum, showcased in the temple architecture and various other aesthetic cultures. Some scholars like S. C. Behera and K. N. Mohapatra claim that Vishnu Sharma who wrote *Panchatantra* in the sixth century CE and Bhattanarayan who wrote *Venishanghara* in the seventh century CE belonged to Odisha. A few other scholars also claim that the *Charya Gitika*, a form of esoteric and mystic poetry by Sahajayani Buddhist tantrics, written during this period, used a language very close to the spoken language of the Odia people. But even then, these can be taken as sporadic manifestation of a literary culture.

Only with the advent of the Ganga dynasty in the eleventh century CE we encounter a vibrant literary culture involving both Sanskrit and Prakrit. The imperial Gangas introduced a language policy similar to that prevalent in South India consisting of three languages, the language of the sovereign, the language of the province and the language of the people and of popular culture. As Telugu was the mother tongue of the Gangas, it naturally became the language of the state. In addition, however, the common language of the people of Odisha was used for administrative purposes. There was an effective transition of Odia from a spoken to a written language or Odia "literization" (Pollock 2007, 4) during this period. A number of epigraphic records bear evidence to this fact (Tripathy 1962). The Gangas, however, encouraged and patronised Sanskrit for the written texts of scripture and literature instead of literized Odia—the language of the people. Thus, the areas of Ganga rule after the eleventh century CE consisting of modern Odisha, Andhra and Telengana witnessed a complex cohabitation of literary cultures of Sanskrit, Prakrit and Telugu, literized Odia and the spoken form of Austric languages, a phenomenon quite distinct from the development of other languages. This is the reason why the development of Odia literary culture was referred to as a fourth category earlier.

This complex interaction gave rise to a lively literary culture in Odisha, but ironically Odia could not participate in it fully. The vibrancy of Odisha's literary culture can be gauged from a statement by the famous Odia scholar Vishwanath Kaviraj who claimed that he was fluent in sixteen languages; he could use both Sanskrit and Prakrit for literary expression with ease. The other iconic texts of the period apart from Kaviraj's *Sahitya Darpan* in Sanskrit and *Kubalaya Carita Kavya* in Prakrit are Vidyadhar's *Ekabali*, Jayadev's *Geeta Govinda* and Chandi Das's *Kavya Prakash Dipika*. Vishwanath Kaviraj's texts (at least eight major texts by him have been identified) could be termed as an apotheosis of a literary culture begun by Vidyadhar and Kaviraj's great-grandfather Chandidas which continued through his father and his contemporary Jayadeva. During this period several knowledge texts in the field of astronomy *(jyotisa)*, *smriti*, etc., were also written along with texts on literature and aesthetics by numerous minor writers (Panigrahi 1981; Mohapatra 1960).

In this multilingual episteme, Odia made progress from a stage of "literization" to "literarization" (Pollock 2007, 5). This progress of Odia towards a language of literary culture was rather slow because of the dominance of Sanskrit.

The situation began to change towards early fifteenth century CE and one of the major reasons for this change was the presence of Islam. Although these areas continued to be ruled by Hindu kings, there were frequent inroads into their territory by the Islamic rulers. The predominant status of Sanskrit as a language of power/culture got compromised to a certain extent because of this development. The South Indian bhasha languages like Kannada and Telugu were being used more widely at the cost of Sanskrit. The "literarization" of Odia was initiated due to a combination of several factors which included a parallel growth of nearby South Indian languages, the presence of Islam resulting in the waning of the importance of Sanskrit, and the three-language policy adopted by the Ganga rulers mentioned earlier. The most important factor, however, was the ascendance of the local chieftains to positions of power due to growing threat of Islamic rulers and weakening of state power. Kapilendra Dev, one of the Odia-speaking chieftains within the Ganga territory, extended his range of influence to such an extent that for the first time in many centuries Odisha became an imperial state.

Kapilendra's rise to power coincided with the rise of competing dynasties in the South like the Hindu kingdom of Vijayanagar and the Islamic rule of the Bahamanis. In the North too, the fledgling Odisha state was under constant threat from expansionist aspirations of Islamic rulers. Like the Gangas before him, Kapilendra was warm to the idea of maintaining a close contact with the South but due to the constant threat of militant Islam he also wanted to strengthen a core constituency of support among Odia-speaking people who could be organised around three distinct markers of identity, that is, common local language, common local religion and local subaltern caste groups. It is instructive to note that a lack of such identity affiliation had resulted in large scale proselytisation into Islam in the neighbouring Bengali-speaking areas. Kapilendra's smart statecraft consisted of elevating the cult of Lord Jagannath into a state religion. Similarly, more space was given to Odia in royal charters and rock-edicts. Sanskrit literary culture however, continued unabated—Kapilendra himself authored a Sanskrit text entitled *Parasuram Vijaya* but it also contained an Odia poem in it. It is as if the king himself was giving legitimacy to Odia literary culture in an episteme so far dominated by Sanskrit. Similarly, Odia replaced Telugu as the second language after Sanskrit in terms of importance in matters of state and public discourse including spiritual matters. This kind of political atmosphere not only consolidated a language- and caste-based Odia identity, it also precipitated the process of literarization of Odia culture. There was a proliferation of literary activity which resulted in the production of several texts of lyric poetry, imaginative *kavya*s and *kavya*s based both on tales from the Puranas and folktales. The process of translation/adaptation also gained momentum.

Apart from *kavya*s and drama the texts in Sanskrit may be broadly divided into three categories, namely, *shruti*, *shastra* and *smruti*. The adaptations and transformations were mainly done of the Puranas which were *smruti* texts. These texts, unlike the *shastr*ic knowledge texts and Vedic *shruti* texts had a wider appeal and were amenable to easy dispersal. Moreover, these texts were always pre-texts, in the process of becoming for a long time, rather than finished master-texts. *Shruti*s and *shastra*s were more esoteric and exact and might have posed greater challenges for an emergent literary language. During the first fifty years of the establishment of Suryavanshi empire, apart from a host of minor writers like Bansidas (Bachha Das) and Markanda Das we come across at least two major writers in Odia, namely Sarala Das and Arjun Das. Among all these authors Sarala claims the pivotal role in terms of his contribution to the growth of Odia literary culture. A close look at Sarala's textual transformations is called for in order to understand the process of cultural negotiation that firmly established Odia as a literary language.

Sarala in his *Chandi Purana* has stated that he wrote the Odia versions of the Ramayana, the *Bharata* and the *Bhagabata* in that order. Historians of Odia literature had for long believed that *Bilanka Ramayana* by one Siddheswara Das was the one Sarala had referred to. But later critics have established that Sarala's first work was *Bichitra Ramayana* and not *Bilanka Ramayana. Bhagabata* which Sarala referred to is actually *Devi Bhagabata* popularly known as *Chandi Purana*. Sarala's *Bichitra Ramayana* is a classic example of the cultural and linguistic negotiation we have been alluding to so far. It demonstrates his scholarly erudition and ideological commitment to domesticate knowledge in the services of an emergent identity discourse. Before Sarala's text, the Ramayana had undergone several mutations according to the ideological imperatives of the authors/rewriters of this ever-evolving metatext. Some of the most important narrators of Ramayana have been Valmiki, Kalidasa and Bhavabhuti in Sanskrit and Vimalsuri in Prakrit. There were also various versions of Ramayana in folk culture (Sen 1972). Sarala drew from several sources like Valmiki and Bhavabhuti's Ramayana, the Jain Ramayana by Vimal Suri in Prakrit entitled *Pauma Chariya* and a variety of Ramayanas in circulation in folk culture. He not only displayed his profound understanding of Sanskrit and Prakrit literary cultures but also reveled in subverting the Sanskritic, brahminical and patriarchal ideology of the dominant strand of *ram katha* encoded in Valmiki and Bhavabhuti. For example, in Sarala's text, Valmiki occupies a marginal space in the narrative. There is also no attempt to glorify the character of Rama; rather, it is Sita who is deified. She has more agency as a person and is more assertive than in the dominant *ram katha*s, including Valmiki's. When she is banished from the court, she goes to Valmiki's hermitage by herself after going through the letter Lakshman has left for her after deserting her in the forest. Unlike Valmiki's Sita, in this version she is part of a reading culture. Here, Sita is not dependent upon Rama, rather it is the other way round. Rama builds a golden replica of Sita to adorn his court in her absence. When he goes to request her to come back Sita scolds him and expresses her anger, saying that she does not want to see his face. She then returns to her mother, the earth's womb and becomes part of nature. By incorporating folk elements like the two-headed deer as Sita's agent of temptation in the forest and some of the motifs of *Pauma Chariya*, Sarala showcases the composite culture and synthetic religious practice prevalent in Odisha. The geographical space of Odia-speaking people has been a palimpsest history of synthesis of various faiths including Jainism, Buddhism, Vaishnavism and Shakti cults. The importance of Sita in Sarala's Ramayana may be due to the widespread worship of Shakti in Odia folk culture.

However, we can glean Sarala's creative dexterity in his use of Odia more than in the many thematic alterations he has affected. In Valmiki or Kalidasa's texts the tone and tenor of the language used by the characters follow proper *kavya*-dharma. The propriety or *auchitya* of the language fits the elevated status of the characters of Ramayana. Since the characters represent the highest ideals of the culture in terms of ethical values and human relationships, the language of the classical *ram katha*s transports the action to an ideal realm unattainable by ordinary human beings. In contrast, Sarala seems to novelise the language à la Bakhtin in order to subvert the notion that the commitment to the highest values should be reflected in every detail of one's outward behaviour. The conjugal commitment between Sita and Rama and the fraternal bonding between Rama and Lakshman is as deep as the earlier versions of the Ramayana but Sarala does not believe that in order to demonstrate that commitment or bonding one has to be consistent or uniform in their behaviour throughout and display an emotional intensity worthy of one's character. For example, Rama, while justifying Sita's banishment from the kingdom in front of Lakshman and elders like Vasistha passes extremely unsavoury remarks about her character and points out her lack of commitment to her marital duties and general waywardness. Similarly, Lakshman scolds his elder brother Rama using foul language quite unbecoming of his stature when he questions his act of deserting Sita in the forest making her vulnerable to Ravana's machinations. Sita's use of base language against Rama, Rama's use of common abusive language against Sita and Lakshman, however, do not make them falter in their commitment to the highest ideals which shape their essential characters. In Valmiki's Ramayana, the need for a golden statue of Sita arises only when Rama has to perform the *ashwamedha yajna* (horse sacrifice). On the other hand, Sarala's Rama has a golden Sita made and placed in the court immediately after her banishment—such is his love for her. Sarala, unlike the classical *ram katha*s, is able to highlight both the highs and lows of his characters, thereby making them more relatable to ordinary human beings. In a manner of speaking, the characters prove that ordinary human beings are also capable of great emotional and ethical commitment. By rooting his characters in the immediacy of their ordinary life and everyday manner of language use and by aestheticising the quotidian, Sarala not only demonstrates that ordinary human beings can legitimately aspire for the highest ethical ideals but also rewrites the *kavya* dharma, the skills of prosody and rhetoric. In fact, he sets out to show that the everyday language of the people can encode the highest cultural and ethical values of a civilisation; there is no need to clothe these values in rarefied ornate terms. Further, unlike Valmiki, Sarala demonstrates that the violation of those high ideals is more common and human. Valmiki's Ramayana depicted sexual transgression as being prevalent only among the untouchable castes leaving the elite characters of his text completely untainted. In Sarala's text, sexual transgression and violation of marital code is common even among the intermediate castes. In the famous episode involving the quarrel between the cowherd and his wife, the former witnesses his wife having extramarital sex. When challenged, she justifies her promiscuity by saying that when a woman enters the workforce and has to contribute to the family income it is natural for her to participate in a wider social network, and this often leads to sexual indulgence. Sarala's assertion of feminine autonomy both in her economic freedom and choice of sexual partner subverts the dominant patriarchal ideology imposed by the brahminical/ Sanskritic culture. In both style and substance Sarala's *Bichitra Ramayana* is therefore, a critical realist rewriting that grounds a pan-Indian cultural knowledge of ideals and ethics in a local and temporal immediacy.

Sarala's rewriting of the Mahabharata brings into sharper focus his strategies of localising a cosmopolitan knowledge system. Traditionally, it is believed that Vyasa (who lived 5000 years ago) composed the original epic, compiled the Vedas and the eighteen Puranas in Sanskrit. Modern scholarship, however, suggests that the text evolved over a period of 1000 years between the sixth and fourth century CE and cannot be fitted into the standard template of text writing and authorship. The epic is an assortment of multiple—often disparate—strands of narrative which balance history, myth, ethical and philosophical reflections, long didactic discourses, innumerable number of *upakhyana*s, anecdotes and legends around a bloody fraternal war. Belonging to the *smruti* tradition in which texts are committed to memory and recited publicly, this text was recited by bards across generations who retained the essence of the text but added and subtracted liberally according to their personal innovativeness and in keeping with the taste of the local public. This process led to various regional recensions and adaptations. Sarala's Mahabharata follows the eighteen *parva* structure of the Sanskrit Mahabharata but there is significant difference in their content and titles (See Appendix for the major structural changes effected by Sarala). A perusal of the content of Sarala's Mahabharata shows that a lot of content has been added, especially in the first eight *parvas*. All of them, except Vana *parva*, are significantly bigger than their Sanskrit Mahabharata counterparts. Along with the additions, a lot of *upakhayanas* and legends have been displaced or dropped. The philosophical content in Sanskrit Mahabharata has been mostly discarded or summaried.

The additional content used by Sarala in his Mahabharata can be traced back to existing literary and scriptural texts, folk ballads and his own ingenuity. Sarala sourced a significant portion of his content from the *Padma Purana*, *Srimad Bhagavata*, and *Skanda Purana* and the literary texts of Kalidasa, Bhattanarayan and Jayadev. Regarding his borrowings from Sanskrit, Krishna Chandra Panigrahi (1975, 28) comments: "On close study his works brings into broad relief his substantial Sanskrit knowledge, though such knowledge does not appear to be a systematic one gained through a regular course of training. Sarala Dasa used both his ears and eyes to gain knowledge in Sanskrit."

Besides borrowing from Sanskrit literature, Sarala also used content from folk ballads and contemporary historical events. The incorporation of content from folk ballads has been discussed by Shyama Sundara Mahapatra (1988) while the historical context has been discussed by Krishna Chandra Panigrahi (1976) and Gaganendranath Dash (1988).

In Sarala's version of the Mahabharata, while some characters from the Sanskrit text have been done away with, a few new characters have been introduced and more importantly the personality of some major characters have also undergone qualitative change. Some of the characters added include Belalsen and Khanikar. Shakuni in this version is pro-Pandava at heart and wishes to destroy Duryodhana and the Kauravas, a far-cry from the character of the Sanskrit original. These changes bring about a substantive transformation of the character of the text as a whole. While Abhinavagupta identified *shanta rasa* as the underlying *rasa* of the Sanskrit Mahabharata, *vira rasa* better explains the essence of Sarala's version.

Sarala's act of translation and rewriting of the Mahabharata, as evinced in his use of language and characterisation, might be construed as an ideological struggle that attempts to subvert the dominant hegemony of brahmins and Sanskrit. For example, in the penultimate Mushali *parva*, after winning the battle of Kurukshetra, the Pandavas are seen undertaking a kind of pilgrimage across Odisha. During this visit, Yudhisthira marries a local girl, the daughter of a pious man named Hari Sahu belonging to the "teli" caste—a subaltern caste engaged in producing and distributing cooking oil. Through similar *upakhyana*s, Sarala has Odianised the pan-Indian Sanskrit text. The last two *parva*s especially, bear the imprint of the attempts of localisation. For instance, in Mushali *parva*, after Krishna's death, his dead body is turned into wood which floats towards the Puri sea-shore. This wood then is reincarnated as *daru devata*, the wood-deity Lord Jagannath of Puri. Although the worship of a wood-deity is of tribal origin, in one deft imaginative transformation Sarala is able to synthesise the ethnic religious ritual of the tribals with the dominant faith of Vaishnavism prevalent in Odisha at the time and connects the pan-Indian Krishna character with the state deity Lord Jagannath.

Apart from bringing together various religious systems which helped in the consolidation of subnational imaginary, Sarala bolstered the regional identity discourse by including the specific place names in Odia geography in literarised Odia, a project which can after Pollock, be called "epicization" of space (Pollock 2004). During the *ashwamedha yajna* after the great war, Arjuna, who is in charge of protecting the sacrificial horse, journeys across the space closer to Odisha. In the last *parva*, before ascending to heaven (*swargarohana*), the Pandava brothers make a pilgrimage across several places in Odisha before leaving for the Himalayas.

The process of epicization of the contemporary political situation is added on to the process of epicization of the space in Sarala's last text, *Chandi Purana*. Here, he makes massive changes to the Sanskrit *Devi Sukta* which is its source of inspiration.

The transformation of the myth in Sarala's subversive imagination clearly encodes the anxiety of a fledgling nation amidst the rising threat of an Islamic takeover. The demon-king Mahishasura of the myth resembles the marauding Muslim rulers around Odia empire in Sarala's hand (Panigrahi 1989). The land Mahishasura has already occupied, a land he has been divinely ordained to establish suzerainty over, is in fact the geographical space occupied by the Islamic rulers of the time. However, the divine boon has a rider. He can be killed only by a naked woman whose exposed genitals will suck all valour off him. In the eventual battle, goddess Durga goes to the battlefield naked armed with this knowledge and destroys him. This riotous and grotesque imagination might be hinting at the general lustfulness of the Islamic warlords and several legends built around the rape and enforced concubinage of Hindu women carried out by them. Sarala's prognosis seems to point out that the lecherous nature of these warlords might ultimately be the cause of their destruction. By valorising the role of an ensnaring yet powerful woman in the destruction of evil forces Sarala seems to be critiquing the narratives of male power enshrined in the traditional discourses of heroism and valour. In this, *Chandi Purana* resonates with the ideology of Sarala's other two texts where pan-Indian brahminical patriarchy is subverted from a matrilineal feminine perspective. The awe and reverence associated with the subject matter of all the three mythical and Puranic texts seem to have been turned on their head by Sarala's iconoclastic and irreverent kaleidoscope. Much like his contemporary Rabelais, through his textual manipulations and use of irreverent language Sarala paints a more realistic and fitting local context. The carnivalesque his language use showcases resembles the genesis of Odia literary culture in its strategies of appropriation and manipulation of and negotiation with other literary cultures.

The genesis and growth of Odia literary culture is thus a demonstration of a complex network of relationships that exist between languages, between languages and structures of power, the genius of an author and the social context and the local aspirations and pan-Indian influences. The early canonical Odia writers were as much a product of that complex network as they helped fashion it. Sarala mined the resources of folk culture, Dravidian and Austric oral aesthetic artefacts, and his own profound command over Sanskrit and Prakrit episteme bequeathed to him by a vibrant tradition of Sanskrit and Prakrit scholarship in vogue in Odishan soil in order to "epicise" the space of a nascent political formation. Being a foot-soldier in Kapilendra's army, he must have internalised the anxiety of a Hindu subject in a Hindu kingdom surrounded by areas acquired by Islamic rulers. His "*kavya*s" (meaning writings and not the genre of *kavya* in the traditional sense) must have served as a metonymy for the "*rajya*" whose consolidation would simultaneously bolster his caste, language and religious identities. His emphasis on *vira rasa* in his epic in place of *shanta rasa* in the Sanskrit original was as much an instrument of inspiration for the warrior caste he belonged to—in order to keep the Islamic proselytising invaders at bay—as it was an ideological tool to subvert the cosmopolitan brahminic hegemony on cultural practices like epic writing. Using the language of the people for literary purposes itself was a subversive and revolutionary act in which he was domesticating cosmopolitan knowledge systems and transforming its tenor and content to suit the local needs. This process of domestication is more radical in his two other texts that substitute the patriarchal flavour of Aryan *kavya*s in favour of local belief systems that valorise shakti. Attributing *vira rasa* to *shakti*, Sarala achieves the double purpose of unifying the people under a national imaginary of a shared belief in the local goddesses of the folk tradition of *gramadevati*s and instilling valour in the subjects who can safeguard their value system and identity within a highly unstable political situation.

With the stabilisation of the state inhabited by Odia-speaking people, subsequent writers like Balaram Das displayed a bold appropriation and domestication of cosmopolitan knowledge systems in the Odia language. The abstract philosophical elements in the Sanskrit texts which Sarala had excised from his epic are reworked into Odia by Das, which challenged the ability of a people's language to articulate the mystical insights and rigorous metaphysical discourses of a highly developed cosmopolitan literary culture like Sanskrit. By involving Lord Jagannath, the state deity, as the source of inspiration for his work, Balaram seems to be replicating his contemporary Milton whose epicization of the space of a nascent English empire prompts him to invoke the holy ghosts as his source of inspiration who were present at the time of beginning of the creation, much before the Greek civilisation which produced early epics. Like Milton, Das was gesturing towards a glorious antecedent of an Odia empire by involving Lord Jagannath who was the *avatari*—the source of all *avataras*, including Krishna, one of the incarnations of Vishnu and the spokesman for the teachings of the Gita. Balaram was trying to demonstrate that the language of the people of Odisha was capable of expressing the most profound knowledge encoded in the *deba bhasha*. In the process, he also brought the people's language closer to Sanskrit.

With his translation of *Bhagabata*, Jagannath Das brought Odia closest to Sanskrit, thereby reversing the process of separation of the identity of Odia initiated by Sarala. Jagannath was trying to reach beyond the dialectal affinities of various kinds of Odia-speaking people under the Odia empire. The various Odia dialects had in the process of their growth more of less assimilated the influence of Sanskrit. By bringing literary Odia closer to Sanskrit, Jagannath was responsible for the emergence of a standard language which had a universal acceptance among the Odia-speaking populace. It strengthened the sub-national imaginary and helped in the protection of indigenous culture that was under threat of militant alternative faiths. The marauding powers of these faiths became all the more menacing as the power of the state was declining gradually. Jagannath's *Bhagabata* espousing brahminical ideology as its core philosophy and the Sanskritic tenor of its language completely overturned the process initiated by Sarala. Jagannath's enterprise was the foundation for a subsequent development of Odia literary culture for two centuries.

Both Balaram and Jagannath had already tested the language and diction of the language and enabled it to appropriate all kinds of knowledge available in developed cosmopolitan cultures like Sanskrit. Now, it was the turn of writers like Upendra Bhanja and his contemporaries to fashion a kind of ornate poetry that dared to parallel and challenge the experimentations accomplished in Sanskrit prosody and aesthetic artefacts. Bhanja could arrogantly claim that poetic diction in his hands would surpass anything that had been attempted in poetics—except Kalidasa, Bhavabhuti, and Sriharsha, the all-time masters of Indian *kavya* tradition. It was not mere unfounded arrogance. The Odia literary culture of the time seemed to portray a maturity that could see itself not in a subordinate role to Sanskrit but as a legitimate competitor. Practised in best courtly tradition, this kind of poetry gradually withdrew from the sociopolitical challenges at hand and concerned itself with the effort of perfection of its own medium. This solipsism and narcissism coincided with the decline of the Odia empire and the literary culture was banished into the privacy of pockets of feudal aristocracy and monasteries. This is a fate similar to the decline of Sanskrit literary culture. A popular regeneration of literary culture and self-conscious identity discourse around it had to wait for a century when new social changes brought about by colonial forms of power/knowledge challenged this situation. The consolidation of colonial power in Odisha unleashed an array of processes that redirected Odia literary culture back to its dialectal roots and multilingual origin. The new form of literary expression in imitation of cosmopolitan literary culture of the West, especially the medium of prose, ensured a mass participatory audience. In order to cater to this need, literary language had to fall back on the early process of negotiation initiated by Sarala. The analysis of this process, however, is a subject matter of a separate essay, which we have attempted earlier (Dash and Pattanaik 2004).

The story of the Odia literary culture much like the story of the Indian bhasha literature is a negotiation between the local aspirations for knowledge and cosmopolitan hegemonic structures of power/culture. Odia bhasha literature is a mirror image of this dynamic. An analysis of the dynamic not only reveals the relationship between *rajya* and *kavya* but in the absence of a self-conscious articulation of a theory, also acts as a clue to aesthetic practices including rhetoric and prosody. By establishing this close connection between historical tradition and political economy, one could build an alternative historiography of Odisha. This is because history in Odisha—like in many traditional societies—is the history of its literary culture where *historiography* is not so much in its encoded documents but in its memory, imbibed through shruti or oral recounting. Literary culture in Odia for better part of its career has been the repository of that memory.

WORKS CITED

Bakhtin, Mikhail M. 1984. *Rabelais and His World.* Translated by Helena Iswolsky. Bloomington: Indiana University Press.

Chatterji, Suniti K. 1964. Artaballabha Mohanty Memorial Lectures, Bhubaneswar Odisha Sahitya Academy.

Das, Chitta R., ed. 1951. *Srimat Bhagavat Gita* (Balaram Das). Shantiniketan: Odia Gabesana Bibhaga.

Das, Nilakantha. 1977. *Odia Sahityara Krama Parinama.* 2nd ed. Cuttack: New Student Stores.

Dash, Debendra K. and Dipti R. Pattanaik. 2002. "Translation as Social Praxis in India." *Journal of Contemporary Thought*, edited by P. C. Kar et al., 75–83. Baroda: Forum on Contemporary Theory.

———. 2004. "Late 19th Century Literary Discourse and Odia Identity." *Utkal Historical Journal* 17. Bhubaneswar: Utkal University.

———. 2006. "Translating Medieval Orissa." *Translation Today* 3, nos. 1 & 2: 20–82, edited by Udaya N. Singh and P. P. Giridhar. Mysore: Central Institute of Indian Languages.

———. 2007. "Translation and Social Praxis in Ancient and Medieval India." In *In Translation*, edited by Paul St. Pierre and P. C. Kar, 153–73. Amsterdam: John Benjamins Publishing Company.

Dash, Gaganendra N. 1988. "Sarala Mahavarata O Itihas." *Esana* 17: 1–26, edited by Krushna C. Behera. Cuttack: Odia Gabesana Parisad.

———. 2008. "History of Oriya Language." *Comprehensive History and Culture of Orissa*, edited by P. K. Mishra and J. K. Samal, vol. 2, 2nd ed., 561–73. New Delhi: Kaveri Books.

Dash, Surya N. 1978. *Odia Sahityar Itihas*, vol. I., 3rd ed. Cuttack: Grantha Mandira.

Despande, Madhav M. 1993. *Sanskrit & Prakrit*. Delhi: Motilal Banarasidass.

Even-Zohar, Itamar. 2012. "The Position of Translated Literature within the Literary Poly System." *Translation Studies Reader*, edited by Lawrence Venuti, 3rd ed., 162–67. London: Routledge.

Jain, Jasbir C. 1987. *Prakrit Narrative Literature*. Delhi: Munshiram Manoharlal.

Kulke, Herman. 1997. *The States In India 1000–1700*. Delhi: Oxford University Press.

Mohapatra, Kedar N. 1960. *A Descriptive Catalogue of Sanskrit Manuscripts of Orissa*, vol. II. Bhubaneswar: Orissa Sahitya Akademi.

Majumdar, Paresh C. 1971. *Samskrit O Prakrit Bhasar Kramabika*. Calcutta: Dey's Publishing.

Mishra, Sachidananda, ed. 1980. *Bichitra Ramayana* (Sarala Das' version). Bhubaneswar: Odisha Sahitya Akademi.

Mohanty, Artta B. 1965–1973. *Mahavarata* (Sarala Das' version). Bhubaneswar: Dept. Of Culture, Govt of Orissa.

Mohanty, Bansidhar. 1984–1989. *Odia Sahityar Itihas*, vols. I-II, 3rd ed. Cuttack: Friends Publishers.

Mohapatra, Shyam S. 1988. *A Study of Oriya Folk Ballads*. Shantiniketan: Visva-Bharati Research Publication.

Panigrahi, Krushna C. 1975. *Sarala Das*. New Delhi: Sahitya Akademi.

———. 1981. *History of Orissa*. Cuttack: Kitab Mahal.

———. 1989. *Sarala Sahityar Aitihasik Chitra*. Cuttack: Prajatantra Prachar Samiti.

Pattanayak, Debi P. 1958. "Aryanisation of Orissa." *Orissa Historical Research Journal* 7, no. 1: 51–55. Bhubaneswar: Dept of History, Utkal University.

Pollock, Sheldon, ed. 2004. *Literary Cultures in History*. New Delhi: Oxford University Press.

———. 2007. *The Language of the Gods in the World of Men*. Delhi: Permanent Black.

Sahoo, Krushna C., ed. 1984. *Chandipurana* (Sarala Das' version). Cuttack: Books & Books.

Sahu, Bhairabi P. 2013. *The Changing Gaze*. New Delhi: Oxford University Press.

Sen, Sukumar. 1972. *Bharatiya Arya Sahityer Itihas*. Calclutta: Dey's Publishing.

Tripathy, Kunja B. 1962. *Evolution of Oriya Language and Script*. Bhubaneswar: Utkal University.

Appendix

Serial no.	Name of *parva* in Sanskrit	Name of *parva* in Sarala Das' version	Remarks
1	Adi	Adi	Many *upakhyanas* have been dropped and some portion of the Adi *parva* in Sanskrit is included in the Madhya *parva*. Many new, original stories have also been added in Sarala version.
2	Sabha	Madhya	Madhya *parva* includes content from Adi and Aranyaka *parvas* along with new descriptions
3	Aranyaka	Sabha	Corresponds to Sabha *parva* with significant additions and subtractions
4	Virata	Bana	Corresponds to Aranyaka *parva* with significant subtractions. Content-wise it is much smaller than Sanskrit Aranyaka *parva*
5	Udyoga	Virata	Corresponds to Virata *parva* with significant additions and subtractions
6	Bhishma	Udyoga	Corresponds to Udyoga *parva* with significant additions and subtractions
7	Drona	Bhishma	Corresponds to Bhishma *parva* with significant changes. The chapters corresponding to *Srimad Bhagavata Gita* have been dropped from Sarala Mahabharata
8	Karna	Drona	Corresponds to Drona *parva* with significant additions and subtractions

Serial no.	Name of *parva* in Sanskrit	Name of *parva* in Sarala Das' version	Remarks
9	Shalya	Karna	Corresponds to Karna *parva* with significant additions and subtractions
10	Souptika	Shalya	It is smaller than Sanskrit Shalya *parva* with some of its contents constituting a separate (Gada) *parva*
11	Stri	Gada	New *parva* focusing on Bhima and Duryodhana's characters and their final fight
12	Shanti	Kainshika	It is a small *parva* where Aishika part of the Souptika *parva* of Sanskrit Mahabharata has been elaborated
13	Anushasana	Nari	Corresponds to Stri *parva* with significant additions and subtractions
14	Aswamedhika	Shanti	It is a concise version of the Sanskrit version with 4 chapters in place of the 353 chapters in the Sanskrit text
15	Ashramavasika	Ashramika	The order of Ashrama and Aswamedha *parva* has been changed in Sarala's Mahabharata. Corresponds to Ashramika *parva* with significant additions and subtractions
16	Mousala	Ashwamedha	Corresponds to Aswamedhika *parva* with significant additions and subtractions
17	Mahaprasthanika	Mushali	Corresponds to Mousala *parva*. It primarily introduces and elaborates on the emergence of Jagannath from Krishna which is missing in the original.

Serial no.	Name of *parva* in Sanskrit	Name of *parva* in Sarala Das' version	Remarks
18	Swargarohana	Swargarohana	Corresponds to Mahaprasthanika and Swagarohana *parva*s with significant additions and subtractions. It also contains a summary of the Anushasana *parva*. An interesting part of the Swargarohana *parva* in Sarala's version is that all the five Pandavas go through a pilgrimage of religious places in Odisha and India.

EIGHT

World Literature and Literary Historiography of Pre-colonial South Asian Vernaculars

Towards a Methodological Model

Sachin C. Ketkar

There seems to be an entrenched Eurocentric bias in the Western discussion on world literature as it appears to conflate literary processes with the processes of the spread of industrial capitalism. Walter Cohen, for instance, has recently argued,

> For if prose fiction from around the world now draws centrally on Western forms, and especially on the novel, why not see all of it as Western literature? The expansionist vocation of European literature thus ends in a self-abolishing contradiction. The history of European literature culminates in the category of world literature.... European literature has a claim on our attention partly because it is the central precursor to contemporary world literature, in which it remains a leading force. (2017, 6)

It is this Eurocentric bias implicit in thinking about literary repertoires in relation to the development of capitalist "world system" that has led several critics like Deckard and Shapiro to see the recent conceptualisation of world literature as an expression of neo-liberalism (2019, 7). The notion of world literature, as Ciocca and Shrivastava note has become a "hegemonic force in the English humanities. It is fast becoming *the* way to theorize any literary field of the contemporary period that has aspirations to a global reach, subsuming postcolonial literature, minority literature, and 'Anglophone'/'Francophone' theoretical models". In addition, it has appeared against the larger neoliberal attempt to monopolise all possibilities of the international into the global life of capital (2017, 10–11).

Commenting on constructions of world literature in colonial and postcolonial India, Vinay Dharwadkar has drawn attention to how the dynamics of *marga* and *desi* were transmuted irreversibly by two substantially reconfigured spatial master concepts, *vishva* and *rashtra* both from Sanskrit and with pre-classical and classical etymologies in the nineteenth century leading to development of notion of world literature in India (2012, 476–77). Dharwadkar seems to imply that world literature in Indian context is largely a by-product of colonial modernity and nationalism.

The link between this conception of world literature and world-capitalist world system underlying colonialism would invariably connect it with the questions of colonialism and modernity. Walter Mignolo has argued that there is no modernity without coloniality and coloniality is constitutive, not derivative of modernity. He points out that non-Western local histories and knowledges cannot be constituted without entanglements with Western local histories. He emphasises that in order to delink and decolonise knowledge and in the process build decolonial local histories thus "restoring the dignity that the western idea of universal history took away from millions of people", one can practice "border thinking". Border thinking requires dwelling in the border, as against border studies, where the knowing subject is an observer and not a dweller in the boundaries (2019, ix–xv).

However, I have attempted to develop an argument that the notion of world literature is not a singular entity or a model; it has multiple models. Certain models of world literature like those proposed by Dionyz Durisin and David Damrosch can be useful for a more nuanced investigation into how individual South Asian vernacular literary cultures like Marathi interacted dialogically not only with larger transregional and translocal cultural spaces like the Sanskrit Cosmopolis to use Pollock's terms (Pollock 2006, 18) or the Persian Cosmopolis (Eaton, "Persian Cosmopolis", 2019) on the one hand but also with other literary cultures on the subcontinent. These models can help us in decolonising the

Eurocentric model of world literature and also assist us in coming up with post-nationalist, post-nativist literary histories of South Asian vernaculars. Damrosch remarks,

> World literature is almost always experienced by readers within the national context in which they live, and more particularly within the national markets in which books are published, reviewed, and assigned in classes. In a kind of figure/ground reversal, it is the nation that frames most experiences of world literature, at least as much as it is world literature that frames any national canon. (2017, 134)

He invites scholars to look more deeply into "the presence of the world within the nation, even as we continue to develop further our exploration of national traditions in the wider world" as "the national literary traditions themselves were never as self-contained, after all, as nationalistic literary histories have often supposed" and goes on to provide an example Ghalib's Persian poetry (ibid.).

While Cohen and Moretti's definitions of world literature seem to imply that it is a recent historical phenomenon, a by-product of Euro-American capitalism, Damrosch's understanding seems to imply that it is as old as literature itself. Damrosch used the idea of world literature to "encompass all literary works that circulate beyond their culture of origin, either in translation or in their original language…a work only has an effective life as world literature whenever, it is actively present within a literary system beyond that of its original culture". He claims that world literature is not an infinite, ungraspable canon of works, but rather a mode of circulation and of reading, a move that is applicable to individual works as well as bodies of material, available for reading established classics and new discoveries alike (2013, 199–200). This formulation allows us to see not only texts like the *Bhagwad Gita*, the epics, vernacular masters like Kabir or Taagore or genres like the ghazal or the novel as world literatures but also allows us to understand the genres of *reading* like literary criticism and literary history as forms of world literature as well.

Harish Trivedi observes that Damrosch's formulation is "empirically innocent of theory, and so readily workable and user-friendly" and goes on to add that this must be world literature "without tears or indeed without breaking into a sweat" (2013, 22–23). However, the manner in which it is deployed in the current project, the post-theoretical consciousness of the contingent historical asymmetries and hierarchies that affect the mode of circulation (along with tears as well as sweat) is brought back, taking away its innocence.

While Damrosch's model does not seem to specify exact modes and mechanisms of circulation and reading, earlier theorisation of world literature by Durisin (1993 and 1984) as a complex, evolving, and dynamic model of systemic interliterary relationships at multiple levels—whose final definition is not possible[1]—is useful for the purpose of historiography of South Asian literatures like Marathi as it subsumes Moretti as well as Damrosch's conceptualisation. Durisin was working within a certain official scientist-Marxist environment, and interestingly, his unwillingness to define "world literature" leaves the history of interliterary processes open-ended, thus overcoming the Hegelian teleology implicit in various versions of Marxism. Durisin's framework here is not deployed in a rigid, schematic sense, but more as a heuristic tool to uncover cultural histories of the South Asian vernaculars.

A note on the term "vernacular" is required here. Somerset and Watson (2003) point out that "vernacular" is often used to talk about three overlapping but distinctive language situations: first, as a derivation from the Latin *vernacular* to describe subaltern, non-elite, local language, or style; secondly, to describe the competitive relation between the classical languages and languages which reflect the cultural, national and political ambitions of the people as well as the rulers, underprivileged and privileged alike; and thirdly, to describe (as in modern English), the universal and the common tongue. Somerset and Watson note that the term is apologetic and assertive at the same time and denotes a language situation in which something is at stake for the user. They also point out that

---

[1] For instructive critical elucidation of Durisin's theory, see Dominguez, Saussy and Villanueva (2015, 20–40).

while the nationalist literary historiographies of the vernaculars focused on canonical writers who sought to create "ennobling language", more recent historiographies seek to break down the divide between high literary and other kinds of texts. They also note how the framework of vernacular studies provides new ways of comparing cultural situations that seem analogous but have never previously been organised within the same frame of reference. Besides, it also has potential to recontextualise "medieval studies" by providing new ways of configuring the relation of the medieval period to the later period, by exploring striking parallels between medieval and postmedieval language theories and practices and long traditions whose relevance to postmedieval vernacular politics often go unnoticed. Vernacular studies also provide a framework where medievalists and modernists can learn from each other. Therefore, this field is fast becoming a force in comparative literary studies (Somerset and Watson 2003, ix–xii). The present paper attempts to build upon these rich insights.

The notion of world literature as conceptualised by Cohen and the notion of vernacularization elaborated by Sheldon Pollock as models of how the transregional space ("world" or "cosmopolitan") engages with the regional or "the national", seems to continue working within the problematic "top-down" framework of Sanskrit-centric or Eurocentric "influence studies", where the peripheral literary cultures and *desi* cultural traditions are assumed to be passive receivers of the cosmopolitan cultures like Sanskrit or English.

The methodological framework of interliterariness and world literature developed by Durisin is also able to eliminate the vulgarisation and one-sidedness implicit in the idea of "influence" or "causality", in the approaches such as Pollock's, Cohen's, or Moretti's as they do not consider or neglect what Durisin terms as "the factors of autonomous individuality" of those literary cultures or their "principle of selectivity" and agency active in the recipient culture. Durisin's model of world literature as a dynamic and evolving construct that models "interliterariness" at several levels is thus, a far more constructive framework as compared to the Eurocentric models like Moretti's or the Sanskrit-centric neo-Orientalist approaches such as Pollock's.

An additional advantage of Durisin's model is that by eliminating the vulgarisation and one-sidedness of influence and causality—by underscoring the principle of selectivity and agency of recipient cultures—it simultaneously enables us to strategically reject the customary reactionary nativist and nationalist accusations of "derivativeness" against the presence and role of "foreign non-native elements" in traditions. Thus, it overcomes the typical postcolonial binaristic paradigm of literary studies, where one is stuck either with the cosmopolitan Eurocentric or Sanskrit-centric approaches or with reactionary nativist-nationalist approaches. Thus, the history of Marathi literature does not remain merely a variety of "national" or "subnational" narrative but emerges as what Damrosch terms as a "figure" against the "background" of the larger world literary processes. At the same time, this approach enables us to see "the world in the grain of sand" in Damrosch's words, alluding to Blake. This "world" in the grain of linguistic sand can also reveal multilingualities and bilingualities within a literary culture, something which is emphasised by Orsini (2014).

Durisin and Damrosch's models of world literature can also allow us to read the pre-capitalist vernacular ecology on the subcontinent as a distinctive interliterary cosmopolis, made up of shared tropes, "miracles" and themes, underpinned by transregional religious movements and *sampradaya*s in conflict and dialogue with each other. The vernacular figures like Namdev and Guru Nanak who are believed to have genetic contatctual relations with multiple bhasha traditions can, in the light of such theorisation, be seen as pre-capitalist cosmopolitans, spiritual cosmopolitans whose sensibility and influence go beyond the boundaries of languages, cultures or *sampradaya*s.

Using Marathi literary history as an instance, one can demonstrate how Durisin's model allows us to conceptualise world literature in pre-colonial South Asian cultures as a historical dynamic category of interliterariness where Sanskrit–bhasha stage of cultural history could be the considered as the earliest stage of interliterary world literature, followed by the stage where the Perso-Arabic linguistic and cultural traditions add to the complexity of interliterary dynamics in the fifteenth and the sixteenth century. There was also an intense bhasha-bhasha interliterary encounter, as seen in the Hindustani compositions of Marathi *sant*s and their engagement with *bhakti* as a vernacular transregional space, which can be thought of as being almost a vernacular cosmopolis in which they drew upon the cultural memories of *bhakta*s widely from the subcontinent.

While emergence of the Marathi language—the central component of Marathi literary culture—predates the age of the Yadavas (1180–1320) by centuries, the earliest Marathi literature emerged in the late twelfth and the thirteenth centuries in the form of devotional, spiritual and hagiographical writings from important sects. Mhaimbhat (or Mhaibhat), Mahadaisa (or Mahadamba [c. 1286]) considered the first woman poet in Marathi, Keshirajbas, Narendra Parshram, Keshiraj and Narendra from the Mahanubhava sect, Dnyaneshwar (1275–1296), and his first great circle of followers consisting of Namdev "Shimpi" (the tailor [1270–1350]), Janabai (Namdev's maid), Gora "Kumbhar" (the potter [c. 1267]), Sawata "Mali" (the gardener [1250–1295]), Chokhamela (the untouchable devotee [d. 1338]), Narhari "Sonar" (the goldsmith [d. 1313]), Sena "Nhavi" (the barber) and Kanhopatra (the dancing girl [c. 1338]) all from the Bhagwat or the Varkari sect and Mukundraja from the Nath sect are the most important composers of the period. There was also a significant body of Sanskrit literature from the royal court, especially by Hemadripandit, Pandit Bopadeva and the Mahanubhava writer like Agneyaraja. Unlike some other bhasha literatures, the emergence of Marathi literature was not due to any direct patronage by the Yadava dynasty, though the question of commercial patronage for sectarian institutions as well as to the language remained critical.

This historical period is significant for South Asia as well as Europe as these places witnessed, in Sheldon Pollock's words, "transformation in ideas and practices that were at once both deeply political and deeply aesthetic" (2006, 435). He argues that for this process, religion was irrelevant and became relevant as a later reaction (ibid., 436). He understands the creation of such a text as part of the process of "vernacularization", or "the historical process of choosing to create a written literature, along with its complement, a political discourse, in local languages according to models supplied by a superordinate, usually cosmopolitan, literary culture" (ibid., 23).

The Mahanubhava ("those of great experience") is a major *sampradaya* that began in the thirteenth century in Maharashtra and is still alive today. Their literature occupies a special place in Marathi literary history, though the existence of this literature is recent discovery. This was largely due to the use of secret scripts like Sakala in which the followers of the sect coded their sacred texts. The *Lilacharitra* (late thirteenth century), the prose biography of Sri Chakradhar is one of the most remarkable texts, not just in Marathi, but also in the entire subcontinent. It is not only one of the earliest and most extensive prose texts in the modern Indian languages, but also quite original in the way it is composed and narrated. The emergence of Marathi prose is not "vernacularization" of any Sanskrit model of prose at all but a development of a new cultural form. The term *lila* literally means episodes of the divine "play" of the Sri Chakradhar and the book consists of approximately 950 such episodes. The book is conventionally divided into approximately 74 *lila*s in *ekanka* (the section of Solitude)—the section is called *ekanka* because it describes the solitary wandering of Sri Chakradhar—358 *lila*s in the *purvardha* (first half) section and around 488 *lila*s in the *uttarardha* or the latter half.

The story behind the composition of the *Lilacharitra* is fascinating; this is described in the *Smriti Sthala* (1313 CE), one of the most important Mahanubhava texts attributed to Narendra Parsharam. The biographer Mhaimbhat was a prosperous brahmin from the Sarale village who went to Vidyanagari in Telangana and studied a *shastra* named *Prabhakar Darshna*. He soon became arrogant due to the knowledge he had gained. When he met Sri Chakradhar, he realised he was in the presence of God and went to Riddhipur and took *diksha* (initiation) from Sri Govind Prabhu. After Sri Chakradhar's departure, his followers mourned his absence and remembered their encounters with him. Nagdev (Bhatobas) instructed Mhaimbhat to meet them and compile these memories in the form of a text. Mhaimbhat wandered extensively meeting Chakradhar's followers and only after meticulously cross-verifying the incidents would he jot down the *lila*s. In one incident, the *Smriti Sthala* says, "There was one Khayibhatt who was a farmer. Mhaimbhat would follow as Khayibhatt worked on the field, narrating his encounters with the lord. Mhaimbhat would bow down to him and then he used to go around asking for alms in order to eat" (Joshi 2008, 145). This method of meticulous literary composition of a biography/hagiography is unique for the period as it is not simply a retelling of a myth from a believer's position. Therefore, the use of the form of prose biography in Marathi cannot be considered as "adoption of any superordinate Sanskrit models" as Pollock would like to believe. Rather, it was the creation of new forms and not vernacularisation of Sanskrit forms.

According to Marathi literary historians like Tulpule, the period of two centuries after Namdev's demise (d. 1350) is *tamoyug* or "The Age of Darkness", a dark period that seemed like it would last forever, not primarily because of Islamic invasion, but because of cultural decadence in which Marathi society lost its "authentic" character (1984, 761). The early period of the Deccan sultanates in Marathi history is referred to as the *asmani sultani* period by historians. This phrase is the title of a poem attributed to Samarth Ramdas (mid-seventeenth century) who describes the invasions by the sultans as "catastrophes from the skies". Such titles indicate the influence of the brahminical Ramadasi *sampradaya* on later historical readings of this period. A typical depiction of this period in Marathi literary history comes from critics like Bhalchandra Nemade who maintained that medieval Marathi literature was "certainly a part of Maharashtrian assertion of independence against Muslim invaders, a part of Indian reformation which began with the loss of political freedom" (1997, 2). Nemade would go on to say,

> The fanatical Muslim powers had reduced the Hindu population to social impotence leading to a total submission to all kinds of authoritarianism. It is no wonder that in such a great disorder caused by the political confusion of the wars, no great literature flourished in Māhārāśtra after the thirteenth century. The fourteenth, fifteenth and sixteenth centuries were the barren period for Marathi literature, and excepting one major poet, Eknāth (1548–1599), the three hundred years did not produce any significant writer. (ibid., 6)

Paranjape and Mirajkar (1994, 8) state that the period following the age of Dnyandev was "an era of darkness"; for about 200 years, till we reach the age of Eknath, no literary work worthy of being discussed was produced. The patronage to Marathi given by the Yadavas ended and the infiltration of the Muslim Sufis into the Deccan was another factor responsible for the "downfall of culture and literature" in Maharashtra. Instead of such biased and evaluative positions, the interliterary world literature model discussed above is a more fruitful way of reading this period. One can discern a subsequent historical stage of interliterary evolution of world literature in Marathi and other south Asian languages, that is, of a prolonged and richly productive interliterary engagement with the Perso-Arabic cosmopolis, apart from continuing engagement with Sanskrit cosmopolis and other bhashas like Hindustani or Kannada.

The Deccan, and later the entire subcontinent, became a part of the larger Islamic cultural world. John Obert Voll has argued that the Islam world can be considered as a special premodern world-system. Despite disintegration of the Islamic imperial system under the Abbasid rulers of the tenth and eleventh centuries and its replacement by a decentralised network of smaller states ruled by military commanders or sultans—who replaced the imperial caliphs as the effective rulers of Muslim areas by the twelfth century—the world of Islam was, in fact, dynamic and expanding, not static and stagnating, or disintegrating. According to Voll, it is possible to see this vast network of interacting peoples and groups as "a social system … that has boundaries, structures, member groups, rules of legitimation, and coherence" (1994, 218). Hence, Marathi literature as well as literature of the Deccan region of this period is a product of interliterary process where the world literature is drawn from Sanskrit cosmopolis, the Persian cosmopolis as Richard Eaton calls it, and also from "folk" and regional narrative traditions.

If the widely accepted year of death of Namdev (c.1350) is taken into consideration, the last three decades of his life coincide with the rule of the Delhi Sultanate in the Deccan. It is unsurprising, given his travels and decades-long stay in northern India that his language and themes reflect the society and culture transformed by the presence of Islam. V.B. Kolte (2014) cites two compositions attributed to Namdev to show his response to the presence of Islam:

> *Deva dagadacha aise dev tehi fodile turki*
> *Ghat le udaki bobhatina*
> *Aisi hi daivate nako daavu deva*
>
> The Turks smash the gods made of stone
> And sink them in water
> And yet the gods do not get angry!
> Do not show me such gods O God!
> (Trans. mine)
>
> The other composition is a Hindustani one, attributed to Namdev:
>
> *Hindu ana turku kana doha te giana siaana*
> *Hindu puje dehura musalmaanu masit*
>
> Both the Hindu and the Turk are supposed to be knowledgeable
> But the Hindu prays in a temple and the Turk in a mosque
> (Trans. mine)

Kolte believes that Namdev's second composition in Hindustani is actually a strategy to contain conversion to Islam by arguing that both the religious modes of worship are futile; hence, conversion is pointless too. Namdev's propagation of *nirguna* philosophy after his return from the North, according to Kolte, is to be understood in the backdrop of Islam as a strategic mode of containing conversion (2014, 38–39). While one may or may not agree with Kolte's explanation, it is well-known that Namdev did turn to *nirguna bhakti* towards the end of his life and his Hindustani compositions embody the same philosophy (Tulpule 1984, 593). One also cannot help but note the shift in language and a kind of bilingualism and multilingualism emerging in Marathi which was distinct from the period of the Yadavas.

Marathi also underwent a massive shift by assimilating Perso-Arabic or Dakhani influences, and this became the language of poets like Eknath. This assimilation was seen as "pollution" by many of earliest nationalist-nativist literary historians like V. L. Bhave. New forms of bilingualism of the Marathi–Hindustani or Dakhani kind emerged with Namdev and can be found in Eknath (late sixteenth century). This bilingualism is obviously of a different kind from the Sanskrit-bhasha bilingualism or Marathi–Kannada bilingualism of the thirteenth century. The diffusion of paper and pen, a technology introduced by the Bahamanis, impacted the "oral-literate" media ecology of the Marathi literary culture profoundly by increasing the significance of reading and writing, without of course, diminishing the importance of oral traditions like folk performances, the *kirtan*s and *akhyana*s.

Namdev's pilgrimages brought him into contact with other cultural regions, languages and their religious and artistic practices. This contact influenced his work and philosophy as he composed in other languages like Hindustani and responded to the social and cultural conditions in other areas. The experiences of trans-regional travelling in South Asia by these writers played a critical role in shaping their poetics and cultural politics. These experiences produced what Durisin terms as "genetic contactual interliterary relations" that would profoundly impact the development of Marathi literary tradition as well as Marathi society and culture. Hence, to see these compositions as simply being modeled on the superordinate Sanskrit cultural forms as Pollock does is inaccurate.

However, this interliterariness and engagement with trans-regional hegemonic Persian cosmopolis is also evident in the rise of the Muslim Marathi bhakti literature as well as the rise of Dakhani literature, especially by the Sufis. As Eaton explains, the sultanates affirmed their Deccani identity by patronising Dakhani language and literature, and their sovereignty by issuing coins and inscriptions in classical Islamic languages. For conducting the routine business of collecting revenue and administrative justice they used the vernacular tongue of the masses. The assertion of indigenous identities resulted in flourishing of Dakhani—a vernacular language of Deccani Muslims—as a literary language patronised by the court. It was the language of northern immigrants who had settled in the upper Deccan area in early fourteenth century and when it emerged in the fifteenth century, it was called Hindavi or Hindi. However, scholars like Sohoni have argued that Dakhani was only mistakenly associated with the Hindi-Urdu continuum and was actually a common vernacular language in the Deccan from the fifteenth through the eighteenth centuries. Both these languages had been continually evolving since the twelfth century, and as it became the new vehicle for spiritual discourse, it turned into the language of the vernacular unified spiritual landscape (2016, 3).

Apart from royal courts, Dakhani literature also flourished in the Sufi shrines where unlike the north Indian Sufis who wrote primarily in Persian, the Deccan Sufi poets wrote in vernacular Dakhani. In Bijapur, Shah Miranji Shams al-Ushshaq (d. 1499) and his son Burhan al-Din Janam (d. 1597) used Dakhani when writing for common audiences. The important genres of this folk literature included the *chakki-nama* or *charkha-nama* sung by village women while engaged in domestic chores like grinding grains or spinning thread. Such songs used simple language to communicate the Sufi's path to spiritual enlightenment. By contrast, as Eaton observes, these authors used Persian when writing expository prose on technical subjects for fellow Sufis. These developments in Sufi literature in the Deccan parallel the sectarian bhakti literatures and dialogic interactions as demonstrated by the genre of *chakki-nama* that is analogous to *jatyavarchi ovi* used extensively by the *santa*s in Marathi (Eaton 2000, 190).

Apart from Dakhani literature, Muslim Marathi bhakti literature is another extremely significant development of the period. A very important Muslim Marathi poet who is Eknath's contemporary is Shah Muntoji or Mutubji Bahamani or "Mrutunjay". He was living in the age of the Bahamani sultans and the name "Mutubji Bahamani" seems to suggest that he was a king of Bidar, but this seems unlikely. While some historians place him in 1620s, others like R. C. Dhere place his dates as 1575–1650. A fascinating book attributed to Shah Muntoji is the *Sidha Sanket Prabandha*, which is in the form of an *anuwad* of the *Padma Purana*, a dialogue on knowledge and spirituality between Rama and Sita. His other books are *Advaita Prakash*, *Prakash Deep*, *Swaroop Samadhan*, *Amrutanubhava* and *Jeevotdharana*. As these books largely express the Upanishadic Vedantic thought, many scholars have questioned whether these venerable men were actually "Sufis" as conventionally understood and accepted.

However, the intellectual effort to find spiritual ground and spiritual equivalences between the Islamic theological terms and Sanskrit in the *Panchikaran* is extremely significant for cultural history of the subcontinent. For instance, it says "Om Ram" is equivalent to "Bismillah", "Sthula deha" is glossed as "Vajbul Vajud," and "Linga deha" is translated as "Mamatal Vajud".[2] The historicity of these texts is unclear. The text says that the glossary was prepared in response to the queries by the great figure of Nagesh *sampradaya*, Adnyan Sidha to Mrutunjay. The characteristic eclecticism of the *sampradaya* as well as its own theological vocabulary is distinct in the book, thus highlighting the importance of the sects and their ideologies as important institutional contexts of most of the precolonial literature. Most of the manuscripts of these works are found in Saraswati Mahal in Tanjore. A note in the *Panchikarana* says, "*Shah Mutubji Brahmani, jin me nahi manmani, Panchikaran ka khoj kiye, Hindu Musalman ek kiye*", translated as, "Shah Mutubaji Bahmani, who did not act

2 For more detailed discussion on the *Panchikarana* see Pathan (2011, 40–50).

as per his whims and fancies, he discovered the *Panchikarana* and united the Hindu and the Musalmans" (Dhere 1967, 35–40).

Texts like these deserve a deeper analysis as they will reveal the cultural complexity of the period. A Muslim saint's Rama-Sita dialogue in the *Sidhha Sanket Prabandha* can throw light on the dialogic relationships, boundaries and cultural transgressions of the society. The cultural need that motivates texts like the *Panchikarana* to seek a spiritual bilingual glossary will help us to uncover significant precolonial models of translation and interliterary poetics that cuts across sectarian and religious affiliations, as well as regional and temporal histories. Interreligious, intercaste, intersectarian, interlingual and interliterary negotiations like these need to be probed extensively.

The economic situation of Maharashtra transformed considerably due to establishment of Shivaji's kingdom in the late seventeenth century. While Shivaji's revenue of his early *jagir* was forty thousand *hon*s (a medieval gold coin whose exchange value was 3 to 4 medieval rupees), it grew into a kingdom of approximately one crore *hon*s, an increase by almost two hundred and fifty percent (Kulkarni 2008, 120). Obviously, the increase in wealth was largely in the hands of the militaristic elites. Maharashtra before Shivaji was largely an under-monetised and less populated agrarian economy. The economic shift, the emergence of new political Maratha elite and the ideology of new patriotism brought about significant shifts in the Marathi literary repertoire, and these shifts can be typically seen in the emergence of new powerful traditions of the bardic *shahiri kavya* in the domain of popular culture and the precolonial historiographic *bakhar* literature in bureaucratic circles. Both these traditions proved essential in the construction of historical as well as popular memory of the Marathi-speaking people.

The term *shahiri* comes from the Persian *shayar*, which means a poet who sings in a *tamasha* performance. Consequently, the composers and singers in this tradition are called *shahir*s. However, the tradition draws upon the existing folk traditions of *gondhal*—a ritualistic performance by the devotees of mother goddess as well as eulogistic-bardic tradition of *bhaats* found in other regions like Gujarat and Rajasthan that celebrate valorous deeds of heroes. In various historical contexts, the emergent theatrical form of the period (*tamasha*) remains one of the most powerful influences on Marathi performative practices till today. The term is Persian, and this folk form is believed to have been used for entertainment for the Maratha armies in the camps during the late seventeenth century (Achalkhamb 2001, 77). It incorporates the *powadas* and *lavani* along with acting and dancing.

Two main genres of the *shahiri* literature, differing largely in terms of subject matter, are the *powada* and the *lavani*. The term *powada* seems to be derived from the Sanskrit *prashashti* or *prastuti*, which means to eulogise and greatly praise something. More specifically, it is a narrative genre like the ballad that eulogises heroic deeds and heroes. Scholars have collected around 300 *powadas* out of which 7 are believed to be from the Shivaji's period, 150 from the Peshwa period and the remaining from the period of British rule.

The *lavani* deals with other emotions, largely erotic and romantic, but also, at times, spiritual. The etymology of the term is unclear. It may have been derived from folk songs sung at the times of harvesting (*lavani*) or derived from *laapnika*, a rural folk song. It may have also been derived from the Sanskrit term *lavan* meaning beautiful or *laavanya* meaning beauty. Like the *powada*, it has deep affinities to the *gondhal* tradition (Kendurkar 1999; Morje 1974). Scholars like Herwadkar would typically "gender" the forms. He says, "If the *Powādā* is masculine in its robust vigour, the *lāvaṇī* is feminine in its tone and tenor" (2001, 665).

Along with *shahiri* literature, we also see an emergence of *bakhar* literature in this period. Many historians have researched this genre as it is considered a historiographical as well as literary form. Herwadkar notes that the term *bakhar* is a metathesis of the Arabic word *khabar* (plural *akhbaar*) and discusses various etymologies of the term. Rajwade is of the opinion that it is written in the style of the *tawarikhs*, but C. V. Vaidya points out that while *tawarikhs* were authentic historical accounts, *bakhars* were based on hearsay. The Molesworth's dictionary defines it as "any history, relation, memoir etc., in Prakrit prose" (quoted in Herwadkar, 2).

Unlike the *bakhar*s and the Mahanubhava prose works, most of the bhakti compositions are poems that are orally preserved and performed, it becomes impossible to draw definite historical conclusions from these works. However, comparing these works to the great predecessors like Dnyaneshwar and Eknath, we notice a significant shift in subjectivity and language that reveals greater influence of the Perso-Arabic and Hindustani and a major shift in the universe of bhakti discourse that includes the saints from larger subcontinent. The subjectivity is brought out by numerous autobiographical references that tie up with the hagiographies to create the image of Tukaram (seventeenth century) in Marathi cultural memory. The shift in the bhakti intertextuality can be demonstrated by a typical composition, for instance, where he says,

> Sacred is the family, holy is the land,
> Where the servants of Hari are born
> Narayana is their *dharma* and Narayana, their *karma*,
> which has made all their three-worlds divine.
> Tell me, has the pride of *varna* made anyone sanctified?
> On the other hand, even those born in the lowest of the low places
> Have crossed the seas of birth and rebirth
> And the Puranas have now become their minstrels.
> This *vaishya* grocer, this potter Gora, this cobbler Rohidas
> Muslims like Kabir, Momin, and Latif, Sena the barber
> Kanhopatra the dancing girl, Khodu the eunuch, Dadu the weaver,
> Chokha and Banka both the untouchables by caste
> All worshiped Hari's feet without discrimination·
> The Lord of All has united them all.
> Who was Nama's Jani, what was her state?
> The King of Pandharpur dined with her.
> Who was Mairal Janak and from what family was he?
> But how can I speak about his greatness?
> The servants of Vishnu have no caste,
> Say the Vedas,

Read the scriptures for yourself, says Tuka,
How many fallen souls are saved?

Abhanga no. 2167

(Nerurgavkar 2003; translated by Sachin Ketkar)

This universe of sub-continental bhakti from non-Sanskrit languages consisting of non-upper caste Hindu composers can be contrasted with Dnyaneshwar's invocation to Ganesha at the beginning of his commentary where he imagines each portion of Ganesha's image as representing various Sanskrit philosophical schools like the Vedanta or the Mimansa and so on. This also highlights the intertextual and multilingual space of bhakti that cuts across cultural geographies, creating an interlingual and intertextual bhakti canon. For instance, later compositions like the Guru Granth Sahib is another instance of sub-continental bhakti canon. Thus, Marathi literary culture that emerged from the interaction with the Sanskrit world literary traditions and Perso-Arabic-Hindustani tradition developed into larger trans-regional intertextual literary worlds over centuries.

It should also be borne in mind that composers like Namdev, Eknath, Tukaram and Ramdas also extensively composed in Hindustani. Tukaram's compositions are classified as *musalmani abhanga*s and Hindi *pada*s by Nerurgavkar (2003, 713–18). These compositions reveal his familiarity with north Indian bhakti poetry, especially that of Kabir, thus unfolding the picture of interlingual and interregional map of bhakti world literature within it.

Marathi bhakti can only be understood in the 'background' of the larger world of bhakti. This interliterary engagement with the Persian cosmopolis is critical to understanding the precolonial Marathi literature. Like many of the South Asian literatures, Marathi culture in the nineteenth century underwent a massive transformation that altered the institutional structures, their ideological orientations, the media, the language, and the literary repertoire due to intense and intimate genetic contactual relation with the colonising culture which inaugurated a new phase of world literature in Marathi. Society underwent a radical shift transforming the Marathi literary culture irreversibly and explosively bringing about multilevel shifts and transformation in society. Thus, the pre-print performative cultural forms like the *shahiri kavan, tamasha*, folk performative forms and *kirtan* were displaced in terms of state patronage, though they continued to flourish under religious sectarian and non-sectarian patronage as well as the forms of entertainment for the non-elites. However, they were modernised in other ways, and were often appropriated by modern social and cultural movements later. They would also be remediated and transposed into the altered media ecology of the period. The transfer of the bhakti texts into print or their remediation in altered media ecology made their legacy critical to the politics of imagining nation. While they were primarily embedded in the publics of face-to-face performance, their entry into the print domain had the effect of altering their mode of circulation and consumption. It is in this context that the concept of world literature proposed by Dharwadker mentioned earlier must be understood.

One another significant interliterary process shaping modern Indian literatures is dialogic social and cultural exchange with Bangla literature and culture starting from the nineteenth century. However, this Bangla-bhasha interliterary relationship is not sufficiently emphasised and studied in literary and cultural histories of other non-Indian languages. It can be argued that the model of Bangla modernity (especially after the Bengal Renaissance) became extremely popular as a model of modern Indian culture in other Indian languages like Marathi and Gujarati, and following the definition of world literature given by Damrosch, the Bangla literature is probably one of the most important "world literatures" in India. Such an analysis would thus complicate the Eurocentric view of world literature and modernity in Indian languages. In the context of Marathi, we can also extend a similar analysis to Hindi or the Hindustani cosmopolis.

Apart from these questions, one can also emphasise the need to look at world literature not merely as a mode of circulation of texts, (re)producing and re-reading texts but also as literature and ideas produced by political, social and intellectual movements like liberalism, conservativism, abolitionism, socialism, Marxism, fascism, nationalism, feminism, cultural avant-gardes and philosophical movements like psychoanalysis, existentialism, phenomenology and so on that have transnational circulation and impact.

Using Durisin's notion of "interliterary communities" defined as "the communities that share interliterary processes", we can also speculate whether it is possible to conceptualise Indian literatures or south Asian literatures as a mega interliterary community made of a range of linguistic literary traditions that share the interliterary processes similar to Marathi. World literary community, then, would be all communities across the planet that historically share interliterary processes.

Works Cited

Achalkhamb, Rustam. 2001. "Tamasha." In *Maukhikta ani Lok Sahitya*, edited by Madhukar Wakode and Sushma Karogal. New Delhi: Sahitya Akademi.

Ciocca, Roscella, and Neelam Srivastava, eds. 2017. *Indian Literature and the World: Multilingualism, Translation, and the Public Sphere*. London: Palgrave Macmillan.

Cohen, Walter. 2017. *A History of European Literature: The West and the World from Antiquity to Present*. Oxford: Oxford University Press.

Damrosch, David. 2013. "What is World Literature?" In *World Literature: A Reader*, edited by Theo D'haen, Cesar Dominguez and Mads Rosendahl Thomsen. Routledge.

———, ed. 2014. *World Literature in Theory*. John Wiley and Sons.

———. 2017. "World Literature as Figure and as Background." In *Futures of Comparative Literature: ACLA State of the Discipline Report*, edited by Ursula K. Heise. Routledge.

Deckard, Sharae, and Stephen Shapiro, eds. 2019. *World Literature, Neoliberalism, and the Culture of Discontent*. Palgrave Macmillan.

D'haen, Theo, Cesar Dominguez, and Mads Rosendahl Thomsen, eds. 2013. *World Literature: A Reader*. Routledge.

D'haen, Theo, David Damrosch, and Djelal Kadir, eds. 2012. *The Routledge Companion to World Literature*. Routledge.

Dharwadkar, Vinay. 2012. "Constructions of World Literature in Colonial and Postcolonial India." In *The Routledge Companion to World*

Literature, edited by Theo D'haen, David Damrosch and Djelal Kadir. Routledge.

Dhere, R. C. (1967) 2014. *Musalman Marathi Santakavi*. Pune: Padmagandha Prakashan.

Dominguez, Cesar Haun Saussy, and Dario Villanueva. 2015. *Introducing Comparative Literature: New Trends and Applications.*

Eaton, Richard M. 2000. *Essays on Islam and Indian History*. Oxford: Oxford University Press.

———. 2005. *A Social History of the Deccan, 1300–1761, Eight Indian Lives.* The New Cambridge History of India I.8. Cambridge: Cambridge University Press.

———. 2019. "The Persian Cosmopolis (900–1900) and the Sanskrit Cosmopolis (400–1400)." In *The Persianate World: Rethinking a Shared Sphere*, edited by Abbas Amanat and Assef Ashraf.

———. 2019. *India in the Persianate Age: 1000–1765*. London: Allen Lane–Penguin Books.

Herwadkar, R. V. 1994. *A Forgotten Literature: Foundations of Marathi Chronicles*. Mumbai: Popular Prakashan.

———. 2001. "Marathi." In *The Maratha Supremacy: History and Culture of Indian People Volume VIII*, edited by R. C. Mujumdar.

Joag, R. S., ed. 1999. *Marathi Vangmayacha Itihas Khand III: 1680 te 1800 ya kalkhandatil Marathi Vangmayacha vivechak Itihas*. Pune: Maharashtra Sahitya Parishad.

Joshi, P. N. Marathi. (1978) 2008. *Marathi Vangmayacha Vivechak Itihas—Pracheen Kaal*. Pune: Snehavardhan Publishing.

Kendurkar, M. P. 1999. "Shahiri Vangmay-Powade." In *Marathi Vangmayacha Itihas Khand III: 1680 te 1800 ya kalkhandatil Marathi Vangmayacha vivechak Itihas*, edited by R.S. Joag. Pune: Maharashtra Sahitya Parishad.

Kolte, V. B. 2014. *Marathi Santanche Samajik Karya*. Translated from Hindi by Sumati Kolte. Mumbai: Lokvangmay Gruha.

Kulkarni, A. R. 2008. *Medieval Maratha Country*. Pune: Diamond Publications.

Nemade, Bhalchandra. (1968) 1997. *Tukaram* (Makers of Indian Literature Series). New Delhi: Sahitya Akademi.

Nerurgavkar, S. K., ed. 2003. *Śri Tukarama Maharajanchi Sārth Gāthā*. Pune: Pracharya Dandekar Dharmik, Shaikshanik va Sanskrutik Vangmay Prakashan Mandal.

Mignolo, Walter D. (2000) 2012. *Local Histories/Global Designs. Coloniality, Subaltern Knowledges, and Border Thinking*. Princeton and Oxford: Princeton University Press.

———. 2019. "Epistemic Reconstitution (s), Colonial/Imperial Differences and Border Thinking." Seventh Balwant Parekh Memorial Lecture 2019, Balwant Parekh Centre for General Semantics and Other Human Sciences, Baroda.

Morje, G. N. 1974. *Marāthi Lāvani Vāngmay*. Pune: Moghe Prakashan.

Mujumdar, R. C., ed. 2001. *The Maratha Supremacy: History and Culture of Indian People* Volume VIII. Mumbai: Bhartiya Vidya Bhavan.

Orsini, Francesca. 2014. "For a Multilingual Literary History North India in the Long Fifteenth Century." In *New Cultural Histories of India Materiality and Practices*, edited by Partha Chatterjee, Tapati Guha-Thakurta, Bodhisatva Kar. Oxford University Press.

Paranjape, P. N., and Nishikant Mirajkar. 1994. *Marathi Literature: An Outline*. New Delhi: Maharashtra Information Centre, Govt. of Maharashtra.

Pathan, Y. M. 2011. *Musalman (Sufi) Santanche Marathi Sahitya*. Mumbai: Maharashtra Rajya Sahitya and Sanskriti Mandal.

Pollock, Sheldon. 2006. The *Language of the Gods in the World of Men: Sanskrit, Culture and Power in Precolonial India*. California: University of California Press.

Ramakrishnan, E. V., Harish Trivedi, and Chandra Mohan, eds. 2013. *Interdisciplinary Alter-Natives in Comparative Literature*. New Delhi: Sage Publications.

Sohoni, Pushkar. 2016. "Vernacular as a Space: Writing in the Deccan." *South Asian History and Culture* 7. Taylor & Francis Online. http://dx.doi.org/10.1080/19472498.2016.1168101. Accessed on 25 June 2024.

Somerset, Fiona and Nicolas Watson, eds. 2003. *The Vulgar Tongue: medieval and postmedieval vernacularity*. Pennsylvania: The Pennsylvania State University Press.

Trivedi, Harish. 2013. "Comparative Literature, World Literature and Indian Literature: Concepts and Models." in *Interdisciplinary Alter-Natives in Comparative Literature*, edited by E.V. Ramakrishnan, Harish Trivedi and Chandra Mohan. Sage Publications.

Tulpule, S. G., ed. 1984. *Marāthi Vāngmayācha Itihās: Khand Pahila: Arambhapasun 1350 Ad paryantchyā Kālakhandātil Marathi Vāngmayāchā Vivechak Itihās*. Pune: Maharashtra Sahitya Parishad.

Voll, John Robert. 1994. "Islam as a Special World-System." *Journal of World History* 5, no. 2: 213–26. Honolulu: University of Hawaii Press.

Wakode, Madhukar, and Sushma Karogal, eds. 2001. *Maukhikta ani Lok Sahitya*. New Delhi: Sahitya Akademi.

NINE

Embodied Inheritance of a Dancing Philosophy

Text and Practice in the Chaitanya Charitamrita

SUKANYA SARBADHIKARY

Introduction

Let us begin with a story from the *Ramakrishna Kathamrita*. Once an ascetic wished to understand whether the lord of the world, Puri's Jagannath, is formless (*nirakar*) or has a divine form (*sakar*). With his *danda* (stick), he thought he could measure god's definite form, but the stick went right through the deity. The *danda* thus literally became a yardstick to conceptualise the simultaneous abstract formlessness and the concrete manifestation of divinity.

I use the term *danda* and varied connotations of it to argue that they tell us of complex ideas of simultaneity such as the above. Bengal-Vaishnava theological distinctiveness lies in the doctrine of *achintya-bhed-abhed* (unthinkable whether the devotee and god share a relation of sameness or difference). The specific term I critically analyse is *ud-danda*, mostly used in the context of dance, to imply ecstatic fervour. I show that the meaning-world of this term is perfectly embodied by the saint, Chaitanya's body, and it in turn becomes exemplary for future devotional collectivities. These collectivities, through the language and practice of *uddanda*, inherit a philosophy which embodies simultaneous sameness-and-difference, monism-and-dualism. The meta-argument which resonates throughout the paper is that language is often able to survive by translating to embodied states. Here, I explore the question of translation at the very productive interface of language and phenomenology. It is a translation born of practise, such that, language and experience resonate with one another in the phenomenon of *uddanda*.

I discuss a tradition in which Sanskrit and Bengali's intermixing through texts, terms and rasaesthetic discourses, informs a (poetic) speech-community. I show that the sustainability, durability, flourish and even intuitive understanding of the language-world is made possible by being woven intrinsically with a religious performance, a specific dance form. The philosophy of language is literally and immediately apprehended, since it is lived through every muscle and pore of the body. Thus, theology and dance, philosophy and body, language and the senses, theory and the everyday, text and practice, metaphor and embodiment, come together in the phenomenon of *uddanda*. This particular kind of engagement of language and dance is being attempted for the first time in the context of Bengal's bhakti landscape.

I focus on a significant episode described in the *Chaitanya Charitamrita* (the main biography of the medieval Vaishnava saint, Chaitanya [1486–1533]), in its *madhya lila*, Chapter 13. The chapter describes Chaitanya's ecstatic dance (*uddanda nritya*) with his followers in Puri, before the deity Jagannath, on Rathayatra day. Bengal-Vaishnavas have a complex devotional lifeworld, such that, they worship Chaitanya not as an avatar of Krishna, but sometimes as Krishna himself, sometimes as Krishna's lover-devotee, Radha, and mostly, as Krishna-Radha reincarnated together for the sake of understanding and enjoying each other's love within and as the body of the saint. For Chaitanya, Jagannath was a dear form of Krishna, and he spent the last two decades of his life in Puri. During this time, biographies state, he exhibited all simultaneous manifestations of *mahabhava*, the most intense form of mixed (even contradictory) divine emotions experienced by Radha herself, towards her lover-god (Marglin 1992, 207–09).

In this paper, I analyse the theology of *achintya-bhed-abhed*, that is, simultaneous philosophical sameness and difference, through the phenomenology of Vaishnava ecstatic dance. This particular engagement of theology and aesthetics has not been explored before. I closely study the phenomenon of Chaitanya's *uddanda nritya*, and argue that its linguistic lifeworld and kinetic anatomy together encase the philosophy of *achintya-bhed-abhed*. Such simultaneous sameness and difference is embodied by the dancing body in three ways: the body is both meditative and mad, divine and human, and of times contemporary and others. I explore all the three ways in which Bengal-Vaishnava theology embodies itself in the saint's *uddanda* dancing body.

Uddanda as madness becomes *uddanda* as meditation, the aesthetics of the arts and love merge into philosophy. Again, during the dance itself, Chaitanya sometimes exemplifies the moods of Radha-like devotion towards Krishna/Jagannath, and sometimes becomes Krishna himself. The metaphysics of this simultaneity also equates the rasaesthetics of multiplicity and dance with the philosophy of union and yoga. The text is especially complex in its spatio-temporal imaginations, where Chaitanya, in Puri, remembers Radha-Krishna's *lilas* in Kurukshetra, and in that *lila* itself, Radha, in Kurukshetra, in turn remembers her encounters with Krishna in Vrindavan. So, Puri-Kurukshetra-Mathura-Vrindavan get tied in chains of simultaneous coeval transportations. Simultaneity has been a critical analytical issue in studies of Bengal-Vaishnavism, and as June McDaniel says, such affective simultaneity is a state "full of wonder and paradox" (1989, 284), but its phenomenology has not been duly developed.

The Textual Fabric

The linguistic universe, texts and terms, have been critical maps of Vaishnava emotional religiosity. The Sanskrit Purana, Bhagavatam (eighth–tenth centuries), the sixteenth century Sanskrit texts of devotional aesthetics, *Bhaktirasamrita Sindhu* (BRS) and *Ujjvalanilamani* by Rupa Goswami, and the seventeenth century Bengali theological biography of Chaitanya, *Chaitanya Charitamrita* (CC) by Krishnadas Kaviraj, serve as exemplary paradigms of complex classifications of emotional religious ecstasy experienced by Radha and Chaitanya. While the CC, to understand

Chaitanya's devotion and divinity, develops the philosophy and literary aesthetics described in the BRS, communities of practitioners—historically and in the contemporary period—define their moods, aesthetics and relations with the divine with reference to all these texts in turn. These Sanskrit and Bengali texts and concepts of emotions have thus been examples for generations of Bengal's bhakti devotees. Aesthetics become textualised, and texts define communities.

The analysis of three Sanskrit terms shall serve as the analytical bedrock of the paper's arguments. They are: *uddanda*, *chitram* and *shavalya*. These terms appear in the concerned chapter of the Bengali biography, CC. The critical philosophical question which binds the Sanskrit/Bengali terms is whether aesthetic and emotional devotional reality is one or many or both simultaneously.

Uddanda

The prefix "*ut*" before a term literally connotes "moving upwards". This includes physical stretchedness as well as psychologically rising above; such verticality expresses a liberating excess. For instance, in the Yoga Sutras, *udan* refers to upward rising breath, and is associated with positive, transformative life-force (see for instance Byrant 2009, 372). Also, the aesthetics treatise by Rupa Goswami is named *Ujjvalanilamani*. *Ujjvala* is a technical term for the *shringara bhakti-rasa* (worshipping Krishna as lover), and which may be broken up as *ut+jvala*: upward inflaming (*jvalati*) of the meditative and passionately-fueled body.

The surplus of "*ut*" corresponds to a frozen-like state of *samadhi*, simultaneous with a vibrant emotional restlessness. It concurrently alludes to an ocean's deep stillness, as well as the innumerable waves which restively arise *from* it, and also dissolve *into* it. The ocean and the waves are both same and different, as are stillness and excess.

The yogic and ecstatic are both states at the limits of human perception. So, the inertia of momentum involved in "*ut*" brings its two paradoxically distinct dictionary meanings close: *unnata* (sophisticated) and *utkat* (weird) (Das 1988, 398). Such extended momentum is phenomenologically similar to the buoyancy of a heavily dancing body, present even after it has stopped dancing.

Now, the term *danda* means stick, and is also, a specific temporal measure. As always held by the god of death, Yama, *danda* also means discipline and yogic rigour. Taken together, *uddanda* could thus mean: a stretched stick-like body which is either caught in meditative stillness or replete with affective excess; or time, which is still in the present and also tightly extended beyond the present. So, the temporal phenomenology is most distinct, such that, the meditative single-pointed concentrated nature of the micro-moment suspends linear time, makes time come to a standstill (*danda*), yet giving it a simultaneous elasticity of momentum or excess (*ut*), thus enabling intensive trans-temporal imagination/embodiment. In this paper then, *uddanda* means a strict yogic disposition, an exuberant emotional body, and time, which is so still in the present, that it also surpasses itself; a stillness which is so pointed that it transcends.

The lexicographer Haricharan Bandyopadhyay defines *uddanda* as that state which extends *danda* (*danda-ateet*). Here *ateet*, as meaning both "beyond" and the "past", implies moving farther than the focused oneness of the body and the present. In defining *uddanda nritya*, he specifically alludes to a tumultuous, spontaneous excess, as well as monistic oneness (1966, 404–05). So *uddanda* approximates an aesthetic sensibility in which yogic oneness cohabits with, and indeed, makes possible, affective excess, and vice-versa; cognitive temporal stillness helps the mind travel to multiple times and spaces. *Danda* (stick/time) is extended, such that oneness and multiplicity are simultaneous.

Thus, while *uddanda nritya* has only been understood as love-mad (*prem-unmad*), ecstatic dance in devotional contexts, I argue that it transcends divisions of madness-meditation, dance-devotion, bhakti-yoga, *utkat-unnata* and aesthetics-philosophy.

This kind of nuanced simultaneity of spiritual emotions (even opposed ones) is also sensed in two other complex Sanskrit terms: *chitram* and *shavalya.* The chapter describing Chaitanya's dance before Jagannath's *rath* begins by saying that his ecstasy caused *chitram* to all people (Mukhopadhyay and Majumdar 2009, 271), and the term *shavalya* is used to refer to a specific emotional condition embodied by him during the dance (ibid., 279). These two terms together conjure the idea of the heart as a painting ground of emotions, and enrich the significant debate about singularity and multifariousness.

Chitram

Chitram means different things: variegated, painting, wonder and even *akasha* (space) (Mitra 1936, 522). The heart-space is thus also called *chid-akasha* (space of consciousness). When clouds/emotions pass through, they are distinct from the passing medium, that is, the sky/yogic heart, but they also dissolve into them since they also exist within them. Thus, they are both distinct and indistinct from the sky/heart. A clear, mono-colour sky/heart does not experience clouds/affects, but nevertheless contains such possibilities of variety within its apparent clarity; so just like white is a blending of all colours, similarly, the range of possible devotional affects merge in yogic consciousness. In the context of *achintya-bhed-abhed*, this would imply the unthinkable distinction between ecstatic differences and yogic stillness, passionate *uddanda* and meditative *uddanda*.

Shavalya

The concept of *shavalya* similarly bridges between ideas of painting and devotional emotions (*rasa*). It refers to the splotchy, spotted, rainbow palate of a painter, where colours are distinct, but not independent of one another (Monier-Williams 1993, 1052). In this, one of its synonyms are *chitram* (*Amarkosh*, 310. See also Monier-Williams 1993, 258). The best example of this phenomenon is of the peacock feather, which embodies a *shavalya* or dappling of colours (such as, blue, green, purple, brown, yellow): it has its own distinct colour, since the thought of a peacock feather always generates a specific colour-image, but that cannot be equated with any one of its separate elements, or even be referred to as a combination/mixture of those. It is a medley with a distinction.

The debate therefore is, whether the colour of the peacock feather is one or many. If we shift the debate to the *rasa* context, we can ask whether devotional emotions are basically one, or variegated. It is not a coincidence then that the peacock feather which adorns Krishna's hair is obsessively referred to in literature as generating the most peculiar passion in Radha.

The resolution may again be sought in the philosophy of *achintya-bhed-abhed*. The mind's stillness is due to the *sattvik* (harmonious) *bhava*, and any emotional movement in it is caused by the *rajasik* (passionate) *bhava*. However, the quieter the water, any slightest movement causes ripples; such ripples are not separate from the water, they dissolve into it, and again create fervour elsewhere, from within it. Thus, it is particularly still water which can feel the ripples' clarity. Similarly, the calmer one is in yogic contemplation, the greater are the felt sensations of Krishna devotion. This itself is *bhaver shavalya* (emotional simultaneity), a continuous supplanting among emotions and their base. The BRS describes emotional *shavalya* (medley) as "a series consisting of a succession of mutually supportive Transitory Emotions" (Haberman 2003, 341).

The Dance before the *Rath*

Select descriptions from the Chaitanya Charitamrita, *madhya lila*, Chapter 13 (paraphrased below) shall help to substantiate the conceptual edifice of the paper.

Lord Jagannath's idol was being pulled by a number of devotees, but it moved only at his own will. When Chaitanya as Radha danced in love, the chariot moved, when (s)he stopped in sulk or meditative thought, Jagannath also waited and watched with still eyes: as if the Lord himself was entranced in simultaneous *uddanda* moods. The Rathayatra and the saint's dance were the direct embodiments of Krishna-Radha's intense dalliance.

Simultaneity was exhibited by Chaitanya's body in different ways. Thus, he danced embodying Radha's different emotions towards Krishna. After many years of wait, Radha came from Vrindavan to meet Krishna, when she heard that he was coming to Kurukshetra from Mathura. When (s)he (Chaitanya) felt intense happiness in meeting Krishna after the long wait, (s)he embodied being *abhed* or inseparate from him, while when (s)he (Chaitanya) experienced the simultaneous agonies of not being with him in their favourite abode Vrindavan however, there were the pangs of separation, *bhed*. However, only very elevated devotees realised that Chaitanya also embodied being Krishna himself, during the same dance. So, there were different groups of devotional musicians dancing before the *rath*, and each such *kirtan* group witnessed Chaitanya dancing in their middle, simultaneously. Each group felt that he belonged to them, while he, in the best possible reminder of the famous Krishna-*lila* in Ras, satisfied all.

Chaitanya Charitamrita's descriptions of the saint's emotions make appropriate discursive sense in relation to the broader philosophy of emotions, theorised in the Sanskrit treatise, BRS. Minute classifications of affect and their subtypes are found in the five chapters of the text's southern quadrant. A broad taxonomy which is relevant here suggests that, "The causes of love, such as Krishna, his devotees, and the sound of his flute; the resulting expressions, such as smiling; the eight reactions, such as stupefaction; and the assisting emotions, such as indifference, are known in the experience of Rasa to be respectively the Excitants, the Indications, the Responses, and the Transitory Emotions" (Haberman 2003, 127).

Chaitanya's dance-description makes abundant references to his *uddanda* state. It talks about many associated expressions: *ananda* (happiness) in *uddanda*, "upward" attention and disregard of all external happenings (*urdha-mukh*), stretched log-like *pranam* or prostration on the ground (*dandavat*), etc. (Mukhopadhyay and Majumdar 2009, 273).

The *rath* and Jagannath stopped and watched the perfected devotees' physical symptoms of intense love during *uddanda nritya*: stupor, sweat, tears, convulsions, paleness, violence, joy, sadness, goosebumps, breaking voice, madness, etc., occurring all together, simultaneously (ibid., 275). These approximate the eight physical responses or *ashta sattvika bhavas* described in the BRS. The term that the author uses to indicate the temporal coincidence of these varied affects in this context is *samakal* (coeval). So again, it is the simultaneity of emotions, moods, selves, and times, which is distinctive in the text's description of Chaitanya's divine dance.

The narrative takes dramatic turns from here. There is a discursive play with references to three distinct but concurrent times: Chaitanya, propelled by the devotional songs or *kirtan*s of the present in Puri, remembered a time when Radha met Krishna in Kurukshetra, and when she was simultaneously overjoyed to meet the kingly Krishna of Dvaraka after long, and also severely estranged from her sweet lover of Vrindavan, thus longing intensely, in turn, to travel to the third time-space in question, Vrindavan. For Chaitanya thus, in his Radha-like mood, the Puri temple as-if became Mathura, the *rath* journey path, Kurukshetra, and Gundicha, where Jagannath travels to eventually during Rathayatra, Vrindavan. Chaitanya's mood thus changed completely. He raised his hands and uttered a *shloka*: "I see the man who stole my virginity. The same beautiful night is here, the air is fresh and even more sweetened with the smell of Malati flowers, I am the same me, but my heart still craves the meeting under the Betasa tree". The operative word here is "still" (*tathapi*). Despite everything, something was amiss. This "still"/*tathapi*, the despiteness, creates the poetic impact (ibid., 275). Completely taken over by Radha's mood, Chaitanya said that the *rath* sounds reminded him of Vrindavan's forest bees, and the devotees reminded him of the lover-flautist's friends (ibid., 276). The poet Rupa Goswami is said to have been present on the same occasion with Chaitanya in Puri, and he composed another very famous verse to the same effect.[1] Once again, the distinctive emotional canvas and the specific affective textures of Bengal-Vaishnavism, find renewed life across different centuries of texts.

---

[1] See: https://www.purebhakti.com/teachers/bhakti-yoga-masters/775-srila-rupa-gosvami-svarupasanatana

However, the contrariness of madness and meditation and the simultaneity of times resolve in the *uddanda* state. This is most persuasively exemplified in Chaitanya's emotional medley. Krishnadas Kaviraj describes in the CC, using the precise discursive grid provided in the sixteenth-century BRS: In the blissful ocean of Chaitanya's heart, a mad storm attacked and insane waves resulted. Sometimes they intensely manifested in the body (*bhavoday:* the eight manifestations of *sattvik bhava*); sometimes like enemies in the battlefield, they combated; sometimes similar or dissimilar emotions united (*sandhi*), sometimes they mingled more abstractly and indefinitely (*shavalya*). These dramatic transformations of emotions and moods resulted in all thirty-three transitory (*vyabhichari bhava*s) or variable (*sancharin*) emotions (affects which assist the eight physical responses) to happily jostle in the body. However, they accompanied and enhanced the basic foundational emotion (*sthayi bhava*) that Chaitanya had in the form of Krishna love. All these mad waves rushed through, only to eventually merge in the ocean of the *sthayi bhava* (*bhava shanti* or resolution) (ibid., 279). *Bhavoday, sattvik bhava, sandhi, shavalya, vyabhichari bhava, sancharin:* all these constitute critical Sanskrit rasaesthetic vocabulary, used by Krishnadas Kaviraj in the Bengali text, to convey the saint's emotional exuberance. As explained earlier, however, among these many strong embodied manifestations, this paper particularly focuses on the peculiar affective state of *shavalya*, and the *chitram* it causes, to understand the phenomenology of the saint's *uddanda* being. However, Rupa Goswami further designates four states in which the transitory emotions primarily exist. They are: manifestation, combination, medley, and resolution (Haberman 2003, 337–43. See also Das 2014, 557 and Dimock 1999, 531).

Exemplary Emotions

The philosophy of simultaneity extends its life through texts and practices of subsequent generations of ecstatics in Bengal. The term *uddanda* and all associated rasaesthetic discourses and embodied experiences percolate, diffuse and sustain across different kinds of sects and devotees. It is important to remember that *uddanda nritya* is not a dance-expression in the usual performative sense of the term. It is a kind of yogic effusiveness which expresses itself as an exuberant total corporeal ecstasy. It is thus a state of dancing or literally rigorously jumping up and down, with hands upraised, and stiffened body and limbs (Dimock 1999, 522), trying almost to desperately reach "up" to one's own sense of divinity and devotional truth. Embodied inheritance in this context thus implies a philosophical identification with the simultaneity of monistic yoga and dualistic devotional ecstasy, which Chaitanya exhibited in his *uddanda nritya*, and which others imbibe in their bodies and language, and discursively perpetuate through a unique technique of metaphorising by the lived sensations of the skin.

So, Chaitanya's *uddanda* state becomes exemplary for others. Once again, the phenomenon of *uddanda* derives this sustainability due to the peculiar linguistic sensitivity of its meaning-worlds towards intense corporeal devotional experiences, and since these are embodied fully, in all their potential epistemological and ontological dimensions, by Chaitanya, and then other practitioners. The language thus finds a kinetic life in the dancing ecstasy of the devotee's body, and therefore carries on a distinct form of embodied intellectual culture. From another equally powerful affective perspective, the stretched vibrancy and calm tremor of the *uddanda* body immediately and automatically understands, identifies with, and inhabits the philosophy of Bengal's bhakti emotions and theology of simultaneity. Language, meaning, sensation, affect, emotion and philosophy are thus spontaneously meshed in the experience of *uddanda*.

Bengal-Vaishnava theology accords a most complex place to Chaitanya. He is sometimes worshipped as Krishna himself, and sometimes, as Radha and Krishna delighting in each other's taste within the saint's own body. Thus, only Chaitanya is said to have embodied all of Radha's simultaneous emotions towards Krishna (*mahabhava*). There is an interesting lineage of emotional inheritance within the sect, such that, Chaitanya's *uddanda* emotions and texts describing them, are considered exemplary for future generations of devotees, each however being able to embody them only partially. *Mahabhava* cannot therefore be embodied fully by any single Vaishnava devotee, but several among them are said to have experienced many of Chaitanya's emotions, sensations and moods. These devotees have in turn become exemplary. Similarly, classifications of emotional states in texts such as biographies, philosophical analyses and literary tracts are also treated as blueprints for devotional embodiment. There is thus a rich trans-temporal intertextual field defining bhakti devotionalism (Vaishnava and otherwise) in Bengal: from the ancient *Bhagavata Purana*, to the philosophical/aesthetic corpus including *Bhaktirasamrita Sindhu* and *Ujjvalanilamani*, to medieval biographies such as the *Chaitanya Charitamrita*, to even modern biography anthologies, including the famous *Ramakrishna Kathamrita* (originally published in 1902).

The *Gaudiya Vaishnava Jivan* (originally published in 1951) by Haridas Das, is a compendium of short biographies of Bengal-Vaishnava practitioners. It describes innumerable instances of devotional ecstatic states embodied by disciplined practitioners. For instance, a certain practitioner, Gourkishor Shiromoni Mahashay, would cry, have a broken voice, and goosebumps, when discussing theology with fellow-devotees (Das 2003, 77). He also had the most humble habit of doing *danda-vat pranam* (straight prostration on the ground) to every living creature he met on the way, since he considered them to be Krishna's devotees (ibid., 64).[2] His realisation of Chaitanya himself as Radha-Krishna breathing in the same body was expressed in a most peculiar incident, when, while reading aloud the deities' *lila*s during a certain Bhagavatam meeting, he was able to witness the exact corresponding *lila*s of Chaitanya written in golden letters in the white spaces between

---

[2] Another renowned practitioner, Gaura Kisora Dasa Babaji, would also cry intensely, his body would become stiffened and red, and he would chant continuously for up to two weeks at a stretch. (McDaniel 1989, 292)

the printed lines (ibid., 58–60). The golden letters were visible only to him, and not others.

Bijoykrishna Goswami was another exemplary figure. Once during the birthday celebrations of the Vaishnava saint, Advaita Acharya, in Dhaka, a *dhulot* festival (a ritual Vaiṣhnava festival in which devotees lie around on the dust, to commemorate and feel the grounds as embodiments of the Vrindavan soil which received Krishna's feet-dust) took place. Goswami did *uddanda nritya* for a long time, and as he stood still in *samadhi* (meditative trance) at the end of the dance, his matted locks also stood up straight (*khara*), and only after a long time, settled to their normal state (ibid., 338). This implies that his *uddanda* embodiment was so intense that it affected every pore of the body, extending from his limbs to his hair. This intensity indicates both strict yogic stillness and spontaneous sensational ecstasy.

In a philosophically distinctive way, Chaitanya was also an exemplary model for the famous nineteenth century saint-mystic, Ramakrishna. This is apparently theologically incongruous, since Ramakrishna's persona is considered by his sect as an embodiment of Advaita Vedanta principles (essentially monistic, which consider the mortal and divine worlds as indistinct, such that human perfectibility is understood as one with divinity), while Chaitanyaite devotion is an expression of *achintya-bhed-abhed* (where the relation between the devotee and God is one of simultaneous sameness *yet* difference).

Ramakrishna's most significant biography, the *Ramakrishna Kathamrita*, has many references to his embodied states which are not merely similar to Chaitanya's, but which directly make Ramakrishna indistinguishable from Chaitanya's *mahabhava* (Gupta 2017, 189). So just as *uddanda* states make Chaitanya's trans-identities as Radha, Krishna and Radha-Krishna possible, they also enable Ramakrishna to become Chaitanya.[3] Also, while

[3] Thus, the phenomenological state of *uddanda* and its accompanying experiences of space-time stillness and simultaneous translocation, may explain the theology of avatarhood in a distinct way.

Bengal-Vaishnavas would not acknowledge anyone other than Radha/Chaitanya claiming to exhibit *mahabhava*, followers of Ramakrishna deem him as the possessor of the highest saintly dispositions and capacities, including *mahabhava*.

So sometimes, when struck by intense devotion while listening to scriptures or *kirtans*, or during the festival of Rathayatra, Ramakrishna would dance and enter into *samadhi*. Devotees would then feel he is Chaitanya himself (ibid., 149–50, 502). At other times, while listening to Chaitanya's stories, he would directly embody his *uddanda*-like states: for instance, he would stand upright (*dandayaman*), his sight would be directed upwards (*urdha-drishti*), his hands would be stretched upright, his eyelids would not move, and his breath would become infrequent (ibid., 28, 442, 526). He even said that he could see Chaitanya standing before him at these times (ibid., 872). Again, in the trans-temporal capacities of *uddanda*, Ramakrishna would claim to be transported to Navadvip then, where Chaitanya performs *kirtan* with devotees, or to Puri's Rathayatra.

A parallel discourse also informs the phenomenology of these states. This pertains to a fourfold philosophical understanding of the spiritually cultivated body. These corporeal states are: *sthul* (gross physical body), *suksha* (subtle body: of dreams, imagination, etc.), *karan* body (the physical sense which stays awake when we sleep; when all senses are in a seed-like state and which progressively project outward as we wake up), and *turiya* (beyond all senses of human embodiment, when the self is one with universal consciousness or God). Corresponding to these, there are three further *dasha* or states. According to Ramakrishna, Chaitanya embodied all three. Thus, in *bahya-dasha* (the external state) he would do *kirtan* with devotees; in the *ardha-bahya-dasha* (half-external state) he would be unable to talk and would dance in a love-struck manner; and in *antar-dasha* (the internal state) he would become still like a painting, and enter what is known in religious discourse as *samadhi*. The external state would correspond to the *sthul* and *suksha* bodies, the half-external one to the *karan* body, and the internal one to what is called *nirvikalpa samadhi* or *maha-karan* (ibid., 317, 615, 635), the *turiya*. Chaitanya is thus exemplary for Ramakrishna's devotional order, and they believe that Ramakrishna also embodied all these states.

Vikalpa means alternative. Thus, *nirvikalpa* would correspond to a state wherein there is literally "no other". It implies a condition of total merge and oneness. *Kalpa* is also a measure of time. So *nirvikalpa* also apprehends the temporal *uddanda*, in which time literally comes to a standstill, allowing the two contrary possibilities of time stopping, and (thus also), time extending itself towards any possible space-time zone.

So, during Chaitanya's *uddanda nritya*, he was in between his *karan* (when physical and all other senses are in a seed-like condition) and *turiya* states. His dancing body was thus not one with ordinary physical sensibilities then. It was already divine, yogic but full of love.[4] The *antardasha* or *mahakaran* state corresponded to the situation when his dance turned from divine twists and swirls to another most nuanced layer of the *uddanda* condition: stiffly straightened and uncomplicatedly one with God. The moments (*danda*-s) of ordinary time would not be experienced then, and "other" times and selves would be enabled and even activated. Chaitanya then embodied either Krishna, or Radha, or Radha-Krishna, or the perfect devotee.

The subtle debate that is present at this stage then is about whether the devotee becomes God (*brahmananda*), or the perfect devotee of God (*bhajanananda*); whether the blackness beyond the black impenetrability of the *karan* body is of nothingness, or divine consciousness, or the colour of Kali/Krishna who Ramakrishna/Chaitanya serve as devotee. Ramakrishna himself uses two beautiful metaphors to explain these distinct states. Once a salt-doll entered the ocean with the intent to return

[4] Ramakrishna calls this body the *premer sharir* or *bhagavati tanu* (Gupta 2017, 64; 181).

to tell what the ocean tastes like. It was obviously never able to. This signifies the loss of the self in *nirvikalpa samadhi.* In another metaphor, no matter how much one rubs off gold, a tiny part always remains, akin to a dust-like particle of fire. This signifies the tiny sense of devotional self which remains only to be able to realise and serve the dark deity (Gupta 2017, 159). In these two senses coming together, one may meditatively feel at this culminating point that Kali and Gauranga (the golden skinned one, Chaitanya) are the same (ibid., 379), that is, the god and devotee become one, and to use a metaphor of luminosity, black (Kali) itself then shines like gold (Chaitanya), since black then does not signify the absence of ordinary colours, but the brilliant radiance of divinity (*jyoti-darshan*), the *mahakaran* enlightened luster hitherto veiled by the dark (*a-gyan*) *karan* body. It is the light of (simultaneous) stillness and ecstasy, oneness and multiplicity. And in another interpretation thus, the devotee's *karan* body realises divinity, yet does not merge with it, but remains active in serving it.

While the Advaita Vedanta doctrine would favour the former position and argue that in *antar-dasha* all linguistic and differential possibilities are dissolved, I think Chaitanya's body would fall between what Ramakrishna called *jara-samadhi* (when there is no sense of self, and one becomes god) and *chetan-samadhi* (when the difference between the devotee and god remains) (ibid., 481). This would approximate the Bengal-Vaishnava position on *achintya-bhed-abhed.* Similarly, Chaitanya's *uddanda* dancing body would then transcend *utkarsha* (yogic) and *unmad-vat* (madness) states (ibid., 39).

Conclusion

This essay has tried to understand ways in which a text (CC) represents the pulsating, living experience of a devotional dance (*uddanda nritya*). It has analysed the discursive foundations and inheritance of *uddanda nritya*'s linguistic and phenomenological universe: in a number of texts informing and influenced by the

CC over centuries, and in felt *uddanda* sensations of practitioners. It has shown how philological-philosophical subtleties in Sanskrit and Bengali form a web within which embodied representations make perfect blending sense. It has argued that the language and body of dance together exemplify the Bengal-Vaishnava philosophy of simultaneity and theology of *achintya-bhed-abhed* (unthinkability about whether sameness/stillness or difference/dynamicity is the primary ontological principle). The tradition of texts and lived dynamics of *uddanda* have survived through bodies of generations of bhakti ecstatics, and become exemplary in the making of devotional collectivities. This is both because language is thoroughly embodied, and the body too is discursively emplotted in rasaesthetics.

Works Cited

Amarasimha. 1969. *The Amarakosa*. Mumbai: Nirnaya Sagar Prakashana.

Bandyopadhyaya, Haricharan. 1966. *Bangiya Sabdakosh: A Bengali-Bengali Lexicon*. Kolkata: Sahitya Academy.

Byrant, Edwin F. 2009. *The Yoga Sutras of Patanjali: A New Edition, Translation, and Commentary*. New York: North Point Press.

Das, Haridas. 2003. *Sri Sri Gaudiya Vaishnava Jivan*. Navadvip: Haribol Kutir.

———. 2014. *Sri Sri Gaudiya Vaishnava Avidhan*. Kolkata: Sanskrit Book Depot.

Das, Jnanedramohan. 1988. *Bangla Bhashar Avidhan*. Kolkata: Sahitya Samsad.

Dimock, Edward C., Jr., tr. 1999. *Caitanya Caritamrta of Krsnadasa Kaviraja: A Translation and Commentary*, edited by Tony K. Stewart. Cambridge, MA: Harvard University Press.

Gupta, Mahendranath. 2017. *Sri Sri Ramakrishna Kathamrita*. Kolkata: Udbodhan Karyalaya.

Haberman, David L., tr. 2003. *The Bhaktirasamrtasindhu of Rupa Gosvamin*. New Delhi: Indira Gandhi National Centre for the Arts and Motilal Banarsidass Publishers Pvt. Ltd.

McDaniel, June. 1989. *The Madness of the Saints: Ecstatic Religion in Bengal*. Chicago: The University of Chicago Press.

Mukhopadhyay, Harekrishna and Subodhchandra Majumdar. 2009. *Sri Sri Chaitanya Charitamrita*. Kolkata: Deb Sahitya Kutir.

Marglin, Frédérique. 1992. "Jagannātha Puri." *Vaisnavism: Contemporary Scholars Discuss the Gaudiya Tradition*, edited by Steven J. Rosen. New York: Folk Books.

Mitra, Subol Chandra. 1936. *Saral Bangla Abhidhan*. 7th ed. Kolkata: New Bengal Press.

Monier-Williams, M. 1993. *A Sanskrit-English Dictionary*. Delhi: Motilal Banarsidass.

TEN

Visual Poetics of the Vaishnava Literary Culture of Assam

Towards a Multimedial Exposition

DHURJJATI SARMA

Introduction

The cultural geography of Assam provides a rich medley of forms and expressions tracing their provenance and features to multiple traditions of social and religious practices prevalent in the region for centuries. These practices have mostly derived their philosophies from pan-Indian cultures of devotionalism, namely, Saktaism, Shaivism and Vaishnavism, thereby also localising them in accordance with the beliefs and customs of the people. The dynamics of response and dissemination vis-à-vis these philosophical–religious systems provided the impetus and rationale behind the consolidation of a veritable corpus of literary works in various Indian languages, including Assamese, encompassing the domains of the oral, textual, performative and visual. Taken together, these domains constitute the literary culture of a language, and, by extension, of a region. The present study attempts to focus on the visual aesthetics of the Vaishnava literary–devotional culture of Assam that developed and prospered between the fifteenth and eighteenth centuries of the Christian era. The period signified a major exposure of Assam to the pan-Indian Bhakti movement, and two visionary-saints, namely, Sankardeva (AD 1449–1568) and his disciple Madhavdeva (AD 1489–1596) took on the mantle of fashioning a new devotional order in Assam called *nava-vaishnavabad* or neo-Vaishnavism. It was a significant social–cultural event in the history of medieval and early modern

Assam, and it still continues to exert a deep and sustained impact on the expressive cultures of almost all the major and minor communities of Assam.

Amongst the many possible reasons that contributed to the growth and sustenance of the Vaishnava literary culture for three centuries prior to the onset of colonial modernity in Assam in the nineteenth century, the most crucial one is the creation of a huge corpus of devotional literature in the vernacular under the able enterprise of Sankardeva and Madhavdeva, which included composition of *bargeet* (songs), *ankiya bhaona*s and *jhumura*s (plays), and translations of several *skandha*s (books) from the *Bhagavata Purana*, alongside philosophical treatises in Sanskrit on Vaishnava bhakti. In accordance with the missionary nature of this sectarian devotional order, primarily engaged in proselytisation, a marked inclination towards the visual–performative medium of dissemination was visible right from the onset of the neo-Vaishnavite movement towards the closing decades of the fifteenth century. From 1481 to 1493, Sankardeva carried out his first pilgrimage along with select disciples to the important centres of religious and cultural importance across the country and came in contact with saints, philosophers and artists belonging to diverse sectarian orders and communities of that time. The new devotional order that he founded in Assam after his return from his first pilgrimage was based on a gradual refashioning of the existing modes of *bhakti* into a more vibrant and dynamic culture of multimedial engagement. The development of a new visual poetics, embedded within plural epistemological frameworks, was a significant component of this process, and, on the basis of this understanding, the present essay takes for its study two illustrated Assamese manuscripts, namely, the *Chitra Bhagavata* and *Gita-Govinda*. In the process, the study shall also touch briefly upon the oral and performative elements within the precolonial Vaishnava literary culture of Assam as well as the institutional structure of this sectarian order and its interface with the Ahom royal culture, all of which were interconnected through a network of vigorous cultural exchange and negotiation.

Visual Poetics: A New Approach towards Multimedial Analysis

The concept of "visual poetics" is juxtaposed with that of "word and image" by Mieke Bal to constitute the larger domain of "comparative arts", which according to her, is "an attempt to expand [the principle of] interdisciplinarity to the entire range of 'arts,' or interpretive disciplines: art history, literary studies, film studies, but also cultural anthropology and history" (1988, 177–78). She further notes that, "[a]cknowledging the profoundly spatial and visual input indispensable in all cognition and the subsequent impossibility of severing the visual domain from the verbal, a visual poetics tries to overcome the word–image opposition implanted into our culture from antiquity on" (ibid.). Visual poetics is therefore understood as "acknowledging [again] the profoundly discursive nature of all semiosis and the subsequent impossibility of basing the analysis of visual art on a specific ontology or substance" (ibid.). As such, the study of "visual poetics" opens up manifold possibilities for a collaborative understanding between the study of literature and the visual arts through one or more kinds of "medialities" that we should be able to identify and differentiate, namely, "multimediality", "transmediality" and "intermediality". Quoting from Kattenbelt (2008), Satyanath defines them in this manner: "'multi-mediality' refers to the occurrence where there are multiple media in one and the same object; 'trans-mediality' refers to the transfer from one medium to another medium ('media change'); and 'inter-mediality' refers to the co-relation of media in the sense of mutual influences between media" (2021, 64). However, we must note that it is difficult to segregate them as distinct types of medialities, and hence they often merge and integrate with one another. All three modes of medialities assume a kind of movement between the associated media or mediums, and, at the same time, visualise them as tied by a symbiotic relationship with each other. They cohabit with and supplement each other. Therefore, for the sake of our understanding here, we shall use "multimediality" as a convenient term representing the three types of "medialities", while being conscious at the same time of their respective denotations.

As far as the study of illustrated manuscripts from a multimedial perspective is concerned, it can be argued that the integration of diverse expressive registers gives rise to a polyvalent situation where images, sounds and gestures originating from various sources interact with one another. Likewise, the coming together of multiple mediums of expressions (oral/written/performative) vis-à-vis the narrative text leads to the generation of new insights and perspectives which would not have been possible had the narrative remained ensconced within a single medium. To these three coordinates, Satyanath adds another position, which is that of the societal structures (which he refers to as "social epistemologies") represented by factors like caste, family, locality, etc. (2020, 73–74). Tangible social structures like the courts, temples, monasteries and even marketplaces were strong epicentres of social epistemologies throughout medieval and early modern Indian history. These factors (both tangible and intangible) might seem external to the text, yet they have markedly influenced the manner of articulation as well as reception of the same within a cultural geography. One only has to look at the literatures composed in various Indian languages during the Bhakti period to get an idea of the manner in which the diverse coordinates of form and meaning were fused and integrated to give rise to a host of multilingual and multimedial textual traditions in the country. It is within this broad theoretical framework that the conception, production and dissemination of illustrated manuscripts within the Vaishnava literary culture of Assam will be located, mapped and understood.

Literature and Visual Arts: The Assamese Context

The *Harshacharita* (c. 640; "The Life of Harsha"), which describes the life and reign of the seventh-century king Harsha, records the list of presents sent to him by Bhaskarvarman, the then heir apparent of Assam-Kamarupa, among which there were "volumes of fine writing with leaves made from aloe bark and of the hue of the ripe pink cucumber" and "carved boxes of panels for painting, with brushes and gourds attached" ("The *Harsha-carita* of Bana, Chapter VII"). Furthermore, in the Uttarbarbil Copper Plate Inscriptions of Balavarman III, who reigned in Assam-Kamarupa in the last quarter of the ninth century AD, there is reference to an earlier king Vanamaladeva's many palaces which were both *akritavichitra* ("devoid of non-uniformity in colour") and *sachitra* ("containing pictures within") (Sharma 1978, 134). Amongst the literary sources there is the classic instance from Pitambar's sixteenth-century poetic work called *Usha-Parinaya* where Chitralekha, the master-painter, undertakes the giant mission of drawing the images of all gods, kings, princes, *vidyadhara*s, *gandharva*s, *kinnara*s and the like inhabitants from the three worlds, so that her friend Usha can identify the person of her dreams. Referring to the task at hand, Chitralekha resolves to prepare a scroll within seven days ("*eka pata prothame koribo nirman*") upon which she intends to bring to life the three worlds for her friend to witness ("*tribhuvan lekho sokhi dekha bidyaman*") (Pitambara Kavi 1955, 51). Once during the early years of his preaching, Sankardeva had presented a performance involving the depiction of the seven *baikuntha*s through scenes painted upon a backdrop. This performance was called the Chihnayatra (performance via signs), which incidentally also signified his belief in the efficacy of multiple genre-based forms (dance, music and painting) symbiotically juxtaposed to create an integrative artistic experience. At a later stage of his life, Sankardeva undertook a massive project of weaving a 120-cubit-long and 60-cubit-broad tapestry upon which various scenes depicting the *lila* or the divine sport of Krishna during his days at Brindavana were painted. This unique masterpiece came to be known as the *Brindavani Bastra*, a specimen of which is presently being preserved in the British Museum. These select examples point towards a continuous engagement in Assam-Kamarupa with "visual poetics" as a means to integrate the varied potentialities embedded within literature and the visual arts for a wide variety of services and purposes, both secular and religious.

Chitra Bhagavata and *Gita-Govinda*: Representing the Pervasiveness of Vaishnava Literary Culture in Early Modern Assam

The *Chitra Bhagavata* and *Gita-Govinda*, along with *Hastividyarnava* (an illustrated treatise on elephant lore), are notable among the illustrated Assamese manuscripts epitomising the joint engagement between literature and visual arts in medieval and early modern Assam.[1] The royal courts (of the Ahoms, the Koches and the Kacharis), and the *sattra*s (the institutional base of Vaishnavite devotional order) were the two prime sites from which emerged the artistic and literary compositions in Assamese during the stated period. Whereas *Chitra Bhagavata* was produced and subsequently preserved in the Bali Sattra of Nagaon, Assam, both *Gita-Govinda* and *Hastividyarnava* were composed under the Ahom royal patronage. For the purpose of our study here, *Chitra Bhagavata* and *Gita-Govinda* have been selected not only for their affinity with the larger Vaishnavite literary culture, but also for representing respectively two marked yet related styles of painting that emerged in Assam between the seventeenth and nineteenth centuries, namely, the Sattriya and the Garhgaon or Rajaghoria (royal) styles/schools of painting.[2] The Sattriya style

---

[1] Other examples of illustrated manuscripts in Assam include *Lava Kushar Yuddha* (preserved in Kamarupa Anusandhana Samiti [KAS] Library; *Sankhachuda-vadha* (preserved in the Department of Historical and Antiquarian Studies [DHAS], Govt. of Assam; Ananta Acharya's *Ananda Lahari* (preserved in DHAS) and *Brahmavaivarta Purana* (preserved in the British Library, London). A number of literary and religious–philosophical works composed by Sankardeva have been reproduced by his disciples within the format of illustrated manuscripts, and a few of them are presently extant in the *sattra*s of Assam. These manuscripts were composed between the seventeenth and nineteenth centuries. (Neog 1986, 2–5; "The Assam School of Painting")

[2] Along with these two styles of painting, there are two more, which are referred to as Darrang school and Tai-Ahom school. With reference to the Sattriya school, Mridu Moucham Bora (2018) notes that, "Mahapurush Sankaradeva had initiated Neo-Vaishnavism in Assam and it was under the

had its genesis during the early years of the seventeenth century, and the *Chitra Bhagavata* is one of the earliest specimens of the school. At one place in the manuscript, the Saka year 1461 (or AD 1539) is mentioned as the date of its composition. However, Kalita questions the truthfulness of the information and considers the date to be an insertion by someone at a later time (2014, 22). He is of the opinion that the text was possibly composed and illustrated sometime after 1662, around the time of Mir Jumla's invasion of Assam (ibid., 28). On the other hand, the *Gita-Govinda* was composed during the reign of the Ahom king Rudra Singha (r. AD 1696–1714) by a poet called Ramanarayana Kaviraja Chakravarti, and the illustrations were possibly carried out within the court itself by *khanikar*s (painters or sculptors) employed by the king (Neog 1986, 1; Vatsyayan 1986, 15; Kalita 2014, 30, 33). According to Kalita, Rudra Singha welcomed skilled *khanikar*s not only from the *sattra*s where there was already a vibrant tradition of producing illustrated manuscripts, but also from the *bhati* areas, that is, from western Assam, thereby facilitating the arrival of many artists and craftsmen from Mughal India (2014, 33). It may be noted in this regard that, for *Hastividyarnava* (AD 1734), the text was composed by Sukumar Barkath, and the illustrations were carried out by Dilbar and Dosai, two skilled artists hailing from the Mughal capital, under the orders of the Ahom king Siva Singha (r. AD 1714–44) and his queen Ambika Devi. Looking at the trajectory of these three illustrated manuscripts composed roughly within a space of seventy years (between 1662 and 1734), one can argue that, consequent upon

---

influence of this movement that a strong tradition of writing manuscripts had begun. In order to spread the ideas of the movement among people, such manuscripts were also decorated with paintings along with the text. The style of painting that had begun within the ambit of Satras in order to support Sattriya text and literature is known as the Sattriya School." On the other hand, the Rajaghoria school, of which the *Hastividyarnava* is the best example, appropriated elements from the Sattriya and the Mughal miniature painting tradition.

the movement of artists across sites of commission/patronage and also cultural geographies, the Sattriya and Rajaghoria styles gradually converged and adopted common characteristics thereby collectively signifying what came to be referred to as the Assam school of painting.

The immediate source for the illustrations of the *Chitra Bhagavata* was Sankardeva's translation of selected portions from *dashama skandha* (tenth book) of the Sanskrit *Bhagavata Purana* into old Assamese. He was particularly interested in translating those passages which depicted the childhood *lila* of Krishna. In addition to the tenth book, he also translated in full and parts from the first, second, third, sixth, seventh, eighth, ninth, eleventh and twelfth books of the *Purana*. Many of these translated narratives were simultaneously refashioned by him into *kavya*, *kirtana* and *ankiya nataka*s thereby expanding the reachability of the narratives amongst the masses through the textual, oral and performative modes alike. The aspect of the visual, as we have noticed with reference to the Chihnayatra performance and the weaving of the *Brindavani Bastra*, was a crucial component of Sankardeva's missionary enterprise and contributed immensely towards the realisation of the multimedial experience that he sought to create and disseminate among the people. With reference to the *Chitra Bhagavata* manuscript recovered from the Bali Sattra, Neog notes that, "[t]he technique and finish of the work exhibit Rajput–Mughal influences, although here and there local conventions are naturally to be expected inasmuch as practices in Assam amounted to an independent school" (1986, 7). At the same time, he is careful not to posit the Assam style as an extension of the Mughal school; he, however, concedes that the influence of the Rajput–Mughal features did exist within the courtly style of paintings, by which he meant the Rajaghoria subset of the Assam school of painting. The *Chitra Bhagavata*, on the other hand, reflected the efforts of an artist who inherited the vision propagated by Sankardeva himself, thereby emphasising the centrality of Krishna and his divine agency vis-à-vis the artistic endeavour. At times, this is visually represented by magnifying the persona of Krishna over other characters drawn within a single folio of the manuscript. The following image may be taken as a case in point.

Source: Baruah 1951, 8

This is the scene where Krishna appears in his magnificent form before Vasudeva and Daivaki in the prison cell and informs them about his impending birth as their son. The corresponding lines in the Assamese *Bhagavata Purana* are:

> *kamala lochana chari bhuje chari ashtra/*
> *kanthat koustava shove gawe pita bastra//*
>
> The lotus-eyed [appeared] with his four arms adorned with the four insignias/
>
> The *koustava* gem is shining on the necklace around his neck, and so is the yellow garment on his body. (Translated by Dhurjjati Sarma)

The image of Krishna is drawn frontally as against those of Vasudeva and Daivaki, which are presented in profile. In this regard, Neog notes that, "The figures [in the *Chitra Bhagavata*] are mostly in profile. Sometimes the face part is profiled and silhouetted against the deep background while the body stands frontally" (1986, 7). Following this argument, it may be deduced that while the front-on vision of the characters enables the artists to capture the body in motion (whether in conversation, in combat, or in dance/performance), the face-in-profile helps in navigating the gaze of the onlooker across the length and breadth of the visual panel inscribed within the folio. It must also be remembered here that, upon the horizontal oblong folios, the artist draws a sequence of succeeding events from left to right thereby presenting a linear visual text for the onlookers. At times, the succeeding images on the horizontal panel also signify movement of characters indicated by changes in postures or hand/leg positions.

As a representative text of the Vaishnava order, the *Chitra Bhagavata* is also inscribed within the multimedial universe perpetuated by the crusaders of the mission, spearheaded by Sankardeva. The image below depicting a *gandharva* dance (in the Sattriya style) will provide a perspective in this direction:

Source: Baruah 1951, 68

Against the monochrome red background in the image above, the figures are drawn upon the *alekhya-sthana* in shades of various colours which capture them in a state of performance using musical instruments, namely, the *khol* and the cymbals, thereby expressing a shared semiotic field of dance, music and colour. The singularity of the human figures is emphasised by the arch patterns which seem to enclose them as if to fix our gaze upon their individual identities. The limited facial expressions of the figures are counterbalanced by highly meaningful use of *mudras* and *bhangimas*. As Neog notes, "[t]here is a rhythm in the scenes of musical and dance performances of Gandharvas, Vidyadharas and Apsaras. Attempts at symmetry are evident. Movements of groups are dynamically depicted" (1986, 8). These illustrations provide illuminating insights into the practice of representing the *lila* or the divine sport of Krishna—more specifically, his childhood acts in the case of the *Chitra Bhagavata*—through performance. The Sattriya dance form provided the most effective platform for the articulation of this divine–performative discourse, and as one could see in the modern context, it has broadened the scope and outreach of the said discourse from its original location within the *sattra* to the secular public sphere. Here, as Satyanath notes, "the text moves in to open space and anyone could be its audience, thereby further diversifying the public sphere" (2021, 70). This expansion into the public sphere is also characterised by the representation within the "text" of body-centric dimensions of the Vaishnava culture, as evident from the pictorial representation of the *gandharva* dance.

Complementary to the illustrations as seen in the manuscripts is the presence of paintings, motifs and reliefs depicting anecdotes and incidents from the *Bhagavata Purana* as well as from the massive vernacular corpus of Sankardeva and Madhavdeva inscribed upon the walls of the *sattra*s and *namghar*s, both being dynamic sites of religious and sociocultural interaction and activities among the Vaishnavite communities of Assam. Referring to the *Chitra Bhagavata* manuscript, Basil Gray attempts to contextualise the art-form vis-à-vis the earlier and contemporary schools of painting prevalent in eastern India. He observes that,

> [t]he heirs of the medieval Pala tradition were in Nepal and Assam, as is indicated anew by the recently published series of miniatures to an Assam MS. of *Bhagavata Purana*, dated 1539 A.D. These show the figures in silhouette, the faces always in profile, against a strong red ground, and beneath carved arches. They clearly look back to the Buddhist MSS. of the Pala period, which are organised in the same way with figures in architectural niches. (1953, 20)

This visual presentation of the narrative in a style and matter resembling the architectural patterns provides a seamless transition of the viewer's perspective from the "text" embedded within the manuscript to the one "seen" as depicted on the walls of a Buddhist or a Vaishnavite monastery. Here, what happens is that, as Satyanath notes, "in the absence of a verbal text, it is the viewer's mental text(s), through a dense intertextuality, that facilitates its mental reading, which is closer to Indian aesthetic experience, the *rasanubhava*" (2021, 71). At the same time, these sites also become emblematic of the pluralistic social epistemologies in place since concerns of caste, gender and even heredity and social status have also factored prominently in the continuation and sustenance of the sectarian ideology of Vaishnavism in Assam since the last five centuries or so. It may be noted in this regard that a great number of manuscripts continued to be preserved in the *sattra*s or in personal collection of the devotees. These manuscripts were zealously guarded by the custodians in both individual and collective capacities, and it required a lot of efforts on the part of early twentieth-century Assamese intellectuals engaged in the process of collecting and cataloguing old manuscripts to convince the owner(s) to part with their collections.[3]

The pluralistic epistemology of manuscript-painting in Assam should also be studied within a broader sphere of influence and reception, particularly in its relation with the Mughal and Rajput styles of painting. In this regard, it will be appropriate to consider another illustration from the *Chitra Bhagavata* manuscript.

---

[3] Hemchandra Goswami (1872–1928), a foremost literary historian and antiquarian investigator of modern Assam, undertook an extensive mission during 1912–1913 of collecting Assamese *puthi*s, most of which were almost or partially destroyed. During this period of searching for manuscripts across the state, Goswami visited the *sattra*s, *tol*s and families in the then districts of Goalpara, Kamrup, Nowgong, Sibsagar and Lakhimpur, and also Cooch Behar. Among the many significant manuscripts recovered from the Vaishnava monasteries was an illustrated treatise on elephants called the *Hastividyarnava*. From Barpeta, which was a seat of Vaishnavite learning during the sixteenth century and after, he managed to procure a great number of manuscripts which were translations of episodic *kavya*s from the Mahabharata and the Bhagavata.

Source: Baruah 1951, 119

The figures in the image above are cloud-gods who are instructed by Indra to let loose a torrential deluge upon the inhabitants of Brindavan. However, one's attention is immediately drawn towards the turban worn by and the facial features of the characters which betray a visible Rajput–Mughal influence. It may be noted in this regard that even though present-day Assam (particularly the Ahom kingdom) as a geopolitical unit was never part of the pan-Indian Mughal Empire, yet a series of Ahom–Mughal conflicts over a period of eighty years throughout the seventeenth century (AD 1615–82) provided an opportunity for artists, poets and musicians, mostly belonging to the various Sufi orders, as well as merchants and traders, from the Mughal heartland to migrate into the Ahom and the adjoining kingdoms. Kalita notes (2014, 25–26) that the headdress depicted above was referred to as the *mughlai-pag* or even *aurangzeb-topi* based on the historical fact that Aurangzeb had presented a *churpao-pag*[4] to the Ahom monarch Chakradhwaj Singha (r. AD 1663–70). He further observes that the headdress worn by performers during an *ankiya bhaona* is a simplified form of the *mughlai-pag* (ibid., 26), thereby hinting towards the popularity of the Mughal-style head-dress as a cultural symbol in seventeenth-century Assam. Interestingly, at another place in the manuscript, the cloud-gods are also shown wearing a *jama* with a *mughlai-pag*, thus emphasising further upon the

[4] *Churpao-pag* is the corrupted form of the word *sarpech-pag* originally used to refer to the turban with a jewel or an ornament fixed at the front, which was popular within the Mughal court.

growing influence of the "Persian cosmopolis" (a term popularised by Richard Eaton) upon the artistic and cultural worldviews of the artists engaged in manuscript-illustration within the cloistered confines of the Vaishnavite *sattras*.

The *Chitra Bhagavata* thus signifies an important milestone in the history of illustrated manuscripts in early modern Assam. In the absence of any early history of painting within the Assam school during the period anterior to the sixteenth century, the *Chitra Bhagavata* provides a veritable window to the tradition of manuscript-painting as it could possibly have existed in the preceding centuries. At the same time, it also captures a moment of flux within the devotional–cultural history of seventeenth-century Assam that witnessed a significant turn towards accommodating a more secular sensibility in the areas of art and literature. This transition was further boosted by the gradual adoption of Hinduism by the Ahom kings in the seventeenth century. With Jayadhvaj Singha (r. AD 1648–63) becoming the first Ahom king to formally adopt Hinduism, the "hinduisation" of the Ahoms became a significant factor in the increasingly mediatory role played by the kings in the monastic–missionary enterprise of neo-Vaishnavism. As noted by Kalita, the reign of Rudra Singha was marked by a cordial relationship between the Vaishnavite *sattras* and the royal house (2014, 33).[5] In addition to embracing

[5] The years during the lifetime of Sankardeva (AD 1449–1568), particularly the first few decades of the sixteenth century (1516 to 1543), were rife with tension and prolonged hostility between the proponents of the neo-Vaishnavite movement, which was on the rise, and the brahmins, whose ritual authority the movement allegedly purported to challenge and subvert. The brahmins solicited the mediation of the Ahom kings, and, as a result, Sankardeva and his followers were constantly on the move in their efforts to escape being persecuted by the Ahom kings. Sankardeva ultimately fled westward and was granted a safe haven under the Koch king Naranarayana, in whose court he spent the remaining years of his life from 1543 to 1568 in relative peace and security. These latter years constituted a productive period on the part of Sankardeva in his mission to construct a substantial corpus of Vaishnava literature in the vernacular, including extensive translations

pan-Indian influences, as already noted, the king was also attentive towards expanding the horizons of Vaishnava art and literature in the post-Sankardeva period. The Assamese *Gita-Govinda*, as we shall see, is the product of this coming together of the Sattriya and Rajaghoria styles towards the close of the seventeenth century under the patronage of Rudra Singha. In this connection, Neog notes that, "[a] new and secular branch of the art of painting thus seems to have been established in Eastern Assam under the Ahoms," while, at the same time, stating that, "there was no hiatus between the religious (Sattriya) branch of painting and the Court (secular) branch" (1986, 10). One can argue that one style seamlessly merged with the other, minor variation notwithstanding, to present a holistic vision and perspective on the Assam school of painting that developed as a joint enterprise between the *sattras* and the Ahom court.

The Assamese *Gita-Govinda* manuscript was recovered by Hemchandra Goswami from a person named Dhareswar Barua in 1912 and was deposited by him in the library of the Kamarupa Anusandhana Samiti (Assam Research Society) in Guwahati, Assam. The composer of the poem, Ramanarayana Kaviraja Chakravarti, is often regarded as a major representative poet of the post-Sankardeva Assamese literary culture. It may be noted that he follows the Rasikapriya commentary of king Kumbha for his interpretation of the Sanskrit verses composed by Jayadeva. The versification is carried out in the prevalent *payara* and *tripadi* metrical styles of the Assamese Vaishnava poetry of the sixteenth and seventeenth centuries. In this regard, the composition of *Gita-Govinda* in Assamese, with its erotic mysticism, signified a remarkable departure from the earlier philosophy of poetry practised and propagated by Sankardeva and his disciple Madhavdeva, which advocated total abstention from longing and

---

from the *Bhagavata Purana*, composition of the "Uttara Kanda" of Madhav Kandali's *Sat Kanda Ramayana*, composition of *bargeet* and *Bhakti Ratnakar* (a treatise on Bhakti), and five *ankiya bhaonas*, namely, *Kaliya Damana*, *Keli Gopala*, *Rukmini Harana*, *Parijata Harana* and *Rama Bijaya*.

desire as the means to attain liberation from worldly ambitions. Neog provides an interesting twist to the discussion when he observes that, "the erotic ring is very much characteristic of this period of Assamese poetry [in the late seventeenth and early eighteenth century]; and that is perhaps why the *Gita-Govinda* tradition found a niche in Assamese literature of the day" (1986, 2). A possible reason behind the efflorescence of this sensibility could be increasing proximity of the Ahom kings, particularly Rudra Singha and his immediate successor Siva Singha to the literary cultures of Bengal and Mughal India. It was during the reign of Siva Singha and his first queen Pramatheswari Devi that, in 1714, Ananta Acharya produced the illustrated manuscript of *Ananda Lahari*, which is a Sakta-Tantric text, and reflected the king's interest in the subject. About twenty years later, the same king commissioned the composition of *Hastividyarnava*, as has already been noted above.

Apart from its more secular treatment of the sentiment of love in terms of visible attributes, the significance of a work like the *Gita-Govinda* also derives from its engagement with various *raga*s and *tala*s employed in order to render the verses into music. The Assamese *Gita-Govinda* manuscript has two parts: the first part contains Ramanarayana Kaviraja Chakravarti's selective translations from the *prabandha*s and *ashtapadi*s from the original Sanskrit text of Jayadeva, whereas the second part provides the *ashtapadi*s in original Sanskrit (in the Assamese script though) in a way that the text actually becomes a kind of "song book" with the *raga*s being mentioned at the beginning of every folio. In both the parts, the text is generally inserted as a horizontal panel on the upper part of the folio; however, there are occasions when portions of the text are presented as columns thereby dividing the illustrations into multiple blocks within the folio. While some folios have textual matter predominating; a few others have part of the illustrations touching the upper margins of the folio thereby segregating the text presented into distinct chunks. Two representative folios are presented below for reference:

Source: Vatsyayan and Neog 1986, 223

The folio depicts the three *avatara*s or incarnations of Vishnu, namely, the Varaha, the Narasimha and the Vamana *avatara*s. Each of them is represented in three horizontal blocks with distinctive arches signifying their individual attributes posited against the monochrome red background.

Source: Vatsyayan and Neog 1986, 227

This images in this folio depict Krishna in his three different manifestations. In the first one from the left, he is seen dancing with the *gopi*s; the next image however shows him as the four-armed god; and the third image brings him back to his human form, as the cowherd-boy milking the cow. The enormity and significance of the central image is suggested by an arch in the form of clouds occupying the whole vertical part of the folio. Unlike the folio above, the images here are not segregated by blocks; the divine image of Krishna in the middle provides the necessary perspective to the viewers.

With respect to the *raga*s, Neog notes that, "[s]ome of the names of the astapadi ragas [presented in the second part of the manuscript] are vernacularised even along the Sanskrit text of the manuscript" (1986, 185). Examples include *gunjari* for *gurjari*, *gondagiri* for *gondakri*, and *ramagiri* for *ramakri*. Within the neo-Vaishnavite movement under the leadership of Sankardeva and Madhavdeva in fifteenth–sixteenth-century Assam, the *bargeet* became the most popular genre of devotional music in Assam.[6] As noted by Neog and Chankakati (2008, 5–6), "[the] bargit and ankiya git may be classed together as representing the classical mode of Assam's Vaishnava music. Each of the songs of these varieties is connected with some *raga*, the word *ragini* being nowhere applied". He further argues that the Vaishnava music of Assam shares certain elements with the *dhrupada* (Indian classical music) style, for instance, in the division into *anibaddha* and *nibaddha* as well as in the indication of specific *raga*s and *tala*s with the songs. However, it also had its own style of performance accompanied by its own set of *raga*s which marks its distinctiveness from both the Hindustani and Carnatic schools of music (ibid., 7, 16). A few representative *raga*s used by both Sankardeva and Madhavdeva are namely, *ahira*, *asowari*, *gauri*, *dhanashri*, *varari*, *vasanta*, *belowara*, *bhatiyali*, *lalita*, *syama*, *sindhura* and *suhai* (ibid., 18–19). The *raga*s of *bargeet* are also attached with certain *tala*s or rhythms like the *ekatala*, *paritala*, *yati*, *kharman* and *manchok*. These *geet*s are then performed with the accompaniment of musical instruments consisting mainly of the *khol* (a large barrel-shaped drum) and cymbals, though *kali* (a kind of pipe instrument) and *nagara* have also been used at some places (Neog and Chankakati 2008, 22, 42; Richmond 1974, 157). Placed within this context, the Assamese *Gita-Govinda* carried forth this musical tradition into the eighteenth century, albeit

---

6 There was an unbroken continuity of several musical genres within Assamese and its adjoining literary cultures from about the eighth till the sixteenth century and continuing till the present time. Most of these genres (with the exception of the *bargeet*) straddled across multiple sectarian traditions, as evident in the case of the *charyapada*s (Tantricism and Buddhism), *dehabicharar geet* (Tantricism, Buddhism, and Vaishnavism), and also the *oja-pali* songs (Saktaism and Vaishnavism). However, we must keep in mind that these sectarian traditions often had overlapping areas of operation and interaction across the larger cultural geography of eastern India specifically during the first half of the second millennium CE.

with changes in terms of subject matter, the presence of Radha, and the dominant sentiment of the poem being *shringara bhava*. The following folio may be seen as an example of the observations noted above:

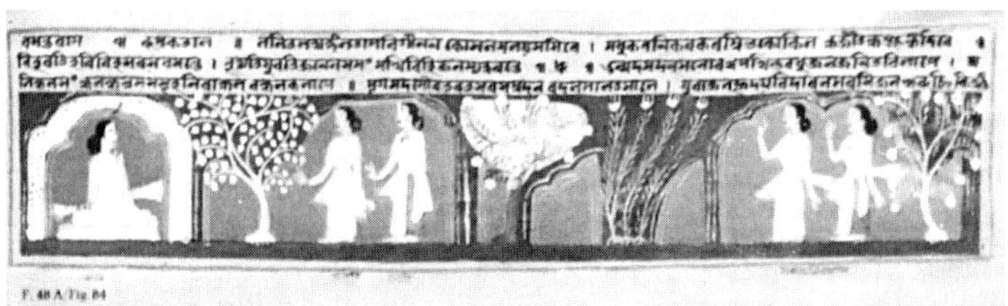

Source: Vatsyayan and Neog 1986, 263

In this folio, the *raga* mentioned is *vasanta* and the *tala* used is *rupaka*. The folio is divided into four horizontal sections; the first shows Radha sitting within an enclosed arch, possibly suggesting her state of *viraha*. The second and fourth sections depict two of her *sakhis*; in both cases, they are displaying *hasta mudras*, and the changed positions of their hands between the second and fourth sections could possibly also imply the continuity of the dance movements. The overall ambience depicted within the folio signifies the arrival of *basanta* (spring) with the trees in full blossom. Also, against the monotonous red monochrome background, the colours of the trees in varying shades of green and white amply illustrate the mood indicated in the text presented in the horizontal panel above the images. With the dynamics of textual poetics qualified by the suggestion of the particular *raga* and *tala*, the element of performativity expressed through the presentation of the series of images together evoke a multimedial experience on the part of the reader/viewer. Furthermore, while preserving the artistic conventions of the Vaishnava culture, the infusion of *shringara bhava* into the semiotic universe of the illustrations diversifies the process of *rasanubhuti* (or the experience of *rasa*) beyond the *bhakti rasa*.

It would be worthwhile at this point to refer to the processes of manuscript-preparation and inscription (both written and illustrated) as vital components of social epistemology within the Vaishnava literary culture of early modern Assam. The manuscripts were prepared from basically two kinds of materials, namely, the *sanchipat*, that is, bark of the *sanchi* tree (aquilaria agallocha) and *tulapat* (made by pressing cotton); even though *talapat* (palm leaves) and *muga* cloth were also used on rare occasions (Nath 2016, 215). It may be appropriate to note here that the *Chitra Bhagavata* was preserved in the Bali Sattra of Nagaon in the form of a *tulapat* manuscript; whereas the *Gita-Govinda* was discovered by Hemchandra Goswami as a *sanchipat* manuscript. The *mahi* or ink was prepared from *silikha* (terminalia citrina), cow-urine, *amlaka* extracts (phylanthus amblica) and soot. The colours applied on the manuscripts, particularly for the illustrations, were primarily *hengula* (*hingula*; vermilion; mercury sulphide), *haitala* (*haritala*; yellow orpiment; arsenic sulphide), *mohi* (bluish green ink), *kajal* (carbon black), and *nila* (indigo) along with a host of other materials, including various colours of *mati* (clay). It may be noted that the application of *hengula* and *haitala* extended beyond the manuscripts to be also used in adding colour to the masks (used in performances like the *ankiya bhaonas*), artefacts of cane, bamboo, terracotta, and also handicrafts (Dutta 2016, 253). Instead of opting for herbal pigments, the use of colours extracted from minerals, which had antifungal properties, aided in extending the longevity of the *sanchipat* manuscripts for centuries (ibid., 255–56).

Implications and Conclusion

A study on the aspects of multimediality conceptualised and practiced within the Vaishnava literary culture of early modern Assam brings forth revealing insights on the symbiotic interplay between the oral, textual, performative and visual dimensions—all integrated to present a cohesive aesthetic–religious experience to the *bhakta*s and the *rasika*s alike. The present study has endeavoured to locate and map a transitional process whereby the artistic and literary experience traditionally embedded within the Vaishnava culture gradually moved out of the monastic confines and commingled with a more secular vision of creating art and literature under the patronage of a royal authority. The *Chitra Bhagavata* stands on the threshold of this transition, to be followed by the *Gita-Govinda* where one can locate a happy blending of the monastic and royal styles. The *Hastividyarnava*, a text which is outside the scope of the present study, signifies a higher degree of artistic elegance and craftmanship, and a more direct and visible involvement of the Mughal court in its execution. The period following the death of Sankardeva in 1568 witnessed visible schisms within the sectarian structure of the Vaishnava devotional order, and such a situation consequently led to the weakening of its ideological–religious hold upon the collective sensibility of the people. However, at the same time, the blossoming of cordial relationship between the *sattra*s and the Ahom royalty was a positive step towards the secularisation of the artistic endeavour, as evident in the works discussed in this study. A multimedial approach towards the study of *Chitra Bhagavata* and *Gita-Govinda* thus opens up exciting possibilities in the study of "comparative arts" with a more sustained focus on the twin aspects of influence and reception as regulating the interaction between the visual and verbal domains of expression. Furthermore, one also needs to pay attention to the aspect of social epistemology and its close interface with the areas of traditional knowledge systems involving multidisciplinary discourses relevant to the culture and society in question.

Works Cited

"The Assam School of Painting." *A Tribute to Sankaradeva*, https://www.atributetosankaradeva.org/manuscript_painting.htm. Accessed on 12 July 2024.

"The *Harsha-carita* of Bana, Chapter VII." *Project South Asia*, 24 March 2022, http://www.columbia.edu/itc/mealac/pritchett/00litlinks/harshacharita/chapter07.htm. Accessed on 26 August 2024.

Bal, Mieke. 1988. "Introduction: Visual Poetics." *Style* 22 (2): 177–82. Penn State University Press. http://www.jstor.org/stable/42945703. Accessed on 26 August 2024.

Baruah, Harinarayan Dutta, ed. 1951. *Chitra Bhagavata*. Guwahati: Dutta Baruah Publishing Co Pvt Ltd.

Bora, Mridu Moucham. "Manuscript Painting of Assam: In Conversation with Mridu Moucham Bora," interview by Meghna Baruah, *Sahapedia*, 04 July 2018, https://www.sahapedia.org/manuscript-painting-of-assam-conversation-mridu-moucham-bora. Accessed on 26 August 2024.

Dutta, Robin Kumar. 2016. "The Science in the Traditional Manuscript-Writing Aids of Assam: *Sancipat*, *Mahi* and *Hengul-Haital*." In *Religious Tradition and Social Practices in Assam: Essays on Popular Religion, Buddhist Tradition and Writing Culture*, edited by D. Nath, 239–62. Guwahati: DVS Publishers.

Gray, Basil. 1953 (June). "The Development of Painting in India in the 16th Century." *Marg* 6 (3): 19–24.

Kalita, Naren. 2014. *Asamar Puthichitra*. Guwahati: Publication Board Assam.

Kattenbelt, C. 2008. "Intermediality in Theatre and Performance: Definitions, Perceptions and Medial Relationships." *Culture, Language and Representation* 4: 19–29.

Nath, D. 2016. "Pre-Modern Writing Culture in Assam: The Tradition of Manuscript Writing." In *Religious Tradition and Social Practices in Assam: Essays on Popular Religion, Buddhist Tradition and Writing Culture*, edited by D. Nath, 207–38. Guwahati: DVS Publishers.

Neog, Maheswar. 1986. "Introduction A." *Gita-Govinda in the Assam School of Painting*, edited by Kapila Vatsyayan and Maheswar Neog, 1–14. Guwahati: Publication Board Assam.

Neog, Maheswar, and Keshav Chankakati. 2008. *Rhythm in the Vaishnava Music of Assam*. Guwahati: Publication Board Assam.

Pitambara Kavi. 1955. *Usha-Parinaya*, edited by Maheswar Neog. Guwahati: Lawyer's Book Stall.

Richmond, Farley. 1974. "The Vaiṣṇava Drama of Assam." *Educational Theatre Journal* 26 (2): 145–163. *JSTOR*, www.jstor.org/stable/3206631. Accessed on 4 July 2024.

Satyanath, T. S. 2020. "Mapping Transmediality in Medieval Indian Writing Culture: Formalistic and Social Epistemologies." In *Indian Multilingualism and Language Behaviour: A Festschrift for Prof. H.M. Maheshwaraiah*, edited by L. Manjulakshi and M. Mahendra, 72–84. Dharwad: Neelaparvat Prakashana.

———. 2021. "Towards Comparing Indian Writing Culture." In *From 'Vishwa' to 'Bharatiya': New Essays on Comparative Indian Literature*, edited by Dilip Borah, 62–82. Guwahati: DVS Publishers.

Sharma, Mukunda Madhava. 1978. *Inscriptions of Ancient Assam*. Guwahati: Department of Publication, Gauhati University.

Vatsyayan, Kapila. 1986. "Introduction B." In *Gita-Govinda in the Assam School of Painting*, edited by Kapila Vatsyayan and Maheswar Neog, 15–19. Guwahati: Publication Board Assam.

Vatsyayan, Kapila, and Maheswar Neog, eds. 1986. *Gita-Govinda in the Assam School of Painting*. Guwahati: Publication Board Assam.

ELEVEN

The Social Imaginary and the Evolution of Modern Indian Literature

P. P. RAVEENDRAN

There are two broad ways of looking at the evolution of Indian literature in the twentieth century, ways that a critical reader might take in mapping its recent history.[1] One of these is to regard the specific traditions of writing in particular languages as molded essentially by the hegemonic culture in the language and see how the discourse of literature, in turn, provides a context for analysing the changes in sensibility that are assumed to have shaped the dominant forms of literary expression. Twentieth-century Indian literature, in this view, goes through a history of sensibility shifts in which the successive attitudes of the progressive–nationalist, the modernist and the post-modernist have acted as pivots in the development of the dominant literary culture, formed by and large under global and colonial cultural influences. Such a reading would provide a kind of "extrinsic" literary history, where literature is defined in terms of its ability to represent the issues of the time that are deemed important by the more articulate segments of the community, who hold tremendous symbolic capital and wield enormous symbolic power in the society. In the context of a sensibility that in effect captures a community's structures of feeling as framed by the dreams and desires of its more powerful segments, these readings are partisan and sectarian. Writers here act, to paraphrase a well-known maxim, as the antennae of the race,

[1] "Indian literature" here is convenient shorthand for referring to the Indian language literatures, sometimes described as bhasha literatures, which by their very nature are pluralistic and multiform.

where the term "race" does not represent the heterogeneity of the community, but merely its most dominant segment, producing a "rational" site which excludes from the realm of artistic experience the aspirations of large sections of the society.

There is a second and equally important position that one might take in looking at the question of the sensibility shifts in Indian literature and in evaluating the relative significance of the progressive, modernist and post-modernist—and whatever other trends the critic might deem important in evaluating a given field of cultural production—elements in its evolution. This is to consider literature as a relatively autonomous discourse, immanent and this-worldly inasmuch as it is wedded to the language's inbuilt creative, unconscious and "irrational" realms, which do not validate the semantic distinctions and ideological contents that inform the counters dispensing the "nationalist", "modernist" and "post-modernist" fare in their vintage forms. The discourse of literature can arguably be realist, progressive, nationalist, modernist, post-modernist, and whatever else the resourceful critic might suggest it to be, all at the same time. As a consequence, the sensibility shifts implied by the first interpretation do not make sense in considerations of literature as an expression of the dreams, desires and pains of a community that is heterogeneous, pluralistic and polyphonic. This view recognises literary imagination as a dynamic and open-ended force that shapes individual and collective identities through practices and symbolic representations. Literature in this view is a manifestation of the social imaginary,[2] which exercises its power through its discursive autonomy and its status as the language geared to the society's progressive potential. The position in some sense overlaps

[2] In talking about the "social imaginary", I am certainly aware of the complex network of ideas that the concept invokes in the writings of theorists such as Cornelius Castoriadis and Charles Taylor, but I am using the term here with the inflection that it will receive when placed in the conceptual world of Pierre Bourdieu, especially where he theorises a "field of literary production" that works in tandem with a particular "habitus".

with Seamus Heaney's argument regarding a poetic tongue that is self-governed, but would not corroborate his somewhat non-political stance (Heaney 1988, 92–93). Writers here indeed are the "antennae" of the race, as Heaney affirms quoting the Polish poet Anna Swir, but the manner in which these antennae capture the race's profile is considerably different from how it has been conceived in the first interpretation.[3]

The present paper, which is essentially about India's literary history of the modern period, purports to map the geography of the Malayalam poetry of the past century as a prototype of the history of modern Indian poetry and examine how the two positions detailed above intervene in its construction and delineation. While the first position is what usually passes for standard literary history in most Indian languages, the second position exists in a buried form, as nothing more than a footnote to most histories, which can be unearthed only by a close critical and symptomatic reading of these narratives. It is also to be remembered here that the two positions are not mutually exclusive and that in real situations, in considerations especially of the larger Indian reality, they sometimes overlap with and inter-penetrate each other. This is why critics often speak of "phase-lags" and "time-lags" between languages and sensibilities, which, as literary historians note, make it difficult for one to visualise a uniform history of Indian poetry with successive phases across linguistic boundaries

[3] The statement was originally made by Ezra Pound who proclaimed in his study of modern French poetry titled *Instigations*: "Poets are the antennae of the race, but the bullet-headed many will never learn this" (1920, 109). Compare this with Anna Swir's statement, which Heaney quotes: "A poet becomes then the antenna capturing the voices of the world, a medium expressing his own subconscious and the collective subconscious. For one moment he possesses wealth usually inaccessible to him, and he loses it when that moment is over" (Heaney 1988, 93). Certainly, Pound's original interpretation is double-edged and can, even as it promotes literature's polyphonic impact on the world, act as an expression of open and elite contempt for the material world and the general public, as is illustrated by second part of his statement.

(Das 1995, 180). As is well-known, Indian languages demonstrate vast heterogeneities in terms of poetic trends, forms and structures of response in the modern period, so that it becomes practically impossible to talk about a common course of poetic evolution with common phases of development. However, historians of Indian poetry also point out that poetry in all Indian languages, irrespective of their phases of development, slowly converge in the period of modernity on a single object which, according to Sisir Kumar Das, constitutes the "inspiration", "imitation" and "appropriation" of elements from Western poetry, especially from modern English poetry, for its onward journey (Das 1995, 180, 185). It is this context of reception and appropriation that becomes the breeding ground for the first perspective, and in fact it is as part of this appropriation that the forces described as progressive, modernist and post-modernist gain significance in the evolution of Indian poetry.[4]

"Progressive" here is to be read as an Indian variant of the romantic phase in the history of Western poetry. One need only take a close look at the theories of romanticism to see the connection between the romantic and the progressive.[5] The best description of romanticism I have seen in recent times has been given by Duncan Wu who, in his introduction to a revised edition of his closely researched work *Romanticism: An Anthology*, provides the following definition for it: "The unquenchable aspiration for universal betterment, the reclaiming of paradise" (Wu 1998, xxxv). This of course is a statement on literature's "progressive" function, upheld by radical writers of all languages. Most Indian

---

4 I am not going into the larger domain of international literary history in which the history of modern Western poetry is presented as getting unfolded through the successive phases of romanticism, modernism and post-modernism, or related variants of these. There are a number of literary historical accounts that deal with this question. As examples, see Gregson (1996), Nicholls (1995), North (1994) and Wain (1972).

5 Critiques of theories of romanticism are legion. See Day (1996) for an introductory and comprehensive account.

progressive writers of the 1930s and later, whether part of the Progressive Writers Association or not, were essentially romantic in temperament and were deeply influenced by Western romantic writers of diverse hues. Though romanticism in its avatar as the revival and idolisation of the past and the primitive could be treated as anti-progressive, the sense in which the progressives could draw inspiration from the romantic visualisations of an improved and egalitarian world has remained undiminished. Philologically and historically, both the "progressive" and the "romantic", moreover, partook of the same environment of political and philosophical debate and both acquired their present associations and shades of meaning as part of this debate in the early nineteenth century. The complex history of the word "progressive", as scholars like Raymond Williams have pointed out, should be understood in the context of the new senses that words like "civilisation" and "history"—and "romantic" as well, apparently—acquired in the late eighteenth and early nineteenth centuries. Though the word "progress" has always been associated with a journey or a movement, as is indicated by the title of Bunyan's *Pilgrim's Progress* (1678), for example, it acquired its sense of an improved moment, the sense of a change from a somewhat uneasy state of affairs to one that could be deemed better, in the eighteenth century, when it was reduced to an impersonal, historical concept. Williams recognises this when he notes: "It was the abstraction of this movement as a discoverable historical pattern that produced progress as a general idea" (1976, 206). The shift in meaning is also bound up with its re-incarnation as a term of political description, where its dynamism is opposed to the idea of a stable condition associated with conservatism. The parallel development of romanticism as a dynamic principle opposed to the more stable and stabilising notion of classicism comes about as part of this. Current critical scholarship defines romanticism as a composite term that embodies within itself a range of sliding meanings, some of which are in contradiction to the others. The progressive, the visionary, the imaginative, the liberal, the secular, the reformist and the nationalistic, though not mutually exclusive, are recognised world-wide as aspects of the romantic mind, appearing in theories of romanticism as universally relevant principles. Inasmuch as romanticism itself is the crystallisation in the subjective world of the more generalised condition of modernity, some theorists would also like to present it as a precursor to literary modernism as well.[6]

To go back to the first of the two competing interpretations of poetic history, the conclusion becomes inevitable in the context of the above discussion that all modern poetry written in Indian languages, that is, all Indian poetry written in the period of modernity, cannot but follow the historical paths delineated for Western poetry, whose inspiration becomes crucial for the evolution of Indian literary history. Sisir Kumar Das's account of the progress of Indian literature up to the mid-1950s articulates this position in a fairly elegant fashion:

> There are at least two distinct phases of transition in Indian poetry from its traditional moorings to its culmination in 'modern'. The first stage has been identified by the literary historians of different languages as 'romantic' and the second stage as 'nationalistic'. The former represented a particular attitude to nature and society, to man and God, and is to a great extent comparable to the romantic temper of the European poetry which inspired it. The nationalistic phase coincides with the Indian political movement: its tone is essentially patriotic, occasionally revolutionary, and quite often didactic. Both phases however coalesced in most of the languages and [were] quite often indistinguishable. (Das 1995, 183)

To be fair to Das, it should be mentioned here that he is merely compiling information gathered from individual languages

---

6 There is a sense in which Edgar Allan Poe, Charles Baudelaire, Arthur Rimbaud, Walter Pater, Paul Valery and W. B. Yeats can all be seen as rendering irrelevant the popular distinction between the romantic and the modernist sensibilities. Comparable poets from the Indian context would be Tagore in Bengali, Bendre in Kannada and R. Ramachandran in Malayalam. For an elaboration of this position with respect to European literature, see Bayley (1957); Kermode (1957).

and that the analysis does not in the strict sense represent his own theoretical position on the nature of Indian poetry or its evolution in the modern period. Having no prior model of a multilingual and multi-literary history before him, he obviously had to depend entirely on the interpretive inputs received from individual language histories. In his Preface to the volume, he has made a reference to this practical difficulty (see Das 1995, xv for details).

What all this implies, in sum, is that most Indian languages imagine their literary histories as going through the successive phases of the romantic, the modernist and the post-modernist. Most literary histories too talk about two major sensibility shifts taking place in the twentieth century in all Indian languages, first, in and around the 1950s, which has been hailed as marking the emergence of poetic modernism, and then again after the 1970s, which has been described variously as post-modernism, retro-modernism, counter-modernism, and so on. The phase prior to modernism in most Indian literatures is generally characterised as a period of lyrical imagination, spontaneous passion, nationalistic fervour, and progressive attitudes to life, all qualities identified with European romanticism. The historical accounts of Indian modernism would like to see the poets appearing on the scene after the period of romanticism and progressivism as fighting a battle against a bygone tradition in the name of the living ethos of the present. The modernists are shown to be the initiators of a new culture of revolt against the obsolete literary forms and practices associated with the romantics and the progressives. This is a standard narrative about the development of modernism routinely reiterated in language after language, in Hindi, in Bengali, in Kannada, in Marathi, in Urdu, and other languages. To give just one example of such a narrative from Telugu, look at the way in which poet Sri Sri, a radical exponent of new poetry in that language, is represented in one of these accounts: "As a romantic he revolted against the classical tradition; as a progressive, he revolted against the romantic school [and] as a revolutionary he revolted against the 'progressive' establishment" (Anjaneyulu 2014, 472).

The role of imagination in the construction of collective identities—which was described above as the social imaginary—is often elided in these narratives. As a result, one feels compelled to revisit the earlier phases of literary history to gauge the extent of social imagining and experience that was left uncharted by official literary sensibilities. This is also the reason why after the end of modernism in the late 1970s, most Indian literary histories started talking about a massive upsurge of counter-modernist tendencies—some of them covered by the expression "post-modernism"—from the 1980s, which led to an unprecedented assertion of new voices and subjectivities that were linked to the poet's somewhat self-conscious concerns about such issues as globalisation, environmental depredation and the sense of social marginalisation in terms of caste, gender and ethnicity.

This, needless to say, is the kind of narrative fostered by the first perspective. And Malayalam to be sure has kept pace with the developments outlined in this narrative. Almost all literary histories in Malayalam, from the earliest to the most recent, are inclined to adopt the story of modern Malayalam literature's evolution and growth in terms of sensibility shifts represented in this narrative.[7] The stage for this perhaps was set in some of

---

[7] This has invariably been the case with literary histories published before 1980, such as that of Ulloor (Iyer 1953), but even histories from the period after 1980 have continued to use this classification. Look, for example, at the histories of poetry in M. Leelavathy's *Malayala Kavita Sahitya Charitram* (A History of Malayalam Poetry, 1980) and D. Benjamin's history of modern Malayalam poetry (Section 1 'Kavita' in George 1998, 1–88). Chapters 12, 13 and 14 of Leelavathy's history are devoted to romanticism in Malayalam poetry. She talks about the "romantic age" in chapter 12, which is titled "Kalpanika Yugam", and follows it up with discussions of major romantics in the subsequent chapters. Chapter 15 of her history is devoted to the modernists. Benjamin's history has two chapters on romanticism, one (chapter 2) devoted to the poetic trinity of Asan, Ulloor and Vallathol and the other (chapter 3, titled "Kalpanikatayude Vikasam") devoted to the subsequent developments in romantic poetry. Benjamin's chapter 6, titled "Naveena Kavita", is devoted to modernism. Both historians agree on romanticism being upstaged by modernism in the later period. There is a

the early literary histories written in the colonial period itself. The intervention of the social imaginary does not seem to be a matter of concern for any one of these histories. All of them are vocal articulators of the first perspective, though closer scrutiny would reveal some of them to be concealing a coded subtext that can be decoded to disclose meanings that are closer to the second perspective. Look, for example, at this early twentieth-century work, the second literary history in Malayalam, titled *Malayala Sahitya Charitra Samgraham* (A Short History of Malayalam Literature), written in 1922 by P. Sankaran Nambiar (1892–1954), a very perceptive literary historian and a competent scholar, one of the most rigorous critics of his generation. In the Preface (written originally in English) to the first edition of his history, Nambiar states, echoing the words of Matthew Arnold on high culture, that his book embodies "in a nutshell the best that has been thought and said in the much-neglected mother-tongue of my native land" (Nambiar 2001, 8). He is more open about his affinities to the method of writing adopted by English literary historians of the time when he states: "As regards the plan of my work, it is almost the same as is generally adopted by renowned writers of English literary history" (ibid., 8–9). The principal account of this literary history reiterates much of what has been canonised by P. Govinda Pillai (1849–97), the first literary historian in Malayalam, the shortcomings of whose analysis in terms of chronological arrangement and historical accuracy are sought to be corrected by Nambiar in his narrative.[8] Nambiar does not seem to be worried about the canonical approach of Govinda Pillai, but

---

more recent history of poetry in Panmana Ramachandran Nair's self-styled *Sampoorna Malayala Sahitya Charitram* (A Complete History of Malayalam Literature, 2008). Chapters 2 and 3 in Part 5 (Nair 2008, 731–87) of this history are devoted to romanticism and modernism respectively. Chapter 2 is by K.P. Sankaran (731–68) and chapter 3 by P. Soman (769–87).

[8] I have discussed the shortcomings of this history in some detail in the chapter titled "Literary Historiography in Malayalam" in Raveendran (2009, 62–73).

is concerned only with the "correctness" and "accuracy" of the material that has gone into his predecessor's literary history. His history does not claim the advantage that it can rightfully claim over the earlier history that comes from Nambiar's considerable and more sophisticated interpretive skills. In the Preface, Nambiar is modest in talking about the superiority of his work over that of Pillai: "If I have in any way been more correct and precise than Mr. Govinda Pillai of revered memory, it is because I have been able to take advantage of the years of research that have elapsed between him and me" (ibid., 8). The years of research however do not embolden him to make detailed comments on the writers of his own day, as is indicated by his history that comes to an end with a detailed consideration of Keralavarma Valiyakoyi Thampuran (1845–1914), a scholar poet of the late nineteenth century with classicist tastes. Chandu Menon (1847–99) and C.V. Raman Pillai (1858–1922), both pioneering novelists of the nineteenth century, are only sweepingly mentioned. Potheri Kunhambu (1857–1919), the author of *Saraswati Vijayam*, today regarded as a founding text of the Dalit narrative consciousness in Malayalam, is not mentioned at all. Kumaran Asan (1873–1924) or the other poets of the early twentieth century, often described as the harbingers of romanticism in modern Malayalam poetry, do not figure in the main narrative of this history.

What has been outlined above is an illustration of the first perspective as it is embodied and textualised in a specimen history of Malayalam literature of the colonial period that witnessed the institution of the protocols of literary historiography in the language. True to the presuppositions associated with the first perspective, Nambiar's history views literature as a symbolic institution constituted by the best of what has been thought and done in the language. There is a focus on the past which is supposed to grant glory and canonical honour to literary works. That literature could be a living practice in the present or that it could be a representation of the everyday or that it could be an expression of the social imaginary that would help the reading community to construct an identity for its members is seldom recognised by this history. This conspicuous disdain for the present is what prompts the historian to leave out of account living writers, including Asan, who by 1922, the year of publication of Nambiar's history, had emerged as a major and radical voice in twentieth-century Malayalam poetry. But the present is not totally banished from the unconscious of the book's textual narrative. It appears in the concluding chapter of Nambiar's book as a coda, so to say, where the author talks, in an obvious reference to Asan and other younger writers of his time, about the radical changes that the Malayalam poetic scene has been witnessing over the decade preceding the publication of his book, and this constitutes a virtual subtext that in effect negates the canonical perspective sought to be upheld in the larger part of the history:

> But now, over the past ten years or so, Malayalam poetry is seen to go through a process of reform. Conventions regarding subject matter, style, language, metrical pattern, the manner of treating the subject and the rhyme scheme are no longer held sacrosanct. The writers of today flout these conventions with the purpose apparently of liberating the poet from the shackles of tradition and making poetry more natural. Here, they also seem to triumph in securing their purpose. The changes that are happening to Malayalam literature today are comparable to the kind of transformations that happened to English literature in the early nineteenth century. This is aided and abetted by the new culture of English education and the writers' increasing familiarity with English literature. (Nambiar 2001, 134)[9]

Though Nambiar does not specifically name the emergent radical writers of his own time, it is clear that he has the British romantics in mind when he talks about the writers' perceived affinities with the poets of the nineteenth century. His history was perhaps too close in time to the period of Asan, but he lived long enough—Nambiar died in 1954—to see the rudimentary sensibility change that he had anticipated in *Malayala Sahitya Charitra Samgraham*, almost in spite of himself, flourish into

---

[9] Translations from Malayalam, here and hereinafter, unless otherwise stated, are by the present writer.

a major literary "movement" in the subsequent years. He does indeed make a note of this in one of his later essays. In a short, five-page account of Malayalam literary history that he wrote later under the title "Malayala Sahityam" (Malayalam Literature), he refers to the poetry of Kumaran Asan, Ulloor S Parameswara Iyer (1877–1949) and Vallathol Narayana Menon (1878–1958) as an offshoot of the Malayali literary imagination's successful integration of the formal lessons learnt from Western romantic poetry (Nambiar 1993, 127).

Critics in general, however, were a little late in comprehending the full significance of the literary revolution ushered in by Asan's poetry. Conservative critics were only too glad to misread his poems as carrying forward what was described as the neo-classical tradition of A. R. Rajaraja Varma (1863–1918), whose death Asan had mourned in an elegy, *Prarodanam* (Lament), written in 1919. There is a notorious review of *Karuna* (Compassion, 1923), in which P. K. Narayana Pillai, a conservative critic of the time, finds Asan's innovative work to be composed in imitation of Ramapurath Varier's *Kuchelavrittam Vanchippattu*, a long narrative poem belonging to a somewhat traditional genre of writing. T. K. Krishna Menon, who published a history of Malayalam literature in English in 1939, puts Asan in the company—this might sound greatly ironic—of the same Narayana Pillai as well as of Vadakkunkur Raja Raja Varma, both of whom, though deeply respected as accomplished scholars, are not treated as poets worth mentioning today (1939, 68–69). Critics who did notice the formal innovation and the freshness of approach embodied in the new poetry talked about a *khandakavya* genre that was getting consolidated as part of the development.[10] One of the earliest to talk about the change

---

[10] *Khandakavya*, to be distinguished from *mahakavya*, is a poem of medium length that deals with an episode in a person's life or a fragment of life. Though the fourteenth-century Sanskrit poetic theorist Viswanatha has used this term in his *Sahityadarpana*, *khandakavya* is not a standard literary form sanctioned by ancient Indian poetics. There are no models to follow for an ideal *khandakavya* in Sanskrit poetry.

in a systematic manner was Joseph Mundasseri (1903–77), whose critical interventions have played a crucial role in consolidating a romantic phase in twentieth-century Malayalam poetry with Asan as the centre-piece. In *Mattoli* (The Echo, 1943), his first attempt at critically explaining the genius of Asan's poetry, Mundasseri reads Asan in comparison with his contemporaries Ulloor and Vallathol, and claims Asan to be in possession of a mysterious and marvellous poetic power that excels Ulloor's felicity of diction and Vallathol's image-making skills. Mundasseri was also the first to speak at length about the radical and revolutionary aspect of Asan's poetry. In an essay included in *Manushyakathanugayikal* (Bards of the Human Tale, 1967), Mundasseri describes Asan as the "lodestar" of social revolution, thus providing a progressivist twist to the poet's romantic bent. In this essay Mundasseri also reminds the reader of Asan's call for a radical change in social customs, and declares that Asan had been a revolutionary right from his initial foray into the world of serious poetry-making (Mundasseri 2004, 167, 171).

Though the identification of Asan as a romantic poet comparable to the nineteenth-century British romantics might have been a radical step to take for the literary scholar of the 1920s and 1930s, viewed from the larger perspective of Indian literary history, this does not seem to have been a wholly salubrious development, especially in the context of assessing the poetic merit of a complex Indian artist whose genius can in no way be reduced to the principles of European romanticism. This unfortunately was what literary history had in store for Asan, whose poetic genius cannot be separated both from the traditions of Indian philosophy that he had internalised from his mentor Sri Narayana Guru, and the Sanskrit poetic culture that he had assimilated through his reading of the ancient Indian classics and who, apart from writing poetry, was also immersed actively in the social reformist work of his day. Though Asan's public image was an extension of his image as a poet, his critics invariably viewed him as a subjectively-oriented romantic, who, like Keats, Shelley and Byron before him, allowed his political persona to be collapsed into a vaguely conceived cosmic poetic vision. This had the deleterious effect of limiting the political dimension of Asan's irrefutable imaginative powers.[11] Even Mundasseri, who as a critic was deeply sensitive to the sociopolitical dimension of imaginative writing was inclined to regard him, for all his complexities, as a scion of British romanticism. In a comprehensive study of Asan's poetry that he wrote toward the end of his life, Mundasseri sums up his general assessment of Asan in the following words: "All of Asan's characters from *Nalini* onwards possess these romantic traits. Only the themes differ in individual works. All of them are subject to the virtues and limitations of their English counterparts" (quoted in Govindan 2014, 207; trans. A. Radhakrishnan).

Mundasseri's indeed is a literary historical statement made from the first of the two competing perspectives cited. But this statement, significant as it is in the canonical installation of Asan as a major voice in twentieth-century Malayalam poetry, does not exhaust the creative potential of Asan's poetic genius. Mundasseri, the far-sighted and resourceful critic that he is, recognises this, and that is why after referring to Asan's limitations arising from his British romantic connection, he adds as an afterthought, and almost as an articulation of his own unconscious: "If, on account of these limitations, we consider Asan's heroes and heroines as distorted characters who have little in common with the normal human beings, and if we reckon their feelings as alien to the human character, we will be committing a great injustice to the poet's imagination" (Govindan 2014, ibid.). In fact, a close perusal of Asan's major works such as *Nalini* (1911), *Leela* (1914), *Chintavishtayaya Sita* (Sita Immersed in Thought, 1919), *Duravastha* (The Tragic Plight, 1922) and *Karuna* (Compassion, 1923) would reveal the poet to be extending his vision to areas and experiences that cannot be grasped by the limited poetic idiom of Western romanticism. Describing Asan as a romantic

---

[11] Recent Malayalam critics, especially those working within a "post-modern" critical tradition, are aware of these limitations in the past critical readings of Asan. See Pavithran (2002) for a representative analysis.

would certainly help one to talk critically about certain aspects of his new writing, part of which indeed must have been inspired by his reading of the British romantics. But there is a poetic and experiential surplus in Asan's poetry, ineffable and ungraspable, which cannot be explained in terms of the romantic mindset. P. Pavithran, a critic of the present generation who interprets Asan with the help of Lacan's theories, points to this surplus without naming it so, when he refers to the regional and subaltern roots of Asan's poetry that cannot just be reduced to the Western impact (2002, 254). This surplus is what makes Indian bhasha literatures uniquely Indian. One might perhaps take a close look at Asan's poetic reinterpretation of the Ramayana story in *Chintavishtayaya Sita* to see how the poet develops the character of the much-wronged Sita, retrieved from Ravana's clutches by her mythical husband only to be abandoned in the forest, as a symbol of woman's struggle against patriarchy for equality and gender justice.

It is possible that the above-mentioned surplus was sometimes highlighted as an aspect of the progressive literature in Indian bhashas. This certainly has been the case with Malayalam, where progressive literature invariably articulated the miseries, dreams and desires of the depressed classes through this surplus. Literary historians of the time seem generally to have been blind to this surplus, though Sankaran Nambiar did allude to it obliquely in some of his essays. One such essay where he links Asan to progressive literature is particularly interesting in this context. At a time when writers with Marxist leanings alone wrote in praise of progressive literature, here is Nambiar, a liberal-minded critic, choosing to write a scholarly piece on it under the title "Jeeval Sahityam", which provides an informed overview and critical appreciation of the literary landscape that emerges in the wake of the new poetry of Asan. Nambiar defines progressive literature as "forward-looking" (*mun nokki*), the kind of writing which brings into the ambit of literary scrutiny the events of the everyday and the concerns of the present, in place of the themes and concerns of the past that traditional literature often chose to celebrate

(Nambiar 1993, 26). But what makes Nambiar's essay unique is his critical far-sightedness that permitted him to see the caste, class and gender concerns that arguably were being articulated by progressive literature. The repressed unconscious of literary histories that we mentioned earlier comes out into the open in the following words of Nambiar:

> Progressive literature is more about caste than about a person. It is not the individual who matters in it, but the class to which he belongs. The progressive writer's sympathies are for the common man who suffers under the step-motherly treatment of a cruel mother nature [...]. In these matters, one possibly can see some relation between the history of literature and the history of women [...]. Today's woman does not run away from life's realities. She faces life boldly, fights it and finds a solution to its problems. This is true of 'kavyangana' [poetry imagined as a woman] too. (Nambiar 1993, 27–29)

The modernist phase in Malayalam poetic history is also well-charted. In the histories of M. Leelavathy and D. Benjamin, poetic modernism appears as a phase that lies sandwiched between romanticism and post-modernism. Both Leelavathy and Benjamin devote a chapter each to the modernists in their respective histories (Leelavathy 2002, 370–501; Benjamin 1998, 66–88). Here too the story is that of the sensitive writer getting frustrated with the outdated practice of writing associated with the poetry of the previous phase and resolving to take poetry back into the arena of real life, which is perceived as being full of conflicts. Though the poetic scene of the 1950s–1960s represents a confluence of currents drawn from diverse sources, the modernist domination of the scene in the later years is seen as almost complete. Poets like N. N. Kakkad (1927–87), Ayyappa Paniker (1930–2006), Akkitham Achutan Nampoothiri (1926–2020), Attoor Ravivarma (1930–2019) and Madhavan Ayyappath (1934–2021) are key players in the new development. These poets brought about a new sensibility that arguably was formalist, anti-romantic, aesthetically intense and highly intellectualised. These perhaps are the characteristics of literary modernism in general and, as suggested by K. P. Appan, one of the major advocates of modernism in Malayalam, these characteristics also led to the creation of "a new style of art" that turned modernist literature into a distinctive discourse (Appan 2000, 70). It however did not take long for the readers to get frustrated with this new style. Paniker, an architect of modernist poetry, was also one of the earliest to announce the demise of poetic modernism in Malayalam. An essay published in 1979 opens with the following unambiguous statement:

> The most important fact concerning present-day Malayalam poetry is that the modernist verse which arose in the 1950's in the post-Independence world from the ashes of the romantic-progressive movement, and which became a major force in the 1960's and guided the poetry of the 1970's, has fulfilled its historic duties and is now transforming itself into the postmodernist verse that has taken birth in the closing years of the 1970's and is anticipating a large role for itself in the 1980's. (Paniker 1985, 140)

Paniker's statement is literary history narrated from the first perspective, compressed into a sentence. The sentence however can be said to subsume within itself a plethora of questions—literary, historical and literary historical—that can render its transparency problematic and sow the seeds for the germination of the second perspective. For one thing, though Paniker himself is often regarded as an important architect, successively, of the modernist and the post-modernist sensibilities in Malayalam at different stages of his life, one cannot overlook the perennial influence of the romantic culture in the making of his poetic personality. If one is not keen on seeing this development as a case of linear evolution, one might even consider the romantic in him to be equivalent to the indigenous "surplus" that we noticed in Asan, and which surfaces periodically in his poetry. In an essay ("Why Write") written in the early 1990s on why he wrote poetry, Paniker makes a statement that can be interpreted as deeply romantic in import: "There is an element of vagueness about all works of art. Even in the appreciation of art there might be elements that one cannot fully understand and share with another"

(Paniker 2005, 279).[12] His life-long fascination for such Malayalam romantics as Changampuzha Krishna Pillai (1911–48) and Edappalli Raghavan Pillai (1909–36) has often been commented upon. Though Leelavathy proclaims that Paniker's poetry of the 1950s was essentially romantic in spirit and that the sensibility shift attributed to him comes only later (2002, 374), one might also argue that the spirit of romanticism is all-pervasive in Paniker's work and that it would be unrealistic to regard his modernism as something that is opposed to the fundamental romantic element in poetic creativity. Leelavathy herself, it is useful to remember, is inclined to regard modernism in Malayalam as an "afterglow" of romantic poetry (2002, 370). Even Appan, a diehard apologist of literary modernism in Malayalam, is willing to recognise, albeit belatedly, that modernism's "radical" subjectivity is in many ways related to the romantic persona (Appan 2000, 74).

There are two other important questions that one might raise in connection with the conceptual world surrounding literary histories. One of these concerns the idea of progress as it is theorised by literary history and the other is related to the problem of dealing with writers who are described as "maverick". Though descriptions of the romantic phase loom large in most literary histories, the concept of progress does not seem to receive proper analysis in any one of them. Progressive writing to be sure is documented by them, but most literary histories share an inherent bias against this literature, which is often regarded as non-art.[13] One reason for this perhaps is the fact that most

---

12 For an English version of Paniker's essay in P. P. Raveendran's translation, see Alexander (2018, 187–89).

13 Leelavathy's history does not discuss the question of progressive writing per se, though she discusses the poets such as Vayalar Ramavarma, P. Bhaskaran, O. N. V. Kurup and others, generally regarded as progressive poets, along with a few others who cannot be easily classified, in a separate chapter (chapter 14). Benjamin's history discusses these poets in the chapter titled "Arunayugavum Yatharthyabodhavum"(The Pink Era and the Sense of Reality) (George 1998, 36–54).

literary histories of the post-1960s era are produced from the point of view of modernism, which considered progressive writing to be built on the false opposition between art and life. Progressive literature, obsessed as it was with the life of the downtrodden, in this view, never cared for the autonomy of art. The organic connection between the romantic temperament and the idea of progress is never sought to be elaborated in the discussions on progressive literature carried out in Malayalam literary histories. As pointed out above, there indeed is a relation between progress and the theory of romanticism on the one hand, and progress and modernity on the other. Duncan Wu seems to recognise this two-fold relation when he, after naming "the unquenchable aspiration for universal betterment" (a euphemism for progress, one might say) as the most distinctive feature of romanticism, goes on to explain its relevance for the age of modernity:

> Today, when the world seems so inexorably drawn to global destruction of various kinds, such hopes may seem ludicrous. But two hundred years ago, when the world was gripped for what seemed like, for the first time, by successive revolutions in America, in France and even South America, it was possible to believe, just for a brief period, that improvement, both on the physical and spiritual planes, could be made real. (Wu 1998, xxxv)

Progress, in other words, is to be understood as "improvement" on "the physical and spiritual planes". This romantic idea of progress seems to have resonated particularly well with the Indian mind of the 1930s and later. The Indian Progressive Writers Association, which embraced a broad spectrum of society, was a direct outcome of this resonance. It was a broad platform of writers and intellectuals—Gandhians, liberals and Marxists—who were held together by their opposition to orthodoxy and a common interest in the values of modernity. There was an inherent pluralism in its ideological composition at the national level, where it was able to reshape the idea of progress as an important aspect of social re-organisation with a pronounced thrust on a possible alternative to colonial modernity. This apparently was what Sankaran Nambiar was suggesting when he referred to caste, class and gender issues as receiving a new visibility in the then upcoming progressive literature in Malayalam. One might argue that it is this romantic connection with progress as a desirable idea that persisted in literary modernism, especially in the Malayalam modernist poetry of the 1970s, when literature underwent a massive process of political radicalisation at the hands of poets like Kadammanitta Ramakrishnan (1935–2008), K. Satchidanandan (b. 1946), D. Vinayachandran (1946–2013), and K. G. Sankara Pillai (b. 1948).

Maverick poets who defy classification are a serious challenge to any literary historian. Malayalam has a substantial number of poets in the last century who cannot be classed either with the romantics or with the modernists. This, needless to say, betrays the unreal or inadequate nature of the frame of reference used by the historian that excludes several important poets from its ambit. The literary historical practice of naming them without classifying them, a practice that Leelavathy perfects in her history, is one easy way of dealing with this problem. Edasseri Govindan Nair (1906–74), Vailoppilly Sreedhara Menon (1911–85), N. V. Krishna Warrior (1916–89), and M. Govindan (1919–89), who all figure prominently in chapter 14 of Leelavathy's history, are among the poets who came to maturity at the time when the "spirit" of romanticism was at its peak, but chose to stay clear of its shadow. None of them can be said to have sought its shelter, although their poetry in individual ways was shaped and molded both by the vast and heterogeneous culture of Malayalam's traditional resources as well as by the colonial cultural resources that came to them through modern education. The "excess" that we noticed in predecessor poets like Asan seems to have been the standard substance in them, though each makes sure that it is deployed and developed in individual and original ways. Leelavathy, however, is at a loss to decide where to place them. It is this uncertainty that forces her to state that M. Govindan belongs to modernism in thought and to romanticism in poetic sensibility (2002, 317), that Vailoppilly's poetry moves spontaneously from romanticism to realism with great ease (ibid., 301), and that Edasseri's poetry represents a confluence of diverse cultures (ibid., 295). Poet O. N. V. Kurup is bewildered by the fact that Changampuzha and Vailoppilly, hailing from adjacent villages in central Kerala and born in the same year into families of comparable social standing, could be so widely different from each other in matters pertaining to literary taste and poetic culture (Kurup 2010, 15–16). The two poets, according to Kurup, traverse parallel lines of poetic experience. Though the romantic enthusiast in Kurup would have us believe that the two poets represent two divergent aspects of romanticism, it is clear from his account of Vailoppilly that he considers the latter to be unique in his poetic practice. It is the unconscious in literary history that speaks through Kurup when he defines Vailoppilly's poetry, specifically, as "poetry that is inconclusive", though by the end of his narrative he expands the phrase and makes it embrace all great poets. Referring to the new significance that each succeeding generation discovers in Vailoppilly, Kurup says: "This inconclusive poetry dissolves into the cultural essence of a people. Here poetry is in dialogue with infinite time, and will continue to do so as long as the rivers flow and the mountain peaks hold their heads high" (ibid., 71). Here indeed is the literary historian's attempt to canonise a writer who cannot be pigeonholed into received categories of literary culture, but there is also an unconscious recognition of the social imaginary as a dynamic and open-ended force that works through poets and artists to shape the cultural identities of a people. Inasmuch as the recognition also constitutes a confirmation of poetry's discursive autonomy and its status as the language geared to the society's progressive potential, it signifies a vindication of the second of the two perspectives that were cited at the beginning of this paper.

WORKS CITED

Alexander, Meena, ed. 2018. *Name Me a Word: Indian Writers Reflect on Writing*. New Haven: Yale University Press.

Anjaneyulu, D. 1974. "Sri Sri: Portrait of an Angry Poet." In *Poetry and Renaissance: Kumaran Asan Birth Centenary Volume*, edited by M. Govindan, 471–74. Chennai: Blaze Media.

Appan, K.P. 2000. *Innalekalile Anweshana Parishodhanakal.* Kottayam: DC Books.

Bayley, John. 1957. *The Romantic Survival: A Study in Poetic Evolution.* London: Constable.

Benjamin, D. 1998. *Adhunika Malayala Sahitya Charitram: Prastanangaliloode,* edited by K. M. George, 1–88. Kottayam: DC Books.

Bourdieu, Pierre. 1993. *The Field of Cultural Production.* New York: Columbia University Press.

Castoriadis, Cornelius. 1998. *The Imaginary Institution of Society.* Cambridge: MIT Press.

Das, Sisir Kumar. 1995. *A History of Indian Literature 1911–1956.* New Delhi: Sahitya Akademi.

Day, Aidan. 1996. *Romanticism.* London: Routledge.

George, K.M., ed. 1998. *Adhunika Malayala Sahitya Charitram: Prastanangaliloode.* Kottayam: DC Books.

Govindan, M., ed. (1974) 2014. *Poetry and Renaissance: Kumaran Asan Birth Centenary Volume.*Chennai: Blaze Media.

Gregson, Ian. 1996. *Contemporary Poetry and Postmodernism.* London: Macmillan.

Heaney, Seamus. 1988. *The Government of the Tongue.* London: Faber.

Kermode, Frank. 1957. *The Romantic Image.* London: Routledge and Kegan Paul.

Kurup, O.N.V. 2010. *Kavitayile Samantara Rekhakal.* Thiruvananthapuram: Chinta Publishers.

Leelavathy, M. (1980) 2002. *Malayala Kavita Sahitya Charitram.* Thrissur: Kerala Sahitya Akademi.

Menon, T.K. Krishna. (1939) 1990. *A Primer of Malayalam Literature.* New Delhi: Asian Educational Services.

Mundasseri, Joseph. 2004. *Mundasseri Kritikal,* vol. 2 Thrissur: Current Books.

Nair, Panmana Ramachandran, ed. 2008. *Sampoorna Malayala Sahitya Charitram.* Kottayam: Current Books.

Nambiar, P. Sankaran. (1943) 1993. *Sahitya Nishkutam.* Thrissur: Kerala Sahitya Akademi.

———. (1922) 2001. *Malayala Sahitya Charitra Samgraham.* Thrissur: Kerala Sahitya Akademi.

Nicholls, Peter. 1995. *Modernism: A Literary Guide.* London: Macmillan.

North, Michael. 1994. *The Dialectic of Modernism: Race, Language and Twentieth Century Literature.* Oxford: Oxford University Press.

Paniker, Ayyappa. 1985. *Ayyappa Panikerude Lekhanangal 1950–80.* Kottayam: DC Books.

———. 2005. *Ayyappa Panikerude Lekhanangal 1990–2005*. Kottayam: DC Books.

Pavithran, P. 2002. *Asan Kavita: Adhunikanantara Paathangal*. Thiruvananthapuram: Department of Cultural Publications.

Pound, Ezra. 1920. *Instigations*. New York: Bony and Liveright.

Raveendran, P.P. 2009. *Texts Histories Geographies: Reading Indian Literature*. Hyderabad: Orient BlackSwan.

Taylor, Charles. 2003. *Modern Social Imaginaries*. New York: Duke University Press.

Wain, John. 1972. "Poetry." In *Twentieth Century Mind*, vol. 1, edited by C.B. Cox and A.E. Dyson, 360–413. London: Oxford University Press.

Williams, Raymond. 1976. *Keywords: A Vocabulary of Culture and Society*. London: Fontana.

Wu, Duncan. 1998. "Introduction." *Romanticism: An Anthology*, edited by Duncan Wu, xxx–xxxvii. Oxford: Blackwell.

TWELVE

The Search for Form and Authenticity in Bangla Novels

A Reading of Debes Ray's Tistaparer Brittanta

Subha Chakraborty Dasgupta

The novel, it has been said, is a genre that emerged when a different economic order came into being. As Goldmann states,

> La forme romanesque nous parait être en effet la transposition sur le plan littéraire de la vie quotidienne dans la société individualiste née de la production pour la marché. Il existe une homologie rigoureuse entre la forme littéraire du roman... et la relation quotidienne des hommes... et par extension, des hommes avec des autres hommes, dans une société productrice pour le marché. (Goldmann 1964, 20)

> The novel form seems to us to be, in effect, the transposition on the literary plane of everyday life in the individualistic society brought into being by market production. There is a rigorous homology between the literary form of the novel... and the everyday relations of human beings in general... and by extension between man and other men, in a market society. (Translated by Subha Chakraborty Dasgupta)

In other words, the novel came into being when human relationships came to be governed by elements or values related to the exchange of commodities—when meaningful social relations declined. The search for an authentic set of values lay at the origin of the novel. But Goldmann's statement can only have relative pertinence in the context of novels in India as social conditions differed and a host of literary traditions were responsible for contributing to the form of the novel in several different ways. Yet, it cannot be denied that the novel in Indian languages too was predicated upon a search for authentic values. There was, in novels written in India, an anxiety of form as also in other places of the world, because of its entry as a latecomer in the history of literature, because of the somewhat alienating structure of the printed form and the world of which it was a product and a fear of inauthenticity generated by drawing away from participatory forms of communication. For many writers in India, it was evident that authenticity could enter the domain of the narrative only if they were able to write the story of the marginalised, "the 6.7 crore poorest people" (Ray 1988, 491) as they lived it, and that the well-being of the entire community depended on bringing forward that story for which there had to be a search for a new form and a new language. The margins were created by sociopolitical and economic structures in history, and it was the same history to which the writer also belonged. My focus in this essay will be on a particular novel by Debes Ray entitled *Tistaparer*[1] *Brittanta* that has not been translated into English and that perhaps does not lend itself to translation.

Debes Ray, who has written extensively on the novel, believed that it was important to draw upon indigenous narrative forms for giving shape to the Indian novel. The idea was present in many novelists belonging to the second phase of novel writing in India when, in some languages, there was a greater experiment with form. There is, for instance, in Bibhutibhusan Bandyopadhyay's *Pather Panchali* (1929) a very conscious endeavour to bring into being a novelistic form and at the same time an engagement with a different sense of time and a different set of relationships not just between human beings but between human beings and the cosmos. Here too, the novel is invoked as a *panchali*, a folk form of storytelling in song.

In the early 1940s, the country was going through a large upheaval and there were ongoing debates around the place of

[1] The name of the river Teesta is usually spelt with double 'e', but the name of the book as it appears on the copyright page is *Tistaparer Brittanta* and I have retained the spelling for the title.

the marginalised castes and groups. During this period and a little later in the 1950s, several novels emerged which related the experiences of groups, castes and tribes from the margins. Regarding one such novel, Tarasankar Bandyopadhyay's *Hansuli Banker Upakatha* (various versions between 1946–51) identified as a regional novel, the translator Ben Conisbee Baer states that the novel "is an account of a much more general problem of literary representation: it is an experiment in how to 'do' novels in India, of how to make tale (*upakatha*) into novel (*upanyas*) across divisions not specifically defined by region" (2011, ix). *Upakatha* is a tale and also implies a "subnarrative, a smaller tangential thread woven into the dense texture of an epic" (Baer 2010, 623); as a character in the text comments, the love stories in the text are just rhymes in the *upakatha*. The canvas is large. Suchand Kahar, the oldest woman resident of the Kahar community, tells the narrator towards the end that the tale would end with her, but, if possible, he should keep it in writing. The alternative postcoloniality of *Hansuli Banker Upakatha*, Baer writes, "consists of a possible call and response across the partitions of class and caste" (ibid., 627). He further demonstrates in his essay titled "Creole Glossary" how the narrator's constant glossing of words used by the Kahars with the term "arthat" or "meaning" fills the texture of the novel with meanings from a different space. Suchand's call implies a "possible survival as reelaboration" (ibid., 631). The narratorial story which is that of the disintegration and proletarisation of the Kahar community in a brutally industrialised society is constantly interrupted by stories from Suchand, with songs and performances and with shifts in rhetorical registers. These stories along with the invocation of the past, of what had taken place, are all part of a form that tries to weave different worlds together and that is important to reinstate the dignity of all lives in history. At the end of the novel, Karali, the protagonist on the side of the modern, is seen digging away at the banks of Hansuli trying to cut a path for "tale's Kopai to merge with history's Ganges" (Baer 2010, 373).

If *Hansuli Banker Upakatha* struggles to transform the *upakatha* into a novel following a possible "call and response" across gaping divides of class and caste, Satinath Bhaduri's *Dhorai Charit Manas* (1949 and 1951, Parts 1 and 2), a much commented upon text, tries to carve out a novel from a *charit*, a genre going back to the medieval period eulogising the lives of saints and in this case bearing traces of the immensely popular *Ramcharitmanas* and all the emotive memory associated with it in that particular region in the minds of the people. The medieval form gets linked with the Gandhian ideals that are primarily village-oriented and tells the story of Dhorai from the marginalised Tattma community, who has nothing to fall back upon and who gradually acquires agency—of a kind, however fragile—and thinks of himself as the proverbial squirrel doing his bit to further the cause, in this case the ideals of Gandhi. Gandhi, of course, appears in many different ways to the people in accordance with their understanding and reaction to social processes, and later, changes in people's understanding of Gandhi are manipulated by self-seeking corrupt individuals. The novel through its form and its mixed language authenticates the message that it is necessary to involve the marginalised in the process of nation building, and that the process of democracy would have to engage deeply with the informed participation of the people and new orders of political justice.

The search for authenticity and form to link the history of the middle-class author with that of the marginalised continues decades after independence and probably with greater urgency. Along with many others, there is Mahasweta Devi, for instance, who often seems to be writing from the other side of the divide, focusing on the "speakerly" and the performative, juxtaposing ancient stories and their modern coordinates.[2]

Let us now come to Debes Ray's novel *Tistaparer Brittanta* that came out in 1980 and 1981 in *Saradiya Baromas*, in 1984 and 1986 in *Kalantar*, in 1987 in *Pratikshan* and in book form in 1988. The nature of a narrative that gets published over several years in three different periodicals is bound to be different. It does not have a structured plot or a causal sequence, but there is a deep

---

[2] See also Dasgupta (2002–2003)

sense of unity in the different episodes held together by a place, the borderlands of the river Teesta next to Apalchand forest and beyond, and the lives of the people at different hierarchical levels. Ray looks at narrative from a large, open perspective and tries to find a way to move away from the European model and rigid structures that, he feels, hinder a writer's attempt to understand his fellow-countrymen and their lives. In Ray's opinion, one does not always need a beginning and an end in the novel, all one needs is a pathway. He asks whether the novel is all about "creating a circuit, breaking it, freeing events and characters, and then drawing them back within the borders" (Ray 2006, 96). He, of course, is in favour of a more open form.

The narrative begins with a map and has a map within the text as well, bringing in a marker from the world of non-fiction, but ironically there will be questions in the novel regarding the drawing of a map. At certain points the wind would blow away the map to the top of a tree. Bagharu, Gayanath Jotedar's man, would have to climb the tree and bring it down holding it in his mouth. The map, however, is useful in framing the narrative. The division of the narrative into *parvas* is reminiscent of the Mahabharata as also the verbal pattern and the titles of some of the episodes within the *parvas*—*nirbasan* (exile) or *Bagharur astralabh* (Bagharu gets his weapon), for instance. There is humour in the titles and sometimes irony and Ray believes that a down-to-earth humour is a key element of narrative as is also evidenced in various folk forms. Epic resonances are brought in with a light touch, but also dissolved or subverted, enacting a process of remembering and forgetting. The former, Ray states, becomes necessary in the colonial context and the latter to get back to the contemporary.[3] If there are resonances from the Mahabharata, there are stronger resonances from the world of contemporary politics, the subversion of certain typical terms and the recurrence of slogans in the body of the narrative. A cluster of chapter headings, for example, is as

[3] See Debes Ray, *Upanyaser Natun Dharaner Khonje* (2006).

follows: "Discussion between Farmers and Labourers", "Exchange between Farmers and Labourers", "Class Struggle between Farmers and Labourers", "Speech Struggle between Farmers and Labourers", "Face to Face Struggle between Farmers and Labourers", "Struggle for Unity between Farmers and Labourers", "Is this a farmer or a labourer?" The scope of the novel is large, going back to the history of the local people, the Rajbangshis, a careful chronicling of the different turns of sociopolitical history leading to the present moment, and also sometimes an impression of a further expansion of time. The novel is dedicated to four individuals from four villages who will never read the text but who will continue to live their many lives on the banks of Teesta, while the epilogue ends with Bagharu and the child Madari walking out in quest of a new forest and a new river. Let them, comments the narrator, "walk, walk, and walk" (1988, 504). In the context of space as well, though each specific locality has its own characteristics, the vast expanse of the river, forest, mountains and the sky sometimes described by the writer in detail brings a rhythm of expansion in the narrative space.

The text begins with a *bibaran* (description in minute detail), and this detailed rendering is a particular stylistic aspect of Ray's writings, as also of several Bangla novelists. The description is that of people going to the *haat* (village market), of their clothes, the objects they carry and their gait. There is a small boy carrying a pumpkin on his head, a goat that a person is taking to the market, not really dragging or cajoling, but following its rhythm, picking it up as he clambers on to a boat, keeping his neck safe from the droppings of the goat; a man carrying three small hens holding them upside down, etc. In the quiet forest road, the people do not look at each other's faces, nor do they talk, but their fast breathing fills the space as they run along the road. They dash towards the *haat* almost like a solid mass. Images of crowds and people fill the pages of the narrative foregrounding a semblance of a community life, a life lived together. It is reminiscent of but also different from the village *haat* of older narratives with Japanese terylene pieces and Seiko watches along with a whole range of products usually available in village markets, a cattle market including one for selling stolen cattle, a place for the sale and consumption of country liquor and so on.

A separate chapter brings into focus the different kinds of markets in the locality. There are two signboards that, according to the narrator, unite the crowd going to the fair just as slogans bind processions—one that is huge announcing a "Centre for the Artificial Breeding of Cows" and the other "Halka Camp" and both have government logos on them. The description continues across several short chapters and here as elsewhere there seems to be a desire to bring an indelible quality to a space that is vulnerable with the weight of the details. The details are both informants and indicators although they are not directly linked to the sequence of action, nor are they present to give an "effect of the real" (Barthes 1968, 84–89)—they constitute the novel, hold up a frame of the human in a fragile zone along with those of the natural and agricultural world that will soon be transformed. An example of such a detail that does not have any link with the ongoing action is the introduction of a tired old horse and its old slouching master slowly going round and round the empty space of the market, winding in and out of the small lanes between stalls at the end of the section. The horse rider is no longer holding out his small bag tied to the end of a stick for alms and the narrator comments that perhaps both him and his steed are blind or probably asleep, or that they are slowly making their way back to their village across many fields by the riverside. The narrator is most often omniscient in nature, but sometimes he chooses to be a mere observant from the outside and this has a different effect in the narrative. There is a surplus of events as also of details as in life and it is within this surplus that the aesthetic or the creative emerges linked with a vibrant "real".

In the first *parva* the narrative is sometimes presented from the point of view of the survey officer Suhas, who is also an ex-Naxal enabling the staging of an overall critical perspective on events. There are, however, several centres and often the focus is on Bagharu who enters the narrative holding a chair on his head for the survey officer at the bidding of his master Gayanath. Bagharu, the narrator comments, is like a relief map, without any sign of life, colour, or shape, his eyes buried in the depth of his face, with a flat nose and his body immense like a tree trunk. He wears a loincloth which mingles with the colour of his body, and he mechanically does all that his master Gayanath Jotedar asks him to do. He has no name as his name keeps changing—he was called Kuraniyar Choya or The Wood-Picker's Son when he was yet to be born for his mother used to collect wood in the forest—"collect wood and collect wood"—as he explains, and then Kuraliya Kata or Cut with the Axe as his mother cut the umbilical cord with her axe, the only thing she had. He was then called Bagharu as he had to fight with a tiger in the forest. During election season, Gayanath gave him the name Forestchandra Barman, which he later turned into Foresterchandra after seeing a Forestersahib walking in the forest—his name then became Foresterchandra Bagharu Barman. He carries the stamp of the tiger's paw on his buttock and back. There are many Forestchandra Barmans, he tells the Member of the Legislative Assembly as he carries him across the river on his back, but he is the authentic one as the tiger has put his seal on him. He pleads with the MLA to shorten his name—that is all he wants. Later in the narrative he will have other names as well. Novels deal with individuals in society and the problem here, it seems, is the bringing into being of a narrative depicting the story of one who stands for the many who are outside the social system, representing "bare lives" to use Giorgio Agamben's phrase—who have no place, no people, no name, and as Bagharu towards the end will say, no party, no flag. His rare dialogues with people are a series of negations where he declares the above. Even the police, while beating up the people protesting the inauguration of the barrage across Teesta, do not pay any attention to him although he is holding a huge banner. All that Bagharu can do is physically follow the orders of his master. The narrator comments that he has no language, for language implies meaning and he has no meaning; he just "lives and lives, he is only life and life". Where else can one find such a naked language, the narrator asks. Language also means a name and he does not have one. In the first section he goes to the survey camp while it is still dark and after several efforts manages to bring himself to call out to the officer to tell him to strike his name off from a piece of land adjacent to the forest and to insert the name of his master Gayanath Jotedar. His master had sent him there and he had ploughed the land for a while but does not do so any more. His master owns everything in any case, and he declares his own eviction in a loud voice. The scene in the dark hours before the dawn with a flashlight on Bagharu's face from time to time is rendered in a performative mode. It has a strange "unreal" effect reinforcing the pathos of the real, but then the narrator employs a realistic technique showing Bagharu lighting a cigarette as the sequence ends to prove that he is not drunk.

The narrative in Adiparva is organised around a survey related to the settlement of land ownership along the Teesta borders and it is being carried out in view of the construction of the Teesta barrage. The officer in charge of the survey is an ex-Naxal who compares his notion of the place and its dynamics two decades back with the actual situation at hand and finds irony in his close proximity to Gayanath Jotedar who owns a large part of the land around. Jotedar is shrewd and scheming and asks how it would be possible to measure land that has gone under the river; the river changes its course frequently and changes in the map. In fact, he asks Bagharu to go into the swiftly flowing mountainous river and points out territories along his track as he struggles to swim with the current. The officer meanwhile, wondering whether it is a trap set for him, asks Gayanath how he could ask a man to go down into the treacherous river and is given the response that it is only Bagharu who has been sent. A second man has also jumped in, but he is a champion swimmer from the area. The scene gets complicated when representatives from the farmers' union, the workers' union, the communist party leader and several others arrive. A dispute arises and turns violent but at the last minute a fight with bows and arrows is avoided, and people find a solution. That is the larger narrative layer within which many other events are incorporated, such as the Jotedar's attempt to learn to plough, the visit of the MLA and his row with the engineers, etc.

The section entitled Banparva relates to Bagharu's exile from Apalchand forest by Gayanath, who falsely believes that Bagharu has told the MLA to ask Gayanath to give him a piece of land. He orders him to go to his *bathan* or cattle farm in the forest near the river Diana. Bagharu sets out on his journey, finding himself a free man in the forest. The moon casts myriad shadows as he passes through trees and uneven lands. There are then several chapters on the breaking of dawn and the changes in sounds, shapes and colours of the forestland and river, Bagharu basking in the first rays of the sun and laughing with his whole body, his companionship with a dog and his efforts to befriend an early morning bird crying piercingly for a mate. Bagharu sleeps on a lonely rock between the mountain and the bridge, his body appearing like a mound on the rock, and as the narrator comments, in exile between history and geography. He stays motionless at dawn allowing the bird to sit around him and the bird's body is in complete alignment with his. Later he tries to mimic its cry but to no effect. Bagharu then has to pass through crowds of labourers going to the tea estates. He gets caught in the crowd and young girls and boys make fun of him for his almost naked body in the middle of the wide, impressive road.

There are three chapters in between that give details related to economy, agriculture and politics. They relate to the history of the place revealing details of a chain of illegal processes that had remained within small ambits, still allowing for a balanced eco-structure in the forest, but that were eventually getting out of proportion with increasing greed, leading to the felling of trees and the destruction of forests. On the agricultural side, the use of pesticides and the disaster caused to birds and animals are brought out in a few gruesome incidents. There are high profile enquiries and research into the cause of the death of a herd of deer or that of the rhinoceros, but eventually the findings are not made public. As for the political side, the narrator refers to the Sino-Indian war in 1962 that lasted for a few months, but the consequences of which continued for a very long period completely transforming the face of the region. Roads and bridges were constructed, and a large number of military encampments were set up along a considerable stretch of the highway. Military men got all their daily needs from far-away places, through contractors, and their settlement had no effect on the local economy. They, however, had to rely on the local supply of milk and the Jotedars were quick to rise to the occasion, buying new buffalos, and the Forest Department was quick to grant license to the cattle farms and a new system with contractors and middlemen thus started operating.

Bagharu is exiled to one such farm owned by Gayanath and gradually gets completely integrated with the place, befriending the buffalos, travelling on the gigantic back of the largest old buffalo who gets a new lease of life energised by the strength and vitality of the man around him. There is a memorable description of the forest and the behaviour of animals and birds during an eclipse, with Bagharu assisting a buffalo while she gives birth to a calf and then running all the way to the river with the calf to wash himself and the newborn.

The next section titled Charparva crosses over to a different set of characters—migrants from East Bengal who have settled on land created by the silt-depositing river—and the arrival of a flood in Teesta. The people wait for the declaration of the flood and start moving up to the embankment with their cattle, taking decisions without expecting much help from the government. Memories of the devastating 1968 flood are also often invoked. The flood also takes the narrative to the borders of India and Bangladesh and members of the Indian camp are invited to go over to the other side to keep themselves safe. There is no order from the headquarters regarding safety measures as the flood cuts off all communication. Bharat is too big a land for the administrators to remember a camp on its border, comments the narrator. The Commandant is at a loss as to his course of action and eventually decides on marching to the other side with his people in full regalia prompting the Commander on the other side to laugh and say, "Oh you really got us worried." The two commanders settle down with a bottle of whiskey. However, an uneasy element creeps in as the commander from Bangladesh hears of the barrage that is being built—for regulating access to Teesta's water for the people of Bangladesh, but they continue with their drink. And then there is the question of "Chhitmahal", the enclaves along the Indo-Bangladesh border. As the officer from the Indian side goes back to the camp with soldiers to bring back the rice and pulses at night and falls behind the vehicle that is being dragged up by a few soldiers, a girl from Chhitmahal joins him. She is homeless and has no one to call her own. She had fallen asleep, got left behind and is now walking to the camp for flood-affected people. The officer speaks to her a little, turns to her and then makes her lie down on the wet soil, an act that is not unusual for the girl. With this act of a "small rape", the narrator comments, where there almost seems to be mutual consent, ends this section.

The next section titled Brikshaparva begins in Apalchand forest where in the darkness of night and amid the roaring flood and storm Gayanath is busy planning how to make money from the trees that are submerged in the flood water, asking Bagharu to cut the roots of an Arjun tree and then to tie up the trees and float them down the river. He asks Bagharu to go along with the trees so that if they get stuck or when the water recedes, they do not get stolen. The order seems simple enough but floating down in the flood implies certain death. A few climactic chapters follow depicting Bagharu's superhuman struggle in the deadly storm and Teesta's tumultuous flood. After a long night, Bagharu finds himself with the trees near the embankment described in the previous *parva*. The people alert the district office and an officer appears. A series of discussions takes place and eventually Bagharu is rescued. The press and the government officers make much of this "rescue operation"—although the administration plays a very small part in it—taking photographs, being careful not to highlight Bagharu's loincloth, and felicitate him by holding his elbow in lieu of a handshake.

The next section or Michilparva begins with Gayanath's visit to the lawyer in relation to his case with the government over occupied forest land. He knows of a movement called Uttarkhanda for a separate region in the north for the Rajbangshis, but also as the lawyer explains, for others who are now part of the region, and they are many as the novel has depicted. Gayanath wonders whether he should join the movement as it might be beneficial to his case or whether it would go against him. The party leaders try to woo him, telling him that he would need to change his designation from a Jotedar to a *krishak* or farmer and that he would of course, become a leader. The narrative again shifts to the history of the Rajbangshis and the process by which they were losing their small plots of land to corporate farmers in the big cities. The Uttarkhanda unit plans a large convention with cultural functions in the evening and a procession to the shrine of Jalleswar where an oath-taking ceremony would take place along with a small ritualistic worship for Teestaburi. There are attempts on the part of the government to stop the convention and the procession to Jalleswar and they call a meeting of the members of the unit to the Circuit House in Jalpaiguri. The authorities, however, are unable to disrupt the proceedings and the conference takes place. There are lectures on why a separate region is necessary by different people from different places and professions, with different ideological backgrounds, who sometimes speak from self-serving interests. There are also lectures on why there should be protests over the inauguration of the Teesta barrage and how several demands should be made on behalf of the farmers who have lost their land, a critique of certain notions of development, and then discussion on changes in the social history of the Rajbangshis. The background of the speakers sketched in sharp outlines bring different layers and perspectives to the content of their speech. Similarly, the cultural events are also described in detail, in particular the dance of Sreedevi, the renowned Bollywood actress, and the frenzied outburst of the large crowd on the last day. Not too many people join the procession to Jalleswar after the last cultural programme.

As the procession to Jalleswar begins, people start looking for someone to hold the large banner and walk for miles. Gayanath asks the local leader to give it to Bagharu. He is reluctant to do so, but eventually he does and Bagharu leads the procession. In fact, he has to continue to carry the flag to all the processions organised in the next few weeks in the local market, where again few people show interest and where the local CPM leader organises larger processions with tea garden workers and others shouting slogans like "*Kranti haate Uttarkhanda cholbe na, cholbe na*" (There cannot be Uttarkhanda in Kranti *haat*), "*Gayanath Jotedarer bamfront birodhi chakranta khatam karo, khatam karo*" (Put an end to the conspiracy of Gayanath Jotedar against the left front). On the day of the inauguration of the barrage they bring out a procession, with Bagharu leading the small group. The procession is stopped midway by the police who order a lathi charge and the people either run away or get wounded and fall. No one bothers to pay attention to Bagharu standing on one side with the banner. Meanwhile, the narrator reports the third dialogue of Bagharu after ten or twelve years. He reiterates that he has no people backing him, he has no Uttarkhanda, no "joining", he is not a Rajbangshi, nor a *bhatia*, no flag and no party. He is simply holding the flag as Gayanath has instructed him to do so. The narrator asks whether Bagharu with his series of succinct negations is gradually becoming irrelevant to himself.

The last section Antaparva shifts to a different part of the borderland to recount the story of Madari and her sons. The title of the first chapter is "The Independent Nation of Madari's Mother". Madari's mother lives alone on the edge of the forest, a small distance away from the highway. She has constructed a shelter made of leaves near a small spring and has gathered a few small rocks under a *shaora* tree hoping that truck drivers would throw some coins as they pass by. But that does not happen as there is a similar place nearby—herds of elephants had been blocking the road for a few years and so truck drivers installed an idol of Ganesha and began to throw coins as they passed by. Madari's mother has given birth to several sons, for she needs a son to help her survive. Drivers of trucks and buses often stop by to wash their face or to drink water and they give her son Madari, who stands near the huge wheels of trucks, a few coins from time to time. Madari has also started going to the *haat* and cleaning a few vehicles, and sometimes he also washes dishes at the sweet shop that sells tea. His mother knows that as the sons reach the height of the table at the tea shop, they leave the forest and their mother in search of work elsewhere; she has to calculate this every time and beget another son to help her survive. She gets her food from the forest, always looking down as she walks, killing small animals sometimes, but she is often short of fuel and tries different strategies to get hold of a few matchsticks. Her young son, who has almost reached the height of the table, is excited to hear about the announcement that is being made asking people to go to the inauguration of the barrage. The barrage is not yet complete, but elections are round the corner and so the inauguration has to take place and a huge gathering needs to be organised. Madari is also excited that Bahadur at the tea stall has allowed him to make tea and that his mother is also given tea and two biscuits. He asks her to take him to the inauguration; there would be trucks and vehicles to carry them along. His mother reluctantly decides to go as she is afraid that she might lose Madari if she allows him to go alone. The long journey and the moods of the people are described in detail. Nothing has any meaning for Madari's mother, but it has been a while and she likes being among people. The taste of the food that is given to her, the bread, seems to her to come from a different age altogether. At the venue, when ministers are busy inaugurating the barrage, she decides to look closely at every face—Nepali, Madhesi, Rajbangshi—to see if she can find any of her sons. When it is time to return, she is unable to find Madari and returns alone to her leaf hut. The narrator comments that she lives there in full sovereignty and independence. Days do not pass for her; she lives each day fully. But, the narrator notes, there is nothing in her poverty that can be glorified for there is too much shame in it. "In India those who can use the pen and ink, like us, do not know how and in which alphabet to write the story of the poorest 6.7 crore. Hence the more one writes the *brittanta* of which the alphabet is not known, the falser it will be" (Ray 1988, 491).

The epilogue is titled "Reasons for Writing the Brittanta and for Ending it". The narrator indicates that the narrative had begun at a certain point, in the Gajoldoba village of Apalchand forest and ends here with the barrage raising its head like a mountain. Though the barrage is still under construction an inauguration did take place sometime after. Events in the narrative are capable of becoming history, he states, just as the old Teesta, the forest and all that had been narrated are in the process of becoming a part of history. The narrative then sees Bagharu trying to go close to the barrage to find out what the huge wall across the river, the stage and the lights are all about, how they are related to the river and the forest, when the police stop him. They entrust a child who is lost in the crowd to him asking him to take him home, and in exchange allow him to go round the place for a short while. Bagharu has a chance to look around and see the transformation that has taken over the whole place. The child is Madari and since all narratives have to end somewhere, the narrator states, this narrative too will end with Bagharu holding the hands of Madari and walking away from the forest, in the night of his "rejection of development" and its consequences, the destruction of the borderlands of Teesta, the forest of *sal*, hordes of deer, elephants, birds and reptiles. His body will not survive in the new land and forest. He will walk and walk with the child and will stop only if he finds a new forest and a new river and if his body will recognise it all.

The novel can be read from several perspectives as there are varied dimensions to characters and events; this includes the figure of Gayanath Jotedar, who is portrayed in a semi-comic manner. The perspectives emerge from formal considerations, from a particular syntactic architecture with the mixing of languages—mainly Bangla and Rajbangshi[4]—in different ways and degrees in the everyday

[4] There was a critique related to the use of Rajbangshi words and syntax in the text and there were responses as well. It is important to look more closely at issues of representation, but it is equally important to note that Ray often weaves the problematic of "representation from outside" in the narrative through certain rhetorical devices such as questions at crucial points, the presentations of different voices related to an issue, a dense texture of details and through constant subversion of mainstream rhetoric.

speech of people, the use of short colloquial forms along with long complex sentences in descriptive passages, and in the general organisation of the free-flowing narrative structure. But of the many directions in which the narrative is allowed to proceed, a particular area of engagement becomes prominent, and it is that of an intermingling of the novelistic and the historical and along with it a strong critique of the socio-economic-political structure, its failure to provide any assistance to the poorest and to certain sustainable forms of life and to the ecosystem in general. The insatiable greed of some ironically finds a nourishing centre in the apparatus of the State. Against this background the narrative gives form and substance to the concept of "bare lives" in the figure of Bagharu, though in a partial manner. It is true that he is seemingly "expendable"—seemingly because Madari needs him as do the animals and birds of Apalchand forest. Stripped of political significance, this "bare life" finds relevance in the context of nature and the ecosystem. Even within the bare life conditions Bagharu exercises his freedom at the end as he leaves the forest rejecting the unjust processes of "development". The figures of Madari's mother and the girl from Chhitmahal belong to the same category of "bare lives" but without the mitigating circumstances that render the life of Bagharu meaningful. But again, the presence of love in the mother's relationship with Madari and her other lost sons does add a layer, however thin, to her bare life. The story of the girl from Chhitmahal remains stark and unresolved.

The free-flowing form of the novel, moving in different directions and situated at the crossroad of different genres has an aesthetic unity at the centre that emerges out of a "greater ethicality" linked with the authentic. This "greater ethicality", Debes Ray believes, is the birthplace of form in the novel.

Works Cited

Barthes, Roland. 1968. "L'Effet de Réel." *Communications* 11: 84–89.

Baer, Ben Conisbee. 2010. "Creole Glossary: Tārāshankar Bandyopādhyāy's *Hānsuli Bānker Upakathā*." *PMLA* 125 (3). jstor.org/stable/25704460. Accessed on 14 March 2024.

——. 2011. "Introduction." In *The Tale of Hansuli Turn*. New York: Columbia University Press.

Dasgupta, Subha Chakraborty. 2002–03. "Writing the Oral: Issues in Translation." *JJCL XXXX*-JJCL 40.

Goldmann, Lucien. 1964. "L'introduction aux problèmes d'une sociologie du roman." In *Pour une sociologie du roman*. Paris: Gallimard.

Ray, Debes. 1988. *Tistaparer Brittanta*. Kolkata: Dey's Publishing.

——. 2006. *Upanyaser Natun Dharaner Khonje*. Kolkata: Dey's Publishing.

THIRTEEN

Kumaran Asan and the Poetics of Freedom

On the Moral Transformation in the Vernacular[1]

VIPIN K. KADAVATH

> There is no responsibility, no decision, without this inauguration, this absolute break. That is what deconstruction is made of: not the mixture but the tension between memory, fidelity, the preservation of something that has been given to us, and at the same time, heterogeneity, something absolutely new, and a break. The condition of this performative success, which is never guaranteed, is the alliance of these to newness.
>
> Jacques Derrida (The Villanova Roundtable; Caputo 1997, 6)

This paper attempts to lay down preparatory ground for a more focused understanding of the sociopolitical and ethical thought embedded in the work of some of the early twentieth-century thinkers in Kerala. We will look closely at the poetry of Kumaran Asan (1873–1924) uncovering the rudiments of an *im*-possible ethics that spills over into modes of political action reducible neither to a self-assuring individualism nor the colonial technologies of community. We will specifically read his poem *Chinthavishtayaya Sita* (Sita Immersed in Reflection, 1919) along with *Veena Poovu* (The Fallen Flower, 1907) in order to foreground a fundamental issue related to social modernity in Kerala—the inception of a

---

[1] I want to thank E. V. Ramakrishnan, P. P. Raveendran and Rajendra Chenni whose insightful comments on an earlier version of this paper at the Bhasha Literatures Conference in Baroda helped me rework it in the present form.

new relation between language, literature and (moral) subjectivity inaugurated by the opening up of a differential gap within the community, or more accurately the differing of the community with itself. A term that mediates all these, that is, language, literature and ethics is "thought", used here as something that becomes universally available in a particular moment of history while it subsists in the midst of a community as an attempt of transgressing the given historical determination.[2] Thought as "potentiality" is to be understood more loosely, different from reason, yet without losing the rigour the act of philosophical reflection carries.

In the first part of the paper, I will look closely at the poem *Chinthavishtayaya Sita* in relation to the retelling of the Ramayana in order to explore the articulation of liberal freedom in these texts. In the second part I will try to unravel a more complex structure of Asan's aesthetics which carries the weight of an ethical opening—permeating his notions of language, literature and the subject—understood as assuming a sense of responsibility not reducible to the liberal subject of rights-bearing, autonomous individual. The last part will briefly discuss Asan's own prose writings as a site where, in both a paradoxical continuation of and departure from his aesthetics, this ethical experience of responsibility transmutes into a form of political action.

Retelling the Ramayana: Claiming Liberal Freedom

Elsewhere, I have analysed the modern vernacular re-tellings of the Ramayana as a site for the reappropriation and re-interpretation of the epic narrative for articulating the idea of liberal freedom

[2] Evan as we emphasise the universality of thought, it needs to be remembered that every language contains internal tensions. As Sudipta Kaviraj remarks, "People 'having' the same language do not have it in the same way. Socially, linguistic competence confers on people capacities, and their absence correspondingly takes them away" (Kaviraj 2010, 128). The creation of standard language and dialects can be cited as an example for such social power that language can exert and is exerted upon language. Still, what I want to emphasise is "openness" as fundamental to the nature of language.

(Kadavath 2019, 226–39). The character of Sita is presented in these re-tellings not as an icon in the nationalist discourse of imminent self-rule (that is, i. as a response to colonial scholarship of Indian society that stressed the inferior status of women, and, ii. the re-imagination of women as the repository of national difference) but as a locus for the elaboration of a critical subjectivity, which undergirds the continuous deconstruction of the patriarchal postcolonial state. In the play *Sita Agnipravesham* (Sita Enters Fire, 1924) written by the renowned Telugu writer Gudipati Venkata Chalam (1894–1979) Sita asks Rama at one point,

> So, in the end, only you have dharma? A woman is not even a living being to you. She has no breath, no heart, no dharma. What if I accept that it is only you that have dharma? You are dharma-bound to your father, mother, brothers, the people of your domain, animals and stones—everybody except your wife! Does the dharma you had to your wife disappear with a single word? (Chalam 2008, 62)

The context for Sita's indignation is this: she comes to know about Rama's decision to disown her on account of her abduction by Ravana which had caused the suspicion that she is no longer "pure", that is, untouched by another man. In the words of Chalam's Rama, he must abandon Sita "to continue his family line, and to keep it pure" for which purpose Sita has now become unfit (Chalam 2008, 60). Rather than a passing reference to dharma, the entire text is a fierce and sometimes a bitter debate between Rama and Sita on what counts as dharma—at stake is the very meaning of the word "dharma". The play starts with the reunion of Rama and Sita after the defeat and death of Ravana where Sita in her excitement advances to embrace and soothe the war-worn Rama, who only indicates disinterest and asks her to stop. Sita is further told that since she was loved and abducted by his enemy, she was "impure" to be the queen of Rama's great empire. Sita in return asks: "Is it my fault that he loved me?"—a question that would resonate in many of the contemporary texts including *Chinthavishtayaya Sita*. Rama tries to defend his action saying that a king's dharma gains precedence over a husband's. To this, Sita unleashes innumerable questions presenting her counter-arguments and exposing Rama's self-contradictions. In a fit of anger she asks, "Don't I have dharma? My dharma as a wife, my dharma as a mother, my dharma as a queen—what happened to those? [and] doesn't leaving your wife damage your integrity?" (ibid., 60).

It is in a very similar strain that Asan's Sita speaks out her mind in *Chinthavishtayaya Sita*. This particular episode in the Ramayana and Sita's portrayal in it as a woman conscious of her identity and dignity and who doesn't bow down to the rules laid out by dharmashastric discourse was not particular to Gudipati Venkata Chalam or Kumaran Asan.[3] A collection of translations of works in different south Indian languages edited by Paula Richman (2008) exhibits the intense creative churning that all these languages underwent in the form of re-tellings of the Ramayana. The question of historicity is very important in the case of these writers who sought to reflect on their societies by re-telling such stories. These re-tellings were enabled by new conceptions of the literary public and the possibility of collective reasoning resulting from the emergence of print technology. As Richman argues:

---

[3] One such episode that has been widely discussed is that of the *agni pariksha*. Linda Hess (1999), for example, has examined the reception of the *agni pariksha* by Indian audiences across time. A survey of different literary presentations of the *agni pariksha* shows that this particular episode was a matter of moral confusion for Ramayana authors across history. Kamban, for example, "did not feel any compulsion to mitigate Rama's cruelty in the agni pariksha scene" whereas, in the *Ramcharitmanas* of Tulsi Das "an elaborate plot device explains it away" by introducing *chhaya* Sita. (ibid., 9) Similarly, the cruel speech by Rama before the episode is also removed. Hess points to the reinsertion of the episode by the Ramlila writer Harishchandra and the toned down presentation of the same by Ramanand Sagar's TV serial. An interesting incident in relation to the Uttarakanda of the Ramayana is narrated by Mangharam. She says: "Sanitation workers in Jalandhar, in the northern state of Punjab, went on strike because the serial was due to end without depicting the events of the seventh and final book of Ramayana. The strike spread among sanitation workers in many major cities in north India, compelling the government to sponsor the desired episodes in order to prevent a major health hazard." (Mangharam 2009, 75)

> [The modern re-tellings of Ramayana] was preceded by three major transformations: the growth of educational institutions, the availability of relatively affordable print technology for India's regional scripts, and an increase in a regular readership for printed serials and monographs in regional languages. These historical changes allowed writers of literature in regional languages to tell Rama's story in their own way for their own time. (Richman 2008, v)

In fact, in vernacular literatures, the lineage of feminist politics is often traced back to these texts, even though they were written by men. In the broader context of colonialism and social reform, this "event of literature" can be placed within a comfortable narrative of social transformation from tradition to modernity. Sita in this narrative becomes the prototype of the rights-bearing citizen that feminist politics invokes. The man who denounces tradition by ventriloquising his dharmic questions through the character of Sita—in the name of creating a modern sociality where women will have an equal place—is recognised as the "social reformer". Even when this sociological account is true (in so far as a *general account* of the "arrival of modernity" in our part of the world may be true) there may be conceptual complexities that this straightforward narrative fails to capture. One such central problem for historical sociology (producing an account of how a social formation evolves into something else historically), is the relation between "traditional" and "the modern", which are conceptual tools only subsequent to the social formation of modernity itself. This issue includes the ideological contest and formation of subjectivities. The problem, to put it differently, is of two kinds of descriptions—from the "outside" and the "inside" as it were. While what I call the description from the outside in the manner of social sciences tries to capture "the social" from a higher plane and often uses Western categories of thought, claiming objectivity, a description from the inside cannot aspire for such a transcendent gaze. The description from within, as I suggest, is not a matter of retreating to "traditional"/"indigenous" concepts either, but a retreat to language itself, recognising it as a creative field for the production—which is already at work in all our languages—of such concepts.[4]

Kumaran Asan: Life and Times

Before we set out to read Asan's poetic works let us briefly look at the way he is presented in biographies and literary histories. Asan was born in 1873 in the Ezhava community. During his childhood he learned traditional medicine, Sanskrit literature and astrology under the supervision of teachers like Thundathil Asan and Kochuraman Vaidyar (George 1972, 9). After elementary education he briefly worked as an accountant but his incessant desire for knowledge drove him to join another Sanskrit school called Vijnanasandayini. He had started composing poems at an

---

[4] Scholars have discussed different discourses of Indian modernity. Modernity in the traditionalist neo-conservative language is "understood as an epistemology of the colonial domination—at best as a bunch of sophisticated conceptual categories with alien intentions of subjugation, of both its economy and psychology" (Singh 2018, 110). The nationalist language of Indian modernity, constituted around the nationalist themes of Enlightenment thought, "focused its intellectual endeavors on the question of subjective freedom of the individual, based on their rationality, the liberal view of the rights and obligations" and also "steered the discourse within the domain of state ideology, by recognizing the 'reason of state' and its central autonomous and directing role in the affairs of society" (ibid., 113). Singh proposes a third possibility of discourse to overcome the tradition-modernity conundrum: the hermeneutical discourse. She argues: "The hermeneutical discourse of modernity contested, challenged, and absorbed features of modernity by reinterpreting its rational contents, and more than that, by extracting meaning from various Indian philosophical texts, to re-establish a practical ethics, and to live out the modern life—an ethics rooted in communitarian social relationships, as opposed to individualistic ethical practices of the Enlightenment modernity" (ibid., 120). Though Singh presents the third approach as more nuanced than the neo-traditionalist and modernist positions, the hermeneutical position is still haunted by the division of Western and indigenous. Language, on the other hand, is neither traditional nor modern in a strict sense; it is a space where the "synchronic" and the "diachronic" can and do co-exist.

early age though he later remarked that his attention was mainly on prosody and other poetic devices (ibid., 11). Asan had picked an early interest in Tamil and Sanskrit which he continued to study throughout his life. A decisive moment in his life, at the age of 18, was his meeting with Sree Narayana Guru who had become an important spiritual figure for the Ezhavas. Narayana Guru encouraged Asan in his poetic endeavour but is reported to have advised him "against an accent on erotic sentiment" (ibid., 14). It was under Narayana Guru that he learned Vedanta and Yogic culture and began writing devotional poems.[5] In 1895, Asan went to Bangalore for further studies under the auspices of Guru who had managed to get Palpu to attend on Asan (Palpu [1863–1950] was a prominent leader of the Ezhava community who took initiative to establish the Sree Narayana Dharma Paripalana Yogam (SNDP) that organised the Ezhavas socially and politically). During this time Asan's preferred subject was *tarkashastra* and *nyayashastra*. He also travelled to Madras and Calcutta as part of his studies. Asan's stay outside Kerala during the period of 1895–1900 had a very fundamental influence on his later life. He was exposed to various literatures, both in Indian languages and English, acquainted with people from different walks of life, and had very closely read the literature of the Romantic Movement.

---

[5] The biographical information on Asan's early writings is contentious. P. K. Balakrishnan, for example, has questioned the details concerning the meeting of Asan and Narayana Guru. He claims that Asan had not indulged in writing erotic poems and Narayana Guru, therefore, did not have to advise him against it. In Balakrishnan's account (2009) Asan was already a mature young poet committed to writing devotional songs. Asan had written poems and plays like *Sivastotramala* and *Vichitra Vijayam*, and translations such as *Soundarya Lahari* and *Prabodha Chandrodayam* during the first phase of his literary productivity. Most of them were spiritual in nature but some had drawn from the Sanskritic literary conventions of erotic literature. Balakrishnan agrees that he paid utmost attention to prosody and poetics, imitated Sanskrit classics and used both Sanskrit and Malayalam.

The Ezhava Memorial[6], an important event in the history of Ezhava movement, happened when Asan was at Bangalore. When he came back, he took up the position of the general secretary of the newly formed Sree Narayana Dharma Paripalana Yogam (generally known as SNDP Yogam) in 1903. A magazine was started under Yogam named Vivekodayam and Asan was appointed the editor. He also organised two industrial exhibitions, first at Quilon in 1904 and then at Cannanore in 1906 as part of the annual celebrations of SNDP Yogam. Asan rose to prominence with his poem *Veena Poovu* (1907), considered as the first lyric romantic poem in Malayalam. He subsequently wrote longer poems such as *Nalini* (1911), *Leela* (1914), *Chandala Bhikshuki* (1922) and *Duravastha* (1922). Reigning at the height of literary repute Asan tragically died in 1924 in a boat accident in the Pallana river.

This biographical narrative shows not only how Asan is presented as a poet, but how he is situated within a larger narrative of social transformation in Kerala. His meeting with Guru—considered a defining moment in the poet's life—sanitizes him of the eroticism accrued in vernacular literary cultures and moves him closer to the social and ideological movement Guru represented. It further adds to the career of the poet who demonstrated through his later poems the greatness of the abstract notion of *sneham* (love) as opposed to that of physical desire. The travel outside Kerala prepared him for the many "influences" he would carry from those places which eventually inaugurated the strain of romanticism in Malayalam poetry. By writing poems with sharp social criticism such as *Duravastha* and *Chandala Bhikshuki*, Asan was eventually endowed with the status of a modern poet-reformer in Kerala's social and literary history.

The critical reception to Asan's poetry has been generally divided into two groups: one which valorised the aspects of different themes

---

[6] Ezhava Memorial was a memorandum signed by members of Ezhava community and submitted to the Travancore maharaja in 1896 citing the social backwardness of the community and requesting the extension of governmental jobs to the Ezhavas who were excluded from it.

Asan has dealt with in his poems such as *sneham* (which earned him the approbation of *snehagayakan* or "the bard of love"). This reading of Asan directly draws on his biographical details and canonises him as the greatest Malayalam poet-reformer of innate insights. The other group engaged in social criticism tried to place Asan in the broader context of social transformation.[7] The prism of an idealised notion of love is sometimes a strategy by which Asan's poetry is inserted into a liberal–literary intelligibility that defies its inner tensions. E. M. S. Namboodiripad's understanding of Asan's poetry, for example, was informed by such a historicist framework (Namboodiripad 1995). He understood Asan as a "bourgeois poet"—and by extension Asan's *sneham* can be read as an antecedent of modern conjugality. What I want to suggest here is that Asan can be read in a way other than simply the poet of an idealised notion of love, as one who dramatised the experience of the impossibility of deciding between the extremities of physical desire and an ascesis that is grounded on renunciation and abandonment of the pleasures of the phenomenal world. Nor is he a poet who resolved the tension between past and present and thereby produced a form of poetic expression that combined the old and the new, but rather one who explored an irresolution between historical memory and the possibility of a future as an ethical opening for the experience of freedom.

The Moral Aporia in *Chinthavishtayaya Sita*

Chintavishtayaya Sita[8] depicts Sita in her most decisive moment—at the end of twelve long years spent in the Valmiki's

---

[7] See the essay by Yacob Thomas "Adhunikathayude Sareeram Veena Poovu: Oru Punarvayana" in *Veena Poovinte Nootand* edited by C. A. Anas (2007). Thomas includes critics like M. Leelavathy, M. K. Sanu and M. M. Basheer in the first group and E. M. S. Namboodiripad, Joseph Mundassery and Thayattu Sankaran as belonging to the second group (Thomas 2007, 107).

[8] Though Asan started composing the poem in 1914, *Chinthavishtayaya Sita* was finished only in 1919. In the preface to the poem Asan says that the first 80 stanzas were written during the first five years but the rest of the poem

ashram after she was rejected by Rama. Her grown-up sons have accompanied Valmiki to Rama's court. Rama would recognise his sons when they recite Ramayana to him and he would remember his past life. This thought makes Sita uncomfortable and she seeks solitude in the garden. The initial part of the poem presents Sita surrounded by vegetation where she enters into a dream-like state. The total immersion and identification of Sita in the surrounding nature suggests a deep ecological meaning as well. Sitting in the garden she engages in an autobiographical reflection as her mind is troubled by countless questions. She begins by taking note of the very contingent nature of the world: Nothing is certain/ our fortunes and fleeting/ we plod along our feverish ways, yet/ the world reveals its mysteries to none.[9]

Recollecting each and every moment of sorrow in her life she slowly begins to closely evaluate and analyse those situations. But the critical introspection instantly gives way to bitter feelings toward Rama who has wronged not only to her but so many others as well, like the "untouchable" Sambuka. The poem which started with the quietude of the ashram garden moves to a point where Sita vents her turbulent feelings. Towards the end of the poem Sita comes to the realisation that Rama as a person could not be the sole reason for her plight; the poem ends with a sense of calm after she overcomes her bitterness toward Rama. She realises that though Rama is the king, he is only a cog in the machine of the dharmic order. But she never thinks of going back to him even when she is able to rationalise her love for him. She asks:

> Why would I endure this? Does the king intend
> that I should appear before him, prove

---

was written in a few days while he underwent a creative surge. He comments that the subject of the poem is Sita's thoughts on her past experiences and her immediate future. The poem is written in the Sanskrit meter called *viyogini* which also means "a woman separated from her husband".

[9] The lines are taken from the translation of the poem by Rizio Yohannan Raj in Richman (2008).

my innocence and live as his consort again?
Does he take me for a puppet? (Asan 2008, 86)

The repeated use of the word "I" is noteworthy here since this kind of usage for self-reference was something rare in the social context of late nineteenth-century Kerala. There were specific honorifics to be used when one was referring to persons of different castes or social positions. This social etiquette of addressing and self-addressing is erased in Sita's speech where the "I" becomes so articulate. This repeated use of the and the self-possession that it indicates give a definitiveness to the final part of the poem that depicts a resolute and unhesitant Sita who accompanies Valmiki to Rama's palace and, there in front of Rama, vanishes to the ground. Asan very skillfully compresses this last sequence into a few words, "and then, she left the world" marking out for Sita a moment of decision. She salutes Rama and bids him farewell, comparing herself to a bird that leaves the bough of Rama's arm and flies off into the sky undaunted (Asan 2008, 86). The vast space—existing outside of time and space—that receives Sita into itself is imagined as one prior to the origins of the phenomenal world.

The mass forming the cosmic spheres
is absent here. In this pure dwelling
of peace, beyond day and night,
is only the radiant Primal Principle. (ibid.)

The word that Asan uses, which is translated as "Primal Principle" above, is *adidhamam* (ancient place/site) and may be understood in line with the *advitin* notion of Brahma, the true ontological reality that is omnipresent in the phenomenal world. This transformative moment is in continuation with Narayana Guru's own argument about finding the true ontological basis of differentiation of the humankind (into male and female) which Asan, through his poetry, supplants with an interiority of the self (Kumar 1997). The crucial point for this transformation is marked by an experience of the limits of the body and relocating the self in the soul. This moment of transformation in the case of Sita also gestures towards a new actor—other than the momentary glance that Rama and

Sita exchanges—within the structure of gaze. The last stanza of the poem reads:

> … she reached the Royal Court,
> went upto Rama in silence,
> and in one glance saw her lord
> amidst the nobles, looking remorseful;
> and then, she left this world." (Asan 2008, 87)

The reference to the nobles that look remorseful (Asan uses the term *poura samaksham*) creates a new interlocutor as it is the group of citizens that now becomes the transferred site for conflict. The site of moral legitimation is no more confined to (or even has now been divested from) the sovereign embedded in the dharmic order but relocated in a citizenry that is capable of experiencing the feeling of remorse or shame. The poem at this point becomes allegorical of Asan's own political vocation as a representative of the Ezhava community in addressing the king on the one hand and the wider public on the other, seeking redressal for the wrongs committed against the community.

To further dwell on the question of the nature of self-transformation that marks Sita's self-destructive critique let us consider how the monologic form becomes a prominent site of the exploration of the self in Asan's work. The solitude and quietude that Sita experiences, which lends her an extraordinary capacity for thought and reflection, is fundamental to her criticism of Rama. Udaya Kumar (1997) has argued that Asan's preferred medium for this expression of thought was monologue which is the central device for the articulation of self. On this subjective interiority of Sita, Kumar remarks that

> *Chinthavishtayaya Sita* … marks the most mature articulation of the monologue in Asan's work. Monologue in Asan is the site of a self-practice which seizes the self in a moment of recognition and transformation … Through the monologue, Asan develops a language for 'the secrets of the mind', a language of thought (vicharabhasha), and provides an elaboration of the notion of 'inner sense' (anthakaranam). (1997, 267)

Sita's subjective immersion could find a fuller expression only in her self-destruction. The aporetic moment of subjective impossibility also defies acceding to the demand of social normativity, and in fact, marks a return to itself from the social world which it cannot inhabit. This introspective intensity of Sita's character is found in other poems as well—as the liminal moment of consummation of desire meets with the finitude of the body (Kumar 1997), but the passage from one to the other does not necessarily involve an analysis, or an awareness of the fallibility or transformative nature of self-representation. What is specific to Sita is this careful self-analysis and the act of its suspension (in her death) itself.

It is to be noted that the moment of "moral dilemma" presented in the poem is not between dharma and adharma (say, which is the ground for the conflict between Rama and Ravana) where the reader would eventually be given an answer as to what dharma is. The monologic form captures "the social" in its dialectical totality and through an act of self-criticism and scrutiny pushes the established moral order to its own limits culminating in the subject's implosion. The subject's implosion is common to other poems by Asan as well, but in Sita we see that this implosion is prefaced by an act of moral critique rehearsed in the monologic form, touching on a point of no return indicating a rupture with the past. Asan does not propose a new ethics for the changing times in his poetry, but tries to show the implosion of the subject under the pressure generated by an immanent movement of thought. The exhibition of this implosion, unable to recoil into another order of ethical assurance, becomes an indistinguishably ethical, aesthetic and affective act. Further, the moral subject of Asan's poetry is built on a heightened awareness of the contingency of law. As Sita begins her reflection, she takes a deep exhale which is described as a breeze that has fled from the law (*niyamam vittoru thennal mathiri*, 6). Sita's own reflection convinces her that there is no certainty to anything (*oru nishchayamillayonninum*). Moreover, the secrets of the world (Asan 2018, 7) are not knowable to anyone. Asan's moral subject is not one who simply adheres to socially accepted principles (*maryada* or *keezhvazhakkam* as it was called in early twentieth-century Travancore) but the one that recognises that the very condition of the possibility of morality is its impossibility and its unknowability. *Chinthavishtayaya Sita* dramatises this implosion of the subject. Morality is shifted away from the *shruti* or *shastras* and re-founded on a notion of conscience as presented through the image of a "remorseful citizenry" which is closely tied to the capacity for thought.

E. V. Ramakrishnan has suggested that Asan's poetry "exceeds the contexts of its origin" (Ramakrishnan 2011, 119). Asan's greatest achievement as a poet is "to have fashioned a poetic mode and voice to embody the social energy unleashed by a moment of radical reforms" (ibid.). The kernel of this poetics, according to Ramakrishnan, was an emphasis on selfhood, "a moment of self-revelation that entails a critique of existing value systems" (ibid.). We have already seen that Asan's poetry becomes a site for the subject's elaboration of self-possession, but what Ramakrishnan points to as an "excess" requires a further detailing. The modes of excess work in Asan's poetry in different ways, the self-imploding intensity of desire (in the case of poems such as *Nalini* and *Leela*) and a radical moral critique which culminates in the destitution of the subject (in the case of *Chinthavishtayaya Sita*) are specific expressions of this excess. Here, we are interested in another way the "excess" figures in *Chinthavishtayaya Sita* in relation to the act of thinking itself. There are many words that refer to "thought" in the poem: *athichintha* which can be translated as "excessive thought" (Asan 2018, 3), but as meta-thought or thought-on-thought as well, as the prefix "*athi*" is often used to refer to "meta" as in the case of *athi-bhouthikavadam* or meta-physics. *Chinthayam kadal* (the ocean of thought; ibid., 6), *vichara bhasha* (the language of thought, 6), *manam chalippu* (the mind moves; ibid., 7) etc., are examples of a new connection Asan establishes between language and thought. Thinking takes a brief rest from the phenomenal world and turns itself into an object.

Sita's mind is stirred uncontrollably and is often in a state beyond linguistic presentation of thoughts. *Vichara bhasha* expresses this impossible relation of the act of thinking to "the unthought". She often expresses her concern over the growing uncontrollability of her mind: "I no longer want the monkey of madness to enter the virtuous garden of my wits" (Asan 2008, 70).

The subject that emerges in *Chinthavishtayaya Sita* is an equally split subject between the conscious and unconscious—a separation that is marked out by the incessant activity of thinking and its *im*-possible linguistic presentation. Sita has to wrestle with an excess within her which—analogous to her modes of excessive speech—acts even as she recognises the limits of language. She remembers her rude behaviour to Lakshmana and says: "Is there any wicked path into which an unruly mind may not wander!" (ibid., 71).

The *athichintha* the poem presents is Sita's efforts to analyse the contents and movements of her own mind. *Vichara bhasha* thus, may not, in this sense, just be "the language of thought", but language-as-thought as well.

Redefining Language and Literature

The mark of modern subjectivity is visible in Asan's earliest poem *Veena Poovu* which we may look at briefly to elaborate on the emerging field of language and literature as well. A very significant event in Asan's life was the publication of *Veena Poovu* in 1908 at the age of 35. This poem marked Asan's complete break from the "convention-bound poems" (George 1984, 27) and also inaugurated a new era of literary appreciation in Malayalam while setting new norms of verse composition. It was first published in the magazine *Mithavadi* published by Moorkoth Kumaran and later republished in *Bhashaposhini* along with a note by the writer C. S. Subramanian Potti who tried to "clear some mistaken notions about the function of poetry which led to a kind of stereotyped, artificial composition of verses" (ibid., 32) and to which Asan's poem was a corrective. George remarks that "every major poem that Asan has written is a sequel or revised version of the Fallen Flower" (ibid., 39). Let me quote at length how Joseph Mundassery, an important literary critic of the period, explains the experience of reading Asan's poetry:

> I happened to come across Asan's "Veena Poovu" (Fallen Flower) and "Nalini" when I was reading in the secondary school. Those were the days when some of my classmates and myself had been captivated by the dexterous style of Ulloor and the versatile writings of Vallathol, inlaid with beautiful imageries. Our admiration for them stretched beyond mere appreciation of their works to an attempt at imitating their styles. But on reading through "Veena Poovu" and "Nalini" we sensed a totally different experience. Despite the fact that we tumbled against a number of difficult stanzas we were tempted to go through those poems several times. What confounded us and rendered it difficult to assimilate the substance on the very first reading were not the tough and incomprehensible Sanskrit expressions, usually found in Ulloor's works. The meaning of difficult words could be referred to in dictionaries. As a matter of fact, we did not come across many such words in "Veena Poovu" and "Nalini". But the magnitude of the imagery infused in each line, compelled us to hold our breath and ponder deeper and deeper. And as we pondered, we were overwhelmed by the expansiveness of the meaning and the unfolding of the poet's imagination. Yet at that time none of us could analyze and determine as to how on reading "Veena Poovu" and "Nalini" we sensed a feeling so different from that experienced on going through the works of Vallathol and Ulloor. All that we could make out was that Asan's poetry heralded a new style. (Mundassery 1974)

In this long reflection, Joseph Mundassery points to an experience that is produced by a rearrangement of language. This internal reconstitution of language is comparable to the changes in the semiology of attire that Udaya Kumar (1997) detects in the transformation of the body, from the one that is marked by a specific set of signifiers to one which is suggestive, which works more with a minimalism in representation than the excess of exhibition. Asan's language, as we understand from Mundassery's words, shuns the decorativeness and ornate embellishment of classical poetry and relies mainly on its simplicity. Further, this linguistic transformation is accompanied by a wonder produced at the level of reception as is clear from the words of Mundassery—even though the poem is written in a simple and unembellished language it presents itself as elusive and demands to be interpreted.

Poetry now acquires a sense of depth, where what is said at the surface is contrasted to something only available at a deeper level. This is further related to the experience of time in poetry as well. Reading of Asan's poem involves "duration" as opposed to the classical modes of comprehension where reading is an instance of the recognition of the "wit" in poetry. It is within this relation to a new temporality—and its repetition—of understanding that the poem carries out the work of disclosure. It is within these modes of experiencing depth, duration and world disclosure that the new sensuous subject of Asan's poetry finds itself placed.

Another characteristic that critics have pointed out is an acute recognition of death and the contingency of life in *Veena Poovu*. It is as if death becomes the background against which one sees life. The poem begins with an acknowledgement of loss and the necessity to mourn. It is at the moment of surpassing a deadlock between life and death that the modern subject can be narrativised and presented in the image of a flower in a striking comparison to the memory of a lost human life in its life cycle of birth, growth and decay. *Chinthavishtayaya Sita* also displays an accentuation of the autobiographical volition in contrast to the imminent possibility of death—or even suicide—of Sita. But what is to be noted is a structure of vision that Asan deploys in many of his poems. Poetry for him becomes a form of "thanatography" which involves a complex structure of "compassionate witnessing".[10] It is quite reasonable to think that Asan was influenced by the Buddhist notions of suffering (*dukha*) and radical contingency (*anatta*) though a general line of reading has established him closer to the *advitin* tradition. But the self in Asan goes through

[10] See Kumar (2016) for a discussion of these terms in Asan's poetry.

an experience of diminution and vanishing; the process which the poem becomes an act of exhibition and cognition for the reader. Thus, the reader identifies with the poet's gaze that takes cognizance of the impermanence of not only the wilted flower but all that exists in *Veena Poovu*. In *Chinthavishtayaya Sita*, the poet creates a structure of gaze where the reader secretly beholds Sita immersed in her monologic thoughts and witnesses her self-annihilation.[11] Sita is presented as immersed in her thoughts where the reader is positioned as someone watching her interior world without Sita being aware of it. Asan's poetry, even when it is a site for the explorations of the self, becomes a site for an ethical opening, and encountering an irreducible other that cannot be reappropriated into discourse. Though Asan did believe in the notion of soul (*atman*) and its afterlife, his poetry may be drawing more prominently from the recognition that death is the absolute finitude of human possibility, and that literature is a specific mode of this recognition.

Sankatam: From Poetry to Politics

In a speech made in Sree Moolam Praja Sabha in the year 1909, Asan presented a grievance that the rights of the Ezhava subjects to study in the government schools ought not be hampered just because some members of caste-Hindu communities do not approve of it. He said that many members of the upper-caste communities have expressed their willingness to accommodate Ezhava children in the schools where their own children are studying. The plea made by Asan was that the Maharaja should

---

[11] For lack of space I have excluded other poems from this discussion, but this structure, one may see, is fundamental to Asan's poetry. In *Karuna* the final scene presents the dismembered body of Vasavadatta before Upagupta, *Nalini* and *Leela* dramatises the deaths of heroines seen through the eyes of Divakaran and Madhavi, *Prarodananam*, an elegiac poem written on the death of A. R. Rajaraja Varma, becomes a sit for taking cognizance of human finitude and mourning, etc. These are examples of this gaze that Asan's poetry explores.

bring forth a law which guaranteed that no discrimination was forced upon Ezhavas in the realm of education. Five years later, in another speech delivered in the same Sabha, Asan said that even though the law had been passed favouring Ezhava boys' entry into schools run by the government, the upper-caste people had adopted a policy of creating difficulties for the implementation of the law. That is, the very social forces that Asan declared as willing to, and even desirous of, Ezhavas' entry into schools had now become reactionary and were going against the Maharaja's own proclamation. It might be the case that Asan was referring to two different constituencies in the two instances—the reformist section among the upper-castes in the first case, and the reactionary, in the latter. Whatever the case may be, what interests us here is the notion of *samudayam* and *sankatam* that Asan uses in his speeches. *Samudayam* was the word used to refer to community in the political discourse—a word that could be located in a wider spectrum of signification: from the human community to a specific community.[12] This term can be understood as having two interrelated aspects: on the one hand there is the notion of a good life (*kshemam*) which works as a generative ground for the aspirations of associational life, and on the other, *sankatam* which may refer to the suffering or historical wrong that specific communities have undergone. The word *sankatam* unites within itself three distinct sets of meaning: as moral dilemma or a situation which demands a decision as in the word *dharmasankatam*, the idea of grief and bereavement at the loss of someone, which may invoke sense of mourning and melancholia, and the notion of a grievance presented before the sovereign or to a governmental office. Though the interrelatedness of these concepts requires a further elaboration, what we are interested here in is the affinity that Asan's use of the term *sankatam* invokes with the structure of his poetry itself. Asan's expression of *sankatam* involves an ethics of compassionate witnessing demanded from the sovereign

12 See Kumar (1997) for a discussion of this term in the context of the Ezhava movement.

or the general public but also includes within its purview the sense of moral decision in the form of law. *Samudayam*, seen through this sense of *sankatam*, is remarkably different from its governmental counterpart, though eventually it is subsumed by the governmental logic. Communities are usually understood to be the traditional hierarchical castes re-articulated through a creation of technologies of colonial census within the grid of governmental power. But these communities, or what came to be called *samudayam*, are not mere socially sanctioned "subject positions". One may call these refigured communities as "critical communities" that come to be seen as the bearers of rights in the colonial context. What accounts for this transformation? It cannot be a movement merely from the forms of reified caste-community into the reified governmental-community. This has to be mediated by a subjective transformation that is not reducible to its own telos in governmentality. It is this invention of a moral subject that Asan's poetry addresses. Without this mediation—what happens in the middle of this passage—we may simply mistake the newer forms of community for a mere continuation of earlier forms of castes. *Samudayam*, therefore, is not to be understood as the ultimate end of Asan's ethical thought either. Its unraveling of the notion of *sankatam* acts as a permanent source of negativity for modes of communitarian attachments and political action.

Works Cited

Asan, Kumaran. (2007) 2018. *Kumaranasante Kavithakal: Sampoorna Samaharam*. Kozhikode: Poorna Publications.

Asan, Kumaran. 2008. "Sita Immersed in Reflection." Translated by Rizio Yohannan Raj. In *Ramayana Stories in Modern South India: An Anthology*, edited by Paula Richman. Bloomington: Indiana University Press.

Balakrishnan, P. K. (1970) 2009. *Kavyakala Kumaranasaniloode*. Kottayam: DC Books.

Caputo, J. D, ed. 1997. *Deconstruction in a Nutshell: A Conversation with Jacques Derrida*. New York: Fordham University Press.

Chalam, Gudipati V. 2008. "Sita Enters the Fire. " In *Ramayana Stories in Modern South India: An Anthology*, edited by Paula Richman, translated by Sailaza Easwari, 58–63. Bloomington: Indiana University Press.

George, K. M. (1972) 1984. *Kumaran Asan*. New Delhi: Sahitya Akademi.

Hess, Linda. 1999. "Rejecting Sita: Indian Responses to the Ideal Man's Cruel Treatment of His Ideal Wife. " *Journal of the American Academy of Religion* 67 (1): 1–32.

Kadavath, Vipin K. 2019. "The Refiguring of Sita: Notes on Kumaran Asan's Poetics of Freedom." In *Gendered Ways of Transnational Un-belonging from a Comparative Literature Perspective*, edited by Indrani Mukherjee and Java Singh, 226–39. Newcastle upon Tyne: Cambridge Scholars Publishing.

Kaviraj, Sudipta. 2010. "Writing, Speaking, Being: Language and the Historical Formation of Identities in India." In *The Imaginary Institution of India*, 127–66. Ranikhet: Permanent Black.

Kumar, Udaya. 1997. "Self, body and inner sense: Some reflections on Sree Narayana Guru and Kumaran Asan." *Studies in History* 13 (247): 247–70.

———. 2016. "Intensities and the Language of Limits: Marking Gender in the Poetry of Kumaran Asan." In *Writing the First Person: Literature, History and Autobiography in Kerala*, 86–119. Ranikhet: Permanent Black.

Mangharam, Muktilakhi. 2009. "Rama, Must I Remind You of Your Divinity? Locating a Sexualized, Feminist, and Queer Dharma in the Ramayana." *Diacritics* 39 (1): 75–78, 80–96, 98–104.

Mundassery, Joseph. 1974. "Roots of Asan's Poetry." In *Poetry and Renaissance: Kumaran Asan Birth Centenary Volume*, edited by M. Govindan, 206–08. Madras: Sameeksha.

Namboodiripad, E. M. S. (1995) 2012. *Asanum Malayala Sahityavum*. Trivandrum: Chintha Books.

Ramakrishnan, E. V. 2011. "Plotting Memory, Modernity and Desire." In *Locating Indian Literature: Texts Traditions Translations*, 119–30. Hyderabad: Orient Blackwan.

Raveendran, T. K. (1996) 2015. *Nairyantharavum Parivarthanavum Asan Kavithayil*. Kozhikode: Mathrubhumi Books.

Richman, Paula, ed. 2008. *Ramayana Stories in Modern South India: An Anthology*. Bloomington: Indiana University Press.

Singh, Savita. 2018. "Three Languages on the Discourse of Modernity in India." In *Exploring Indian Modernities: Ideas and Practices*, edited by Leila Choukroune and Paul Bhandari, 107–27. Singapore: Springer.

Thomas, Yacob. 2007. "Adhunikathayude Sareeram Veena Poovu: Oru Punar Vayana." In *Veena Poovinte Oru Noottand*, edited by C. A. Anas, 102–25. Cochin: Pranatha Books.

FOURTEEN

The Lives of *Aithihyamala*

Textuality, Region, History

BINI B. S.

The paper examines *Aithihyamala* or the garland of legends and myths, a twentieth-century compilation of regional lore in Malayalam by Kottarathil Sankunni from three perspectives: first, I look at the very process by which *Aithihyamala* came into being as an attempt to conserve, showcase and circulate "ancient" and "timeless" narratives as printed texts for posterity. Secondly, I read *Aithihyamala* as a supplement to and an interpretative site for history since some of these legends and myths claim to be based on actual historical events and people. Lastly, I map the arrangement of narratives in *Aithihyamala* in which animals, humans, demi-gods and gods feature to get a sense of implicit hierarchies and interconnections.

Textual Transitions and the Rationales of Conservation and Circulation

The oral-textual-visual transitions of the narratives compiled in *Aithihyamala* are numerous and diverse: disjunct oral narratives gathered and serialised in popular literary magazines, printed multi-volume formats with an implicit logic behind grouping and arranging the stories, later, a downloadable e-book retaining the same order of arrangement, select stories in comic book form in English and Hindi translations, stories adapted into television series and films, *kathaprasangam* (a performance featuring music and story-telling, usually staged during temple festivals) and several theatrical adaptations.[1] The rationale behind these attempts of collection, compilation and reinterpretation of *Aithihyamala* stories appears to be the conservation and circulation of *aithihyams*. These narratives are gathered and put together by Kottarathil Sankunni in Malayalam but the range of spatio-temporality is not limited to the histories and folktales of the Malayalam-speaking regions. In other words, these *aithihyams* may seem rooted in a specifiable regional and linguistic domain but they branch out to undefined and boundless realms of time and space. The closest synonymous expression for an *aithihyam* in Malayalam is *pazhamkatha*, which can literally be translated as "an old/ancient narrative". Distinct forms like folklore, *sthalapurana* (narratives based on places), *mahacharitam* (biographies of great beings—real or imagined), events from an indefinite past filtered through collective/popular memory, fables, legends, myths, yarns, and the like fit into the expansive terrain of the *aithihyam*.

While probing the cultural as well as the linguistic conditions behind the compilation of *Aithihyamala*, one cannot overlook the complex rationale and aesthetics of the transition from the oral to the literary, followed by the visual, the performative, and the digital. Most of the legends and myths in *Aithihyamala* were part of an oral tradition spanning an indeterminable temporality and perhaps existed in many narrative variations. Sankunni was open to the polysemic fluidity of the process of gathering accounts and then reminiscing and narrativising them for posterity by presenting them as written stories. *Aithihyamala* came out in the book form in 1909 as the consequence of an endeavour commenced by Kottarathil Sankunni for collecting, recording, organising and serialisation of narratives in *Malayala Manorama* newspaper and then *Bhashaposhini*, a literary magazine published

---

[1] There had been films in Malayalam based on the stories of *Naranathu Bhranthan* and *Perumthachan* from the long *Aithihyamala* narrative titled *Parayipettu Panthirukulam*. The stories of Kadamattathu Kathanar, Kayamkulam Kochunni, Thacholi Othenan, Unniyarcha, many goddesses and elephants have inspired cinematic and theatrical adaptations.

by the Manorama group of publications. Sankunni worked with the chief editor K. I. Varghese Mappila of the Kandathil family that founded the *Manorama* newspaper and had many occasions to share the lore and legends he had heard and memorised with Mappila during their myriad conversations. Mappila was so taken in by the stories narrated by Sankunni that he suggested the need to record the same. He told Sankunni:

> It is not enough to narrate and forget these *Aithihyams*. The narratives contain humour, exaggerations and absurdities that defy logic, yet they are remarkably rich in ideas and philosophical principles that everyone should get to know. The text would benefit those who would be entertained by it; the ones who are capable of engaging with the deeper vision of the narratives would become wiser by it.[2]

Mappila saw the potential of *Aithihyamala* as a text that could enlighten while it delighted. The propelling and driving force behind the original compilation was a realisation about the entertainment and didactic value of cultural legacy. When Mappila willed and facilitated it, Sankunni found himself rather enthusiastically fulfilling the wish of a scholarly entrepreneur friend. When the stories started appearing in *Malayala Manorama* and *Bhashaposhini*, there were a few detractors and numerous adulators. "Parayipettu Panthirukulam", a story that sheds light on the caste-gender dynamics and social hierarchies invited some criticism perhaps because of its subversive force and incredibility. But Kerala Varma Valiya Koyithampuran and Sheshagiri Prabhu who was renowned for his astute writings in *Manorama* publications, along with several other literary stalwarts appreciated the effort. After Mappila's death, Sankunni stopped compiling the stories and only later resumed the compilation in a book form for a series, *Lakshmibai Granthaavali*, respecting the request of the manager of the series, Vellaykkal Narayana Menon.

---

[2] Author's statement dated 17 April 1909, *Aithihyamala* (vol. 1, xi–xii). I have used the two-volume print version published by Kottarathil Sankunni Memorial Committee in 1974 for this study, which has all 8 books. Volume 1 has the first 4 books and the second volume has books 5–8.

The text eventually transitioned from the serialised version for a popular magazine to a compilation into eight books comprising 126 stories. Its popularity continues to date and many go back to reading it with much nostalgia. The text has been reprinted in several formats including the popular two-volume version which comprises four books each, complete and unabridged. There also exists a translation of select narratives into English. A few stories are available in Hindi as well. A project to digitise the book was initiated in 2011 and completed in 2013. It is also available in a downloadable eight-book format on archive.org. Now a single volume complete and unabridged format with illustrations brought out by Sayahna Foundation is available for free download. There is a comic book version of select stories in English in the series "Myths, Legends and Folktales from India" translated by Rukmini Sekhar and illustrated by Subir Roy.

I have, in the past, narrated in great detail the lives and journeys of *Aithihyamal*a as a disjunct assemblage of narratives and eventually a compiled text to illustrate how tightly intertwined it is with the life-worlds, memories, cultural imaginings and fantasies of a region and a people. *Aithihyamala*, being tales told in their language and idiom, was an integral part of the childhood reading repertoire of the people of many generations in Kerala. The lives contained in the stories of the text, long and multifarious, testify how Mappila's vision and Sankunni's efforts for conserving and circulating the *aithihyam*s and providing a pleasurable and instructive reading experience had not been in vain.

Stories, Contexts, and Reconceptualising Temporality

In this section of the paper, I examine how *aithihyam*s provide an interpretative and analytical site for revisiting our notions about history and historical truth. As mentioned in the previous section, the very idea of *aithihyam* comprises a wide range of epistemic and methodological possibilities as it could imply history, lore, anecdotal accounts, hearsay, legends, mythology, imagination, and even make-believe. *Aithihyam* can also represent collective memory, which includes both the official and popular variations. The processes of narrativising weave together all the conceptually disparate possibilities of an *aithihyam* and this compels us to revisit the notions of truth and method that are taken for granted. There could be a subtle or conscious politics in the selection and omission of numerous stories that had existed and circulated in the regional and linguistic oral tradition by Sankunni. In fact, he may have had to deal with several versions of the same story and thus may not be innocent of conscious aesthetic, ethical and political plans and strategies while choosing the mode and style of narrating. Sankunni was aware that his work based on *aithihyams* deserved to be categorised as *sahityam* ("literature" suggesting imagination and emplotment) and *charithram* ("history", which also embraces the strategies of informed speculation and emplotment). Hence, he had to adhere to a notion of truth that did justice to these categories which in his mind were never totally disconnected.

The creation of region as a linguistic space in *Aithihyamala* defies the structuralist logic which privileges structure over agency in unequivocal terms. I would go with the view of Henri Lefebvre[3] that language and the narratives that it could produce need not necessarily precede space, but production of space and spatiality follows the production of language and narrative. We see a unifying of the physical, the mental and the social domains as spatiality is constituted and shaped through discourse. The lived space is not limited to a concrete physical entity that can be mapped and defined by boundaries; it is an amorphous cultural location with indeterminate coordinates. Language, communication and narratives which compose that location play a vital part in making sense of temporality in relation to that lived space or life-world.

Sankunni as a collector, compiler and organiser of stories from the Malayalam-speaking regions under the umbrella term *Aithihyamala* or "garland of *aithihyams*" negotiates with concepts

---

[3] See Lefebvre's *The Production of Space* and *Critique of Everyday Life* to make sense of the interfaces of space, language/narrative and micro moments of life, experienced day by day.

of truth that are seemingly antonymous, that prevail independent of pedantic demands of verifiability. Sankunni's narrative philosophy and techniques have illustrated how ostensibly opposing views about truth can coexist. He keeps the spatio-temporalities of *Aithihyamala* narratives rather ambiguous and malleable, despite being occasionally daunted by the notions of truth and authenticity, a conflict that he comes to terms with by asserting that there could be truths more significant and pertinent than factual, documented historical truths. As Foucault extensively argued in *Archaeology of Knowledge*, historical space expands beyond a limited empirical sphere of documented happenings to a socio-psychological epistemological domain or a discursive field where the subject constitutes the objects of discourse and the truth of their life-worlds. Sankunni as the one who has taken up the task to narrate, constitutes such truth through informed imaginative processes, and his "truth" borders on poetic truth as it ties together documented knowledge, speculations based on available knowledge, sensitivity, and intuition.

Aithihyamala provides a macro view of the Malayalam-speaking region and takes us through the domains of grand temporality while also giving vivid details of the microphysics of everyday by ushering us into intimate private, domestic and psychological spaces. It is a reading experience marked by deep involvement—almost a shift in space and time as Michel Certeau (1989, xxi) points out:

> A different world (the reader's) slips into the author's place. This mutation makes the text habitable, like a rented apartment. It transforms another person's property into a space borrowed for a moment by a transient. Renters make comparable changes in an apartment they furnish with their acts and memories; as do speakers, in the language into which they insert both the messages of their native tongue and, through their accent, through their own "turns of phrase," etc., their own history; as do pedestrians, in the streets they fill with the forests of their desires and goals.

The conjoining of the macro and micro modes of life without leaving much space for distinction is a remarkable feature of

Aithihyamala narratives. We read about the rise and fall of powerful dynasties and monarchs, the coexistence of and conflicts between the political and religious authority, warfare and conquests, modes of land distribution, management of temples including allotment of land and other kinds of property to temples by the rulers, British colonialism, economy, and merchants and tradesmen. We also come to know about everyday routines and rituals, food and cooking, livelihoods and occupations including sorcerers and robbers, conversations happening at homes and in congregations of friends, jealousies and grievances, romances, betrayals, art and entertainment, animals, birds and plants that are integrated to the life-worlds, and magic and miracles that meld so well with the everyday. The interconnectedness and complicated juxtaposition of specific, localised, quotidian, and intimate micro-history with capacious and more general aspects of collective existence is explained by Susan Stewart:

> We cannot speak of the small, or miniature, work independent of the social values expressed toward private space—particularly of the ways the domestic and the interior imply the social formation of an interior subject. And we cannot speak of the grand and the gigantic independent of the social values expressed toward nature and the public and exterior life of the city. (1992, 95)

The micro-history that ties together the everyday and the experiential invariably necessitates a different approach to knowledge, method, and truth falling within the disciplinary domain of history. One may notice Sankunni's iterated claim of being located in a domain of "layered" truth far richer, more vibrant and having infinite possibilities. The idea of historical knowledge is often challenged by Sankunni's convictions about unknowable mysteries or metaphysics. While he acknowledges the magic and mystery of history, he also demonstrates a sense of the mindscapes and affective realms of lives around him. As far as the region is concerned, the text gives a glance at the social while capturing the historical by mapping the private and public domains of people's everyday lives: their customs, modes of being and doing, and existing social hierarchies. The notion of "everyday history", while striving not to limit itself to a narrow disciplinary range of history, straddles several disciplinary domains as it aspires not to leave out the experiential, social and anthropological. In other words, history becomes far more than narrative manoeuvring of those who wielded temporal or spiritual authority, which invariably would erase, silence and make invisible those who are conventionally unaccounted for in "official" legitimised histories.

History of everyday life has an expansive narrative and disciplinary scope to resist the furtive strategies of deletion and silencing. *Aithihyamala* engages with the everyday in great depth and detail by presenting varied perspectives on the life-worlds that it captures. Narrated with verve, elements of fantasy and unharnessed imaginative liberties characteristic to legends and mythology, the text illustrates such tropes of writing that are far removed from what we traditionally consider historical, making the claims to accuracy—frequently raised by the writer—sound almost paradoxical. The truth claims made by Sankunni form a recurrent feature of his narratives. These claims are often reinforced by references to divine or temporal authority or alluding to the opinions of sages or scholars. He adheres to a vision of the grandeur of truth which transcends the standards of historical authority. However, on the other hand, the details of the microcosmic life-worlds and temporalities that *Aithihyamala* provides would compel one to reconsider how a bhasha text of this kind could be brought to use in enriching the notion of history as a discipline and discursive practice.

The notions of space and time in a narrative like *Aithihyamala* are far removed from how spatio-temporality is conceived in history as a disciplinary practice. Very few *Aithihyamala* narratives have timeframes mentioned in them. Certain narratives suggest timelessness while certain others go by the norms of accepted historical periodisation, as happening in medieval times. There are also many narratives that capture the author's acceptance of and unease with the emergence of modernity.

The textualising of *Aithihyamala* coincides with a time in Kerala wherein existing social alignments and practices depending on caste, class and gender hierarchies were beginning to be analysed and questioned. Social institutions including marriage, family and norms of inheritance were at the threshold of major changes. The text often emphasises the immutability of certain hierarchies, beliefs, values and customs by narrating an origin myth, divine interventions, and the like. At the same time, mechanisms of mutability and subversion are not unknown to the narrator. He acknowledges change as an inevitability, often with pain and sometimes in triumph.

The narratives weaving together life-worlds and domains of experience are seldom innocent of the influences of ideology. Althusser explains that the selecting and deploying of the experiential as a narrative is an extended project of ideology. He further elaborates that a writer narrativising a life-world thus,

> only makes us 'see', 'perceive' or 'feel' the reality of the ideology of that world. When we speak of ideology, we should know that ideology slides into all human activity, that it is identical with the 'lived' experience of human existence itself.... This 'lived' experience is not a given, given by a pure 'reality', but the spontaneous 'lived experience' of ideology in its peculiar relationship to the real. (Althusser 1971, 223)

As it happens in the process of narrativisation, the readers' interpretations in and across spatio-temporalities also get coloured by the hues of their ideological spectrums. As an illustration of narration that is ideologically coloured, one may look into the stories about important human beings, dynasties, conquests, places of worship, and social ordering in *Aithihyamala.* Ideology in Althusser points to the processes or structures meant for perpetuating and validating systematised perspectives and patterns of domination and control. These processes and systems are both political and epistemic and resist any opposing point of view or procedures. Ideologies often turn into closed systems presumably complete in themselves. Loosely used, ideology can refer to a set of principles seeking constant validation and adherence, which also demonstrates an aversion to radical change and challenge. In *Aithihyamala*, the stories are founded on several recurring tropes and perspectives, which gain the gravity of defining principles or moral norms. For example, the greatness of the ruling class follows certain standards, of which devotion to deities and contribution to temples is an integral component. What the ruler does for gods is more important than what beneficial contributions she or he makes for the mortal subjects. This standard is expected to be followed by not only Hindu kings, but also rulers and conquerors from other religions. In fact, to prove the powers of a deity, Sankunni often highlights an incident of a Muslim conqueror or ruler turning into a devotee and making considerable offerings to the temple.

The principles built around values and morality percolate into the life-worlds and mindscapes irrespective of the theme and characters across narratives. The worlds of animals, gods and goddesses are anthropomorphised as Sankunni attributes human-like emotions, patterns of ordering the domestic and the social spaces, and behaviours to the divine and the animal (for example, the goddess and elephant stories wherein the divine and the animal often behave like human beings). Celebration of such virtues as obedience, piety, fidelity, women's chastity and love for the ruler run through the narratives. Qualities that Sankunni deems virtuous are often rewarded by divine and temporal powers, while deviance from the norm invites the divine wrath or the ruler's ire. Sankunni's personal opinions and convictions, often bordering on prejudices and stereotypes are reaffirmed through iteration, especially his views on castes, genders, social institutions, ideals and morals. This could make one wonder about the extent to which his personal opinions and proclivities have influenced the selection and omission of narratives for *Aithihyamala*.

An implicit conformity to customs, traditions and conventions is a dominant feature of *Aithihyamala*. Sankunni often validates the hierarchies of social division and has notions of superiority attached to caste, social position, economic status and the like. The politics of respect and contempt is too conspicuous to miss our attention. The subversive potential of individual and collective actions challenging exploitative hierarchies are portrayed in greyer shades of suspicion than brighter hues of hope. Sankunni's stories suggest that behind the existing hierarchies of religion, region, caste and gender, there is a preordained, unquestionable and mysterious logic. The next section will examine the rationality of cosmic/social ordering in *Aithihyamala*.

Hierarchising the Cosmic/Social Scheme: Ordering the Life-Worlds and Narratives

Aithihyamala captures social divisions by laying out telling instances of class, caste, and gender dynamics and how such equations affected the everyday lives of people and percolated into their psyche. An interesting factor about the narratives is that not many people are given a first name in the stories; characters are referred to in terms of their religion, caste, gender, age and social rank. We may come across references to an old Muslim woman, a Kanakkan, a young Parayi, and a powerful Nair chieftain and the like. The author also gives ample instances to illustrate how structures of hierarchy could be detrimental to an equitable social arrangement; however, we get a sense that these structures are not erected and preserved without conscious attempts to disrupt them. In the narratives of *Aithihyamala*, there is an ambivalent attitude towards the mutability of social hierarchies as the author expresses his shock and a sense of triumph rather simultaneously when systems fall apart.

The legend about the text, *Adhyatma Ramayanam*, a bhasha Ramayana text written by Thunchathu Ramanujan Ezhuthachan illustrates how the prevalent culture hesitated to acknowledge the scholarly and literary contributions of someone from a caste considered to be lower in the hierarchy. Ezhuthachan is now celebrated as the father of Malayalam language and the *Adhyatma Ramayanam Kilippattu* text is lauded for its originality, literary beauty, mellifluousness and philosophical depth. The legend is a telling example of the brahminical desire to appropriate Ezhuthachan's accomplishment. It affirms that the *Adhyatma Ramayanam* text was originally written by a scholarly and devout brahmin who took certain creative liberties and deviated from the other well-known versions of the Ramayana. He was aggrieved as not many found his work appealing though it was remarkably rich in bhakti *rasa*. The reason for the rejection of this text was that it was not retold by a sage. The brahmin meets a quaintly luminous being during his pilgrimages who advises him to go to Gokarnam during the next Shivaratri (a major festival of the Hindus) to present the text to a brahmin who would appear with four dogs. When the brahmin who authored *Adhyatma Ramayanam* did so, the brahmin accompanied by the dogs revealed his identity as the sage Ved Vyas whom the loyal Vedas follow as dogs. He blesses the author and text, but curses the Gandharva who advised the author to resort to such a strategy. The cursed Gandharva was born as Thunchathu Ezhuthachan, a shudra who wrote *Adhyatma Ramayanam* from his memory. The text becomes well-known and he gains his contemporaries' respect and his name is remembered by future generations as well. In short, the legend drives home the fact that even though wrongly assumed to be written by a shudra, the original author of *Adhyatma Ramayanam* was a brahmin blessed by none other than sage Ved Vyas.

The story "Parayipettu Panthirukulam" or the narrative about twelve clans birthed by a Paraya woman beautifully captures the permeability of divisions and mutability of hierarchies based on caste and gender. There are quite a few stories in *Aithihyamala* about the twelve abandoned children born to a scholarly brahmin Vararuchi and spouse, a Dalit woman (Parayi). The children—ten boys and one girl—were abandoned in the forest immediately after their births and adopted by parents from different castes. The youngest one turned into a hill deity. All these children had to face predictable social and familial situations in which they were either revered, insulted or oppressed on the basis of the conventional attitudes towards their caste and gender. Yet, the subversiveness that dismantles hierarchical divisions surfaces in moments when these sons and daughter affirm their superiority as wise, knowledgeable, talented individuals to those who treat them with disdain. These incidents shed light on the fact that an individual's respectability and dignity has the potential to rise above the prejudices and derogatory social attitudes about caste, class and gender. The tactics the oppressed adopt to deal with their condition without passively resigning to their plights give powerful lessons about challenging and disrupting hierarchies and asserting one's dignity as a human being. Subversive potential is woven into the very fabric of our life in an intricate manner, as Michel Certeau argues:

> Many everyday practices (talking, reading, moving about, shopping, cooking, etc.) are tactical in character. And so are, more generally, many "ways of operating": victories of the "weak" over the "strong" (whether the strength be that of powerful people or the violence of things or of an imposed order, etc.), clever tricks, knowing how to get away with things, "hunter's cunning," maneuvers, polymorphic simulations, joyful discoveries, poetic as well as warlike. (1989, xix)

In "Parayipettu Panthirukulam", the annual meeting of the siblings belonging to different castes for performing the *shraddha* rites (memorial event for the ancestors) for their biological parents becomes an occasion for the wife of one of the siblings Mezhathoor Agnihotri, a brahmin, to understand that even those who are considered to be untouchables and unclean are manifestations of divinity. There is a moment in the story when the Antharjanam (wife of a brahmin; the term means the one who is always indoors) who complains about having to accommodate in her home the unclean siblings of her husband witnesses the Advaita (the inseparability of the *jeevatma* and *paramatma*) as all the siblings sleeping in their beds manifest in front of her eyes as reclining Padmanabha or Lord Vishnu.

One may wonder why innumerable stories in the text are about temples and people associated with them. Sankunni belonged to a community broadly grouped as Ambalavasi that was involved in responsibilities of the temple and perhaps had access to the legends concerning the temples, the origin myths, the rituals, allotment of land and other kinds of property to the temples by the kings and the like. He was a devout follower of the Shakta cult and the worship of the goddess. As elephants who fulfilled a major role in the temple rituals, Sankunni must have been fascinated by the stories about elephants who attained their own share of fame or notoriety in their time. Between the goddesses and elephants, he has collected stories in which the protagonists are scholars, writers, *vaidyas*, astrologers, merchants, conquerors, people with magical powers and the like. Though most of the stories deal with the Hindu—especially Namboothiri life—in both reverential and satirical way, Sankunni opens the world to the lives of people from other kind of faiths.

The stories about famous scholars, literary figures, traditional medical practitioners and artists adept in music and performing arts are hagiographic in tone. Most of these stories affirm the principle that human talents are rendered useless if the divine grace and blessing of elders are absent in life. The accomplishments of the underprivileged get only a passing mention or are completely erased. In the gallery of stellar achievements, very few women (except the queens) and individuals from communities considered 'lower-class or caste' find space. Talented individuals like Perumthachan (the chief carpenter) or Naranathu bhranthan (madman from Naranathu) transcend the limitations of their caste because of their devotion to certain deities or the benevolence of their patrons.

The very pattern of arranging the narratives suggests the social and ritual hierarchies extant at Sankunni's time. The structure of the text blatantly reflects the social structure. Even a casual reading gives a sense of the power equations. In the original eight-book series, except the first book which opens with a legend about the king of Chembakasseri, all other books start with the story about a goddess and end with the story about an elephant.

To conclude, the stories compiled in the volumes of *Aithihyamala* had a well thought out agenda of conserving and circulating a particular vision of cultural legacy. This legacy, founded on a certain philosophy of cosmic/social schema of existence, fleshes out through narratives that capture the grandeur and simplicity of everyday lives and experiences. Such an approach that juxtaposes the macro and the micro features of an indefinite temporality calls for paying attention to the possibilities of making sense of history, in a way that ventures beyond the scope of history's disciplinary and methodological confines. Making sense of and interpreting the life-worlds of people far removed in temporality, for Sankunni, had an underlying ethical pedagogy—of reinforcing the timeless values that he held in high esteem. Sankunni and his mentor, Kandathil Varghese Mappila had faith in the values represented by the *Aithihyamala* narratives. *Aithihyamala*, inspired by Mappila's vision, has been an influential text for many generations of readers in Kerala. Their mission of saving the narratives from slipping into oblivion has been remarkably successful, considering the many lives and new avatars of *Aithihyamala* stories in other narrative, visual and performative traditions.

WORKS CITED

Althusser, Louis. 1971. *Lenin and Philosophy and Other Essays.* Translated from French by Ben Brewster. London: Monthly Review Press.

Certeau, Michel De. 1989. *The Practice of Everyday Life.* Translated from French by Steven Rendall. Berkeley: University of California Press.

Foucault, Michel. 1971. *The Archaeology of Knowledge.* Translated from French by A.M. Sheridan Smith. New York: Pantheon Books.

Lefebvre, Henri. 1991. *The Production of Space.* Translated from French by Donald Nicholson Smith. Oxford (UK): Blackwell.

——. *Critique of Everyday Life.* 1991. Volume 1. Translated from French by John Moore. London: Verso.

Sankunni, Kottarathil. 1974. *Aithihyamala* (Volumes 1 & 2). Kottayam: Kottarathil Sankunni Memorial Committee.

Stewart, Susan. 1992. *On Longing: Narratives of the Miniature, the Gigantic, the Souvenir, the Collection.* North Carolina: Duke University Press.

FIFTEEN

Adaptation/Transformation

Locating Amar Chitra Katha's Mahabharata within Indian Bhasha Narratival Traditions

TONISHA GUIN

It is commonly accepted within constructionist critiques of culture that mainstream systems of knowledge are deeply embedded in ideological structures and perpetuate sociocultural hierarchies. This holds true for the cultural maps of the modern citizen-subject and the intersectional domains of culture that they inhabit (Hall 1997, 15). There has been a steady attempt to problematise these normalised, unequal power relations and how they make certain discourses more visible and render others marginalised, especially within the discourses of colonialism, postcolonialism and contemporary modernities. The constitution of these systems of knowledge are questioned along the lines of their implicit politics of representation. This affects what is coded as high culture (Williams 1958, 49), as well as the cultural continuums of colonisation in social imaginaries decades after the political independence of nation-states like India, and how they manifest themselves within discursive practices of identity formation and cultural production.

This criticism also engages with how terms like globalisation, neoliberalism, cosmopolitanism inform our understanding of our subject positions vis-a-vis the wider network of cultural relations that transcend national or regional limitations. Terms like "subaltern elite", "waiting room of history", "modular nationalities", "imagined communities", and on the other hand, a revival and revision of terms like "world literature" and "shared knowledge" have been coined in an attempt to de-centre mainstream structuration(s) of value. While the effects and lasting influence of colonialism on Indian culture and literature is indubitable, the European trend of deracinating the white man and recreating him and his very particular perspective as the universal, leaves one with very peculiar problems. Western critical theory lacks the tools to properly engage with and analyse much of the Indian canon or culture(s). As a part of the possible responses to this problem, this paper explores the manner in which the *Amar Chitra Katha* (Immortal Illustrated Series) graphic novels reiterate and transform the Mahabharata for a particular moment within the Indian middle-class' modern, English-speaking identity project.

Identity projects allude to the ongoing and conscious narrativisation of self-identity in relation to perceptions of past, present and future. While identities have always been both plural and constructed, modernity "not only breaks down the traditional forms of identity but also increases the levels of resources for identity construction, so we are all faced with the task of constructing our identities as a project" (Barker 1990, 96).

Identity is here treated as something always in process, towards which one moves without ever arriving at. The identity project asks and answers the question of how to conduct oneself and approach personhood, often through narratives of the perceived past and promised future, relative to the present. While cultural theory understands identities as fragmented, the identity project creates a coherent narrative of the self, especially as narrativised for children.

There has been a wide-ranging academic consensus regarding the mainstream popularity of *Amar Chitra Katha* (henceforth ACK) as the quintessential "Indian" comic book for children for the last three decades. Its readership openly acknowledges its pedagogical functions, not just in tutoring Indian children about myths, historical figures and extraordinary moments marked by mainstream history writings, but also as texts that facilitate a moral compass aligned with the "Indian" version of ethical values of courage, sacrifice and consideration. The extant scholarly work on ACK comic books may be read as directly contributing to and examining the ways in which it works as a disciplinary-pedagogic tool of a modern, Indian identity project. There has even been a body of work on its art and its influences like that of Rijuta Sawant's *Emergence of a National Popular Visual Culture: Influence of Raja Ravi Varma on the Aesthetics of Amar Chitra Katha.*

Besides art, commentaries on its popularity within the Indian mainstream talk in universal terms, but pinpoint a particular intersection of economic affluence, middle-class identification, literate, urban-oriented—if not always located—esotericism. Thus, for instance, Karline McLain in *India's Immortal Comic Books: Gods, Kings, and Other Heroes*, draws exhaustively upon the feedback received from her NRI and immigrant Indian students, how they identify and are extremely familiar with the texts of ACK and consider it a very important conduit in helping them identify with the imagined community of India (McLain 2009, 49, 58, 64). Though she doesn't explicitly use the term "imagined community", McLain's commentaries on the way the diasporic and resident Indian community identifies with and promotes the ACK comic books implicitly hints at it. There is a volume of work by authors like Deepa Srinivas which explicitly links ACK to an emergent Indian middle-class and its homogenising projects when it comes to the disparities increasingly evident in the post-Nehruvian developmental rhetoric in the Indian public domain, in books like *Sculpting the Citizen: History, Pedagogy and the Amar Chitra Katha*. Commentators like Shaan Amin (2017) take this a step further to talk about caste, class and colour biases within the overarchingly mainstream, idealised Hindu notions that the ACK comics tend to propagate and proliferate further. In fact, while early engagements with art in the ACK discussed the ways in which it draws from the Raja Ravi Varma school, later discussions focus on the ways in which the women are portrayed, the skin colour of the villains, the ways in which Aryan and Dravidian biases are shown or *asura*s and *deva*s are portrayed, in ways that conform with discriminatory norms of beauty, caste and class intersections.

As a prime example of popular culture in our lived modernities, there are different ways of treating the genealogy of a cultural text like ACK: its relation to nineteenth- and twentieth-century Indian art, especially, as some have pointed out, to the Ravi Varma school, its engagement with Sanskrit traditional texts and their many later adaptations in Indian languages, the Indian print industry, the fact of its circulation in a largely Hindi/Devanagari-speaking belt, the locations of its concentrated circulation, and the ways in which it is treated as Indian sometimes, rather more Indian in favour of other texts and forms of children's literature produced within different parts of the principality of India, but considered provincial in comparison, to name a few. Its reception and criticism has been as hybrid as the heterogeneous sites of Indian modernities it inhabits. Yet, a persistent thread of engagement focuses on how popular social imaginaries within mainstream India tend to treat it unproblematically, as an unsullied, absolutist text perfectly suited to act as a pedagogical tool of morality and information for children.

While the category of childhood is now ingrained in our conceptualisation of life, this was far from the case till the sixteenth century. The seventeenth century witnessed what Foucault calls a major epistemological rupture in the history of the modern West (Foucault 1973, xxii) which resulted in a reimagination of children as something other than proto-adults, and a relocation in material and discursive practices that led to the construction of childhood as a distinct portion of life that preceded adulthood. The late-eighteenth century was marked by the creation of disciplinary and surveillance practices that monitored the child while furthering the concept of childhood as an autonomous state. By the mid-nineteenth century, childhood had been firmly established as a unique part of life. The child was constructed as being marked in terms of nation, gender, race and class, such that childhood was no longer homogenous. Significantly, a similar if lesser break witnessed the construction of teenage as distinct from both childhood and adulthood in the mid-twentieth century.

One may see this plurality and heterogeneity of childhood reflected in children's literature of the period. In India, the development of the new child, the markedly "Indian" (and usually Hindu and male) child, proceeded alongside the development of the new Indian woman, who found her place in a family restructured to suit the needs of modernity. The new woman was given somewhat unprecedented prominence in the new family, even as her role centred on the upbringing of the child. As Partha Chatterjee (1996) argues, the project of "producing disciplined citizens for the new nation took root in the inner spaces of the community, especially in the restructured everyday life of the new family", was evident in the newly-etched out domain of the woman as the domestic and spiritual heart of the family and nation. One may note that colonial thinking entrusted the creation of the future citizen to educational and other institutes while nationalist thought sought to mould the citizen in the "purity" of home, and that the education and empowerment (such as it was) of the modern Indian woman was in service of the future citizen: implicitly a boy.

But this was not left entirely in the hands of the mother, however educated. As in England, so too in India, children's literature was accorded a prime position in the task of moulding the child who would grow into the model citizen. Post-independence India saw the creation of children's literature initiatives like Children's Book Trust, National Book Trust, Nehru Bal Pustakalaya and Bal Bhavan: all part of the Nehruvian endeavour to mould the national child. This efflorescence of children's literature included the then-nascent Amar Chitra Katha, which narrativised the past from an elite, upper-caste and fairly masculine perspective as part of the identity project that enmeshed the child in its toils.

The Dominant Communication System (DCS) of a culture alters over time, with the oral/gestural epoch being replaced by the scribal systems, which give way to the medium of print, which is replaced successively by the audio-visual and finally the digital DCS. European intellectual histories favour a smooth linear progression of the DCS and further—in a familiar move—universalise that progress, in a manner grading cultures in accordance with their adoption of various systems so that digital cultures are considered least, and mnemonic cultures, which utilise the oral/gestural DCS, most "backward". Mnemocultures, when found embedded within a hypermedial culture which has by and large made the shift to later, "better" Dominant Communication Systems, are largely disenfranchised and treated as cultural fossils; this attitude entirely ignores the fact that mnemocultures have their own apparatus of memory and of performance, as surely as print or audio-visual cultures do.

As Rajasekhara says, the *kavya-purusha* marries the *sahitya-vidya-vadhu* and this union creates literature, which is therefore not alienated from, but is rather a product of the convergence of poetry and philosophy (Rajasekhara Ch. III, 10). This difference of attitude towards philosophy and poetry marks only one of many differences between Indian and Eurocentric cultures, and points out the essential futility of using European critical theories in order to engage with Indian texts, whether or not mnemocultural.

So, cultural artefacts/practices which may not register as mnemocultural, or are in fact not mnemocultural, may still possess a mnemocultural artefact or appearance. While the West as the "universal" is a false and fallacious notion, the ramifications of our 250-year engagement with the West cannot be ignored, lest it render us culturally amnesiac. So, it is not sufficient to simply locate mnemocultures in the cradles of their genesis; also, if the umbilical cord of modern, hybrid cultural artefacts located in the current, popular cultural domain is not traced back at least partially to mnemocultures, there will be a gap evident in the map of mnemocultures which is being constructed and a dissonance will remain.

The epics are especially productive in exploring the limits of and a break from the Sanskrit literary tradition because they escape the travails of limited access. The canon of the Sanskrit *vangmaya* comprises the Vedas, Upanishad, the Brahmanas and the epics.

Access to the first three has been highly restricted even among brahmins. However, the epics are deeply influenced by and import from Vedic texts, while also moving beyond them in terms of accessibility. They—especially the Mahabharata—are transgressive in their availability to "*stri-shudra-dvijabandhunam*" (Srimad-Bhagavatam 1.4.25). The Mahabharata, free of brahminical custody, thus appears in many iterations and genres. It is marked by collective authorship and non-didactic, transformative pluralities, so much so that these three traits have become fundamental to its constitution. The early genres of Sanskrit *vangmaya* do not privilege narratives, though they are not necessarily anti-narrative. Rather, they use narratemes, or *upakhyana*, embedded within the larger non-narrative structure, for instance in the *Panchatantra*.

Within the Mahabharata, compositional structure is of three types: narrative, non-narrative and dialogue which tapers into non-narrative. These compositional strategies manifest in various ways in different iterations, because of the pluralities present in the Mahabharata. It is interesting to note that, at least in the Bangla canon, the scribal and printed iterations of the Mahabharata largely focus on "children's Mahabharata", which are prominently illustrated. Illustrated Mahabharatas, even texts which eschew written text primarily in favour of storytelling through art, are by no means a minor or ignored compositional strategy, as evidenced by the *potua* tradition of scroll-painting in Bengal, or the Andhra *kalamkari* tapestries that depict episodes of the Mahabharata.

The origin of the comic or the graphic novel in its modern iteration can be traced to the early decades of the twentieth century, at which point it was disregarded as a later contemporary of the lurid pulp novels and paperbacks which proliferated the American market between the wars. The critical attention it has received has conflated medium and content, and discussed the former only in relation to the latter. Scott McCloud (1994, 9), one of the few to critically engage with the medium, defines comics as juxtaposed pictorial and other images in deliberate sequence, intended to convey information and/or to produce an aesthetic response in the viewer.

The comic medium has been used for topics as divergent as autobiographies and political parody, accounts of the Holocaust and of adolescent infatuation, and the retelling of epics. According to McCloud, comics aim to reduce art to its most symbolic, so that it approaches text, and simultaneously reduce text to its least symbolic, so that it approaches art, and then combine them to tell a story which, due to its apparent simplistic nature, can have the widest and most immediate impact on readers: this allows it to be the popular, even the populist medium, a story told in which can reach the masses (McCloud 1994, 31–32).

Stuart Hall (1981) conceptualised the popular cultural domain as a site of both tradition and resistance, resonating with Judith Butler's notion of the performative as both reiterative and transformative. Now, obviously Butler talks of performing subjecthood (Butler 1990, 25) while Hall is looking at cultural artefacts, but the way both these notions talk of the simultaneity of reiterating and transforming is very crucial for us. "Commonsensically speaking, popular culture [is] regarded as inferior both to the elevated cultures of Art or classical music on the one hand and to an imagined authentic folk culture on the other [and] is accused of standardization and a levelling down that encourages, and indeed demands, conformity" (Barker 1990, 147–48).

Graphic novels are a perfect fit as popular cultural examples. One of the most prominent modern iterations of the comic book in India is the *Amar Chitra Katha*. The ACK books, while not trivialised in popular social imaginaries as having no substance, are instead infantilised as being, in effect, picture books for children.

A tension exists between children's prose adaptations of the epic in Indian languages and the ACK rendition: where ACK is both treated as a higher prestige and simultaneously, more diluted version in terms of quality. Within Bengali mainstream literary traditions, for instance, the most popular renditions of the Mahabharata—Kaliprassanna Singha's (1886), Rajshekhar Basus's (1949) and the formally acknowledged children's adaptation by Upendrakishore Roychoudhury (1904)—are all deeply revered, homogenised despite their production across more than six very eventful decades in the Bengali print industry, and considered dated and quaint by most publishers and readership alike. There is a call for a collector's edition, but definitely not one that can be given to a child anymore compared to an ACK rendition. This, however, itself marks a marked improvement in the status of the comic book in India—exceptions were made for ACK because of its religio-moral subject. ACK books figure lower in the hierarchy when compared to the deemed sacred, higher prestige Sanskrit texts and their direct translations and adaptations because they are marketed as children's literature. Yet, in a curious subversion, they are considered superior to cinematic media adaptations because they are perceived to be a pedagogical tool.

The style of the ACK comics made them peculiarly well-suited to depicting the Indian epics, which might not be didactic, but do certainly hold to a notionality of good and evil, though good men might commit evil. The compositional strategy of the ACK Mahabharata largely foregrounds art, conveying layers of information through it; the accompanying text is nearly rudimentary and often banal, and frequently omits the nuances and ambiguities of the original epic, perhaps judging it unsuitable for the intended readership.

Kajri Jain's "The Efficacious Image: Pictures and Power in Indian Mass Culture" (2007) begins with an instance of what might be called sympathetic magic, whereby artist S. M. Pandit felt that his paintings of the Kurukshetra were inciting riotous acts of violence. He did not believe this to be a case of direct influence, but felt that the content of his works inspired a similarity of feeling in the "real" world; interviewed about it by a skeptic who attempts to reduce his beliefs as essentially naive and superstitious, Pandit retaliated by recontextualising them as part of the "high" philosophy of Hinduism. As Jain says,

> In a dilute, barely perceptible register, this little exchange enacts a tension around the efficacy of the sacred that has permeated public culture in post-colonial India. This tension can be broadly seen as emanating from a dichotomy between religion as "good" faith in

> its "cultural" avatar as "tradition", philosophy and so on; and "bad" ideology, i.e., the manipulation of "meaning in the service of power" […] as long as it stays within a delimited sphere and takes on a certain accepted format, religion (like "culture") is tolerable, but its direct involvement in political economy and the public performance of power is a very dis*taste*ful business. (2007, 146)

While her article concerns chromolithographs on commercial art (especially of the sort Mazzarella [2003] dubs the commodity image) it is possible to apply her findings to the ACK Mahabharata, which similarly combines the sacred imagery of the epic with the commercial context of the comic.

The new technology evident in the creation and distribution of comics does not create a distinction from more traditional divine imagery. However, neither are they treated initially or intrinsically as sacrosanct objects, instead occupying a somewhat tense positionality whereby they are lesser than traditional iterations of the epic, but greater than other stories told in the comic medium. One might hazard that they are on par with *potua* or *kalamkari* versions of the Mahabharata, but even these traditional visual iterations are sanctified by age.

Further, the ACK comics, and not simply the Mahabharata series, are connected to the project of identity-building through an imagination of the past, most traditionally through the retelling of heroic and patriotic lives and events. Common even in more straightforwardly mythic comics is the use of a divine image that is connected to a very nationalist definition or model of valour and is always in an auspicious aspect/form: Goddess Kali slaying demons, for instance.

Evident in these comics is a sort of tension that Mazzarella (2003) describes as characteristic of commodity images: they are the product of particular commercial institutes but at the same time inspire a very personal and often visceral reaction in the viewer which has little or nothing to do with the commercial establishment. It is the sort of agitation that Barthes (2009) feels when looking at pictures of his mother, but complicated further by applying to images that are neither private nor truly commodified.

Further, the very private reaction is anticipated and banked on by the publisher, and it is the power of these images to inspire that reaction which ensures the continuity of ACK's reputation as a trustworthy institution of good moral fibre, which may be trusted with pedagogical tasks.

Objects in general and images in particular, are not exemplars or evidences in the background of events, politics or modes of discourse, but form their own narratives, and this is especially seen in this cluster of articles in the way—at every stage—different kinds of lines have been effectively blurred: for Appadurai (1986) the line between commercial and social, for Pinney (2004) the line between public and private presentation, etc. So, what emerges from this discussion is the fact that, going back to what Appadurai said, methodologically speaking, looking at objects in circulation illumine their contexts and politics, and this is important, looking at not just the object in discourse, but looking at the object in intersections—spatially, temporally, across subjects, across subject-positions—which isn't really synonymous to but flows into the former and forms a significant part of it (Appadurai 1986, 32).

Two things emerge from a brief survey of the ACK comics: that it employs a style of art that is recognised in the mainstream as "Indian"—though of course the notion of a monolithic, unfractured Indian-ness is itself troubling/illuminating—and has a claim to telling Indian stories largely due to the acceptance of this art form; the other thing is that because the language used is stripped to the bare minimum (though sometimes they are loose translations of the original) the ways in which this text acts like a critical response can be measured rather in terms of what they omit, and how they omit it. Within the comic book, the sense of morality follows a very black-and-white scheme of victims/heroes and villains, as opposed to Vyasa's Mahabharata, where each character is painted in shades of grey; everyone is represented as human and consequently fallible.

Within the ACK's compositional strategy of foregrounding the art, the narrative style adopted is essentially dialogic. Though graphic novels with text have managed to coax out a variety of narratival styles, ACK limits itself to dialogue and to tags describing the action depicted in the art. Parts of the original composition, which may not have been dialogic, are perforce translated to this form; for instance, all the panels of the *Bhagwad Gita*, despite its original, non-narrative structure, are displayed as an extended conversation between Arjuna and Krishna against the background of the war, with the two participants and their immediate surroundings rendered in greater detail than the rest of the scene. The comics also use this technique later to incorporate popular lore attached to the original: one iteration of the text, which says that Ganesha was approached as a scribe, is not included in the original, but finds a place in the ACK Mahabharata, presumably due to its popularity.

The language, even in the stripped-to-bones dialogues, is extremely revealing. Archaic tags like "thee" and "thou" are reserved for sages and holy men; the heroes, here the Pandavas and their associates, usually use passives; the Kauravas, and Bhima among the Pandavas, use direct, often imperative speech. Karna's moral complexities are marked by his use of both modes of speech, while Krishna's diplomacy is marked by his use of various modes of speech with various people and situations.

The art proves strangely evasive. That it looks like the mainstream expects art for an epic to look is clear enough, but it is difficult to further pinpoint sources. The artist of the Mahabharata series, Dilip Kadam, vociferously protests that there are no inspirations for his work, other than the images in his own head. Tellingly, Kadam's imagination closely resembles the art of Raja Ravi Varma, and the calendar art of the early twentieth century—significant tools of consolidating the target imagined community during the Indian freedom movement and latter sociopolitical agitations.

The ACK Mahabharata functions not only as an adaptation of, but a response to Vyasa's epic, aimed towards children. The medium—and the intended audience—requires a certain level of bowdlerisation, and certainly the epic in its entirety cannot be included. In the *dyutakrida* section, three glaring omissions serve to illustrate the differences in plot and characterisation beautifully, especially since they are clustered close together, largely occurring around the foci of Draupadi being used as a wager. At the moment of the *dyutakrida* the participants are dependent on Yudhishthira's nature as a gambler and his decision to play dice with Shakuni.

In the epic, Yudhishthira knows or guesses that the Kauravas have conspired, as is apparent from his comment to Shakuni "*tadvai vittam matidevirma jaishih shakune param*"; in the ACK comics he believes it an innocent game. Further, his status as an inveterate gambler is repeatedly referenced in the epic, and despite that addiction, his actions even during the game are governed by a strict sense of dharma, which does not allow him to abandon the game, even though he clearly knows that he is being cheated. This juxtaposition of a gambling addiction with a deeply virtuous nature is not regarded as contradictory in the epic. In the comic, Yudhishthira is shown as the trusting fool who keeps on hoping: a significant reading-down of the character.

Finally, just before he wagers Draupadi, Yudhisthira in the epic spends some time praising her attributes, describing her hair, height and physiognomy, calling her "*naiva hrasva na mahati natikrishna na rohini,*" and referring to her as "*yamicchetpurushah striyam*" (Sabha *parva*, 53. 9). In the comic, he is far more restrained and seemingly reluctant to wager his wife: the dialogue alters to "Alas, Shakuni! With the daughter of Drupada, as a bet, I play." This, along with the emphasis laid on the actions of the Kauravas, transforms the episode into a teachable moment rather than one revealing the flaws of an otherwise righteous character. It is also illustrative of ACK's use of art and elision to delineate the desirable "modern" moral position: characters are flattened out in order to be more easily identified as virtuous.

Yet, despite this moral censoring, the subsequent *vastra-harana* is shown quite explicitly, perhaps because omitting it would cause the adaptation to become untrue to the spirit and story of the original. However, there are two ways to look at this omission: the adapters might have considered the scene crucial to furthering the plot of the Mahabharata, and therefore unomittable, even despite the inappropriateness of the matter at hand; some bowdlerisation was permissible, but the *vastra-harana* had to at least be mentioned. However, as looks more likely—considering that the disrobing occurs over several panels—because of the black-and-white morality of the story, Yudhishthira's deeply inappropriate praising of Draupadi is neatly omitted, while Dhritarashtra's eagerness to know the results of the throw of dice, and, some pages later, Karna's edict to disrobe Draupadi, are both not just included but also emphasised to some extent. In this context, emphasising Draupadi's disrobing marks the Kauravas as irredeemable villains; there is a consensus regarding the immorality of lechery especially when the latter is directed towards one's female relatives.

The violation, of course, is not simply physical; Draupadi here lacks what we might call the regalia of queenship, and is exposed as simply a vulnerable woman, and the attack on her symbolises and exemplifies the rapacious attitude of the Kauravas, whether towards land, wealth or women.

The ACK Mahabharata comics were serialised from 1985–89 and anthologised in three volumes upon completion. The run therefore overlapped in its last year with Doordarshan's B. R. Chopra's *Mahabharat* TV serial. It might be more productive therefore to look at these as working in tandem in the sociopolitical contingencies of their time: the particular need for a modernised and accessible secular Hindu, coded "Indian" tradition.

Chopra's *Mahabharat* was immensely popular—the streets would be deserted at the times when it was being broadcast—and immensely theatrical: the costumes, set-design, as well as the gestures and voice-modulations adopted by the actors were melodramatic at the least, and would today classify it as high-camp. The audience that watched the show had by and large no way of retaining it except in memory—video-recording was not at the time an easily-available technology—and this undoubtedly contributed to the emptying-out of the streets; in this way, it was rather mnemocultural in effect. The sources of this show do not constitute an interest of this paper, but it must be noted in passing that the costumes—and often the garish make-up—seem to owe more to the thirteenth or fourteenth century CE rather than the third millennia BC. Because of the limited scope of the paper, there will be a brief comparative examination of the way in which Chopra's *Mahabharat* and the ACK Mahabharata depict the first round of dice-playing in Hastinapura, which devolves into the *vastra-harana* episode.

This episode constitutes a crux for the plot and further is important because of the way in which people behave during it—not simply the putative villains, but also those who have been variously lauded as embodying virtue, here revealing their deeply fallible natures. Given the tone of storytelling usually adopted by both the TV serial and the comic, which clearly distinguishes between absolute good and absolute evil, this episode constitutes a paradox of sorts, since it on the one hand reinforces the status of the villains, while on the other hand also creating internal dissonances in the image of the heroes. It constitutes a half-way point of sorts for both Chopra—where it features in episodes 45–47 of a 94-episode show—and for ACK—where it constitutes the middle portion of the second book of the Mahabharata trilogy—and further constitutes a crux, as mentioned earlier, not only for the characters, but for the plot. The seeds of the Kurukshetra battles, though they will take several more years to flower, are sown here, with Bhima's promises of destruction. What strikes one about the Chopra adaptation, not just visually, but also and even primarily aurally, is that since the TV serial deals with "real" people and cannot differentiate between the heroes and villains—who dress similarly and look not unalike: there is a certain family resemblance between Bhima and Duryodhana, Bhima and the twins, and even Arjuna and Yudhishthira—it does so through voice modulations and a heightening of the various affectations of the characters, such that Duryodhana's temper fits or Shakuni's jeering reach farcical levels, and Vidura's appeals to his brother would have made any political demagogue proud in all its sweeping gestures. Contrarily, the ACK series, though it visibly follows the television serial as regards costuming, achieves the difference between heroes and villains visually—lacking the aural dimension—by making the Pandavas, and especially Yudhishthira, look constantly serene, while the Kauravas have a permanent stamp of cunning and covetousness imprinted on their faces.

The *dyutakrida*, for both Chopra and Kadam, begins with introducing the main characters in a very similar setting—Dhritarashtra on a raised throne surrounded by the elders of the court, the courtiers on their thrones around the hall, and the players in the centre, facing each other across the *chaupar* board—both the serial and the comics depict only a single game between the Kauravas and the Pandavas, where Vyasa's epic records several games.

In the *dyutakrida* section, however, three glaring omissions serve to illustrate the differences in plot and characterisation beautifully, especially since they are clustered close together in the continuum, largely occurring around the foci of Draupadi being used as a wager. The continued moment that holds them all is interesting also because, despite their backstories and motives and presences in linear or durational time, at the moment of the *dyutakrida* the participants—arguably all of them, but certainly the Pandavas and the Kuru elders—are dependent on Yudhishthira's nature as a gambler, and his decision to play dice with Shakuni.

In Chopra's adaptation, it is Karna, rather than Shakuni, who suggests wagering Draupadi, an interesting divergence since the serial usually attempted to keep Karna markedly ambiguous—the best of a bad lot, if not actually good. In the epic, Karna affects disinterest, even apathy, throughout the proceedings, only rousing himself after the wager on Draupadi has been laid and won—then he laughs harshly on Duryodhana's usage of *dasi* as an appellation referring to Draupadi, and further incites the Kauravas to disrobe her; he also reprimands Vikarna's attempt to argue on behalf of Draupadi. In the serial, he laughs along with the Kauravas when Duryodhana wins, and, in marked divergence of his behaviour till then, suddenly grows affectionate towards Duryodhana, clasping his hand and gripping his thigh in approbation. In the comic—in line with its depiction of a black-and-white morality, with Karna largely on the side of right, save by association—he is present throughout, but his active vocal participation is limited to reprimanding Vikarna indirectly and directing Duhshasana to disrobe Draupadi: this in effect restricts his interest in Draupadi entirely and without respite. Gender sensitivity might be one of the aspects closely analysed and criticised about both. However, gender roles work very differently within the Mahabharata. Its modern appropriations, in the neo-Victorian regressions of the 80s and 90s either sentimentalise, or put it in a stereotype formula. It's not like women lacked agency, but it was a very different kind of agency, not necessarily made available through men. In the crucial scene of attempts of disrobing Draupadi, Chopra very interestingly emphasises the bruised male honour of the royal family—Vidura chides Dhritarashtra for allowing his daughter-in-law's name to be evoked in court in the manner in which it has been. While it is of course one of the most decisively heinous moments in the epic, magnified tenfold by the compelled silence of the elders, the very different stance of Karna as the provocateur—in contrast to the ambiguous tragic hero—is a classic instance of an exposé of the convoluted workings of an undeservingly tortured, unexpectedly rewarded, above all human mind. Whatever the nature of his initial interest in Draupadi, it has morphed—whether solely due to the initial rejection, or in confluence with subsequent events—into the twisted impulses that urge him onto the one petty—though perhaps not the only "evil"—thing he does in the duration of the epic. Interestingly, speaking of stereotyping, Karna's actions during the *dyutakrida*, at least as represented by the comics—and to an extent the serial and even arguably the epic—are stereotypically feminine, insofar as he takes no action himself, but leverages those of the men around him to achieve his own aims, and also incites them to further action. In contrast, Draupadi, to the mainstream Indian mind, behaves rather mannishly after she has been dragged into court, neither collapsing in tears, nor in hysterical rage. Rather, she attempts to debate points of law with the Kuru elders—interestingly, she does not appeal to dharma, or virtue, but questions whether Yudhishthira, himself a slave, had the legal right to wager anyone else—which they cannot satisfactorily answer, whether in epic, or comic, or serial. Duryodhana's actions, though depicted faithfully in both adaptations, gain a very different hue in accordance with how the actions of those around him have been depicted and/or omitted. In the epic, he repeatedly ignores Yudhishthira's allegations of cheating—both in practice and principle, since the one who lays the wager should also be the one to roll the dice—and carries on regardless; in the comic, of course, there are no such allegations, and in the serial the charges are laid by Vidura. He is not represented as someone who is politically immature in the serial, unlike his depiction in the comic-books and the source material. Of course, Duryodhana, even in the epic, is easily swayed, as we see after they have won Draupadi in the wager: his joy in winning her is not at this initial moment sexual, but is rather of the same category as his joy in winning her husbands. Duhshasana and Karna—though not the latter in the ACK adaptation—make explicit the sexual dimension to Draupadi's potential slavery in the Kaurava household, urging her to abandon shame and look at Duryodhana, "*duryodhanam pashya vimuktalajja*" (Sabha *parva* 60.20) and to pick a new husband from among the Kauravas "*anyam vrrinishva patimashu bhamini*" (Sabha *parva* 63.3). Duryodhana subsequently—and perhaps consequently—bares his thigh and urges Draupadi to be seated on it. Interestingly, while the gesture itself smacks of lewd obscenity, the epic makes it clear that he is doing it due to a desire to further humiliate the Pandavas, an interpretation also followed by the comic, though that also adds "desire" as at least a secondary motive. However, since the egging on by Duhshasana and Karna is absent in the comic—though the sexualisation of her slavery is present in Duhshasana's comments to Draupadi, and in Karna's directive to disrobe her—Duryodhana's action stands alone and must therefore be judged in isolation, rather than in the intoxicating atmosphere of victory that permeated the Kaurava party at the moment. Despite this, it is clear from subsequent pages that even in the comic, Duryodhana's chief interest is in humiliating the Pandavas and in gaining power over them, by whatever means necessary.

These are but some of the various differences to be further noted among the different adaptations of the Mahabharata, to show the manner in which the ACK Mahabharata functions as both a critical and a creative response, certainly to Vyasa's epic, but also to the B. R. Chopra serial, which in a way embodied the epic for the late 80s. Interestingly, the decade-long gap between the serial and the comics shows itself in the way in which morality is treated in them—in the serial, man is ultimately shaped by the society in which he lives, and though the Pandavas eventually succeed in going beyond their environment, they certainly have behavioural and psychological issues parallel to those of the Kauravas and their associates. Thus, Bhima's righteous anger parallels and resembles Duryodhana's fits of temper and Arjuna's love affairs—though legitimised by eventual marriage—are typologically similar to the background hints and allusions of Karna's easy lust and his tortured yearnings for Draupadi; in effect a man's inherent nature is allowed to matter far less than the uses to which he devotes himself. In the post-liberalisation comic, good and evil are treated as innate to the individual, the social environment is treated as exerting minor influence, if it exerts any at all—this affects the treatment of Karna, and in effect often renders him mute, since to give him the lines he utters in the epic or even in the serial would be to acknowledge his status as a "bad" man, and to be evil is, in this situation, to be irredeemably evil. In the epic, of course, all the characters are treated as essentially flawed since they are essentially human; all lessons about morality are open-ended and acknowledged as subjective and neither Duryodhana nor Yudhishthira truly learn *rajadharma*, though both are taught it.

Though popular culture is a loaded term that can be appropriated in many ways, if we look at it as Raymond Williams (1958) does, as cultural artefacts and practices which are disenfranchised but widely shared mass cultures intrinsically entwined to the life and aesthetics of a community, then one can perhaps safely say that mnemocultural artifacts are embedded in the popular cultural domain of a community. If so, while neither the graphic novel in question, nor its inspirational television serial technically meet the definition of mnemocultures, being exclusively invested in and manifested through surrogate bodies as discussed previously, nevertheless they constitutionally resemble each other in the shared memory that is evoked in both. As such, perhaps the ACK Mahabharata may very legitimately be called one of the continuums of Ved Vyas's original oral epic. While investigating mnemocultural forms, it is imperative to keep in mind that the dialogue(s)—whether it is between the Indian aesthetics and the West, the Hindu pantheon and all the others, or pre and postcolonial—isn't a frozen, finished entity but continues and manifest itself in multifarious ways, as appropriated by the strand of popular culture it manifests itself in. One of the reasons why Amar Chitra Katha and its immediate predecessor in a very different medium—B. R. Chopra's *Mahabharat* (as aired on Doordarshan)—are thus bowdlerised, even oversimplified in essentialising virtue and vice in particular characters, as opposed to Vyas's emphasis on a larger scheme of things, and the non-didactic fallible humanity of nearly all the actors of his epic, could be the internal conflicts and balancing acts they are required to perform to create a single, uniform (to be passed as universal) "Indian" narrative in the wake of liberalisation and globalisation. The multifarious ways in which traces of mnemocultures manifest in what is called "the contemporary," along with all the ways in which their contexts permeate and shape them are no less significant than mnemocultures themselves.

Works Cited

Amin, Shaan. 2017. 'The Dark Side of the Comics That Redefined Hinduism'. https://www.theatlantic.com/entertainment/archive/2017/12/the-comics-that-redefined-hinduism/539838/ Accessed on 15 August 2024.

Appadurai, Arjun. 1986. "Introduction." *The Social Life of Things: Commodities in Cultural Perspective.* Cambridge University Press: London.

Barthes, Roland. 2009. *Mourning Diary: October 26, 1977–September 15, 1979*. Trans. Richard Howard. Hill & Wang.

Barker, Chris. 1990. *SAGE Dictionary of Cultural Studies*. London: Sage.

Bose, Pradip Kumar. 1996. "Sons of the Nation: Child Rearing in the New Family." In *Texts of Power: Emerging Disciplines in Colonial Bengal*, edited by Partha Chatterjee. Calcutta: Samya.

Chatterjee, Partha. 1996. "The Disciplines in Colonial Bengal." In *Texts of Power: Emerging Disciplines in Colonial Bengal*, edited by Partha Chattcrjcc. Calcutta: Samya.

Foucault, Michel. 1973. *The Order of Things: An Archaeology of Human Sciences*. New York: Vintage Books.

Hall, Stuart. 1981. "Notes on Deconstructing 'The Popular'." In *People's History and Socialist Theory*, edited by Raphael Samuel. London: Kegan Paul-Routledge.

Hall, Stuart ed. 1997. *Cultural Representations and Signifying Practices*. London: Open University Press.

Jain, Kajri. 2007. "The Efficacious Image: Pictures and Power in Indian Mass Culture." In *Gods in the Bazaar: The Economies of Indian Calendar Art*. Durham: Duke University Press.

Mahabharat. Created by B. R. Chopra. 1988–1990.

Mazzarella, William. 2003. "Elaborations: The Commodity Image." In *Shoveling Smoke: Advertising and Globalization in Contemporary India*. Durham: Duke University Press.

McCloud, Scott. 1994. *Understanding Comics: The Invisible Art*. New York: HarperCollins.

McLain, Karline. 2009. *India's Immortal Comic Books: Gods, Kings and Other Heroes*. Bloomington: Indiana University Press.

Pai, Anant et al. 1998. *Mahabharata 2: The Pandavas in Exile*. Edited by Anant Pai. Illustrated by Dilip Kadam. Mumbai: Amar Chitra Katha Pvt. Ltd.

Puri, Gaurav. *Reading History in Comics—A Case of Amar Chitra Katha Visionaries*. Unpublished Dissertation. https://www.academia.edu/6153810/READING_HISTORY_IN_COMICS_A_CASE_OF_AMAR_CHITRA_KATHA_VISIONARIES_Dissertation_Report. Accessed on 15 August 2024.

Sawant, Rijuta. 2014. *Emergence of a National Popular Visual Culture: Influence of Raja Ravi Varma on the Aesthetics of Amar Chitra Katha*. https://www.academia.edu/6275615/Emergence_of_a_National_Popular_Visual_Culture_Influence_of_Raja_Ravi_Varma_on_the_Aesthetics_of_Amar_Chitra_Katha. Accessed on 15 August 2024.

Srinivas, Deepa. 2010. *Sculpting the Citizen: History, Pedagogy and the Amar Chitra Katha*. New York: Routledge.

Srimad-Bhagavatam 1.4.25. https://vedabase.io/en/library/sb/1/4/25/. Accessed on 15 August 2024.

Williams, Raymond. 1958. "Culture is Ordinary." In *Culture and Society*. England: Chatto and Windus.

SIXTEEN

Quest for a New Discourse in Literary Criticism in the Nineteenth Century

Interface between Gujarati and English, 1850–1890

HIREN PATEL

The influence of a new understanding regarding the very concept of literature, acquired through contact with the "superior" Western literature, is clearly visible in the nineteenth-century Gujarati poets' and writers' evaluation of not only their literary past but also the literature produced in their own time. A new and different critical consciousness regarding Gujarati language and literature can be observed emerging in this period. This can be attributed to Gujarati writers' and poets' reading of classical theoretical works on literature such as Aristotle's *Poetics*, essays by English Romantic poets such as Percy Bysshe Shelley and William Hazlitt, and Sanskrit critical practices and works on poetics. It can also be observed that translation played a significant role in this inevitable process of epistemic negotiation.

In the process, Gujarati writer-critics coined new critical terms and also redefined familiar literary terms in a new way. As Western concepts of literature had not gained currency during the time and there was an increasing interest in Gujarati, these writer-critics either adopted words from Sanskrit poetics or near-meaning words from their own Gujarati. Though they adopted critical terms largely from Sanskrit poetics, they redefined them most of the time, following Western literary concepts and tradition of literary criticism. It has to be noted here that it was not simple imitation or direct borrowing from the West. In fact, the concepts borrowed were merged with existing ones and given different, nuanced shapes.

This paper examines essays and articles of two important Gujarati writer-critics of the period: Navalram Pandya (1836–88) and Narmad (1833–86). Pandya's essays on literary criticism and book reviews, which were published mostly in the magazine *Gujarat Shalapatra* during his tenure as its editor, were collected and published as a book titled *Navalgranthavali* by Govardhanram Tripathi in 1891. Narmad's essays and articles were published mostly in *Buddhivardhak Granth* (1856–69) magazine and in his own magazine *Dandiyo* (1864–69).

Let us begin with the word "*ras*" since it came to be considered the most important element of the literature produced during the period. In his critical review of *Karanghelo* (1866)—the first Gujarati novel—Navalram Pandya states that an interesting (*rasik*) book has three aspects: *ras*, *ritbhat* and *suvichar* (a good thought) (Parikh 1937, 4). He further states that poetry, drama and the novel (or stories) try to present a whole picture, as per their capabilities, of internal and external nature[1] (*kudarat*); the distinction (*khubi*) of each of these forms rests on the truthfulness of the picture it gives (*chitra ni sacchai*) (ibid.). By the word *ras*, Pandya means: "the appropriate delineation or description of various passions that arise in mind through different experiences" (ibid.). He also uses the English phrase "delineation of passions" to explain the term *ras*. Moreover, he argues that there should be "truthfulness of nature" (*kudrat ni sacchai*) in the description of these various passions (ibid., 7). Now, Pandya argues that the book which is rich in description of *ritbhat*[2] (manners) and *ras* is merely sprinkled or sporadic can be called a novel (ibid., 4). Hence, Pandya praises *Karanghelo* for its rich description of *ritbhat* such as the palace of Madhav, court, animal fights, military exercises, etc. However, he

[1] Internal nature means "passions, mental instincts, feelings, emotions, etc." and external nature means "objective environment, behavior, interaction between characters etc." See Shukla (1988, 49).

[2] By the word *ritbhat* (manners), Pandya meant the ordinary passions (among the above mentioned "various passions") which emerge in keeping with different times and places.

criticises the novel for its "inappropriate delineation of passions" and "absence of truthfulness of nature", evident in the queen Rupsundari's one and half page long wailing on her abduction by Karan and the mourning by Karan's queens on his death in the form of recitation of his glory (ibid., 4–9). Pandya finds the behaviour of both Rupsundari and the queens inappropriate to the occasions mentioned and argues that the reader (*rasikjan*) would find it quite contrary (*viparit*) to the related occasions (ibid., 8). What Pandya emphasises here is aspects like "real" or "real like" and the idea of probability (*sambhavasambhav*). There are certain other examples available where Pandya has criticised literary works for their inappropriate "delineation of passions" and absence of "truthfulness of nature". In Manibhai Nabhubhai Dwivedi's drama *Kanta* (1882), the protagonist Sursen gives a necklace to his wife Kanta and promises her that he will remain safe and secure as long as this necklace is safe and intact (ibid., 41). However, as the drama progresses, the character named Tarala cuts this necklace while Kanta is asleep in order to make her think that her husband is dead. When Kanta sees the broken necklace, she starts wailing feverishly and prepares for self-immolation (ibid., 42). While reviewing *Kanta*, Pandya criticises this aspect of the drama on the basis of the argument that the necklace cannot be shown getting broken or cut as Sursen is alive. He wonders how Kanta can be intensely possessed with the desire to be a *sati* when her husband is still alive. Pandya argues that the tragic drama (*karunparinamak gambhir natak*) *Kanta* seems to turn into a farce (*prahasanrup*) because of this particular reason (ibid., 42). In the same drama, he also criticises the author for showing the king distributing glasses of wine to his friends on the basis of the argument that it is completely contrary to the customs of a kingdom (*rajvada ni ritbhat thi ultu*). The king is not supposed to serve his inferiors in this manner (ibid., 52). It can be observed here that Pandya gives prime importance to *ras* in creative literature. Moreover, in his opinion, there should be truthfulness in the depiction of nature (both internal and external) that the creative literature is attempting to portray. For Pandya, the nature related to both plot and characters should seem "real" or "probable", it should not be represented without convincing sense of reality. Thus, Pandya's explanation of the term *ras* emphasises the idea of "truthfulness of nature" (*kudrat ni sacchai*) in creative literature and failure in adhering to this principle, according to him, is failure on the part of a work of literature. Though Pandya adopts the term *ras* from Sanskrit poetics, he explains the term according to the basic doctrines of Aristotle, especially the principle of imitation. In fact, Pandya's evaluation of Gujarati literature shows great influence of Aristotle's discussion regarding the importance of "the law of probability and necessity", "consistency", "universality", etc., in literature in *Poetics*. Now, Pandya's redefinition of the term *ras*, coloured by the doctrines of Aristotle (especially the principle of imitation), also influences his understanding of other literary forms and various aspects of literature.

Pandya coins the term *rupakgranthi* or *maharupak* for the form of allegory in Gujarati by using the Gujarati word *rupak*. The word *rupak* is used for one of the figures of speech in Gujarati, namely the metaphor. Discussing Keshavlal Motilal's *Buddhi ane Rudhi ni Katha* (The Story of Buddhi and Rudhi, 1883), Pandya tells the readers that the book, though it seems to be in the form of a story, is an allegory (*rupakgranthi*) (ibid., 22). The word *rupakgranthi* is completely new for readers and not a single word has been written on this matter in Gujarati until now. Hence, in his opinion, an explanation of the word becomes necessary. He argues that in an allegory, the author personifies (*sajivaropan*) abstract and invisible human qualities such as virtues, thoughts, manners, etc., and describes them as per their character (*lakshan*) as if they are walking human beings (ibid., 22). Now here, Pandya's understanding of the term *ras* in creative literature too influences his definition and notion of the term "allegory". He argues that if *ras* is not there in an allegory in the form of life (*jiv*), then the skeleton made merely of philosophy and preaching is unreal (*mithya*) and quite monotonous (ibid., 23). In *Buddhi ane Rudhi ni Katha*, Gurjardas, a Bania merchant, divorces his wife Buddhidevi and throws her out of his home as per the evil instruction of his new and second wife Rudhidevi. Buddhidevi, along with her brother Gnandev, flees to the West and marries Europeraj. She comes back with her children (from Europeraj) to Gurjardas' home, claims her rights and achieves them by the end of the story. According to Pandya, to show a noble (*kulvan*) woman like Buddhidevi getting remarried when her former husband is alive and to show her making claims over Gurjardas' home is a big mistake in the composition of the allegory (ibid., 25). These observations clearly indicate his conservative attitude. However, Pandya is right in finding Buddhidevi's behaviour improbable (*asambhavit*) in the allegory as his assessment here is being guided by his very own conception of the term *ras*.

The last but not the least is his discussion regarding the principle of "humour" in literature. This too follows his conception of the term *ras* and the Aristotelian principle of imitation. Pandya in his article "Hasya ane Adbhut Ras" (The Sentiments of Laughter and the Marvellous) observes that humour does not get generated out of the imitation of the nature (ibid., 264). We do not laugh, Pandya argues, when we behold a beautiful landscape or when we read its appropriate description. There is an imitation of nature in all other types of *ras* but in humour, according to Pandya, there is a "distorted" (Pandya uses the English word in the text) imitation of nature or mere imitation (*nakal*) as we say in the ordinary language (ibid., 264). It can be observed here that the general Aristotelian demand on the part of literature, that "all poetry is to be defined by the presence of probability or necessity in its imitation" (O'Sullivan 1995, 47), clearly influences Pandya's coinage of new critical terms in Gujarati as well as their explanations. Though Pandya borrows critical terms from Sanskrit poetics or coins new ones using the near-meaning words from Gujarati, he defines them, most of the time, following the tenets of Western literary criticism.

Narmad also defines the term *ras* in an almost similar manner as Pandya does. Narmad's explanation of the term too bears the influence of Aristotelian doctrines. In his article "Kavi ane Kavita" (Poet and Poetry), published in *Buddhivardhak Granth* in September 1858, Narmad argues that *ras* is a kind of "internal delight/happiness" (*andar ni maza*), where pain too can be included (1858a, 264). He further observes that the natural affection (*satvikbhav*) that arises in our mind when we see someone suffering is also a kind of *ras* (ibid.). This explanation of the term reminds us of Aristotle's comments on poetry in his *Poetics*. Aristotle observes: "Objects which in themselves we view with pain, we delight to contemplate when reproduced with minute fidelity" (1902, 15). It can be observed here that both Narmad and Pandya's explanations of the word *ras* follow Aristotelian doctrines, especially his views on the principle of imitation and poetry. Though the term *ras* has been derived from Sanskrit poetics, both these writer-critics define it in an entirely new way. It indicates the degree to which the new critical language being formulated came to depend on Western critical concepts. Moreover, their redefinition of the term also influences their evaluation and understanding of other literary genres in Gujarati.

The familiar Gujarati terms for "poet" and "poetry", namely *kavi* and *kavita*, were also redefined during the period. The redefinition of these terms bears the combined influence of Aristotelian doctrines, English Romanticism and Sanskrit poetics. Moreover, the concept of *ras*—as has been discussed above—too influences this redefinition of Gujarati terms. Let us begin with the term *kavi* (poet). Both Pandya and Narmad emphasised "scholarship", especially knowledge regarding prosody (*pingal shastra*) and aesthetics (*ras shastra*), as an important requisite for being a good poet. The new conception of a poet, proposed by these Gujarati writers, was quite different from the previously understood conception of a poet as a *mugdha kavi* (emotionally charged) (Yashaschandra 2003, 587–89). Pandya, in his review of Manibhai Dwivedi's play *Kanta*, observes that poetic genius is innate and one must cultivate pure "taste"[3] (*shuddha rasagnata*) in order to be a good poet (Parikh 1937, 34). However, he argues that the cultivation of good taste requires higher education and profound study of aesthetics (*ras shastra*) (ibid.). He argues

[3] Pandya uses the word "taste" in the text.

that poetic genius is of two types: "subjective" (*svanubhavi* or *anthsthita*) and "objective" (*sarvanubhavi* or *bahyasthita*) (ibid., 35–36). He further claims that lyric poetry, such as that of bhakti poets of Gujarati, results from the subjective poetic genius. Drama and other types of poetry, on the other hand, requires the objective poetic genius. He gives more importance to objective poetic genius as it requires the ability to describe different incidents as felt by people with different natures (ibid., 36). It is not enough to describe *ras* as one feels inside oneself (ibid., 36). He laments that most of the Gujarati poets have been "subjective" in their literary output and considers Premanand, the medieval Gujarati poet, as the only poet having objective poetic genius. In his article on Premanand, Pandya observes that the power of his poetic genius was extraordinary and he never missed creating an exact picture of the subject on which he was writing in front of the reader (1937, 179). The other medieval poets such as Shamal Bhatt and Dayaram were praised for their "imagination" (*tark*) and the sentiment of love (*shringar ras*) respectively, but were given secondary position because of their inability or lack of competency in the matter of *ras* (ibid., 187–88). It has to be noted here that Aristotle's principle of imitation does influence the way Pandya defines the word "poet" and evaluates the Gujarati poets from the past. However, Pandya's proposed new definition of a poet attempts to establish a dialogue between two separate lines of thoughts on the term.

In his analysis of Navalram Pandya's highly cryptic essay "Manana Vicharo" (Thoughts from the Mind), Ramesh Shukla observes that Pandya expresses his wish to propound his own doctrine on aesthetics—*ras shastra*—in this essay (Shukla 1988, 53). Pandya, in fact, wishes to introduce a new standard for *ras* which will be an assimilation of Aristotle's principle of imitation, Francis Bacon's principle of improvement on nature and John Stuart Mill's principles of pragmatic intellectualism (1937, 54–55). His doctrine on aesthetics or *ras shastra* in a way would be a conciliation between "classicism" and "romanticism" (ibid., 53). Shukla argues that Pandya uses the word "radicalism" for "romanticism" in the article under the influence of Western philosophers such as Bacon and Mill. Now, Pandya describes Gujarati poets Shamal Bhatt and Narmad as "radical" and Premanand and himself as "conservative" (ibid., 54). In his opinion, radicals are action-minded and conservatives like him are brooding in nature (54). In the above context, he considers Shamal Bhatt as *nagar* (romantic) and Premanand Bhatt as *shastri* (classical). The poetry of Premanand possesses "organic unity" (*akhandlahari*) and Shamal's poetry lacks it as it seems to be formed in parts (*khandlahari*) (ibid.). He further observes that romantic poets like Shamal are read by common people in general while classical poets like Premanand are read and preferred by a particular class of people only (ibid.). Here, in this particular context of introducing a new *ras shastra* of his own, Pandya imagines a new poet who would imbibe the best elements of both romantic and classical poetry of the Gujarati literature. He imagines this new poet as a sage, a seer poet like that of the Vedas (ibid.).

Like Navalram Pandya, Narmad also believed that in order to be a poet some natural potential (*svabhavik buddhibal*) is required and he too emphasised the need to have scholarship in order to be a good poet. In his article "Kavita Bhed" (Types of Poetry), Narmad does not consider *bhakti* poets of Gujarati such as Narsinh Maheta, Meera, Dheero etc., as "poets" as he believes that they did not have the knowledge of prosody (Dave 1858b, 202). Narmad considers these Gujarati poets *git kavi* (lyric poets) and their poetry "ordinary" (*samanya*)[4], and argues that even one who does not know the *kavya shastra* can compose such poems with just proper practice (ibid.). In his essay "Kavi ane Kavita" (Poet and Poetry) Narmad says that all are appreciative of or sensitive to beauty, all have the artistic taste (*rasgnan*) to a certain extent (Dave 1858a, 262). But all are not endowed with this faculty to the same extent. It differs according to occasions, nature of people, observations, time and place (ibid.). According to Narmad, a person whose *rasjnan* is energetic, who controls his feelings, who knows what anger is

[4] According to Narmad, *vir kavita* (epic poetry) is the best poetry.

and what love is, who is able to speak and express whatever he sees or hears in language or in some other way (e.g., painting) is a poet (ibid., 262–63). In the same essay, Narmad observes that a poet is someone who presents the clear/exact form of the original thing (*asal vastu nu chhokhu swarup jnan karave te kavi*) (ibid., 272). Narmad's redefinition of the term "poet" is also influenced by the views of English Romantic poets such as William Hazlitt and Shelley. Narmad uses Hazlitt's views on "poet" in order to explain his own conception of the same. He observes:

> One who provides immense maturity to our thoughts regarding nature or provides strength to the passion of our heart is the best poet. He can be known as the best poet, who has great imagination, whose passion of love is the best, whose knowledge regarding the *rasas* and divine beauty is awakened, and who has insights into the perversions of the feelings in the human heart. (Singh and Mukherjee 2005, 132)

Narmad's new conception of "poet" rejects the popular and traditional relationship between a poet and a patron. In his opinion, a poet is not someone who composes poetry on the request of his patron and on any occasion (1858a, 276–77). He observes that in case someone (say a patron) demands a poem to be composed for him and a person says "give it to me, I will do it for you", the person who wishes to be called a poet should go and wash his face[5] (ibid., 277). This is the reason why Narmad does not accord the status of poetry and poet to extempore/impromptu poetry (*sheeghra kavita*) and its composers respectively. He argues that

5 Pandya also vehemently criticises this popular and current tradition of composing poetry on request, especially in honour of a patron where he pays money or gives some kind of gift out of his pleasure. In his review of the poem *Dharmpurvarnan*, Pandya lambasts the poet for writing a statement on the front page that provides information regarding the amount the poet has received from the person in whose honour the present poem has been composed. Pandya considers this as *bhikhariveda* (an act of beggary) which is quite disreputable to the notion of a *granthkar* (writer or a poet). See Parikh (1937, 108–09).

mere ability to recite/compose poetry impromptu is not enough, what is additionally required is "thought" (Dave 1858c, 152–53). Mere intellect in composing poetry on an occasion, in his opinion, is meaningless (ibid.).

Narmad also argues that poets are not only those who do/express poetry merely through the medium of language. He asks us to include the singers, dancers, masons, sculptors, painters, legislators, etc., within the purview of the term "poet" as they also express their *rasjnan* in different ways, on different matters (1858a, 265). According to Narmad, the task of the poet is not to merely show what has already happened but also to show what might happen (ibid., 269). In short, to acquire all joys/pleasures of the nature and to express them in the same manner is the task of the great poet (ibid.). Narmad's new conception of the term "poet" here clearly indicates the influence of Aristotle's discussion on poetry in his *Poetics* as well as thoughts and concepts borrowed from English Romantic poets.

Let us now turn to another familiar Gujarati term *kavita* (poetry) as it undergoes a sea change in its conception in the concerned period. Narmad has expressed his views on poetry in his essays and articles such as "Kavi ane Kavita", Kavita Bhed" and "Kavi Charitra Vishe". It has already been observed that his new conception of poetry discarded medieval Gujarati poetry's peculiar characteristics (recitable and predominance of music) and emphasised the beauty of *arth* (meaning) and *vichar* (thought) in poetry (Dave 1858b, 202). Narmad does not accord the status of "pure" poetry to the poetry of medieval Gujarati poets as it does not utilise and follow the rules of prosody. In fact, Narmad asserts that pure poetry (*shuddh kavita*, in which one finds syllabic verse or *akshavrtta* and quantitative verse or *matravrtta*) emerged only after 1856 (ibid., 204). His conception of poetry also differentiates between *git/gayan* (song) and *kavan/kavita* (poetry). Narmad opines that a song (*gayan/git*) that is merely meant to be sung appears as a poem merely on the surface but the one which is full of thoughts deserves to be called poetry (*kavita*) (1858a, 272).

Narmad's long essay "Kavi ane kavita", published in 1858 in *Buddhivardhak Granth,* is an important document to understand the way he redefined the term "poetry".[6] In this essay, Narmad's new notion of poetry bears the combined influence of the Aristotelian principle of imitation and English Romanticism and Sanskrit works on poetics. His arguments in the essay that the aim of poetry is to provide joy, that it is an "expression of imagination" and his emphasis on *josso* (impulse) and *tarkbuddhi* (imagination) in poetry clearly indicate the influence of the views of English Romantic poets such as Shelley and Hazlitt. Finally, Narmad gives a new definition of poetry: "Poetry is something which effectively and in a concealed way converses with our mind, awakens benevolence and stimulates compassion in us, brings out impulses of love (*je pritina joṣṣane bāhar kādhe chhe*), improves/ cultivates our feelings and makes them worthy, gives consolation in bad times, forgiveness in good times and small pleasures in life" (ibid., 264).

However, when Narmad argues that the aim of poetry is to provide joy, he is following the views expressed by not only English Romantic poets but also Sanskrit texts on poetry. He quotes a definition of poetry in Sanskrit (*vakyarasatmakam kavyam*) from *Sahityadarpan* (a Sanskrit text by Vishvanathkaviraj published in West Bengal in 1850–53) in order to explain that even a sentence

---

6 In a footnote to this essay in his *Narmagadya*, Narmad observed: "Gujaratis being uneducated, their understanding of 'poetry' is very limited. For them, the meaning of poetry is the musical composition of famous and old stories from *puranas*. Even *kavi* Dalpatram also believes that the function of poetry is to present ordinary and known matters in a good style and to ornate them with figures of speech. Moreover, it is generally believed that poetry cannot be there in prose, only rhyming composition can be called poetry. Considering all these misconceptions regarding 'poetry', I published this essay in *Buddhivardhak Granth* in September 1858. In this essay, I have included my views on poetry along with views of English scholars and Sanskrit scholars. That is why I accord a sign *mishr* (a mixed one) to my essay." See Dave (1858a, 128).

out of which *rasa* (here, pleasure) is produced in the writer, reader, speaker and listener can be called poetry and that the aim of the poetry is to provide joy (1858a, 267–68). His further observations that poetry does not imitate nature but shows it in a wonderful, different and new way, that poetry is more serious and respected than history, that poetry is something that a person is born with and it is brought out in the form of a painting, a poem, a piece of sculpture, dance or a song, etc. indicates the influence of basic doctrines of Aristotle as discussed in *Poetics.*

Pandya redefines poetry in a somewhat similar manner as Narmad does. In his essay "Kavyashsstra Sambandhi Vicharo" (Thoughts on Poetics), he argues that the *kharekharu* (true/real) picture of the form of *maya* or *kudarat* (nature) is poetry (Parikh 1937, 270). He asks us to consider the meaning of "picture" in his definition as an instrument to make others understand the form of nature (ibid., 272–73). In his opinion, a singer or a painter can also be called a poet as they have the capability to make others understand the form of nature through their respective arts. In another article, "Kavi Narmadashankarni Kavita" (Poetry of Narmad), Pandya observes that poetry is there in meaning; meaning which creates a picture in the mind and influences one's sensibilities (ibid., 186). The success of poetry, in his opinion, depends on *the truthfulness and completeness* (*sacchai ane sampurnata*) of that picture (ibid.; emphasis mine). Like Narmad, Pandya also emphasised the beauty of "meaning" and "thought" in poetry as against the beauty of grandiose words. He argues that for the so-called appreciators of good poetry of the present time, only sound is important and "a versification with a few swift, bursting, bustling, heavy sounding alliterated words" is also considered poetry (Shukla 1988, 52). His definition of poetry also emphasised the idea of "organic unity" and compactness of language in poetry. Discussing the poetry of Narmad in his article "Kavi Narmadashankar ni Kavita", Pandya stresses on appropriate tuning between meaning and word, and the uniqueness of the suggestive power of a word which cannot be replaced with another one. He observes:

> Gujarati does not have poetry in which every single word of a sentence has a unique purpose, with the result that removal or replacement of that word may destroy the picture of meaning and affect the *ras*. Where the figures of speech seem the integral part of the poem and meaningless elaboration is absent. Written with such brevity that the scholar would not like to add even a single word to it. Where not a single rule of prosody is inappropriately followed. Such meaningful and suggestive poetry is absent in Gujarati. Such excellence is only there in English and Sanskrit poetry. Such type of *shashtriy* poetry has begun to be produced in Gujarati by Narmad. (Parikh 1937, 196)

Pandya proposes to divide Gujarati poetry into three schools on the basis of the style (*shaili*) in which it has been composed: Dalpatshala (old school of poetry represented by Kavi Dalpatram), Narmadshala (modern school of poetry represented by Narmad) and Navalshala (the school of poetry represented by himself) (Parikh 1937, 96). In his opinion the poetry of Dalpatshala is characterised by its emphasis on "word" and the poetry of Narmadshala is characterised by its emphasis on "meaning" and "thought" (ibid.). The poetry of Navalshala, according to him, would be characterised by the combination of elements of the poetry of both Dalpatshala and Narmadshala. In his opinion, the poetry of Navalshala would give equal importance to "meaning" and "diction", and would employ "concise" style (ibid., 97). According to Pandya, style reflects the mind of the poet and so he emphasises proper understanding and profound study of the poetics of "style" in order to avoid flaws in poetry (Dadawala 2004, 28). In his review of *Subodhchintamani,* Pandya discusses "concise" (*sankshipt* or *ekagra shaili*) and "diffused" (*sarvagradashti shaili*) styles in poetry (he uses English words "concise" and "diffused" in the text). He explains to his readers that the concise style in poetry emphasises compactness where every word is meaningful and useless elaboration and repetition are absent (Parikh 1937, 97). In his opinion, this style is difficult to achieve and requires practice and natural capabilities (ibid., 97–98). Pandya also evaluates the contemporary as well as past Gujarati poets on the basis of the style that they employed in their respective works. For example, he observes that Premanand Bhatt is the only Gujarati poet who has succeeded fully in achieving this style. The style of Shamal Bhatt, another important Gujarati poet, on the other hand, is "diffused" and elaborate. In his opinion, the composition of Akha Bhagat[7] is meaningful and he employs concise style in his poetry but, in doing so, ends up deforming the language (ibid., 98).

"Natak" is another term that came to be redefined in this period following the principle of Western dramaturgy. It has to be noted here that plays that started to be produced in Gujarati from the 1860s onward as well as Sanskrit dramas were evaluated and analysed following the views expressed by Aristotle in *Poetics*. Pandya in his review of *Kanta* and *Shravan Pitru Bhakti Natak*, for example, observes that *ras, patrabhed* (characters) and *vastusankalana* (plot) are the most important and inevitable ingredients of good literary texts (*natak, kavya*, etc.) (Parikh 1937, 34; Tripathi 1891, 155). He explains that the story on which the whole *kavya* (literary text) is based is called subject (*vastu*) and the art of arranging different parts of the same story, by editing or expanding them appropriately, is called *vastusankalana* (plot) (Tripathi 1891, 155). *Patrabhed* (characters), in his opinion, is to describe manners and mentalities (*mati ane riti*) of men and women of the text in different ways according to the difference in their nature (ibid.), and the whole *ras* (interest) of the text, he argues, depends on *patrabhed* and *vastusankalana*. Though Pandya adopts words such as *vastu* and *patrabhed* from Sanskrit and coins the new word *vastusankalana*, he provides explanation of these terms following Western dramatic tradition. Ramesh Shukla rightly observes that Pandya's concept of drama was enriched by Western theories and not by Sanskrit poetics

---

[7] Akha Bhagat (1600?-1655?), popularly known as "Akho", was a medieval Gujarati poet from Jetalpur who later came to reside in Ahmedabad. He is most famous for his more than 750 *chhappa* (a verse form of total six lines that employs a quantitative metre named *chhappo*) that satirised the contemporary ways of life and the traditional ritualism.

(Shukla 1988, 61). The influence of Aristotle's views is clearly evident in Pandya's use of English words such as "action", "plot", "characters" and "triple unities" in his evaluation. In his review of Bhavabhuti's *Malatimadhav*, Pandya argues that the excessive description of nature hinders the "action" of the play (Parikh 1937, 69). He observes that Sanskrit dramatists seem to give more importance to *ras* than action, and this tendency itself, in his opinion, is responsible for the distortion of *ras* (*rasbhaṅg*) (ibid., 69). He further states that Bhavabhuti lacks in attributes of "characterisation" and "probability" (*sambhavitata*). On the other side, Pandya praises the twelfth century drama *Ratnavali* of Harshdev for its observance of "triple unities" (Parikh 1937, 72–73). The influence of Aristotle's doctrines is also evident in Pandya's vehement rejection of plays of professional companies which hardly employed regular script and focused more on entertainment rather than technical perfectness (ibid., 65).

Thus, the Gujarati writer-critics of the second half of the nineteenth century reformulated critical vocabulary available in Gujarati through their epistemic negotiations with the critical concepts of an alien literary tradition. As Gujarati was not cultivated enough to accommodate and express this new terminology, these writer-critics attempted to attain communicability in the language by adopting either Sanskrit terminology or near-meaning words from their own language. However, they redefined these critical terms or coined new ones chiefly following the critical concepts of Western literary criticism. In conclusion, we can say that the language of critical analysis took a shift towards new standards based on Western concepts during the period concerned here and it is through translation that a new critical vocabulary became available.

Works Cited

Aristotle. 1902. *The Poetics*. Trans. S.H. Butcher. Rev. 3rd ed. London: Macmillan and Co., Limited.

Dadawala, Darshini. 2004. "Gujarati sahityavivechan ni bhashano aalochanatmak abhyas, ketlak vivechakona sandarbhe" (The Critical

Study of the Language of the Gujarati Literary Criticism, with reference to critics). Diss. M. S. University, Baroda.

Dave, Narmadashankar Lalshankar. 1858a. "Kavi ane Kavita." *Buddhivardhak Granth* 3.9: 261–80.

———. 1858b. "Kavita Bhed." *Buddhivardhak Granth* 3.7: 201–07.

———. 1858c. "Sheeghra Kavita Vishe." *Buddhivardhak Granth* 3.5: 152–56.

Junu Narmagadya. 1912. Bombay: Gujarati Printing Press.

O'Sullivan, Neil. 1995. "Aristotle on Dramatic Probability." *The Classical Journal* 91.1 (1995): 47–63. *JSTOR*.

Parikh, Narhari Dwarkadas, ed. 1937. *Navalgranthavali*. Ahmedabad: Navjivan Prakashan Mandir.

Shukla, Ramesh M. 1988. *Navalram*. New Delhi: Sahitya Akademi.

Singh, Avdhesh Kumar and Sanjay Mukherjee, eds. 2005. *Critical Discourses and Colonialism: Indian Critical Discourse in the Colonial Period in Hindi, Gujarati and English*. New Delhi: Creative Books.

Tripathi, Govardhanram. 1891. *Navalgranthavali*. Ahmedabad: n.p.

Yashaschandra, Sitamshu. 2003. "From Hemacandra to *Hind Svaraj*: Region and Power in Gujarati Literary Culture." *Cultures in History: Reconstructions from South Asia*. Ed. Sheldon Pollock. Berkeley and Los Angeles: University of California Press.

SEVENTEEN

Domestication of English, Education and Perpetuation of Sexual Difference

A Study of Govardhanram Tripathi's Leelavati Jeevankala

ZARANA MAHESHWARI

> There is a belief among our people that the western education proves to be poisonous for our girls and troublesome for their relatives. It is not that this belief is completely groundless, untenable and incorrect. The lacuna lies not in its education but in the method of imparting education. The poison given in an appropriate manner serves as nectar and the nectar given in an unsuitable manner works as poison. (Tripathi 1894, 98)

The above quoted words from *Leelavati Jeevankala* (1905) by Govardhanram Tripathi (1855–1905) provide insights into ambivalence caused by the historical transition, that is colonial encounter in various domains of the society in the nineteenth century. The present scholarship on colonialism suggests that colonial modernity marked the period with constant dialogue between native and Western mode of constructing knowledge as part of negotiating the other (Gurjarpadhye 2014, 44). The new situation caused by colonial encounter compelled the native intellectuals to demarcate the juncture between internal cohesion and the external difference. As a result, a need arose to keep ethnic boundaries intact. The native intellectuals felt that it was essential to reconfigure earlier patriarchal vocabulary and hierarchical norms within the "dislocations and possibilities created by a colonial context" (Gupta 2012, 13) and hence, various discursive strategies were devised by them in order to negotiate the crisis caused by colonial modernity.

Govardhanram Tripathi was an eminent writer in Gujarati literature. He contributed significantly to Gujarati literature by writing poems, novel, drama, biography, etc. He was an integral part of the native intelligentsia and had completely devoted himself to preparing a new format for the middle class and to perform his duty efficiently, he educated himself selectively (Shukla 2015, 65). He worked out "the rationale of his selection" (ibid.). He took himself seriously and never doubted that he was the most qualified to perform this task. The publication of the biography *Leelavati Jeevankala* was also a crucial part of his larger project of preparing the blueprint for an ideal nation. The present paper attempts to study how *Leelavati Jeevankala* devises various discursive strategies in order to create a commensurable space for native interests to grow and develop; it studies how the biography reconfigures earlier patriarchal vocabulary by legitimising knowledge given by shashtras through their reinterpretation. Moreover, the biography creates a discursive space where Leelavati's virtues derive legitimacy from knowledge imparted by Hindu scriptures. It further analyses how the biography devises various strategies in order to create the discursive space where the knowledge imparted by Western education is domesticated and is made commensurable with that of the native.

The quote in the beginning from *Leelavati Jeevankala* provide insights into Tripathi's oscillation between retaining the traditional institutions and heralding the modern establishment. He uses the metaphor "nectar" and "poison" to refer to both Sanskrit and Western education respectively. He conforms to the notion prevalent in the contemporary society that English education proves to be dangerous for women. The changes brought about by the colonial encounter are looked at as the forerunner of moral crisis and hence, there is a need to negate the harmful effects of Western education and produce "sexual difference to confine English within class and caste locations of the new colonial India" (Chandra 2012, 35). His words "the lacuna lies not in its education but in the method of imparting education" suggest his endeavour of domesticating the Western education by modifying the very method of imparting that education.

Tripathi wrote *Leelavati Jeevankala* to commemorate his daughter Leelavati who died young. He presents Leelavati as an ideal virtuous and ascetic woman to be followed by Gujarati women of the time. He writes: "the essence of your life and your actions are worthy enough to be told" (1894, 52). He carefully chooses the form of "life story" in order to delineate Leelavati's ascetic life. He makes it clear that the articles in his book are written in the form of a life story, and not in the form of a biography. In his view, the heroes of biographies are eminent persons, who have led adventurous lives. The adventurous lives of such great people are usually written in the form called "biographies" (ibid., 82). He further clarifies that *Leelavati Jeevankala* is not governed by any intention of highlighting Leelavati's adventures, as her life does not consist of anything laudable; rather, it comprises subtle asset, that is, her virtues (ibid.). The account draws heavily on the depiction of Leelavati's ascetic life and the role played by education in making her lead such a life. In Tripathi's words, the narrative changes the sequence of the life story by providing detailed account of the events first and not her birth details. He says: "the purpose behind changing the sequence is primarily to present Leelavati's subtle world before the eyes of those beholders, who after savoring the essence of the things wish to explore the roots which have shaped those incidents" (ibid.). It should be noted that "the root" here implies education and specifically, the education provided to Leelavati which played a crucial role in making her handle the sufferings fallen upon her after her marriage. Moreover, it rendered the endurance of suffering as an essential aspect of Eastern knowledge.

Tripathi himself charted out the curriculum for Leelavati, and it was designed in such a way that she naturally developed interest in Sanskrit language and literature and sought refuge in them to handle the crisis. Moreover, she was strategically kept away from the direct influence of English language and literature and her knowledge of English was kept confined to the sphere of practical tasks. Moreover, the English made available to her was domesticated in order to consolidate hierarchies, discipline sexuality and achieve "sexual difference" (Chandra 2012, 58).

The present life story reveals that Leelavati was sent to a girl's school which was situated near Tripathi's sister's house. However, her admission was canceled from that school and Tripathi provides an explanation for the same. According to him, his sister who used to keep an eye on Leelavati, had to move to Junagadh. Moreover, Tripathi was dissatisfied with the kind of education given in that school as in his view, school education at the time focused more on amusement than actual studies. In addition, the school did not offer any other advantages. He further clarifies that he found it inappropriate to burden her with the hard work of studies (1894, 83). Tripathi's thoughts clearly articulate his dissatisfaction with the existing education system. In order to provide education to Leelavati, he made arrangements at home by taking into account her "age, gender and body" (ibid., 86). Here, it is important to take some insights from Charu Gupta. While providing insights into the attempts undertaken by native intellectuals for negotiating the disruptions in domestic space, she argues that women were the significant subjects for their renewed emphasis on conservative hierarchical upper caste domination. In her view, caste and gender inequalities can influence each other in systematic ways. She further posits that women emerged as a powerful means of brahminical patriarchal attempts to hold power, consolidate social hierarchies and express caste exclusivity (2012, 28). John and Nair posit that sexuality has been present as the site of contention in the discourses of social reforms (1998, 19). They are of the view that discourses on sexuality were generated in such a way that they complied with the "broader Hindu national ideal of citizenry" (ibid.). Tripathi designed Leelavati's curriculum in such a way that it contributed to "reordering of the household" (Gupta 2012, 28) and to creating "social difference" (Tripathi 1894, 34).

Tripathi hired shashtriji in order to impart education to Leelavati at home. In addition, he himself instructed shashtriji on how to provide education. As he says:

> While handing over her education to shashtriji Jivram, this author had given some instructions. Shashtriji, Leelavati is supposed to go abroad, where her mother or I cannot accompany her and go there to give lessons on happy or sad occasions. Moreover, it is impossible for the worldly people to do that. When you impart her education, you kindly take into consideration the fact that her education serves as a friend to her intellect wherever Leelavati goes and she stays parented with her own intelligence. (Tripathi 1894, 34)

These words by Tripathi unfold the motif behind providing education to Leelavati. In Tripathi's view, Leelavati's education should be a friend to her intellect once she goes abroad. Here the word "abroad" implies her in-laws' place. Thus, method of providing education is designed by taking into consideration her life after marriage. Leelavati was first provided education in Gujarati which enabled her to read and write in the language. Further, she was taught mathematics and her teacher was instructed to take into consideration the fact that this should enable her handle the accounts of her domestic and household work. Then, Leelavati's mother was appointed to train her in cooking and other domestic chores. One more shashtriji was hired in order to exclusively provide Sanskrit education to Leelavati. The newly appointed shashtriji was also instructed on methodology of imparting Sanskrit education to Leelavati. Shashtriji trained her in identifying different forms of words and inferring their meanings without referring to any grammar book. Then, Tripathi realised the need of introducing Leelavati to Sanskrit literature. However, he realised the need to be attentive to erotic aspects in Sanskrit literature, as in his view, Sanskrit literature drew much on *shringar*. This problem was resolved and it was decided that the parts which contain *shringar* should be omitted and the portions which were free from *shringar* should be taught. She was introduced one by one to Bhartrhari's *Nitisatak*, *Chandkaushakik* by Aryashrenisvar, the fourth act of *Abhigyan Shakuntalam* and the third act of *Uttar Ramcharit*, respectively. Moreover, she also used to read *Savitri* and *Abhigyan Shakuntalam* in her free time and on several instances, drew inspiration from Savitri and Shakuntala and these books refined her taste and exposed her to the ultimate virtues (Tripathi 1894, 90).

Leelavati Jeevankala further reveals that Leelavati was fascinated by Sanskrit and as a result, could not develop an avid interest in English. Tripathi justifies her lack of interest in English by saying: "How can those reading books written in a modern style, proliferated with the subjects which appease children having childlike intelligence cater to the interest of the one who reads *Abhigyan Shakuntlam* and *Uttar Ramcharit* with profound interest" (ibid., 89). Having established the superiority of Sanskrit, he categorises English to be the language of power and domination and hence leaves it up to Leelavati's husband to decide whether she should be further trained in English or not.

Chandra (2012) suggests that native codes of gender and sexuality in colonial India shaped the history and symbolic power of English and English came to the play in shaping intimate sphere of conjugality and desire (ibid., 7). In *Leelavati Jeevankala*, one can notice that English and Sanskrit education are shown to be preparing manuals for sexuality and asceticism respectively. Further, modernity introduced by English language is domesticated to assimilate modern ideas into the discourses established by Sanskrit language. Both English and Sanskrit emerge as signs that dictate behaviour, domesticity and caste dynamics.

In Tripathi's words, Sanskrit literature contributes to ameliorating life's desires and taste and huge trees like *shastras* are required to support and make climb the creeper-like intelligence (ibid., 90). The life-story unfolds several instances in which *shastras* prove to be the guide to Leelavati's intellect and direct her to curb her desires. Comparisons are drawn between Leelavati and Savitri and Leelavati emerges to be an ideal woman to be followed by Gujarati women of the time. She succeeds in leading a life devoid of worldly desires and attains virtues like asceticism. Here, it is important to take some insights from Shefali Chandra. Chandra brings to the fore how knowledge and sexuality remained central to the social upheaval of the time as they were instrumental in soaring up caste formations (2012, 57). She posits that languages derive their identity from their associations to power and access (ibid., 34). *Leelavati Jeevankala* creates a discursive space where Sanskrit restores its identity by reconfiguring old patriarchal vocabulary—inscribing the lexicon of purity, self discipline and self-control. Moreover, Sanskrit is established as the language of self whereas, English is established as the language of the other. The analogy drawn by Tripathi between Sanskrit and mother's milk supports the above argument. He says:

> The Sanskrit proves to be a mother's milk for the children of this country and can easily be absorbed. It protects and nurtures them in the form of education till the end of their lives. If we send the kite which has come to a shape on this earth to the sky of the Western education, which is profuse with different type of sanskara and if we do not tie the kite to the earth using a strong thread, it results into complete mess and there is no doubt about it. (Tripathi 1894, 173)

The above quoted words explicitly institutionalise Sanskrit as the language of the "self". Sanskrit education becomes essential to guard oneself against the influences of Western education. Moreover, he makes it clear that only a glimpse into Western education is sufficient for women and assigns the charge of educating women in English to their husbands. Thus, English emerges as a tool to reconfigure old patriarchal vocabulary and help tame women's sexuality. The argument provided by Chandra helps one understand the point. She argues that the English had power to determine the femininity of vernacular languages but it also had power to determine the native male's desire to determine native female behavior (2012, 35). She further posits that the ideas of sexual difference and standards of desirable femininity were grafted onto English (ibid., 58). In her view, cultural analogies were established between English and Gujarati and then grafted upon the other (ibid.). *Leelavati Jeevankala* disciplines women's sexuality and serves as a conduct book to the contemporary women. It draws analogy between English and Sanskrit, denies social access of English to women and domesticates English in order to retain sexual difference and make it commensurable to the upper caste domesticity.

It should be noted that Tripathi does not completely do away with English. He cannot ignore the usefulness of English in day-today life and calls an education without English "one dimensional" (1894, 91). He is of the view that in order to extend support and provide protection to women from faltering due to severe cold in the dark nights of the winter of the world, there is no other alternative than good education which can offer coziness, sharpen logic and can lead them to a virtuous path. Presence of such might can be noticed in our shastras too, and its amalgamation with western education can render it compatible with the present time. It is to be noted that before blending Western and Sanskrit education, Tripathi strategically domesticates the very language and the methodology of its teaching. *Leelavati Jeevankala* thus unfolds the strategic domestication of English. Tripathi while discussing Leelavati's education, informs the readers that Leelavati developed a dislike for English education and left it midway. However, the section which discusses Leelavati's efforts of overcoming her limitations draws one's attention to a contradictory view. The readers are informed that Leelavati dropped the idea of educating herself in English because she found it inappropriate to receive English education from a male teacher and her efforts to find a female teacher were futile. In order to pursue her unfulfilled dream, she was advised to refer to a book titled "Gujarati" which was written in Gujarati and comprised lessons on English in Gujarati. Moreover, Leelavati was not educated in English much. In order to meet the demand of rationality, she was given access to a handful Gujarati literary journals and books like *England ma Pravas (Travel to England)*. *England ma Pravas* is a travelogue by Karsandas Mulji which records an account of his travel to England in 1866. Indira Karamcheti, while providing insights on how any act of representation becomes an act of translation, argues that any cross-cultural text by definition is translative (1996, 185). She further posits that all acts of representations are perforce acts of translation from being to saying, experience to memory, presence to absence (ibid.). Like translation, it is a twice-written discourse transforming the original by supplementation. Like translation, representation is always referential and like translation, it negotiates dominant subversive relationship. If one considers any travelogue in the light of the above argument, one can consider it a kind of cross culture text and therefore translative. Mulji's account of his travel is thus also a translation. He attempts to translate modernity in familiar terms, as the lack of linguistic means comes in the way of referring to a particular referent. It interprets and translates the culture of the West in domestic terms, in domestic dialects, registers and style. These terms are able to translate modernity in such a way that it does not disrupt the culture of the target language. Thus, the translation in domestic registers and style in *England ma Pravas* mitigates the "dangers" of Western modernity and helps in keeping women away from the direct influence of the West. Tripathi's intention in making Leelavati read such books allowed her to appreciate the rational mode of thoughts.

Tripathi further devises various strategies in order to keep women aloof from the direct influence of English. He acknowledges the importance of the knowledge offered by English education in the arenas of health and sanitation. By citing one example of how English education helped Leelavati in finding remedy for her disease, he further draws one's attention to the benefits of its application in practical life. However, he simultaneously accentuates Leelavati's femininity, chastity and faith in the *shastra*s. He informs the readers that Leelavati had read in one of the English books about the importance of exposing oneself to fresh air in curing her ailment and hence, she was taken to a hill station called Mount Abu. Taking walks around the lake there eventually improved her health. This discussion is followed by an explanation that Leelavati's actions generated religiosity also. In order to get fresh air, she used to take rounds of tulsi plant which served a dual purpose—that of looking after her health while abiding by religious rituals. Tripathi further devises various strategies in order to retain the "sexual difference" established by Sanskrit *shashtras* and mitigate the effects of the threat posed by English education. He provides different interpretations of modern concepts like "travel" and tries to convey the same by taking refuge of referents from Sanskrit language. He cites the advantages of travel by quoting from books by Kalidas and Shakespeare. Cultural analogies are drawn between the two, as he says:

> The men and women who have undertaken travel, are found more experienced, smart, liberal and kindhearted than those who are confined to their home only. An as English poet Shakespeare says: "home keeping youths have ever homely wits" it means that those who are confined to the corners of their house, their intelligence remains blunted. This sentence advocates the advantage of travel for the growth of virtues and wits of those men and women who have undertaken travel. There is a shloka: people who visits more places and pursue the scholars, their intelligence expands like a drop of an oil in the water and those who fail in doing so, their intellect shrinks like a drop of ghee in the water. (1894, 91)

Here Tripathi highlights the importance of travel and eliminates the difference between Sanskrit and English. He further cites another *shloka* from Sanskrit literature and lays down six important advantages of travel such as observation of the place, general knowledge, increasing wealth, observation of attractive wonders, sharpening wit and acquiring acquiring an extensive vocabulary. He further argues that like English, *shastra*s in Sanskrit also advocate travel for women. According to him, the belief that *shastra*s forbid travel for women, is completely baseless (1894, 90). However, he cautions against women availing the advantage of general knowledge. According to him, the benefit of general knowledge can be availed only by taking into account the constraint of gender. He further retains the sexual difference by strategically playing with the word "travel".

The word "travel" is translated as *yatra* which has two connotations. It implies a travel to a religious and sacred place while also referring to travel to any touristic place. When discussing the advantages of travel for women, he refers mainly to the first connotation. He further gives other interpretations of the word, translating it as "the service of the pundits" and argues that it can be done by staying with them or keeping in touch with them. In his view, if the places can be observed by travel, they can be observed by reading the articles written by the pundits as well. This interpretation restricts actual travel for women and by doing so, conforms to women's confinement. He further translates "travel", that is, *tirth* as the elder people of one's country. He says: "The way Sanskrit word *tirth* implies holy and agreeable places, it also implies scholars and saints. We consider the elders of the family as *tirth*. Similarly, the elders of one's country or the community can also be considered as *tirth*. If one can observe both animate and inanimate objects during travel, the same way, the books on geography, travelogues and physics can provide glimpse into inanimate *tirth* to their readers. Moreover, if one reads history books and life stories, one can avail the benefit of the animate *tirth*. The women in ancient times used to be made acquainted with such book in order to take benefits of travel" (1894, 89–91). Thus, the above discussed translations of the word *yatra* confine women's travel only to holy places. Moreover, it restricts their physical movement and prohibits them from transgressing the boundary of their home, thereby maintaining the "sanctity" of their gender. Thus, the domestication of the travel succeeds in inscribing old patriarchal vocabulary by getting legitimacy from the *shastras*.

This paper has thus argued how *Leelavati Jeevankala* projects Leelavati as an ideal woman to be venerated by Gujarati women of the time. It showed how Sanskrit is established as a superior language to English. It also studied how English is domesticated and how the meanings are recreated in order to make them appropriate to the target culture. It further analysed how domestication of English is used as a trope in order to allow native interests to grow and develop.

WORKS CITED

Chandra, Shefali. 2012. *The Sexual Life of English: Languages of Caste and Desire in India.* Durham and London: Duke University Press.

Gurjarpadhye, Prachi. 2014. *Bringing Modernity Home: Marathi Literary Theory in the Nineteenth Century.* Indian Institute of Advanced Study: Shimla.

Gupta, Charu. 2012. *Gendering Colonial India: Reforms, Print, Caste and Communalism.* New Delhi: Orient Blackswan.

Karamcheti, Indira. 1996. "Aime Cesaire's Subjective Geographies; Translating Place and the Differences it Makes" Between Languages and Cultures; Translation and Cross-cultural Texts. Eds. Anuradha Dingwaney and Carol Maier. New Delhi: Oxford University Press.

Mulji, Karasandas. 2010. "Deshatan Vishay." *Oganis mi Sadi nu Gujarati Paravaslekhan Sanchay.* Compiled and edited Patel and Patel, 233–42. New Delhi: Sahitya Akademi.

Nair, Janaki and Mary John. 1998. *A Question of Silence: The Social Economies of Modern India.* Delhi: Kali for Women.

Nemade, Bhalchandra. 1990. *The Influence of English on Marathi: A Sociolinguistic and Stylistic Study.* Saurabh Printers: Noida.

Shukla, Sonal. 2015. "Govardhanram's Women". *Economic and Political Weekly* 22 (1987): JSTOR. http://www.jstor.org/stable/4377664

Tripathi, Govardhanram M. 1894. *The Classical Poets of Gujarat.* Bombay: Forbes Gujarati Sabha.

EIGHTEEN

From the Poetics of Self-Knowledge to the Politics of Social Change

Sree Narayana Guru as a Social Reformer and Philosopher-Poet

E. V. Ramakrishnan

(1)

In this paper I discuss the life and works of Sree Narayana Guru as a social reformer and philosopher-poet and in the process flag certain issues that intersect the domains of Humanities and Social Sciences. More specifically, these issues pertain to the inadequacies of prevailing discourses on modernity in general, and their inability to deal with the experiential component of reality rooted in the relations between the self and the world, in particular. Radical changes within a society are possible only when the imagination of people is stirred by a deep sense of involvement and commitment. Social movements shape the course of sociopolitical evolution of a society enabling its progressive democratisation by mobilising the people in the service of certain ideals and ideologies that have the capacity to redefine the very nature of society. These movements take off only when their objectives capture the imagination of the public at large. It is culture, more specifically art and literature that equip the movements with the necessary means and modes of persuading the people by enlisting them in the service of a higher vision. In her book *Public Emotions: Why Love Matters for Justice*, Martha C. Nussbaum has argued that texts of exceptional imaginative power are necessary in a culture to instill abstract ideas such as justice, equality and liberty in the minds of people, transforming those ideas into sensuous experiences of intimacy, immediacy and urgency in concrete forms, at crucial moments in the evolution of society. In a liberal society political cultivation of emotions has two-fold tasks: the first is to create and sustain "strong commitments to worthy projects that require effort and sacrifice and the second is to keep at bay dark forces such as envy and disgust, the desire to inflict shame on others" (2013, 1). Cultural texts that discharge such functions include not only poems, plays, stories and novels but conversations, pamphlets, speeches and performative acts of great symbolic power that prepare a society for re-imagining reality by cultivating a critical consciousness. Mahatma Gandhi's act of defying the imperial ban on salt-making in 1930, and Narayana Guru's consecration of a Shiva temple in Aruvippuram (in Kerala) in 1887 may be cited as examples of such performative acts that charged the imagination of a whole community and changed the direction of history.

We are here concerned with a moment of radical transformation in nineteenth-century Kerala when the social, political and cultural scene was undergoing a complete transformation. While the first half of the nineteenth century was marked by the standardisation of Malayalam language and the emergence of Malayalam prose, the second half witnessed the spread of periodicals and the rise of new literary forms like the novel, autobiography and the essay. The arrival of print and the introduction of English in Kerala partake of the episteme of colonial modernity as they reorient the protocols of reading and writing which had far-reaching consequences for the entire society. Benjamin Bailey (1791–1871), a protestant missionary from England, established the first Malayalam printing press in Kerala in 1821. By the time translation of the New Testament into Malayalam appeared in 1829, modern Malayalam alphabets designed by Bailey had become the standard prototypes for print and writing in Malayalam. By 1849, both Malayalam-English and English-Malayalam dictionaries were published and the first periodicals in Malayalam had made their appearance. The standardisation of Malayalam led to the creation of prose with a new syntax and vocabulary capable of communicating modern forms of knowledge, giving rise to a public sphere where questions of sociopolitical and cultural significance found articulation in both discursive and imaginative modes (Ramakrishnan 2017, 34–43, 201–17).

We cannot understand the social structure of Kerala of this period without reference to the caste system. Kerala had more than 220 castes which does not include sub-castes. There were 41 sub-castes among Nairs alone, and among the lower castes there were more than 170 sub-castes (Bhaskaranunni 1988, 175–76). By 1805, Kerala was under British domination, and departments such as revenue, public works, judiciary, jail, police, excise and education were actively involved in redefining relations between individuals and political power. Sanal Mohan rightly refers to lower castes as "slave castes" as the system of caste oppression prevalent in Kerala was nothing but slavery of the most ruthless kind (Mohan 2015, 3–7). Slavery in the Malabar region of north Kerala was abolished in 1843, while it was abolished in the Travancore region of south Kerala in 1855. However, this did not make much difference to the material conditions of the lower sections of society. It is important to note that while introducing administrative reforms, colonial authorities left the caste structures alone, thus deepening the contradictions between social change and political aspirations. Nicholas B. Dirks has argued that "caste became the colonial form of civil society, it justified the denial of political rights to Indian subjects (not citizens) and explained the necessity of colonial rule" (Dirks 2003, 16). It is necessary to understand this transformation of caste as a category in the colonial context, its simultaneous social validation and political suppression, to grasp the significance of Narayana Guru's (1856–1928) intervention in the sociopolitical sphere of Kerala. In the absence of its traditional economic and regulative functions, caste now became a ritualistic apparatus that helped the colonial authority to perpetuate their absolute control over their subjects. Taxes levied by the colonial machinery on lower castes increased manifold and there was greater pauperisation of these castes forcing them to even sell their own children (Rajeevan 2011, 289–90). Lower castes including Ezhavas could be forced to render free labour for the upper castes. Mohan in his book, *The Modernity of Slavery* observes:

> Most of the lands used to be controlled by the upper castes, while the slave caste labourers, who were slaves juridically till the mid nineteenth century, carried out the actual cultivation. As a result of this, the untouchable slaves continued to exist in the same structural position for very long time, even after the abolition of slavery in 1855 in the Travancore region of Kerala. (2015, 40)

It is against these abject circumstances of the lower castes that Narayana Guru's roles as a visionary, thinker, writer and social reformer have to be evaluated. The complex undercurrents of the period reflect transactions between an entrenched feudal system (with brahminic hegemony built into it), an emergent public sphere with aspirations for modern values rooted in equality and justice and a repressive colonial regime that set severe limits to social mobilisation, free expression and collective resistance. What Narayana Guru achieved in Kerala's society riven with every conceivable social division of caste, religion, class and gender one can imagine and with limited access to any modern education, was made possible by his grasp of the ideological structures that operated in Kerala society. Mohan notes how the missionaries who tirelessly worked for the abolition of slavery in Kerala failed to understand how the lower castes' subordination "was legitimized by the moral and religious codes articulated through the ideology and practice of 'Hinduism' and caste" (ibid., 41).

(2)

Sri Narayanan was born in an Ezhava middle class family near Thiruvananthapuram in 1856. He was initiated into Sanskrit and Ayurveda in the traditional format that was current in his times, with the disciple staying at the house of the teacher. He acquired Tamil through his own efforts, as it was spoken in the region. He started a school in his village for children but later, after the death of his parents, left home and took to wandering as a mendicant. After 1884, he never stayed in any place permanently; he had the habit of staying alone in secluded mountains and forests. His close association with Chattampi Swamikal (1853–1924), a reformer who challenged the brahmin supremacy in Kerala through his writings and Thycaud Ayya (1814–1909), a scholar in the Saiva tradition of Tamil Siddhars, transformed him into a thinker.

The Siddha tradition in Tamil, strongly radical in its content, questioned the legitimacy of brahminic ideology. David Shulman observes that Siddha tradition which was "egalitarian, iconoclastic, skeptical, and strongly rationalistic" was part of the intellectual and social world of the nineteenth-century Tamil Nadu (Shulman 2010, 310). Though there were many sects within the Siddha tradition, they had in common "hatred for caste-hierarchies and orthodox rituals, a Yoga-oriented universalistic ethic, anti-Brahmin sentiments, a generalized social critique and a Tantric metaphysics of body, self and language" (ibid., 312). Guru came into contact with this Tamil system of thought in his formative period, and this had a lasting impact on his formulation of principles that inspired the social imagination of Kerala. A materialistic worldview rooted in the body, repeated invocations of *jnanam* or *arivu* (knowledge) as the essence of universal truth in all his major poems and rejection of brahminic elements of hegemony in the everyday world, clearly follow from Guru's immersion in an alternative tradition that questioned the prevailing theocratic order.

All biographies of Narayana Guru mention his extensive wanderings across the length and breadth of Kerala, Tamil Nadu and beyond. His first major disciple and close associate (who was to become one of the most eminent poets of Malayalam in the twentieth century), Kumaran Asan (1873–1924) writes: "After his parents' death, it became easy for Guru to escape from the bondage of family relations. His resolve to renounce worldly attachments and devote himself to spiritual enquiry was firm. Having left home, he could be seen in nearby deserted hills, forests and such solitary places, lost in meditation or walking alone" (Guru 2002, 25).

Guru was not a "monk" in the traditional sense—he was not initiated into ascetic life by any master, nor did he follow any one as his mentor. He engaged in conversations with a large number of saints and scholars across south India, wandering from place to place. He dressed in white throughout his life, with the exception being during a trip to Sri Lanka when he was forced to wear saffron due to non-availability of white clothes. He translated several texts from Tamil and Sanskrit into Malayalam, and composed poems of exceptional artistic merit in all these three languages.

In an insightful study, P. K. Balakrishnan, a historian, has argued that Guru was both a prophet and philosopher, but without a prophet's passion for founding his own faith and without a philosopher's disdain for the common people (Balakrishnan 2006, 296). Guru overcame the indifference natural to philosophers towards worldly matters and the missionary zeal seen in prophets to create an institutional framework for their ideas, through his intense engagement with everyday life of people through ceaseless wanderings across south India. Balakrishnan observes that his formative period during the twenties holds the clue to his transformation:

> This unknown period in Guru's life (his life in the early youth) holds the key to understanding his emergence as a fully formed leader of people. Even after becoming a towering figure in Kerala acceptable to all communities, he never lived in one place for more than three days or so. He persisted in this habit, in old age as well. He lived among those considered as 'lower castes', the fisherfolk, Muslims, and marginalized communities of every kind, sharing their food, observing their ways of living. He knew the topology of South India like the palm of his hand, and this is what enabled him to love the communities of Kerala with such openness, not in abstract theory but in everyday practice. (Balakrishnan quoted in Guru 2002, 296–97)

Sukumar Azhikode, a major Malayalam literary critic, has observed that Guru did not become aware of discrimination based on caste after studying Vedanta. He observes: "He sought in Advaita a philosophy that can deny and defy the practice of caste discrimination and he sought in social reforms a practical course of action to eradicate caste discrimination" (quoted in Guru 2002, 304). Asceticism in India led people to renounce life, but in the case of Guru, it only refined his understanding of the social divisions and reinforced his resolve to fight against it.

Once Guru remarked that it was the British who had granted him "sanyas". Gopikrishnan, a Malayalam poet, has pointed out that Guru's "sanyas" was not an endorsement of tradition but an interpretation of modernity: "It was his deviation from the Brahminic code that enabled him to reinterpret 'Advaita' philosophy as expounded by Sankara, from a non-Brahmin point of view in accordance with the demands of Kerala renaissance" (Gopikrishnan 2019, 18). The colonial government had graciously granted him exemption from appearing in the court, when some differences between him and his followers became a matter of litigation. While he would have remained an outcaste in the traditional brahminic scheme of things, the British government recognised his standing as a "sanyasi" in society. This also provided him a vantage point to view society critically from the margins of the existing narratives about Kerala society. The context of colonial modernity is inherent in his radical pursuits of equality and social justice.

The large corpus of Guru's works in Malayalam, Sanskrit and Tamil, mostly poetic compositions, affirms his status as a major writer at the turn of the century in Kerala. He wrote in Sanskrit, Tamil and Malayalam with equal ease and the bulk of his works belong to poetry. Of the 62 works available, 44 are in Malayalam. For the purpose of discussion, we may group them under three categories: hymns and *kirtan*s in praise of Shiva and Shaivaite deities like Shanmukha, Ganesha and Devi, philosophical poems outlining Advaita philosophy or questions of Dharma and finally poems that address contemporary questions of caste differences and oppression. He also translated *Thirukkural* and *Ishavasyopanishad* into Malayalam. Apart from these, he engaged in conversations with a wide range of people from all walks of life, as he was sought out by eminent scholars and common people alike. His conversations with Mahatma Gandhi, Tagore and many other contemporary scholars and leaders from Kerala like Sahodaran Ayyappan and C. V. Kunhiraman have been documented and give us acute insights into his ways of thinking and analysing subjects of contemporary relevance. He also issued statements from time to time, one on the cardinal principles to be followed by his followers in 1909, and another against the consumption of liquor addressed to the members of Ezhava caste in 1920. There were also occasions when he directly intervened and ordered his followers to stop oppressive and outdated rituals such as the sacrifice of animals in the temples.

His poetic works play an important role in reconstituting the social through charged utterances that embody the social energy of the conflictual situations of caste violence and religious strife rooted in social inequalities. His mode of questioning the hegemony of the state and feudal system was radical and unprecedented. In March 1888 in a place near Aruvikkara, he consecrated a temple of Shiva, breaching the brahminic authority to establish temples. This was a gesture of far-reaching consequence as it shifted the idea of the sacred from the domain of religion to that of the secular, entailing a redefinition of the ritualistic apparatus of the brahminic theocratic order. Guru had been frequenting this secluded forest area for many years and people used to throng the place to meet him. He chose the day of Shivaratri to consecrate the new temple. When questions were raised regarding his authority to carry out such an act, he answered that it was "Ezhava Shiva" that he had consecrated. After consecrating the temple, he also wrote the following lines on a wooden plank with lime: *Jatibhedam matadwesham/Ethumillathe sarvarum/Sodaratwena vazhunna/Mathruka stanamanithu* ("This is an exemplary abode of brotherhood where everyone lives in harmony without discrimination of caste or religious hatred"). This is one of his most well-known and earliest poetic verses in Malayalam.

In retrospect, the significance of the 1888 event becomes clear when we recognise that it was part of a series of iconic events that stamped the mark of modernity on the life of Kerala. The first "popular" Malayalam novel *Indulekha* was published in 1889. The government of Madras formed the Marriage Commission in 1891 in response to a bill introduced in the Madras legislative assembly by C. Sankaran Nair demanding changes in the matrilineal customs in Malabar. Again, in 1891, the common people of Travancore, for the first time, submitted a memorandum to the king, commonly described as "Malayali Memorial", demanding equality of job opportunities. Collectively, they point to the churning that was shaping a new idea of the social where several ideas and ideologies were competing for visibility and expression.

(3)

In all accounts of Guru's life and works, his role as a social reformer is at centre-stage while his contribution as a poet is relegated to the background. Canonical literary histories of Malayalam, while occasionally noting his devotional works in passing, have not attributed much value to his literary output. It is, therefore, important to recover Guru as a *poet* and thinker to put his life and works in perspective. Our inability to appreciate his role as a poet and communicator is traceable to the discourses of modernity which give precedence to an empirical approach to reality. While Guru's interventions in the sociopolitical sphere can be "objectively documented", his poetic works bear witness to subjective and sensuous ways of apprehending and relating to the world of reality.

Distrust of the personal and the subjective is inherent in the positivist scientism at the core of modernity. The fact that Guru's poetic works speak of "experiences" which are essentially "mystical" or "spiritual" further complicates this problematic. Here, we are face to face with the ontology of modern disciplines like sociology and political science which cannot accommodate the sense of the sacred as a valid ground for constructing reality. For instance, his performative act of invoking the sacred by consecrating a stone as "Shiva" and the way it altered power relations between castes in Kerala, helps us understand how he used symbolic gestures to shape the inner life of the community. His poetry partakes of the same objective of awakening of the self within.

Guru was fashioning a new subjectivity through his poetic works which held out a new mode of negotiating social turbulence in contemporary Kerala. He was acutely aware of the resonant intertextuality of Bhakti tradition, well-versed as he was in many languages. Wisdom, in this tradition, is a mode of "knowing" embedded in language. Despite the use of the conventions of Bhakti poetry, his individual voice could be heard distinctly in his compositions. Guru's works are held together by a distinctive voice of his own, which communicated his sense of the felt experience of the world despite its formal use of conventional apparatus of bhakti poetry. His locus at the intersection of the traditional and the modern, on the cusp of contested epistemologies ranging from the Sanskritic-Vedic to the colonial-modern imparts him a privileged position of being a participant and critical observer. O. V. Vijayan has observed that Guru's aesthetic was a unique blend of the universal and the personal: "What Guru did was to invest language with spirituality and ground it in the everyday world of untouchables" (Guru 2002, 347).

Caste was at the core of several narratives that emerged in the context of modernity. Pradip Kumar Bose in his I. P. Desai memorial lecture delivered in 2019 comments that "most of the basic treatises on the Indian caste system written during the period 1880 and 1950 were written by men who had important positions either as census commissioners for entire India or for a province" (Bose 2019, 15). Census was part of a new epistemology which used tabulation, classification and quantification as means of assembling knowledge about the people of India. Statistical methods were deployed to create India as a knowledge subject. The taxonomy of observed data decided the foundational principles of knowledge about Indian society. As opposed to this, Guru's deep sense of experiential reality of caste was rooted in his intimate knowledge of the suffering subject. This understanding of caste system not only contradicts the positivist approach of the colonial state but provides a critique of the foundational doctrines of modern disciplines like sociology and political science. His poetry is an affirmation of the irreducible plurality of the social that cannot be normativised. He transforms a traumatic view of history into philosophical reflections on the nature of suffering. By putting the felt life of the mind at the centre of his reflections, he is able to draw into his fold subjects which differed vastly among themselves. Cultural anthropologists and sociologists who study "pre-modern" cultures, proceed on the assumption that we cannot critically see our way of life from the inside without the disciplinary training offered by modernity. In one of the temples Guru consecrated he put a mirror in the place of the deity (In fact, in many temples in Tamil Nadu, this practice of installing the mirror at the centre was prevalent). When Guru used it in Kerala, it was his way of demonstrating the need for critical reflection in a society where caste had reduced people to creatures of habit. He developed the capacity for critical reflection through his efforts of embodying the felt life of the mind in the syntax of poetic form which charged the consciousness of his audience. In poetry he spoke as a critical insider who could evaluate the transient and the contingent from the perspective of the universal. This involved the act of transforming experience into self-knowledge. The Bhakti tradition in India had created a new subject which could be in direct communication with the divine. Guru's invocation of the sacred in his poetry released it from the confines of institutionalised forms of religion, and aligned him with the tradition of dissent and dialogue one finds in Bhakti poetry (Ramakrishnan 2017, 46–64).

Vishnu Narayanan Nambuthiri, a major Malayalam poet, has remarked that Guru's poems convey the anguish and torment he underwent in their composition in their very syntax and diction (Guru 2002, 335–41). In a poem like "Kundalinipattu" (The Song of Kundalini), the snake-charmer and the snake enact several levels of inner struggles for revelation from the sensual to the intellectual. The semantic content here transcends the literal meaning of words because the metaphorical resonance of the dialogue between two parts of the self, reverberates with echoes from several traditions of Bhakti poetry. No contemporary poet could compete with his ability to map minute movements of the mind in its struggle for clarity and revelation. He also brought into currency many prosodic patterns and vibrant rhythms of poetic composition which were obscure or lost. Most of them were from oral traditions with deep intertextual relations with Tamil and spoken registers of Malayalam. Guru's immersion in the semiotic structure of the local is inseparable from the nuanced nature of his expression and action as a social reformer that created the modern Malayalam subject at a crucial moment in the history of Kerala.

Poems by their very nature could contain contradictions and multitudes creating an experiential discourse that persuades the reader through an aesthetic that is rooted in the ethics of difference. Appeals to truth are always concealed attempts to dominate the other. In using Advaita philosophy to question the legitimacy of caste system Guru was reading it against the grain. This was possible in poetry, but not in a philosophical treatise. Here, he belongs to poets like Jnanadeva and Tukaram, who used the power of poetry to stand witness and also propound the truth of their experience. Guru's first-hand knowledge of the social divisions had convinced him that there were no easy and ready solutions to the problems that plagued Kerala or Indian society. While concluding his conversation with Guru, Gandhi had asked him, "We are engaged in a struggle for people's worldly liberty. Won't it succeed?". Guru replied, "It will succeed. However, when we think of the entrenched nature of the problems, Gandhi may have to be born again for the project's complete fulfilment" (Guru 2002, 458). These words do appear prophetic as we are about to commemorate the 76th year of the Mahatma's death. All this goes to prove that it may not be productive to evaluate his work through the binary of tradition and modernity alone. He was one of the few who reconciled their contradictory impulses through grounding his critique of such essentialist ideologies in the utterances of the suffering subject.

Once he was convinced of the unity of human beings through the philosophical explorations of various knowledge systems, Guru chose to articulate his faith in the essential oneness of mankind through his works as a poet. The rare integration of word and deed, continuity between thought and action in Guru's life came about through his long and solitary meditations on the sufferings of the simple rural folk he witnessed throughout south

India. The act of creating a text and addressing a living audience, meant identifying and confronting the other. Ethics meant for him not a set of dogmas but a dialogic relation with the other, to re-invent the self from its perspective. The defining features of his poetic universe are its intertextual relations with Bhakti traditions of dialogue and dissent, his abiding sense of the sacred which transcends the social divisions, and a deeply rooted concern for the other which translates into ethical action. Collectively, these elements bring forth the transformative potential of the social. This is where the poetics of self-knowledge becomes indistinguishable from the politics of social change. In consecrating a stone from a flowing river on a rock as Shiva, he was performing an ethical act of seizing power from the priestly class on behalf of those who were deprived of their voice. Guru had to shape an emancipatory ethic in his poetics before he acted it out as a political project in the public arena of Kerala's divided social world.

(4)

Guru had a critical relation with the existing thought systems and literary traditions. He held Sankara in high esteem, but read Advaita thought against the grain to question the dominant brahminic thought. Sahodaran Ayyappan, who was close to Guru, has commented that he was a rationalist who never blindly followed any text or master, unless he was convinced of their worth (Balakrishnan 2006, 204). B. Rajeevan has argued that what Guru achieved was the "minorization" of the Advaita philosophy (Rajeevan 2011, 251–53). This means that he displaced Advaita from its pedestal of legitimising authority wielding a majoritarian perspective. Guru deployed it as a living thought system to question the very justifications advanced to legitimate the caste system. "Avidya" is a term that has great resonance in Guru's thought system. It must have come to him through his familiarity with the Siddha thought system. However, in Shaivism of the north which continues in the Nath cult of Maharashtra one finds a similar concern with knowledge as emancipator. Guru refutes the idea that the world is an illusion; according to him it is lack of knowledge that creates various types of illusions. The world exists as an impediment to self-consciousness to those who cannot transform their self from ignorance to knowledge. His major poems expounding Vedantic thought such as "Advaita Deepika", "Atmopadesa Satakam", "Darshanamala", "Swanubhava Geeti" and "Arivu" are replete with images of light, waves, sea, river, the sun, the eye, vision, etc., which are deployed to outline moments of sudden illumination and epiphanies that transform consciousness.

One of the recurring themes in his poems and utterances is the nature of knowledge and the relation between the self, the knower and knowledge. Poems such as "Atmopadesa Satakam" (Guru 2002, 157–69) and "Swanubhava Geeti" (ibid., 149–56) convey the sense of torment that accompanies self-exploration. The poet experiences God as an immediate presence and the word becomes the medium of realising His radiance and benevolence. Through the conventional frame of an invocation or "keertan" or "hymn" he is able to convey a sense of personal quest that exceeds the context and content of the poem. To evaluate Guru as a poet it is necessary to keep in mind that he has assimilated multiple traditions from many regions of South India and deploys a vocabulary which is unusual in its range, tonality and texture. He was a complete outsider to the mainstream tradition of Malayalam poetry which was neo-classical and narcissistic. In addressing a large audience consisting of the unlettered masses from the marginalised sections of society, his poems conveyed as much through sound and rhythms creating a sense of transcendence as their profound arguments. Only those who were initiated into philosophy could access his deeper meanings. His works have largely survived through the oral tradition by recitations of his followers. Sahodaran Ayyappan has noted: "He never wrote down his poems. He would compose a few stanzas and will dictate them from memory. He always had people who read to him books or wrote down what he dictated" (Balakrishnan 2006, 202–03). In this sense, he may be seen as one of the last *sant*-poets who spoke to the masses from a sense of personal transcendence that embodied the social in its conflictual form.

In the very opening stanza of "Atmopadesa Satakam", Guru invokes the question of knowledge. One has to control senses to recognise the supreme knowledge that pervades the world; one's inner light determines the way one relates to the world. In the third stanza, he uses the word *vivarta* which is commonly used in Vedanta to suggest that the multiple, phenomenal world is nothing but the manifestation of the essential oneness of the supreme being. One of his recurring metaphors to suggest the flux of life and the unity behind this constant change is that of the waves and the sea which we fail to see as manifestations of the same elemental water. Knowledge, the meanings it produces and the knower of that knowledge cannot be differentiated. The poem continuously juxtaposes the mundane world with its grossness and the eternal world with its emancipatory radiance. It is this inner movement that gradually leads to a significant section dealing with the relation between the self and the other. The arguments regarding the nature of the reality of this world, and an eternal essence that informs the phenomenal world, can never be settled one way or the other. He has alluded to the impulses and desires that accompany our senses and prevent us from realising our potential. At this point, he says that one's preference for a caste should not deny or contradict another's preference. One should harmonise one's desires in accordance with the needs of society. He talks of *sama* which sees the essential unity of things and *anya* which differentiates and discriminates between things. In "Advaita Jeevitham", he had observed that human beings always seek happiness. Guru observes: "Conflict between men arises with their regard to their objects of desires". The larger question he poses is how to reconcile one's actions with those of others. In "Atmopadesa Satakam", in keeping with its style of *sant-vani* (sage's advice), he says: "What one does for one's own happiness/ should bring happiness to others as well" (Guru 2002, 160). He continues: "Remember that any action that ensures one's own well-being but causes suffering to others goes against oneself" (ibid.). The words he uses are *atma sukham* and *atma virodhi*. He uses the word *aparan* to mean "the other", not *anyan* which is commonly used in Malayalam to denote an outsider. The use of *aparan* recasts the question of the relation between the self and the other as an ethical question. Seen against the public context of caste violence, the discourse of the essential unity of the human beings is an attempt to release the caste-marked body from its bondage of slavery and subjection.

The poem reflects on questions of experience in the world, of the world and beyond the world in the next section to invoke the complex process of self-transformation. Towards the end of the poem, he speaks of the conflict between the part and the whole. Here again the question relates to the nature of knowledge. Knowledge is not separate from oneself for those who are free from the illusion of division; this is the only way to reconcile the part with the whole. One can go on to discuss poems like "Swanubhavageeti" and "Advaitadeepika" along the same lines, but for the larger part of my argument, the above discussion shows how his philosophical poems intricately construct a critique of the prevailing social practices by setting the abstractions of the Vedanta against the lived reality of gross injustice. It is important to note that the sense of hurt and pain Guru must have gone through is never spelt out in these poems but it is present in the texture of the lines and also in the tone of address to his fellow human beings. It is the sense of immediacy and urgency conveyed by intensity of emotion that transforms the poem into a revelation about the inherent dignity of all human beings. If there is a key word that unites his entire corpus of works, it is *manushyan* and *manushyatvam* ("human being" and "humanness").

"Arivu" is another poem which may be briefly mentioned in this context. At a time when the imperial machinery was engaged in using knowledge as a means of instrumental control, Guru theorised it from a perspective that defied and denied the primacy of power in the constitution of knowledge. Ayyappa Paniker has commented that the poem "Arivu" is a hymn to the moment of "union between ontology and epistemology" (Guru 2002, 332).

Knowledge is being, and being is what constitutes us from within. The known has a being only when there is knowledge. Guru uses "knowledge" in the abstract to denote the same as absolute and universal. Knowledge in this sense envelopes the knower and the known. In the world, things exist in a disjointed state and we fail to perceive the underlying unity between them. In the absence of Knowledge, the very knowledge that validates existence of the known, would not survive. The act of knowing is compounded by the duality of the subject and object. We become that which is the knowledge of knowledge. He observes: "It is the self-unfolding of the universal knowledge that creates the knower as well as the impression that "I know" or "I do not know". Even the knowledge that I don't know is also an effect of the universal "Knowledge". In one of the verses of "Atmopadesa Satakam", Guru says: "Without knowledge, I do not exist,/Without me there is no knowledge, light alone is".

It is worth noting that a canonical text of Marathi Nath Sampradaya, *Anubhavamrut* by Jnanadev, uses many of the metaphors and images that one sees in Guru's major poems, such as river and ocean, light and shade, mirror and reflection, *vidya* and *avidya*. There is a pan-Indian dimension to Guru's poetic compositions which can be brought out only through detailed comparisons with the dissenting traditions of Bhakti in Tamil, Telugu, Marathi and Hindustani. Dilip Chitre in his Introduction to *Anubhavamrut* comments: "Jnandev's Nath sect, as well as his Kashmir Shaivite precursors, are the philosophical antagonists of Vedanta and neo-Vedanta. All this is heresy to Brahminical ears, whether steeped in the Vedas or schooled in Vedanta" (Chitre 1996, 12). One of the stanzas of *Anubhavamrut* reads like this: "Water and wave either is/Nothing except water: Thus other than the Self/There is no Being" (ibid., 177). In the third stanza of "Atmopadeshasatakam", Guru says: "The world manifests from outside/from the five elements including light/May we recognize that the waves and the sea/are nothing but the same essence" (Guru 2002, 157; my translation)

(5)

Guru transcended the boundary of castes by recasting issues of power relations as epistemological questions. This becomes his mode of negotiating the Hindu caste system as well as the superior power of Western imperialism. The colonial apparatus of power, while using the Eurocentric epistemology as a "mask of conquest", had invested the existing caste hierarchy with legitimacy. His interventions in multiple fields cleared an emancipatory space and defined a community-centric political identity that became the social capital for the making of a modern Kerala. He was a monk with a mass following, a towering presence in the public life of Kerala, mobilising the masses against the evils of caste oppression while building several institutions that embodied his vision of oneness of the human race. Though he was primarily seen as a reformer from Ezhava community, his work exceeded the caste boundaries because he denied primacy to caste in the organisation of the social structure. His idea of *samudayam* (community) progressively included all oppressed castes. Many of the caste organisations in Kerala were fashioned after the model he used in setting up SNDP (Sree Narayana Dharma Paripalana Samgham) in 1903. For instance, Ayyankali, the great Dalit leader of Kerala who was inspired by Guru, named his organisation Sadhu Jana Dharma Paripalana Samgham. Nair Service Society and Yogakshema Sabha (of Brahmins) were also modelled on the principles he outlined.

Guru found *Bhagavad Gita* a problematic text. When a specific question was put to him by a disciple regarding the line from the Gita on "Chaturvarnyam" he replied, "That is not the way it should be" (Guru 2002, 355). It is instructive to remember that Ambedkar held that *Bhagwad Gita* was instrumental in heralding a counter-revolution against the hold of Buddhism in India (Vajpeyi 2012, 235). Guru has more in common with Ambedkar than Gandhi, as a moderniser of the depressed castes, but that is a separate topic that requires more space. Guru's elucidation of the nature of "knowledge" and "known" should be seen as a prelude to his critique of caste. This leads us to two of his famous pronouncements on the nature of caste in society. In "Jatinirnayam" and "Jatilakshnam", Guru proceeds from the premises he has already established in his discussion of the relations between the knower and knowledge and between desire and the other. In both these poems, Guru implies that one becomes human only in the context of community. This larger emphasis on community makes it clear that his enquiries have local, contextual dimensions. "Jatinirnayam" (Guru 2002, 202) begins by citing a Sanskrit sloka: *manushyaanam manushyatwam/ jatir gotvam gavam yadha/ na brahmanadirasyaivam/ ha tatvam vetti ko pi na.* This roughly means that the only *jati* of human beings is humanness. As cowness is to cows, humanness is to humans. Attributing caste to divisions like brahmins has no basis. There is only one religion, one caste and one god for all human beings. All human beings are born of the same *yoni*, have the same human shape and there is no essential difference. Both brahmin and pariah are born in the same *nara jati*. He refers to the story of sage Parasara who was born of a pariah woman. He ends the poem by saying that differences between human beings have nothing to do with caste, they issue from individual's unique qualities and achievements like education and occupation. It becomes clear that for Guru *jati* implies species. This is carried on to the poem, "Jatilakashanam", where he uses *inam* as a synonym for *jati* (Guru 2002, 203). All those who beget offsprings through sexual union belong to the same *inam* or kind. Each kind is characterised by different types of body; one's body reveals one's caste, whether one is a human being or not. Sexual difference belongs to nature. Human differences in the profession, names and ways of living have nothing to do with nature. Guru had asked Ezhavas to change their caste names to Malayalees as Ezhava refers to one who came from "Eezham" or Sri Lanka. In Guru's opinion, human body is the only mark of difference. It may be noted that around this time, ethnography and anthropology had already begun using race as a category to study caste. Udaya Kumar quotes Thurston and Fawcett to show how it was argued that "Namputhiri was the truest Aryan in South India". He shows how Guru's conception of the body "militated against both these ways of 'materializing' caste bodies", the brahminic and the imperial (Kumar 2017, 71). In reducing the site of caste difference to the physical plane, Guru questioned both the Sanskrit epistemology of the Vedanta rooted in *chaturvarnya* and Western epistemology based on racial difference.

Guru's epistemological enquiries were rooted in history and the conditions of his own life in society. As mentioned earlier, he travelled across the length and breadth of South India tirelessly, never staying in one place for more than a few days. Once he was in Sri Lanka for months, and was reluctant to return, as he felt his ideas were not being received in their right spirit. It was a fact that his followers lacked the intellect to comprehend his ideas in their proper perspective and this made him a solitary figure among his own men (Gopikrishnan 2019, 18). He lived a life of struggle, and his poetic compositions are in the form of arguments with himself and others. His works have strong dialogic dimensions in the sense that they are spoken in the context of others' speech. His poems were conversations with the world—attempts to clarify a path forward, when competing ideas of what is good and bad had compounded his choices. Guru could see that knowledge, truth and reality were produced, sustained or displaced through power structures. He was not averse to accepting the benign aspects of colonial modernity and encouraged people to learn English (Balakrishnan 2006, 203). Towards the end of his life, he regretted that his initiative in constructing temples did not have the desired results. He suggested that efforts are required to educate the people, and hence there was need to build more schools (Bhaskaranunni 2005, 251).

In the poems mentioned above, Guru makes a primary distinction between caste and religion, dislodging "caste" from the epistemic structure of Hinduism. He held that *matham*—which is the Malayalam word for religion—merely means "an opinion" and cannot constitute an essential feature of one's self-definition. Commenting on the issue of conversion he said:

> Religion has two sides—the inner and the outer; which of these two needs a change? If the zeal is for a change on the outside, it is no religious conversion. It is only a social change. Change within takes place gradually in anything individual. It is a change that happens naturally corresponding to the increasing knowledge, it cannot be brought about by anybody. One who follows a particular religion like Hinduism or Christianity, should give it up if one comes to lose faith in it. (Govindan 1974, 219)

Here religion is a subjective state of feeling, sensibility and receptivity and not an unalterable code of irrevocable differences. This subtle description undermines the very basis of religion as a symbolic system of knowledge that mystifies everyday world of differences. Guru locates an interior space within the self that gives primacy to knowledge and experience, rather than faith and belief.

(6)

This approach is reflected in Guru's dialogue with Gandhi as well. Gandhi visited Kerala during 8–19 March 1925, primarily to support the temple entry Satyagraha at Vaikkom Temple. His meeting with the brahmin priests of the temple was not a success. When Gandhi met Guru, he initially asked him about the movement and whether there was any need to make any changes in the movement. Guru said, "I don't think any changes are necessary" (Guru 2002, 256–59; my translation). Guru also supported the non-violent mode of Satyagraha. Gandhi went on to ask his opinion on conversion: "Some say that we must resort to religious conversion to attain freedom. Does Swamiji give permission for that?", to which Guru replied: "It is being seen that those who are converting are gaining freedom. Looking at these, people can't be blamed for thinking that religious conversion is good." Gandhi wanted to know specifically if Guru thought Hindu religion was sufficient for spiritual liberation. Guru replied, "There are ways of liberation in other religions too." Gandhiji repeated the question asking him to leave out the question of other religions, and Guru replied that he felt Hindu religion was enough for spiritual liberation. But he added, "but people desire material freedom (liberation) more." Gandhi was insistent and wanted a clear statement from Guru against religious conversion, but Guru was insistent that religious conversion was not necessary for spiritual liberation. The underlying tension in the conversation can be traced to Gandhi's strong faith in Varnashrama dharma. Guru's perspective is a continuation of what we discussed earlier with reference to his poems on Advaita where he does not differentiate between material and spiritual liberations. Guru had pointed at the tree nearby to say that although the leaves are of different shapes, the same sap ran through all of them. For Guru the question of struggle for social freedom was not separate from the quest for political freedom. Unlike Gandhi, Guru speaks from the perspective of the *dharmam* and *samudayam*.

This is where Guru's intertextual relation with the indigenous Bhakti tradition becomes apparent. Once the basis of caste is shown to be a product of distorted knowledge, he is able to create a category of community as the participatory space; here self-awareness leads to community formation. It is by relocating the self, trapped in the discourse of caste and religion in the narrative of community that Guru establishes a new discourse rooted in history and social transformation. Once caste marks are erased from the body, the social customs that legitimate caste structure will lose their foundation. Rajeevan has argued that Guru displaced the theoretical foundation of caste and sub-caste to formulate the idea of community, the framework and details of which present us with an alternative to the Western model of civil society (Rajeevan 2011, 294). However, this mode of studying Guru through the lens of Western formulations may not be productive. What is needed is an attempt to place him in the context of his own struggles and creative dialogues with history that include his poetry.

Since Guru found humanness as the fulcrum of his vision of equality and justice, he could extend the idea of dharma to the non-human plane as well. In one of his philosophical poems,

"Anukampasatakam" (Ten Verses on Empathy) he identifies empathy and compassion as the core values of all religious teachings. He begins the poem with the stanza: "May I cause no harm at all, even to an ant—/ such empathy, O maker of kindliness, and ever/ bless me with such contemplation that/ never strays from Your sacred form" (Chaitanya 2022, 18). A human being can claim to be human only if he is capable of compassion (*arul ullavananu jeevi*). While the idea of *samudayam* was based on shared suffering the need for liberation, the question of dharma that underlines Guru's ideas of knowledge, being, and the universal truth transcends human boundaries.

In evaluating Guru as a central figure of Kerala "Renaissance" we tend to see his contributions through the lens of European enlightenment. This results in the creation of a split figure: a wandering monk given to reflection and meditation, and a man of action who built major institutions to channelise the creativity of lower castes. We have not been able to see him as a unified figure who moves seamlessly from the domain of creative utterance to social action, the one propelling the self towards the other. He devised a system of thought where divisions such as the secular and spiritual, self and the other, body and mind become immaterial. The current debates on the failure of liberal humanism should help us retrieve the visionary epistemology formulated by Guru that had space for a critique of capitalism and its narrow definition of the human. A poem like "Anukampasatakam" would enable us to reformulate the human from the perspective of the non-human. Guru was deeply grounded in contemporary social concerns. In his address to the members of the marginalised castes he always emphasised the importance of cleanliness, education and industry. His interventions were definitive acts of conviction, never leaving any room of ambiguity of his position on issues of social freedom. We need to recognise that he did not see the liberated self as an end in itself—it remains liberated only when it is in a perpetual state of revolt, struggle and regeneration. By carefully aligning himself with the lived and shared religion of the folks grounded in the dailiness of struggle, he could resist the prescriptive violence of organised religion and also leave a possibility of his own critique by future generations. He found a spiritual lexicon to embody the turbulence of a transformative era and created a permanent testament through his poetical and philosophical works to the struggles of the body and mind to break the limits of language set by the prevailing ideologies. We need to return to his mould of thought to reshape our vocabulary of critical thought and face the challenges of the present.

WORKS CITED

Azhikode, Sukumar. 2002. *Guruvinte Darshanam* (The Philosophy of Guru). In *Narayana Guru: Jeevitam, Kritikal, Darshanam* (Narayana Guru: Life, Works, Vision). Compiled and Edited by K. N. Shaji, 301–11. Thrissur: Current Books.

Balakrishnan, P. K. 2002. *Narayana Guru: Oru Padhanam* (Narayana Guru: A Study). In *Narayana Guru: Jeevitam, Kritikal, Darshanam* (Narayana Guru: Life, Works, Vision). Compiled and Edited by K. N. Shaji, 292–300. Thrissur: Current Books.

———, ed. 2006. *Narayana Guru*. Kottayam: D.C. Books.

Bhaskaranunni, P. 1988. *Pathompatham Noottandile Keralam* (Kerala during the Nineteenth Century). Thrissur: Kerala Sahitya Akademi.

———. 2005. *Keralam Irupatham Noottandinte Arambhathil* (Kerala at the Beginning of the Twentieth Century). Thrissur: Kerala Sahitya Akademi.

Bose, Pradip Kumar. 2019. "Population, Statistics and Governmentality", I.P. Desai Memorial Lecture No. 27. Surat: Centre for Social Studies.

Bose, Satheese Chandra and Shiju Sam Varughese. 2015. *Kerala Modernity: Ideas, Spaces and Practices in Transition*. Hyderabad: Orient BlackSwan.

Chaitanya, Vinaya, trans. 2022. *A Cry in the Wilderness: The Works of Narayana Guru*. Gurugram, Haryana: Harper Collins Publishers India.

Chitre, Dilip, trans. 1996. *Shri Jnanadev's Anubhavamrut: The Immortal Experience of Being*. New Delhi: Sahitya Akademi.

Dirks, Nicholas B. 2003. *Castes of Mind: Colonialism and the Modern India*. New Delhi: Permanent Black.

Gopikrishnan, N. 2019, "Nataraja Guruvum Sanyasathinte Aadhunikatayum" (Nataraja Guru and the Modernity of Sanyas), Mathrubhumi Weekly, September, 2–9, 2019, pp. 15–20.

Govindan, M. 1974. *Poetry and Renaissance: Kumaran Asan Birth Centenary Volume*. Madras: Sameeksha.

Guru, Sree Narayana. 2002. *Narayana Guru: Jeevitam, Kritikal, Darshanam* (Narayana Guru: Life, Works, Vision). Compiled and Edited by K. N. Shaji. Thrissur: Current Books.

Kumar, Udaya. 2017. *Writing the First Person: Literature, History and Autobiography in Modern Kerala*. New Delhi: Permanent Black in association with Ashoka University.

Mohan, Sanal. 2015. *Modernity of Slavery: Struggles against Caste Inequality in Colonial Kerala*. New Delhi: Oxford University Press.

Nussbaum, Martha C. 2013. *Political Emotions: Why Love Matters for Justice*. Cambridge: The Belknap Press of Harvard University Press.

Rajeevan, B. 2011. *Vakkukalum Vastukkalum* (Words and Objects). Kottayam: D.C. Books.

Ramakrishnan, E. V. 2017. *Indigenous Imaginaries: Literature, Region, Modernity*. Hyderabad: Orient BlackSwan.

Shulman, David. 2016. *Tamil: A Biography*. Cambridge: The Belknap Press of Harvard University Press.

Vajpeyi, Ananya. 2012. *Righteous Republic: The Political Foundations of Modern India*. Cambridge: Harvard University Press.

Notes on Contributors

Bini B. S. teaches English at the Institute of Law, Nirma University, Ahmedabad. She is the author of *Life Worlds of Cancer: Narratives that Resist and Heal*, a monograph published by the University of Kerala. Her articles, poems, and translations have appeared in journals and anthologies like *An Anthology of Modern Malayalam Literature* (2017). She is the recipient of the 2016 J. Talbot Winchell Award from the Institute of General Semantics, New York.

Rajendra Chenni is the Director of Manasa Centre for Cultural Studies, Shivamogga, and is a former Professor of English at Kuvempu University. He has written and edited eighteen books in Kannada and English, including a novel in English and three collections of short stories in Kannada. He has received the Karnataka Sahitya Akademi's Life Time achievement award for his contribution to literary criticism. He is also known for his participation in several people's movements in Karnataka. His recent book, *State Matters: Kannada Sub-nationalism and State Formation* was published in 2023.

Debendra K. Dash (1954–2022) taught Odia literature at various colleges in Odisha before taking voluntary retirement in 2013 to devote himself entirely to research and publication. In his long career as a researcher, he published definitive editions of the works of Fakir Mohan Senapati, Madan Mohan Pattnaik and Gopalbandhu Das, among others. He won the Fakirmohan Sahitya Sanmanna and Kshetrabasi Sahityabidya Puraskar for his literary criticism. He was felicitated by Odisha Sahitya Akademi for his outstanding contribution to Odia literary culture.

Subha Dasgupta Chakraborty taught Comparative Literature at Jadavpur University for about three decades and was also Joint

Director of the School of Cultural Texts and Records (JU) for a short period. She has published extensively on comparative literature, narrative theory, translation studies and marginality. Her recent edited volumes include *Figures of Transcontinental Multilingualism* (with K. Alfons Knauth), *Critical Discourse in Bangla* (with Subrata Sinha) and a volume of Hindi Dalit stories translated into Bangla (co-editor). She was editor of *Jadavpur Journal of Comparative Literature* for several years and is now the series editor of the French-Bangla translation project of Jadavpur University Press.

Shamsur Rahman Faruqi (1935–2020) was a reputed poet, novelist, critic and theorist in Urdu literature. He was a pioneer of modernism in Urdu, and was closely associated with the journal, *Shab Khoon*, which nurtured modernist sensibility. His *Sher-e-Shor-Angrez*, a critical work is considered a classic in Urdu. His translation of Aristotle's *Poetics* into Urdu was very well received. He received the Sahitya Akademi Award in 1986 for his book *Tanqidi Afkar.* He was also honoured with Saraswati Samman and Padmashri for his contribution to Urdu literature.

Tonisha Guin is trained in English Literary and Cultural Studies. Her academic interests are identity and spatiality studies, popular culture, decoloniality, knowledge systems in the Global South and New Media Studies. Her doctoral research looked at mainstream bhadralok identity formation around Barabazar, Kolkata. For the last few years, she has been looking at biopolitical and ecological concerns around the Sundarbans area in West Bengal, India. She joined the School of Liberal Arts, IIT Jodhpur, as an Assistant Professor in July 2022.

Vipin K. Kadavath is an Assistant Professor of English at Banaras Hindu University, Varanasi. His doctoral work is on the subject, "Historicizing Kshemam: A Study of Vernacular Political Discourse in Travancore, 1880s-1930s" (EFLU, Hyderabad). He co-edited the volume *The Digital Popular in India: Mainstreaming the Marginal*, published in 2023.

Mrinal Kaul teaches Sanskrit philosophy in the Indian Institute of Technology, Bombay. He has several publications in the areas of his expertise such as Philosophy of Indian Aesthetics and Truth and Knowledge in Indian Philosophy. He is a Sanskritist with deep interest in Kashmir Shaivism.

Sachin C. Ketkar is Professor, English, The Maharaja Sayajirao University of Baroda. He is a bilingual writer, translator and academic. His books on criticism include *(Trans) Migrating Words: Refractions on Indian Translation Studies* (2010) and *Changlya Kavitevarchi Statutory Warning: Samkaleen Marathi Kavita, Jagatikikaran ani Bhashantar* (2016). His most recent book is *Vyankatesh Madgulkar: A Villageful of Stories and a Forestful of Tales* (2023), co-edited with Keerti Ramachandra.

Zarana Maheshwari is Assistant Professor at the Centre for Comparative Literature and Translation Studies, Central University of Gujarat. Her research interests include disability studies, translation studies, gender and sexuality, post-colonial literature and travel literature. She has published in the areas of translation studies and disability studies in peer reviewed journals, peer reviewed portals and books.

Hiren Patel is Assistant Professor, English at the Government Science College, Bhilad. His areas of specialisation include nineteenth-century Gujarati journals and Translation Studies with special reference to the role of translation in the creation of literary public sphere. He has published several articles in research journals.

Dipti R. Pattanaik teaches English at Banaras Hindu University, Varanasi. He has won several awards for his creative writing in Odia, including the Odisha Sahitya Akademi Award, Katha Prize and Jhankar Award. He was a Fulbright scholar during 1996-97,

British Council Fellow in 2000, Shastri Indo-Canadian scholar in 2009 and Erikson Scholar in Residence at the Riggs Institute, U.S.A, in 2011. He has several volumes of short stories in Odia. His novel, *Life and Times of Banka Haricharan* (translated into English by Himanshu S. Mohapatra) has been very well received.

Anisur Rahman is a bilingual poet in English and Urdu, translator and literary critic. Formerly a Professor at the Department of English, Jamia Millia Islamia, he has published in the areas of Comparative Literature, Translation Studies, Postcolonial Studies, and Urdu studies. His most recent publications include *In Translation: Positions and Paradigms* (2019), *Hazaaron Khwahishein Aisi: The Wonderful World of Urdu Ghazals* (2019) and *Socioliterary Cultures in South Asia* (2019).

C. Rajendran retired from Calicut University as Professor of Sanskrit. He has extensively written on Sanskrit poetics in Malayalm and English. Among his published works are *Studies in Comparative Poetics, Sisupalavadha of Mahakavi Magha* (2018), *Narratology: Indian Perspectives, Sanskrit in the Twenty First Century* (edited, 2017) and *Nilayude Kayyoppukal* (in Malayalam, 2019).

E. V. Ramakrishnan, the editor of this volume, is a well-known critic in Malayalam and English, besides being an Indian English poet and translator. He is a former Professor and Dean as well as Professor Emeritus of Central University of Gujarat. He has published ten critical works in Malayalam among which are the award-winning *Aksharavum Aadhunikatayum* (1993) and *Malayala Novelinte Deshakalangal* (2018). Among his published works in English are *Indigenous Imaginaries: Literature, Moderniy, Region* (2017), *Bakhtinian Explorations of Indian Culture: Pluralism, Dialogue and Dogma through History* (co-edited, 2019) and *Literary Criticism in India* (edited, 2021). He is a recipient of Kerala Sahitya Akademi Award (1995), Odakkuzhal Award (2018) and Kerala Sahitya Akademi's Vilasini Award (2018).

He received the Sahitya Akademi Award (2023) for his Malayalam work, *Malayala Novelinte Deshakaalangal.*

P. P. Raveendran, bilingual critic and currently the Vaikom Muhammad Basheer Chair Visiting Professor at the University of Calicut, was formerly Professor and Director, School of Letters, Mahatma Gandhi University, Kottayam. His works include *Texts, Histories, Geographies: Reading Indian Literature* (2009), *Kamala Das* (2017), and the co-edited volume, *The Oxford India Anthology of Modern Malayalam Literature* (2017). His latest publication is *Under the Bhasha Gaze: Modernity and Indian Literature* (2023).

Sukanya Sarbadhikary works at the interface of the anthropology of religion, anthropology of embodiment, religious studies, and philosophy. In her first work, "The Place of Devotion: Siting and Experiencing Divinity in Bengal-Vaishnavism" (2015), she did an intensive ethnography among different kinds of Bengal-Vaishnavas, focusing on diverse experiences of religious place and sensory apprehensions of divine affect. She currently works on religious sound and its varied cultural and natural lives in South Asia.

Dhurjjati Sarma is Assistant Professor, Department of Modern Indian Languages and Literary Studies, Gauhati University, Assam. His articles and book reviews have appeared in reputed journals like *Indian Literature, Dibrugarh University Journal of English Studies* (DUJES) and *Margins: A Journal of Literature and Culture.* He translates between Assamese, English and Hindi, and his recent translations include G. N. Devy's *Mahabharata: The Epic and the Nation.* He is presently working on a critical history of Assamese literature.

Nirmal Selvamony was Professor and Head of the Department of English Studies and Dean of the School of Social Sciences and Humanities at the Central University of Tamil Nadu. In 1980, he founded the forum *thiNai*, which introduced *thiNai* as an alternative to the industrialist lifeway, and contributed to the emergence of the "*thiNai* movement" through his numerous publications, talks and conference papers. He developed the new field of "*thiNai* musicology" and revived its philosophical tradition, which precedes the *darshanas*.